# RICHARD III

Richard III.

# RICHARD III

Charles Ross

*Professor of Medieval History*
*University of Bristol*

EYRE METHUEN
LONDON

*First published 1981*
© *1981 Charles Ross*
*Printed in Great Britain for*
*Eyre Methuen Ltd*
*11 New Fetter Lane, London EC4P 4EE*
*by*
*Willmer Brothers Limited*
*Rock Ferry, Merseyside*

*British Library Cataloguing in Publication Data*

Ross, Charles
　　Richard III. – (English monarchs)
　　I. Title　　　II. Series
　　942.04'6'0924　　　DA260
　　ISBN 0–413–29530–3

# CONTENTS

# ILLUSTRATIONS

## PLATES

MAPS

GENEALOGIES

Acknowledgements and thanks for permission to reproduce photographs are due to the National Portrait Gallery for the frontispiece and plate 24a; to Her Majesty the Queen, Royal Collection, for plate 1a; to Queens' College, Cambridge, for plate 1b; to Aerofilms Ltd for plate 2a; to Geoffrey Wheeler for plates 2b, 4a, 4b, 9b, 10a and 23b; to the National Monuments Record for plates 3, 6a and 9a; to the Dean and Chapter of Canterbury for plate 5; to the Bishop of Bath and Wells for plate 6b; to Pitkin Pictorials Ltd for plate 7; to Guildhall Library for plate 8; to the Public Record Office for plates 10b, 11a and 11b; to His Grace the Archbishop of Canterbury and the Trustees of Lambeth Palace Library for plates 12a and 13; to C. V. Middleton & Son, Lincoln, for plate 12b; to the British Library for plates 14, 15, 16a, 16b, 17, 18 and 19; to Her Majesty the Queen, National Gallery of Scotland, for plate 20; to the Property Department, Leicestershire County Council, for plate 21; to the Art Institute of Chicago for plate 22a; to Photographie Giraudon for plate 22b; and to the Dean and Chapter of Westminster for plate 24b.

The maps and genealogies were re-drawn from the author's roughs by Neil Hyslop.

# PREFACE AND ACKNOWLEDGEMENTS

This book is an attempt to take a look at one of the great figures of the English historical saga in a different way from what has been attempted in the past. William Shakespeare himself took a long look, and we have been living with the dramatic consequences ever since, to everyone's satisfaction. Since then, considerations of the life and reign of Richard Plantagenet have been largely concerned to rebut the historical interpretation on which Shakespeare's great play rested. This is not a conventional biography, if such were possible. No attempt has been made to reproduce or improve upon the sweeping, emotive and perfervid narrative of Richard's most widely-read modern biographer, Paul Murray Kendall, nor the rather dour chronological treatment accorded him by that fine nineteenth-century scholar, James Gairdner. Instead, the approach is thematic, in an effort to see Richard in the context of those aspects of his life and reign which mattered most to Richard himself and his contemporaries. Hence the emphatic concentration on the problems of how to gain, and even more of how to keep power in late-medieval England, and on the inevitable centre of these operations, his use of patronage – the main weapon in the armoury of a medieval king. This approach involves a certain degree of repetition, for which apologies are offered to the reader. None, however, should be offered for the apparently relentless concern with historical evidence. Speculation about Richard III's character and motivation is an all too easy game. Arriving at the hard facts about him is less glamorous but no less interesting.

I have many debts to acknowledge in the preparation of this book: to the late (and much-regretted) Professor A. R. Myers, Professor Charles T. Wood and Dr P. B. Wolffe for their comments and criticisms on my account of the events of April to June 1483 (none of them agreed with me – it is in the nature of this subject – and, therefore, any faults are mine and not theirs); to several members of the Richard III Society for their assistance and advice, especially Mr Peter Hammond and Mr W. E. Hampton, who gave me sturdy advice on the logistics and on cavalry charges in the conditions of August 1485, and to Dr R. A. Griffiths for his assistance in the matter of protectorates. Dr Rosemary Horrox kindly allowed me to draw upon her thesis on Richard III's patronage, as did Dr Michael Hicks from his study of George duke of Clarence. My colleague

J. W. Sherborne has listened patiently, but in most scholarly fashion, to my repeated complaints about Richard III; another colleague, Dr A. V. Antonovics, gave me valuable advice on the state of French politics on the eve of the invasion of 1485. Students of mine, past and present, especially those who have shared in successive seminar groups on the theme of 'William Shakespeare and Richard III', have helped a great deal, usually through their capacity to ask challenging, often unanswerable questions – the best antidote known to any scholarly complacency. To my mother I owe a great debt for her help with the Bibliography. Finally, my thanks to my wife, Anne, for living with the preparation of this book, even though, as yet another specialist in this field, she does not always agree with me.

FOR JAMES ALEXANDER ROSS

# ABBREVIATIONS

The following abbreviations are used in the footnotes. Full details of the works cited below and of other books or articles cited by short titles will be found in the Bibliography at the end of this book.

| | |
|---|---|
| *BIHR* | *Bulletin of the Institute of Historical Research* |
| B.L. | British Library |
| *CC* | Croyland Chronicle – 'Historiae Croylandensis Continuatio', in *Rerum Anglicarum Scriptores Veterum*, ed. W. Fulman |
| *CCR* | *Calendar of Close Rolls, 1476–1485* (other volumes in the series identified by date) |
| *CFR* | *Calendar of Fine Rolls, 1471–1485* |
| *CP* | *The Complete Peerage* |
| *CPR* | *Calendar of Patent Rolls, 1476–1485* (other volumes in the series identified by date) |
| *DNB* | *Dictionary of National Biography* |
| *EHR* | *English Historical Review* |
| Gairdner | J. Gairdner, *History of the Life and Reign of Richard III* |
| Gairdner, *L & P* | *Letters and Papers Illustrative of the Reigns of Richard III and Henry VII* |
| *GC* | *The Great Chronicle of London* (ed. Thomas and Thornley) |
| *Grants* | *Grants from the Crown during the Reign of Edward V*, ed. J. G. Nichols |
| Hanham | A. Hanham, *Richard III and his Early Historians* (1975) |
| Harl. 433 | British Library, Harleian MS 433 (fos. 1–105, ed. Horrox and Hammond, 2 vols) |
| Kendall | P. M. Kendall, *Richard III* (1955) |

Mancini            Dominic Mancini, *The Usurpation of Richard III*, ed.
                   C. A. J. Armstrong

More               Sir Thomas More, *The History of King Richard III*, ed.
                   Sylvester

*PL*               *The Paston Letters* (ed. Gairdner, 1904)

PRO                Public Record Office

PV                 Polydore Vergil (*Three Books of Polydore Vergil's
                   English History*, ed. H. Ellis)

*RP*               *Rotuli Parliamentorum*

Scofield           C. L. Scofield, *The Life and Reign of Edward The
                   Fourth*

*TRHS*             *Transactions of the Royal Historical Society*

*VCH*              *The Victoria History of the Counties of England*

*YCR*              *York Civic Records*, ed. A. Raine

# RICHARD III

# INTRODUCTION

## THE HISTORICAL REPUTATION OF RICHARD III: FACT AND FICTION

> Richard the Third, of all the English Monarchs, bears the greatest contrariety of character. . . . Some few have conferred upon him almost angelic excellence, have clouded his errors, and blazened every virtue that could adorn a man. Others, as if only extremes would prevail, present him in the blackest dye; his thoughts were evil, and that continually, and his actions diabolical; the most degraded mind inhabited the most deformed body. . . . But Richard's character, like every man's, had two sides . . . though most writers display but one. . . .

With these words that engaging antiquary William Hutton, whose book, *The Battle of Bosworth Field*, was first published in 1788, lit neatly on the principal characteristics of so much that has been written about Richard III. Many have seen him in terms of unrelieved black and white. Few have been willing to judge him without prejudice and preconception and (so far as this is possible) to see him objectively. These apparent compulsions have made the history of Richard's reputation almost as much a drama as his career and reign themselves. Violent attacks have produced no less violent counter-attacks, full of emotion, scorn and vituperation.

Richard Plantagenet ruled England for a mere twenty-six months. His reign is one of the shortest in English history. Yet few English monarchs have exercised so compulsive a posthumous fascination for the English-speaking peoples. A recent estimate suggested that something has been written about him in every single generation since his death almost five hundred years ago. Nor does this quick-flowing stream show any signs of drying up; indeed, in recent times it has reached flood proportions. Interest in a long-dead king seems greater now than ever before, and Richard III is one of the few Englishmen to revel posthumously in the labours of a Society dedicated to his name, a distinction which he shares with Cromwell, Marlborough and (curiously) his alleged victim, King Henry VI.

For all this, that greatest of English publicists, William Shakespeare, is largely responsible. Shakespeare may no longer be, as he was for the duke of Marlborough, 'the only English history I ever read', but his influence remains deeply pervasive. Shakespeare made Richard into an archetypal villain, exceeded only, in consummacy and subtlety, by Iago in the Shakespearian canon. Yet he was too great a dramatist to paint only in the crude colours of a wall-poster. It is difficult not to share in the sheer witty glee, illuminated by no flicker of conscience, with which Richard sees his plots and 'inductions dangerous' bearing fruit, even against the odds, as in his wooing of Anne Nevill, nor to feel some sympathy for his growing remorse, reaching its climax in his ghost-ridden dreams on the eve of Bosworth. At midnight, as the lights burned blue,

> My conscience hath a thousand several tongues,
> And every tongue brings in a several tale,
> And every tale condemns me for a villain.

Confidence returns on the morrow as he arms for battle:

> Let not our babbling dreams affright our souls;
> Conscience is but a word that cowards use,
> Devised at first to keep the strong in awe;
> Our strong arms be our conscience, swords our law!

Yet a villain, repentant or not, he remains. Abuse is heaped upon him throughout *Henry VI, Part III* and *Richard III*, especially by that trio of widowed and avenging harpies, his mother, Cecily duchess of York, the queen-dowager, Elizabeth Woodville, and (most unhistorically, for she was already in her grave) Queen Margaret of Anjou, relict of Henry VI. He appears in various deeply unflattering forms, as 'a hell-hound from your womb', 'a carnal cur', 'hell's black intelligencer', a 'bottled toad', a 'bottled spider', and (in birth) 'an indigested and ill-formed lump' or a 'lump of foul deformity'. The palm for inventive abuse goes to Queen Margaret:

> Thou elvish-marked, abortive and rooting hog,
> Thou slander of thy heavy mother's womb,
> Thou loathed issue of thy father's loins,
> Thou rag of honour! Thou detested –

(unfortunately, Richard interrupts the flow of venom, pretending he had not heard). His inherent evil makes it easy to predict his fate: 'Bloody thou art, and bloody will be thy end.'[1]

Shakespeare's Richard was far from being a mere dramatic invention. His characterization derives from a whole century of *historical* writing, during which time Richard's name had been, with growing elaboration,

---

[1] *Henry VI, Part Three*, V, vi, 339; *Richard III*, I, ii, 57; I, iii, 227 ff., 241, 244; V, iii, 194–7, 309–12.

consistently denigrated.[2] The sheer power and endurance of the Tudor tradition, especially when consecrated by Shakespeare, makes a sober assessment of its historical value an essential pre-requisite for any consideration of the 'true' Richard. The importance of this exercise is heightened by the fact that the Tudor writers appear to provide us with so much more information about Richard's life and reign than we can extract from the more scanty comments of his own contemporaries. Three questions deserve careful consideration. What motives lay behind the consistent Tudor hostility to Richard's reputation? How reliable was their evidence, so far as it can be checked? How far does their antagonism conform or conflict with the opinions of Richard's contemporaries, so far as these in turn can be evaluated?

To begin with, it would be fallacious to see the Tudor tradition as being in the main a product of official Tudor propaganda.[3] It is true that, in the years immediately following Bosworth, the slandering of Richard's name lay in crudely partisan hands. The Warwickshire antiquary, John Rous, produced, some time during Richard's own reign, a short *History of the Kings of England*, with significant additions and changes made during Henry VII's reign. It is chiefly memorable for the remarkable natal peculiarities attributed to Richard, who was born with teeth in his mouth and hair down to his shoulders (neither medically impossible) and after a confinement of two years in his mother's womb (which would be miraculous). But his account also contained many other elements of the later Tudor tradition. According to Rous, Richard was an Antichrist; he was born under Scorpio, and like a scorpion displayed a smooth front and a vicious swinging tail (he was, in fact, born under Libra); he murdered his nephews, and that 'holy man', Henry VI, was done to death on his orders if not by his own hand, and he poisoned his wife and imprisoned her mother for life.[4] But the fragility of Rous's historical conscience, allied to

[2] For Shakespeare and Richard III, and his historical sources, E. M. W. Tillyard, *Shakespeare's History Plays* (1944), Lily B. Campbell, *Shakespeare's 'Histories'* (1947), Irving Ribner, *The English History Play in the Age of Shakespeare* (1957), G. Bullough, *Narrative and Dramatic Sources of Shakespeare* (1966), III, and P. Saccio, *Shakespeare's English Kings* (1977). More directly historiographical and less oriented to Shakespeare are the pioneering study of G. B. Churchill, *Richard III up to Shakespeare* (still useful despite its date), C. L. Kingsford, *English Historical Literature in the Fifteenth Century* (1913), chap. x, and Alison Hanham, *Richard III and his Early Historians* (1975), a most important study for Polydore Vergil and Sir Thomas More and their sources. See also the specialized works on Vergil and More listed in the footnotes below.

[3] This important point is very well made by Hanham, *op. cit., passim*, but especially pp. 126, 191–2.

[4] *Joannis Rossi Antiquarii Warwicensis Historia Regum Angliae*, ed. T. Hearne (Oxford 1716). A more accessible version of this rare work is printed, in modernized English, in Hanham, *op. cit.*, 118–24.

his wish to attract the patronage of the currently powerful, is most strik-
ingly revealed in the two contrasting versions of his illustrated *History of
the Earls of Warwick*, one in English, one in Latin, and both written
between 1483 and 1485.[5] The English version, which Rous was evidently
unable to recover after Bosworth, praises Richard along precisely the same
lines as Richard himself tried to project a public image:[6]

> a mighty prince and especiall good lord . . . in his realm full commendably
> punishing offenders of the laws, especially oppressors of the Commons, and
> cherishing those that were virtuous, by the which discreet guiding he got
> great thanks and love of all his subjects great and poor.

In the Latin version, however, these sentences were erased. He becomes
merely the 'unhappy husband' of Anne Nevill, and the line-drawn portrait
of him was replaced by that of the Lancastrian Edward prince of Wales,
Anne's first husband.

A prudent if also time-serving concern for his own reputation is perhaps
the most charitable explanation for Rous's *volte-face*. Elegant toadyism
to a royal paymaster is perhaps nearer the mark as a description of the
vilification of Richard as he next appears in the works of Henry VII's
blind poet laureate, Bernard André, who was also Henry's official historio-
grapher. His work has no independent value, and is of interest only for
two reasons: his use (in a restricted sense) of the notion of divine justice to
point the contrast between the Black Richard and the Angelic Tudor
(God's messenger sent to punish Richard's crimes), and the likelihood that
his book represents the view that Henry himself wished to present of the
events leading to his acquisition of the English throne.[7] Much the same
may be said of another humanist court-scholar, Pietro Carmeliano of
Brescia, who served both Richard III and Henry VII, and, like Rous, saw
no problem of conscience in praising Richard when alive and reviling him
when dead.[8]

Such time-serving considerations are of far less relevance to the work
of the twin architects of the Tudor tradition, Polydore Vergil of Urbino
and Sir Thomas More, or to that of their principal plagiarizer, Edward

---

[5] The English version, now B.L. Additional MS 48976, was published by H. G.
Bohn as *The Rows Roll*, with introduction by W. Courthope, in 1859; reprint, with
historical introduction by C. D. Ross, as John Rous, *The Rous Roll* (1980).

[6] See below, pp. 147, 173–6.

[7] Bernard André, *Historia Regis Henrici Septimi*, ed. J. Gairdner (Rolls Series,
1858); Churchill, *op. cit.*, 59–66. It should be noted, however, that André did not
accuse Richard of the deaths of Edward prince of Wales (son of Henry VI), Clarence
or Queen Anne.

[8] For Carmeliano, R. Weiss, *Humanism in England during the Fifteenth Century*,
169–72; W. Nelson, *John Skelton Laureate*; Armstrong's introduction to Mancini, 19
and *n.*; Sylvester's introduction to More, lxx–lxxi, lxxviii.

Hall. It was unfortunate for Richard's reputation that, with Vergil and More, the etching of his villainy fell into the hands of draughtsmen far more skilful, subtle and sophisticated, and, above all, more influential than those of Rous, André or Carmeliano. A careful assessment of the work of Polydore Vergil in particular is of crucial importance not only in the development of the Tudor Saga but also in that his writings, far more than those of More, form a major source for the study of Richard's reign. This is partly because his *English History* covers the entire reign, whereas More's *History* breaks off abruptly on the eve of Buckingham's rebellion in the autumn of 1483, partly because it has much more claim to be regarded as serious and sober history than has More's work, and finally because his book represents by far the fullest account of Richard's reign which has come down to us.

Polydore Vergil was already a humanist of international repute when he came to England in 1502 as a deputy of his Italian patron, Cardinal Adriano Castelli, as a collector of papal taxes. Although Polydore himself says that he was encouraged to write his history of England by a formal request from Henry VII, the various preferments he received in England during the last seven years of the reign owed more to Castelli's influence with the king than to any direct royal patronage. His *Anglica Historia* was not completed until 1513 and not published (after much revision) until 1534, by which time he need give no thought to the possible favours of a Tudor king. The dedication of the manuscript to the new king, Henry VIII, was written during a brief period when Henry looked favourably on him, but he received no royal patronage after that date, and incurred the spiteful hostility of Wolsey. The dedication of Renaissance histories to Renaissance princes was, in any event, a commonplace, given the didactic nature of such works; it was regarded as a positive necessity for princes to learn from the lessons of the past.[9]

Polydore, then, was no official hack. Equally, he could not afford to be wholly detached and impartial. He has been seen in the posture of 'a modern historian of repute who undertakes to write the history of a large business firm'.[10] Tact was necessary in relation to certain incidents and certain persons, some still alive, some dead but with important surviving descendants. Polydore himself always claimed to tell the truth. Indeed, in his view, this was the main function of history, although he was not unaware of the moral content of the subject, so dear to his Renaissance contemporaries. Nevertheless, it is fair to say that 'the implicit purpose of

[9] For Polydore in general, see the major studies by Denys Hay in his introduction to his edition of *The Anglica Historia of Polydore Vergil, A.D. 1485–1537* (1950), i–lxii, and his *Polydore Vergil* (1952), *passim*.
[10] Hanham, 126–7.

the work (which is nowhere deliberately concealed) was to put a favourable interpretation on the rise of the house of Tudor'.[11] Certainly, the pattern of historical development which Polydore imposed on the history of fifteenth-century England tended to lead to this conclusion, although no one has suggested that he invented it for this purpose. Polydore's great invention (apart from writing history designed to be read as literature) was to break with the annalistic tradition of the chroniclers, and instead to divide English history into royal reigns. 'The central thread of continuity lies in the succession of kings, where immutable human nature and mutable fortune play a never-ending game.'[12] In the fifteenth century, however, kings were especially subject to the workings of divine retribution: and here we have the entire schematic framework of Shakespeare's fifteenth-century history plays from *Richard II* to *Richard III*. Henry IV started a chain of calamity by breaking his solemn oath of allegiance to Richard II. His sin was visited on his descendants in the third generation: Henry VI was born to misery. But the agents of retribution were themselves sinful. Edward IV similarly breached a solemn oath, and paid for it in the murders of his sons (by Richard). Richard III, the next agent in the sequence, was even more villainous, and he too paid the necessary price. The victory of Henry Tudor at Bosworth, his marriage to Elizabeth of York, and the accession of their son, Henry VIII, in Vergil's own time, brought the horrid sequence to an end, as Shakespeare expressed it through the mouth of Henry of Richmond in the closing lines of his play:[13]

> We will unite the White Rose and the Red.
> Smile heaven upon this fair conjunction,
> That long have frowned upon their enmity!
> Now civil wounds are stopped, peace lives again,
> That she may long live here, God say Amen!

Within the context of this major scenario, the underlying hostility of Polydore's portrait of Richard was achieved by means more subtle and insidious than the overtly dramatic methods favoured by Sir Thomas More. One example may suffice to show the contrast. At the very beginning of his *History*, More uses Richard's alleged physical deformities and appearance as a signpost to the man's inner evil. More's 'little of stature, ill-featured of limbs, crook-backed . . . hard-favoured of visage' leads on at once to 'he was close and secret, a deep dissimuler, *lowly of countenance, arrogant of heart*, outwardly companionable where he inwardly hated, dispitious and cruel'.[14] This subtle literary counterpoint was not Polydore's

---

[11] Hay, *Polydore Vergil*, 154.
[12] Hay, *op. cit.*, 136, and, for what follows, 141–5.
[13] *Richard III*, V, v, 19–21, 40–1.
[14] More, 7–8 (my italics).

style. Instead, his description of Richard's appearance is tagged on at the very end of his account of the reign. The bias remains: 'little of stature, deformed of body, the one shoulder higher than the right . . . a short and sour countenance, which seemed to savour of mischief, and utter evidently craft and deceit': but Polydore has the grace and honesty to end on a note of muted admiration:[15]

Truly, he had a sharp wit, provident and subtle, apt both to counterfeit and dissemble; his courage also high and fierce, which failed him not in the very death, which, when his men forsook him, he rather yieldeth to take with the sword, than by foul flight to prolong his life, uncertain what death perchance by sickness or other violence to suffer.

The main element of hostility to Richard in Polydore's account lies essentially in his projection of Richard's psychology, especially in the attribution of motive. He uses what Richard's modern defenders might call a 'smear technique', constantly suggesting elements of deceit and dishonesty behind the facade of an outwardly correct and apparently well-intentioned public behaviour. Two examples may serve to illustrate this point. On hearing of the death of Edward IV, says Polydore, Richard 'began to be kindled with an ardent desire for sovereignty' (a claim many modern scholars would dispute):[16]

but for that there was no cause at all whereby he might bring the same to pass that could carry *any colour of honesty, so much as in outward show and appearance*, he deferred the devise [devising] thereof presently unto another time, and the meanwhile sent most loving letters to Elizabeth the queen, comforting her with many words, and promising on his behalf (as the proverb is) seas and mountains. . . .

Summoning together all 'the honourable and worshipful' of the country around York, he caused them to swear an oath of allegiance to Edward V:

himself was the first that took the oath, which soon after he was the first to violate.

Later, as king (asserts Polydore), Richard allowed the rumour that the princes were dead to circulate abroad in the hope that the people would accept his rule, knowing that no issue male of Edward IV now remained

[15] PV, 226–7; see also, p. 200, 'a man to be feared for his circumspection and celerity'. Polydore's references in this same section to Richard's nervous habits of chewing his lower lip and plucking at his dagger clearly show that he had his information from someone who knew Richard well.

[16] PV, 173; and see below, pp. 64 ff.

alive. This merely earned him general unpopularity, since it was believed that he had caused their deaths, and, therefore,[17]

> he fell again from so great felicity into a fear and heaviness of heart, and, because he could not reform the thing that was past, he determined by all dutifulness to abolish the note of infamy wherewith his honour was stained. . . . And so, whether it were for that cause, or (as the brut [popular report] commonly goeth) because he now repented of his evil deeds, he began afterward to take on hand *a certain new form of life, and to give the countenance and show of a good man,* whereby he might be accounted more righteous . . . (to) appease partly the envy of man, and procure himself goodwill, he began many (good) works as well public as private. . . .

Although the note of bias seems obvious, we cannot preclude the possibility that Vergil was merely reporting the truth as he knew it, or at least as it was retailed to him by his informants and his written sources. There is, however, no suggestion of any such change in policy in his most important contemporary source, the Croyland Chronicle.[18]

Despite its author's great reputation, and the justified celebrity and wide influence of the work itself, Sir Thomas More's *History of King Richard III* deserves less serious consideration as a source of information for Richard's life and reign than does Polydore's *Historia.* Quite apart from its dependence on Polydore's work (written about the same time), to which More may well have had access in manuscript,[19] it has long and with some justice been questioned whether More was seriously writing history in the modern as opposed to the classical sense of the word (i.e., drama) at all. As long ago as 1768, Sir Horace Walpole (one of Richard's earlier defenders) was not too far wrong in calling More 'an historian who is capable of employing truth only as cement in a fabric of fiction'.[20] This view has been shared in less extreme form by many modern scholars, for example by A. R. Myers, who observed that 'his history is much more like a drama, unfolded in magnificent prose, for which fidelity to historical fact is scarcely relevant'.[21] More recently it has been seen, with much point but also some exaggeration, as nothing more than a 'satirical drama', but this idea that More was merely indulging in an urge to poke fun at his contemporaries and exercise his own literary cleverness seems to belie the

---

[17] PV, 191–2 (my italics).

[18] Discussed below, pp. xliv–xlvi.

[19] For a plausible argument on this point, Hanham, 146–7. Polydore was working on his MS in 1512–13 and completed it in 1514 (Hay, *Anglica Historia,* xiii–iv). More wrote the first part of his *History* in 1518–19, the second (post-coronation) later, perhaps in 1520–1 (Sylvester, introduction to More, lxiii–lxvi; Hanham, 218–19).

[20] Walpole, *Historic Doubts on the Life and Reign of Richard III,* 116.

[21] Myers, 'Character of Richard III', 119.

essentially serious nature of the work.[22] It is perhaps best seen as a treatise against tyranny, for which, his friend Erasmus tells us, More always had a 'peculiar loathing'.[23] Like many other Tudor writers and dramatists, he turned to the recent English past for exemplars to support his didactic thesis. A second reason why More is of less value to the historian than his contemporary, Polydore, lies in the unfinished nature of the work.[24] More deals in far greater detail than does Polydore with the events of the months from April to October 1483 (Polydore was, after all, writing a general history of England), and he ends abruptly with a scene describing Bishop Morton's subtly flattering exhortation to Henry duke of Buckingham to take arms against his royal master:[25]

> it might yet have pleased God for the better store to have given him [Richard] some of such other excellent virtues mete for the rule of a realm, as our lord hath planted in the person of your grace [Buckingham].

How More might have developed his treatment of Richard's character had he continued his work can only be speculation, but in the period covered by the *History* he emerges as an unrelieved and ruthless villain, lacking any of the lighter touches with which Shakespeare's imagination endowed him.

It has recently been observed of Polydore Vergil's *History*:[26]

> it treated history as literature. . . . In the classical manner, Vergil related his story with all the refinements of the stylist, from elevated rhetoric to the homely proverb; introduced imaginary orations and arguments . . . dramatized established incidents . . . graphically described new ones . . . and attempted to deduce and explain motivations.

All these features in Polydore are writ large in More. Invented speeches, such as Edward IV's deathbed oration and Buckingham's address to the

---

[22] Hanham, 152–90. Although ingenious and stimulating, Dr Hanham's arguments are sometimes overstrained, and to adopt her arguments *in toto* tends to lead to the conclusion that More did not believe a word of what he was writing.

[23] Sylvester, intro. to More, c.

[24] Various reasons have been put forward for More's abandonment of this book (not the only work he left unfinished). In so far as it was designed to 'launch an attack on the *Realpolitik* practised by the princes of his day', he may already have become suspicious by 1518 of Henry VIII's tyrannical tendencies and noted some obvious parallels with the recent past; or his increasingly full-time commitment to the king's service by 1518 may simply have deprived him of the time to write his *History*; and, according to Dr Hanham, an extension of a work originally planned, apparently, to end with Richard's assumption of the throne to cover his entire reign would have created serious literary difficulties (Hanham, 118–19; Sylvester, intro. to More, ci–ciii).

[25] More, 93.

[26] Hanham, 144.

Londoners urging Richard to accept the throne (some six pages in print), occupy in all one-third of the *History*. To a greater degree than Polydore he was influenced by literary precedents in classical authors. Thus the praise accorded at the opening of the *History* to Edward IV as a beneficent and successful king ('In which time of his latter days, this Realm was in quiet and prosperous estate . . . no fear of outward enemies, no war in hand . . . the people toward the Prince in a willing and loving obedience'), immediately contrasted with the dissimulating and malicious personality of Richard, finds an almost exact parallel in the contrast between the beneficent Augustus and the evil Tiberius drawn by Tacitus in his then recently rediscovered *Annals*. Tacitus, it has been claimed, provided More with 'not merely a collection of analogues from imperial history' but also with 'a dynamic narrative that in both plot and pervading atmosphere parallels the basic movement of More's *History*'.[27] He also drew considerably on the writings of Sallust and Suetonius. To some extent, therefore, More's account of the events of 1483 was influenced by admired literary models rather than by an objective concern with truth.

As might be expected of two men writing about the same time and moving in similar circles, More and Vergil shared much the same sources of information, but their attitude towards their evidence is very different.[28] Both made use of such written sources as were available, notably the London Chronicles, and Polydore had the advantage in that he was familiar with a version of the Croyland Chronicle, whereas More had not, except in so far as he derived of it via his likely knowledge of Polydore's work. But, as Polydore himself observed, written sources became scanty after 1450. He spent six years, he tells us,[29]

> in reading those annals and histories [for the earlier parts of his history] during which . . . I collected with discretion material proper for a true history. When, on approaching our own times, I could find no such annals . . . I betook myself to every man of age who was pointed out to me as having been formerly occupied in important and public affairs, and from all such I obtained information about events up to the year 1500.

Although More makes no such claim, both men probably derived much of their information from those who had shared Henry Tudor's exile and

---

[27] More, 4–5, 7–8; Sylvester, intro. to More, lxxxvi–xcviii, esp. xcii–xcv.

[28] For Polydore's sources, Hay, *Polydore Vergil*, 84–95, Hanham, 129–42; More's sources, Sylvester, lxv–lxxx, Hanham, 161–74. Neither Polydore nor More knew of Mancini, but both Armstrong (Mancini, xix–xx, 119 *n.* 6) and Sylvester (intro. to More, lxxiii, lxxviii) were struck by the way in which Mancini's contemporary narrative appears to corroborate More on many points of detail, but as Hanham, 71, points out the divergencies are also impressive.

[29] Quoted in Kingsford, *English Historical Literature*, 256–7.

had later come to hold prominent positions in his council and court, like Cardinal Morton, Bishop Fox of Winchester, Christopher Urswick, Henry's confessor and almoner, and Reginald Bray – sources largely unbalanced by any favourable to King Richard. Polydore seems also to have cast his net wider and sought out information from less partisan lips; he tells us, for example, that in trying to find the reasons for the breach between Edward IV and Clarence, he made inquiries of several of Edward's surviving councillors, though without success. More and Vergil also differ in their handling of popular beliefs and stories assigned to no particular person. Vergil attempts to resolve conflicting interpretations, distinguishing mere rumour from what is believed by 'men worthy of credit', or will observe that a certain story seems plausible when set against other evidence. More also makes fairly frequent use of phrases like 'it is for truth reported', 'this I have by credible information' and 'some wise men also ween', but, at least according to one recent interpretation, these were only introduced by More as stylistic parodies of other historians and were intended as 'danger (or joke) signals to the alert reader'.[30]

More made relatively few 'factual' additions to the development of the Tudor saga, the most notable being the suggestion that Richard planned to make himself king even before the death of his brother, an emphasis on the innocence of the Woodville family, and his delightful digression about Mistress Shore, the first pen-portrait of a living woman in English prose. The great difference between More and Vergil, however, lies partly in the extent to which More embellishes his story with invented details, over and above those already added by Polydore, and partly in the constant hostility which runs through his narrative, condemning Richard sometimes blatantly, sometimes by subtle innuendo. His intention is, in some degree, to heighten dramatic effect. Thus, in his account of the events of 13 June 1483 which led to the arrest of Hastings and some of his supporters, and then to Hastings's execution, More embroiders fancifully on Polydore's account: amongst other inventions, More says that Richard arrives late and then asks for someone to fetch him a dish of Bishop Morton's famous strawberries from Ely House; displaying his withered arm, he accuses the unlikely partnership of the dowager queen and Elizabeth Shore as the witches responsible for his affliction; then Hastings's execution has to be hurried because Richard swore that he would not dine until Hastings's head had been struck off (Richard had eaten dinner three hours before, around 10 or 11 a.m., unless he departed seriously from the customs of his time).[31] Equally, More's highly elaborate account of the death of the

[30] Hanham, 159, 165; cf. Sylvester, lxiii–iv.
[31] For More's handling of the Hastings episode, see the full account in Hanham, 166–74.

princes has long ago been dismissed as contradictory and deserving of nothing but scepticism.[32]

All this makes any convincing assessment of the value of More's work difficult indeed, and it is not surprising that historians have differed widely in their conclusions. No one would nowadays accept the judgement of James Gairdner, a careful scholar whose excessive trust in the value of tradition, without which, he said, the study of history is like attempting 'to learn a living language without a teacher', led him in the end to assert that 'a minute study of the facts of Richard's life has tended more and more to convince me of the general fidelity of the portrait with which we have been made familiar by Shakespeare and Thomas More'.[33] This, of course, is to ignore the special problem of Richard's reign, that is, how much importance should be attached to the Tudor tradition. More's judicious modern editor, R. S. Sylvester, reached the conclusion that[34]

> Richard III, in the pages of the *History*, is indeed evil incarnate; but the portrait More drew reflects an image which his age bequeathed to him. His acceptance of that image stems not so much from his own partisanship, as from the trustworthiness which he attributed to those who had already, both orally and in writing, created the main features of the legend. . . . Few of Richard's defenders would care to deny that More's portrait of the king reflects a view of him current in the court of Henry VII. What they have failed to notice, however, is the remarkably accurate way in which More renders this. Had [Richard's defenders] noticed this, they would not perhaps have dismissed his narrative as mere Tudor propaganda.

On the other hand, Dr Hanham, whilst sharing Sylvester's belief that More was no propagandist, argues that this hard-headed lawyer did not think it possible to know the reasons behind human actions, which were a matter of sheer conjecture, and one might as well 'shoot too far as too short':[35]

> For himself, therefore, he would not be bound by facts (which were, in any case, often unrecorded), but would aim at poetic truth as he deduced it – a life of the tyrant on the lines perhaps of Tacitus or Suetonius, with a liberal admixture of his own sardonic wit. . . . He was writing primarily as a literary craftsman, not as the investigator of historical evidence.

[32] Kendall, 398–405.

[33] Gairdner, xi–xiii, and see the comment of Myers, 'Richard III and Historical Tradition', *History*, liii (1968), 198–9.

[34] Sylvester, intro. to More, lxxviii.

[35] Hanham, 160, 194–5; see also the suggestion of Myers ('Character of Richard III', 119) that More 'may have wished to present Richard as a personified Vice in a Renaissance equivalent of a morality play'.

Whichever emphasis one may prefer, it is important to realize that neither More nor Vergil can be accused of *inventing* the 'Tudor Saga', for propaganda or any other reason. They were 'improving' upon a view of Richard already accepted in their own time, and for some years before. What contemporary fire produced all this Tudor smoke we shall have to consider later.

One other figure in the development of the Tudor version of Richard deserves separate consideration.[36] In 1548 the lawyer Edward Hall published his *Union of the Two Illustre Families of Lancaster and York.* His work was a eulogy of the Tudor regime with Henry VIII as hero, as his introduction reveals:

> What misery, what murder and what execrable plagues this famous region hath suffered by the division and dissension of the renowned houses of Lancaster and York, my wit cannot comprehend nor my tongue declare. But the old divided controversy . . . by the union celebrated and consummated between the high and mighty Prince King Henry the seventh and the lady Elizabeth his most worthy queen . . . was suspended and appalled in the person of their most noble, puissant and mighty heir, King Henry the eight, and by him clearly buried and perpetually extinct.

More clearly than either Polydore or Sir Thomas More, Hall reveals the characteristic 'correct' attitudes of the Tudor Englishman, which were partly the product of his own chauvinism and staunch Protestantism, and partly reflect the propaganda of the regime: these are echoed in Shakespeare, who was acutely sensitive to the political climate of his own time. Civil war was abhorrent; sedition – 'that cankered crocodile and poisoned serpent' – was hateful; rebellion could not be forgiven. According to Tudor tradition, even a bad monarch must be obeyed. But, of necessity, Richard was an exception, since the Tudor usurpation had to be justified, and this could only be done by making Richard a monster from whose rule England was delivered by its saviour, Henry Tudor. His coming fitted into a scheme of divine providence, which ended the long period of suffering and atonement for England's sins, beginning with the deposition of Richard II, and reaching a 'culmination of savagery in the tyrannous reign of Richard III',[37] an idea which clearly owed much to Polydore Vergil. Far from being 'the Welsh milksop' which Richard alleged him to

---

[36] The later chronicles of Richard Grafton (1568) and Raphael Holinshed (1578, 1587) make no significant additions to the Tudor tradition, Holinshed's being very much a copy of Hall in form and content (Churchill, *op. cit.*, 207–23). For what follows, and on Hall in general, see Churchill, 173–206; Kingsford, *op. cit.*, 261–5.

[37] Ribner, *English History Play in the Age of Shakespeare*, 104–5.

be, Henry's goodness showed in his appearance in the hour before Bosworth:[38]

> For he was a man of no great stature, but so formed and decorated with all gifts and lineaments of nature that he seemed *more an angelical creature than a terrestrial personage,* his countenance and aspect was cheerful and courageous, his hair yellow like the burnished gold, his grey eyes shining and quick. . . .

Hall also took over from Polydore the division of history into reigns, but dramatised the method by his chapter-headings: 'Unquiet Times' (Henry IV), 'Victorious Acts' (Henry V), 'Troublous Season' (Henry VI), 'Prosperous Reign' (Edward IV), 'Pitiful Life' (Edward V), 'Tragical Doings' (Richard III), 'Politic Governance' (Henry VII) and, finally, 'Triumphal Reign of Henry VIII' (which last takes up half the space in Hall's book). This histrionic approach, of course, suited Shakespeare well, and was heightened by Hall's exuberant and highly charged style and his lavish embellishment of his sources to strengthen dramatic effect. Although Hall drew upon a number of sources for his fifteenth-century history in general, when he came to the years 1483–5 he relied on Thomas More for the account of the usurpation (it is printed entire), but for the rest of the reign largely upon Polydore Vergil, with some drawing from the London Chronicles. Hall's ability to 'improve' upon Polydore, who seems almost impartial by comparison, may be illustrated by two examples. When Richard was endeavouring to induce Queen Elizabeth to leave sanctuary with her daughters, much persuasion and many promises were necessary, but finally,

> forgetting injuries, forgetting her faith and promise to Margaret, Henry's mother, she first delivered her daughters into the hands of King Richard.

In Hall this becomes:

> And so she putting in oblivion the murder of her innocent children, the infamy and dishonour spoken by [concerning] the king her husband, the living in avoutry levied to her charge, the bastarding of her daughters, forgetting also the faithful promise and open oath made to the countess of Richmond . . . blinded by avaricious affection and seduced by flattering words, first delivered unto King Richard's hands her 5 daughters as Lambs once again committed to the custody of the ravenous wolf.[39]

[38] Hall, *Union*, 416 (my italics).
[39] PV, 210 (the original Latin of Polydore, *Anglicae Historiae Libri XXVI* (Basle 1534), 550, reads 'haud ita multo post oblita iniuriarum, immemor datae fidei Margaritae Henrici matri, primo filias in Ricardi potestatem tradit'); Hall, 192.

Some months later, after the death of his queen, news of Richard's plan to marry his niece, Elizabeth, leaked out. Polydore observes:[40]

> But because the maiden herself opposed the wicked act, all men abhorred it.

Then Hall:

> But because all men, and the maiden herself most of all, detested and abhorred this unlawful and in manner unnatural copulation. . . .

Hall was also capable of deliberately twisting or suppressing facts. Thus in relation to the notorious incident of Collingbourne's lampoon ('The Rat, the Cat, and Lovell our dog/ Rule all England under the hog') he states:[41]

> Yet the wild worm of vengeance wavering in his [Richard's] head he could not be contented with the death of divers gentlemen suspected of treason, but also he must extend his bloody fury against a *poor gentleman* called Collingbourne for making a small rhyme. . . .

The lampoon, widely circulated as it was, would have been enough by itself to get Collingbourne into trouble, but Hall carefully suppresses the fact that the real indictment against him was that he had been encouraging Henry Tudor to land at Poole in Dorset in October 1483 where he and many other gentlemen would cause the people to rise in arms against King Richard. The case was considered sufficiently important to be tried before two dukes, thirteen lords, the mayor of London and nine regular judges.[42] Although Hall makes some material additions to the Tudor Saga, as, for example, the warning pinned to the duke of Norfolk's gate before Bosworth, 'Jack of Norfolk be not so bold/ For Dickon thy master is bought and sold', the main interest of his narrative lies in his interpretation. Its most notable feature is the consistent animus he bears against Richard, shown in his regular embellishment of Vergil to bring out, with blatant lack of subtlety or reservation, Richard's essential cruelty. Indeed, this picture is heightened by the much more important role (by comparison with Vergil) which he assigns to Richard before 1483. He is praised for his bravery, skill and loyalty, and only his lust for the throne warped a nature which had much potential for good, and thereby brought about his downfall. This enabled Hall to echo directly the opinion of the London

[40] PV, 212; Hall, 193. The reference by Hall to 'unnatural copulation' rests upon the then widely-held but mistaken belief that the marriage of uncle and niece was contrary to the laws of the church.

[41] Hall, 398.

[42] CPR, 519–20; Gairdner, 186–91.

Chronicles that Richard's realm might have prospered and he himself might have been praised and beloved instead of reviled, if only he had been content to remain Protector.[43]

With the work of Edward Hall the Tudor portrait of Richard reaches its fullest flowering in the hands of sixteenth-century historians. If we are not justified in seeing in their work any systematic distortion of facts for political or propaganda reasons, the same effect was achieved by their additions and embellishments to known evidence, the tone of their prolix imaginary speeches, their concern with literary projection and above all their animus against Richard to support their essentially didactic purposes. If it was left to the dramatists to add the final flourishes, they were presented with an already theatrical canvas on which to work.

How far did the Tudor tradition reflect the attitudes of Richard's own contemporaries, as expressed in narrative and literary sources written during his lifetime or within a few months after his death? This is the acid test of its validity.[44] It is also a task of no mean difficulty.

The second half of the fifteenth century in England is a period of disquieting hiatus between the traditions of historical writing of earlier centuries and the still developing forms of Renaissance history. Gone are the voluminous chronicles written in Latin by monks or clerks which provide us with so much of what we know about the country's history in the three hundred and fifty years before. At St Albans Abbey, home of the most famous of the historical scriptoria, the tradition struggled on into the early years of Edward IV, but it was an expiring effort: Abbot John Whetehamstede's *Registrum* shows the shrinkage of the monastic horizon in being primarily a record of abbey history, with notices of historical events inserted only when they affected the fortunes of the house. Other monastic annals are mere scrappy jottings, often concerned with exceptional or unseasonable weather conditions.

The vacuum thus created was only imperfectly filled by the development of two largely novel sources of historical information: private correspondence and chronicles written in the vernacular English. Private letters, and the family papers which often accompany them, are of immense value where they have survived in quantity, partly because they are usually contemporary and mostly precisely dated, and partly (not being deliberate works of history) because they are unselfconscious. Unfortunately, their distribution in relation to particular periods of the

---

[43] *GC*, 238.

[44] Record sources are, of course, of immense value as a supplement to and a correction of the testimony of narrative sources, but their very impersonality makes them less valuable for the political attitudes and opinions of Richard's contemporaries.

century is very uneven. Their interest for national affairs depends largely on the changing fortunes of the families concerned. Thus the Norfolk family of Paston, whose papers form by far the largest surviving collection, were involuntarily but deeply involved in the competing interests of the great lords of that region. Local politics interacted closely with national affairs, and their search for influential patrons at court led the Pastons to keep a close eye on the politics of Westminster, especially during the two very disturbed decades between 1449 and 1471. With the return of more settled conditions during Edward IV's second decade, their political interest dwindled along with their political involvement: so, too, did the volume of their correspondence devoted to either national or local politics. Hence their letters and papers, as printed in James Gairdner's six-volume edition of 1904, fill some 414 pages for the decade of 1449–59. The two critical phases of the civil war, 1459–61 and 1469–71, consume 145 and 126 pages. In contrast, the decade from 1475 to 1485 produced only 109 pages of correspondence. Of these, those relating to 1483–5 occupy a mere 14, and only four documents have any political bearing.[45]

The reportage of national events which is a distinguishing feature of the Paston letters is not matched in the surviving papers of the three other families commemorated by substantial collections, although they too had their vicissitudes in an age of civil war. Those of the Yorkshire family of Plumpton, who, like the Pastons, could not be indifferent to the manoeuvres of great lords, are mainly local in interest, and contain only three letters which can certainly be dated to the reign of Richard III. One of these is of some interest as a reflection of northern reactions to the outbreak of Buckingham's rebellion in October 1483.[46] The letters and papers of the Stonor family, landowners principally in Oxfordshire and Berkshire, although of sizeable volume, are similarly short of political interest. This is despite the fact that the head of the house, Sir William Stonor, rebelled with Buckingham and suffered forfeiture of his estates thereby, a circumstance ignored in the correspondence. They do, however, contain two newsletters written to Sir William Stonor from London by Simon Stall-

[45] There are two letters from John Howard, duke of Norfolk to John Paston, summoning him to do military service, one on the eve of Buckingham's rebellion, the other on the eve of Bosworth; the third is a similar summons from Richard himself, while Protector, to Ralph, Lord Nevill, dated 11 June 1483, which a modern editor inserted into the Paston correspondence, and the fourth is one of the two surviving copies of Richard's proclamation against Henry Tudor and his followers, issued on 23 June 1485 (*Paston Letters*, ed. Gairdner, VI, 71–3, 81–5).

[46] *The Plumpton Correspondence*, ed. T. Stapleton (Camden Society, 1839), 45–8; and see also J. Taylor, 'The Plumpton Letters, 1416–1552', *Northern History*, x (1975), 72–87; K. R. Dockray, 'The Troubles of the Yorkshire Plumptons', *History Today*, xxvii (1977), 459–66.

worth on 9 June and 20 June 1483, which have recently been much discussed for their bearing on the events surrounding the death of William, Lord Hastings on 13 June.[47] Finally, we possess the correspondence and business papers of the London wool-merchant family of Cely. These are of great interest for the organization of the wool trade at the time and for the domestic affairs of a trading family, but they are largely barren of any evidence concerning national affairs, except where they bore upon the wool trade.[48] To judge from their correspondence, one might be forgiven for believing that the Wars of the Roses never took place at all. Therefore, for this immediate period at least, private correspondence can at best be used only for crossing the t's and dotting the i's of what we can learn from other sources.

In these circumstances, it is peculiarly galling for the student of the Yorkist period that he misses by a mere thirty years or so the development of that great collection of letters and other material known as State Papers, which add so much to our knowledge of the Tudor age.[49] Although the State Papers were generated by the new demands of government on the king's subjects, they shed much light on individuals, since they themselves wrote many of the letters. The State Papers, as Professor Elton puts it:[50]

add the dimension of individual personality to our knowledge of English history . . . we know throughout this period the names, avocations and fortunes of a great many people in England, but before the State Papers exist in quantity, we know the minds, characters and purposes of only a very few.

Moreover, as he further points out, these records make possible a quite different analysis of events, in that

[47] *The Stonor Letters and Papers, 1290–1483*, ed. C. L. Kingsford, 2 vols (Camden Soc., 3rd ser., xxix–xx, 1919). The abrupt end to the correspondence was caused by its seizure into crown hands as a result of Sir William's rebellion, which in turn ensured its subsequent survival. The Stallworth letters are in vol. ii, 159–61, and for the discussion see further below, pp. 83–4, but especially Hanham in *EHR*, 1972, 237–40 and 1975, 824–5, and Wolffe in *EHR*, 1974, 840–4.

[48] *The Cely Papers*, ed. H. E. Malden (Camden Soc., 3rd ser., i, 1900). A new edition of the letters only is by Alison Hanham, *The Cely Letters, 1472–1488* (Early English Text Society, no. 273, 1975). Some disjointed jottings on political events occur for June 1483 (Malden, 132–3; Hanham, 184–5).

[49] For an admirable description of this class of material, see G. R. Elton, *England 1200–1640* (*The Sources of History*), 66 ff., esp. 69–70. A small number of documents of comparable character exists for the period before 1500, but they are chiefly diplomatic in interest (*ibid.*, 68 and *nn.*).

[50] *Ibid.*, 70.

They go behind the scenes. They introduce the historian to motive, intrigue, policy-making, the daily actions of people involved in affairs. . . . The whole texture of the history that can be written alters.

The possession of a fund of material of this kind for the Yorkist period – so markedly filled with political disturbance, policy-making and intrigue – would transform our knowledge of its inner dynamics. Lacking such material, the student of the fifteenth century must, however ruefully, learn to live without it, but it is worth emphasizing how greatly the scope of his inquiries is limited thereby, forcing him only too often into inference from men's actions in order to explain events rather than working from knowledge of their motives and circumstances.

Vernacular chronicles were by no means wholly new in the mid-fifteenth century, but it is only about that time that they first begin to be of prime value as historical sources, largely because of the decline of the monastic chronicle. Their importance is further enhanced (another negative reason) by the fact that, unlike France, England had no tradition of the 'chivalrous' history, as represented by Froissart and his successors, nor of the official or semi-official histories sponsored by the French crown, such as those emanating from the royal abbey of St Denis in Paris.[51] For English native chronicles we depend, therefore, upon works produced for an audience very different from both that served by these French historical writings and the restricted and educated circles in England to which the Latin chronicles of the past were meant to appeal. Nearly all the surviving vernacular chronicles were of London origin, their distinctive emblem being a method of dating by the London mayoral years. They were intended for an increasingly wide readership of people, mainly laymen, who had benefited from the spread of literacy and from the triumph of the vernacular language over Latin and French as a literary vehicle.

The London Chronicles exist in many different versions and clearly achieved a wide circulation. This is not the place to discuss the complicated story of the inter-relationship of the various texts, but certain broad points may be stated briefly. These chronicles were essentially compilations, the compiler/author making his own selection from earlier versions until he reached his own days, when he commonly added material drawn from his own knowledge and experience. They were also essentially annals rather than true histories, being innocent of any concept of causation or historical explanation and containing no analysis of the events they record. They tend to be uncritical of their sources, making no effort to reconcile differences or contradictions, often incorporating rumours as facts and making

[51] D. Hay, 'History and Historians in France and England during the Fifteenth Century', *BIHR*, xxxv (1962), 111–27.

much play with portents and prophecies (a form of contemporary credulity by no means confined to them). Finally, they were never intended as national histories. They are dominated by events in London, some being merely of civic interest, others, naturally, since they were writing in the capital, of wider interest. They have little knowledge of events outside the capital, and no interest at all in affairs outside the realm. Paradoxically, therefore, these chronicles are provincial, somewhat resembling a modern *Yorkshire Post* or a *Western Daily News*.[52] On the bonus side, however, it can be claimed with some justice that the London Chronicles, or at least the sources from which they were compiled, were written soon after the events they describe and 'thus reflect, to some extent, the popular opinion of these events'.[53]

For the Yorkist period, we have to deal only with three versions of these chronicles, each closely related to the others, and probably drawing on some lost original ('The Main City Chronicle'). These are the accounts known as 'Vitellius A XVI', *Fabyan's Chronicle*, and the fullest and most important of the trio, the *Great Chronicle of London*.[54] As its modern editors have demonstrated, the *Great Chronicle* shares with *Fabyan's Chronicle* a common author/compiler, Robert Fabyan, citizen, alderman and sheriff of London, and freeman and master of the Drapers' Company, who died in February 1513. They have also shown that the portion of the *Great Chronicle* dealing with events from 1439 to 1512 shows a definite unity of style and quality, and that the narrative up to 1496 was written before 1501–2, and perhaps earlier.[55] Hence it represents 'the adverse opinion of Richard III already current in the early years of Henry VII',[56] some time before the main architects of the Tudor tradition got to work, and it is unlikely to have been much influenced by the crude vituperations of Rous and André. It is interesting, for example, that the chronicle makes no mention of the alleged physical deformities of Richard so popular with other Tudor writers. Certainly, it contains distinct elements of Tudor prejudice, much more so than Vitellius A XVI or even Fabyan. For instance, when Richard, soon after his accession, sent his people out to see

[52] For the London Chronicles in general, C. L. Kingsford, *English Historical Literature in the Fifteenth Century*, 70–112, with revisions in *The Great Chronicle of London*, ed. A. H. Thomas and I. D. Thornley (1938), intro., *passim*.

[53] *GC* (as above), intro., xxiv.

[54] C. L. Kingsford, ed., *The Chronicles of London* (1905), 152–263, for Vitellius A XVI; Robert Fabyan, *New Chronicles of England and of France*, ed. H. Ellis (1811); *Great Chronicle*, as above. Although much effort has been spent on the textual relationships and authorship of this group, their historical value has not been critically assessed, hence the rather full discussion below; cf. the somewhat perfunctory and dismissive discussion by Hanham, 111–17.

[55] *GC*, intro., i–lxxvi, *passim*, for authorship; lii, lxiv, lxviii, for dating.

[56] *Ibid.*, and Kingsford, *English Historical Literature*, 101.

that their 'Cuntrees' were well guided and that no extortion be done to his subjects, this earns the comment 'And thus he taught others to exercise just and good which he would not do himself': Vitellius A XVI simply says that, immediately after assuming the throne, he summoned all the judges of the temporal law, 'giving them straitly in commandment to execute his laws justly and indifferently to every person as well to poor as rich'.[57] Not all such apparently hostile remarks need invoke Tudor prejudice as explanation. Some seem to be no more than the result of hindsight: in retrospect, for example, the fair promises offered to the queen-dowager by Richard in May 1483 may well have appeared to be 'manifold *dissimulating* promises'. Others seem to be a genuine record of the fears and rumours circulating in London in Richard's own time, especially during the months of his Protectorate. Unknown to the author of the *Great Chronicle*, many of these had already been recorded by Dominic Mancini, writing before December 1483. Indeed, Mancini tells us that many people believed that Richard was aiming at the throne at least from the time that he entered London; the chronicle states that the idea only became clear in connection with the death of Hastings.[58] Mancini also confirms the chronicler's statement that the original reason advanced to justify the deposition of Edward V in Dr Shaa's sermon from St Paul's Cross was that Edward IV himself was illegitimate (not the princes) and therefore his sons could not inherit the throne: Richard himself was the true son of Richard duke of York, and legitimate successor of his brother.[59] Although the *Great Chronicle*'s author believed that the princes had been murdered by their uncle, and says so twice, he is also at pains to make clear that this was a *general* belief ('men feared not openly to say they were rid out of this world', 'much whispering among the people that the king had put the children of King Edward to death', 'the more in number grudged so sore against the king for the death of the innocents that as gladly would they have been French, as to be under his subjection').[60] But it is the *Great Chronicle*, not Vitellius A XVI or Fabyan, which sets forward the idea that the murder was Richard's greatest mistake:[61]

[57] *GC*, 233; Vitellius A XVI, 191. For another example, see below, p. 173.

[58] *GC*, 231, for the suggestion that Richard's generosity to Hastings was 'all to bring his evil purpose about' and that after Hastings's death 'then was privy talking in London that the lord protector should be king'. For Mancini, see below, pp. xli–xliii.

[59] *GC*, 231–2; Mancini, 97.

[60] *GC*, 234, 236–7.

[61] *GC*, 238; cf. *Fabyan's Chronicle*, 673, which has 'Thus with misery ended this prince, which ruled mostwhat by vigour and tyranny, when he in great trouble and agony had reigned or usurped by the space of two years and two months and two days'. Vitellius A XVI, 193, merely records Richard's death at Bosworth and the dishonourable treatment of his corpse.

And thus ended this man with dishonour as he that sought it, for had he continued still protector and have suffered the children to have prospered according to his allegiance and fidelity, he should have been honourably lauded over all, whereas now his fame is darkened and dishonoured as far as he was known, but God, that is all merciful, forgive him his misdeeds.

But it should be noted that he is quite ready to avoid judgement when he thinks he has no firm information. Many opinions, he tells us, circulated about the manner of the princes' deaths (smothering, drowning in malmsey wine, injection with poison), but he does not care to choose: 'however this may be', the one certainty is that they had been put to death before Henry Tudor's invasion.[62]

The *Great Chronicle* has many of the faults common to its genre. Its chronology is faulty: some events are placed in the wrong years, and, more serious, the sequence of events is, more than once, disarranged on quite important matters. For example, Buckingham's rebellion of October 1483 is explained not only as a reaction to the supposed death of the princes, but also by rumours that Queen Anne had died by poison (March 1485). There are mistakes of fact – Anthony, Earl Rivers, not his kinsman, Thomas Grey, marquis of Dorset, was in charge of Edward V on his journey to London in April 1483 (a mistake shared with the *Chronicle*'s cousins). There are contradictions: Thomas, Lord Stanley (miscalled the earl of Derby, a title he received only in 1485 at the hands of Henry Tudor) is said to have been arrested at the time of Hastings's execution, but immediately released, for the fear which Richard had of possible dangers from his son, Lord Strange, who was at large in Lancashire. Months later, however, he is still in custody, held by the king 'for a season'. There is also the usual concentration on events in London, with details of executions, civic receptions, the loans made by Londoners to the king, and the like.[63] Nevertheless, the chronicler seems to have had some first-hand knowledge of the events he describes, and of some he was clearly an eye-witness. He saw, for example, perhaps with a draper's sharp eye for sartorial splendour, the young king's entry into London in May 1483, describing the mayor and his brethren clad in scarlet, 500 citizens in violet meeting with the king in Hornsey Park, 'his Grace riding in blue velvet and the duke of Gloucester in coarse black cloth', while all the king's servants and his own were clothed in black.[64]

In some respects the penny-plain narrative of Vitellius A XVI may be preferred to the more prejudiced version of the *Great Chronicle*, but it is

---

[62] *GC*, 237.

[63] *GC*, 230–6.

[64] *GC*, 230. He also clearly had direct knowledge of the jewels pledged by Richard as security for loans (pp. 235–6).

going too far to say of these London narratives that 'there is little to suggest that they derive from sound first-hand information, and as they stand they present a baffling mixture of borrowed material and innovations', and there is much to be said for the judgement of the editors of the *Great Chronicle* that 'its narrative, if not that of a highly trained historian, yet gives us a vivid record of events which fell within the author's own knowledge'.[65]

'It is because no sound contemporary history exists for this age,' claims G. R. Elton, 'that its shape and meaning are so much in dispute now', but 'the narrative material does not permit much scope or depth to reconsideration, and those who have tried to rewrite fifteenth-century history from the narratives alone have been beating the air'.[66] If we had to depend for our knowledge of Richard III solely on the vernacular narrative and literary sources, we should indeed bow before this stricture. Fortunately, for Richard's reign we can also draw upon two sources of very different character and of much higher value than any of those discussed so far. They share the advantages of being at once contemporary and being composed as deliberate and critical histories.

First comes Dominic Mancini's account of *The Usurpation of Richard III*, which came to the notice of English historians only as late as 1936, when it appeared in a scholarly edition by C. A. J. Armstrong.[67] The discovery of Mancini's work was an event of major importance for the study of Richard's Protectorate and usurpation: its date of composition and the inherent quality of the work combine to make it an invaluable control with respect to the validity of the Tudor tradition. A successful poet and author, Mancini found an influential patron in the Italian physician, Angelo Cato, who was also a councillor to Louis XI of France and owed his appointment as archbishop of Vienne to royal influence. It seems to have been upon Cato's directions that Mancini was sent to England in the summer of 1482, where he remained until recalled shortly after 6 July 1483. His account of events in England had been completed by 1 December 1483. The value of his report on the state of English affairs during the last months of Edward IV's reign, particularly his description of the court and its leading figures, a subject on which he clearly possessed much direct information, and the subsequent narrative of the events of April–July 1483, is enhanced by his approach to his task. He writes soberly and objectively of the unfolding of the dynastic revolution,

---

[65] *GC*, intro., lxxiv.

[66] Elton, *op. cit.*, 22.

[67] 2nd and revised edn, 1975. Mancini is also usefully discussed by Hanham, 65–73, although her remarks are affected (p. 75) by her views about the date of Hastings's death (below, p. 84).

eschewing the moralizing and invented speeches beloved of many humanist historians, preferring to explain events in his own words. Since he apparently did not readily understand English, it is likely that much of his information came from the Italian community in London, among them probably the humanist Pietro Carmeliano, who could have introduced him to court circles; and Mancini himself tells us that he obtained information from Dr John Argentine, physician to the princes in the Tower and the last of their attendants to be withdrawn (although himself English, Argentine spoke Italian and has studied for some years in Italy).[68]

Since he was a foreign observer, with no foot in any English political camp, we might expect Mancini to be detached to an extent no Englishman was likely to be. His modern editor believed that his account contained little animus or prejudice, 'save in his assumption that Gloucester was all along aiming for the throne'.[69] His views may have been influenced both by hindsight and by his own expressed intention to 'put in writing by what machinations Richard the Third attained the high degree of kingship'. He makes no secret of what he believed to be Richard's true intentions from soon after the time of his brother's death, but he also makes it clear that many other men in the London of May and June 1483 very much shared this conviction.[70] In this sense, he may be seen as a reporter of other men's opinions rather than as one foisting upon Richard's actions his own pattern of explanation. It is the same with his observations about the likely fate of the princes. He tells us that they were withdrawn into the inner apartments of the Tower and were gradually seen no more, that their attendants were withdrawn, and that Dr Argentine reported that the young king himself was in imminent fear of death. These were damning circumstances in themselves, but Mancini does not go on to state, as any Tudor writer would have done, that the princes' lives had already been brought to an end. Instead, he reports that many men burst into tears at the mention of the king's name, 'and already there was a suspicion that he had been done away with'. But, he adds cautiously, 'Whether, however, he has been done away with, and by what manner of death, so far *I have not at all discovered*'.[71]

The importance of Mancini's narrative lies in the fact that he provides direct contemporary evidence that Richard's ruthless progress to the throne aroused widespread mistrust and dislike, to the extent that at least some of his subjects were willing to believe, within a fortnight of his accession, that Richard had disposed of his nephews by violence. He had

[68] Mancini, Armstrong's intro., *passim*.
[69] *Ibid.*, 17.
[70] Mancini, 85, 89, 91 (his own statements); 83, 91, 95 (other men's statements).
[71] Mancini, 93 (my italics).

no good reason to invent this latter story, and his caution in refusing to accept rumour as fact is clear evidence that he was not concerned with embellishing a tale already sufficiently dramatic in order to please his continental literary patrons. On the contrary, it provides a strong indication that such hostile rumours were already circulating from very early in Richard's reign: they were already sufficiently widespread four months later to cause men to rise in rebellion against the new king. Such stories cannot have been mere inventions of Tudor propagandists writing years after Richard's death. Recent attempts to discredit Mancini's testimony by presenting him as a prejudiced foreigner later corrupted by Tudor agents rest upon mere biassed speculation and do not deserve serious consideration.[72]

Whatever the value of Mancini's work for the period of the Protectorate, the most important single source for the reign as a whole, and indeed also for the entire second decade of Edward IV's reign, is the history generally known as the 'Second Continuation of the Croyland Chronicle'.[73] Despite its name, this was no chance late survivor of the monastic chronicle tradition, although in form it is preserved as a continuation of two spurious chronicles associated with the Fenland abbey of Crowland or Croyland. Instead, it is a sophisticated piece of history. Its author claims that he was a doctor of canon law and a councillor of Edward IV and that he had gone on embassy to the court of Burgundy in 1471. There is no good reason to doubt his further claim that his history was 'done and completed at Croyland within ten days', ending on the last

---

[72] To take but one recent example, Audrey Williamson, *The Mystery of the Princes* (An Investigation into a Supposed Murder) (1978), esp. 17 ff. Despite clear evidence to the contrary, Mancini's account of the Yorkist court in 1483 is dismissed as 'garbled ... largely based on gossip ... in many cases by Lancastrian sympathisers'. Apart from the fact that a *Lancastrian* sympathiser would indeed have been a *rara avis* in the London of 1483, no evidence is adduced to support these statements. Similarly, Mancini's suspicions about the death of the Princes are rejected with an *ex cathedra* statement: 'There is *no doubt* that at the time Mancini left England the princes were still alive' (p. 17, my italics). Sharing Markham's suspicion on all things French, especially information alleged to come from across the Channel, Miss Williamson actually credits Angelo Cato with being the head of 'a French spy ring' (p. 20), whose purpose, it seems, was mainly to forge evidence.

[73] 'Historiae Croylandensis Continuatio' in *Rerum Anglicarum Scriptores Veterum*, ed. W. Fulman (1684), 549–92; English translation by H. T. Riley, *Ingulph's Chronicles* (1893), 453–510. The chronicle has been discussed by C. L. Kingsford, *English Historical Literature*, 178–94, and, most usefully, by Hanham, 74–102, especially as regards the corruption of the later part of the text, but her account is spoilt by her acceptance, in part, of some of the conclusions of J. G. Edwards (see next note).

day of April 1486.[74] Good evidence exists to support the suggestion already made by more than one recent historian that the author was none other than John Russell, bishop of Lincoln (1480–94), who was not only a doctor of canon law and a royal councillor but also keeper of the privy seal to Edward IV (1474–83) and chancellor of England to Richard III himself (June 1483–July 1485).[75] Even if this particular identification is not accepted, it can be shown from the internal evidence of the chronicle that the author was a well-educated clerk, possessing knowledge of the chancery, who was present at a number of meetings of council, parliament and convocation, and who was clearly on several occasions an eye-witness of the events he describes.[76] We are dealing, then, with a man of quite

[74] This was generally accepted until challenged by J. G. Edwards, 'The "Second" Continuation of the Crowland Chronicle: Was it Written in Ten Days?', *BIHR*, xxxix (1966), 117–29. Edwards questioned the date on the grounds that the phrase 'Acta sunt et expleta apud Croylandiam A.D. 1486 per spatium decem dierum' (the last of which was 30 April) refers not to the chronicle but to a legal process between Crowland and Peterborough abbeys inserted into the later pages of the Continuation. It can, however, be shown that the same phrase was used in other works by the most likely author, Bishop Russell (see following note). If he were the author, then he can also be shown to have been in the right place at the right time (in the course of an episcopal visitation), and, further, it is unlikely that, if the chronicle were written *after* April 1486, it should not have contained any reference to later events, particularly the northern rebellion of 1486, of which the author had heard but did not know the outcome, although it had already been suppressed by the end of that month.

[75] The suggestion was made by A. R. Myers, 'Richard III: A Correspondence', *History Today*, iv (1954), 710, and by P. M. Kendall, *Richard III* (1955), 432–3. More recently, Hanham, 88–95, has advanced a number of plausible reasons for regarding Russell as the author, but other evidence (which Miss M. M. Condon and I hope to publish shortly) exists which seems to put the matter beyond all reasonable doubt. For Russell's career, see A. B. Emden, *Biographical Register of the University of Oxford to A.D. 1500*, iii, 1609–10. Russell was said to have been reluctant to take office (Rous, *Historia*, in Hanham, 119), but Hanham, 89 *n.*, is wrong in saying that he was dismissed from office in July 1485 (R. L. Storey, 'English Officers of State', *BIHR*, xxxi (1958), 86). Hanham, 89 ff., suggests some reasons to explain why a man who served Richard as chancellor throughout almost his entire period in power should nevertheless have produced a distinctly hostile portrait of his former master.

[76] E.g. his description of the Christmas festivities at Richard's court in December 1484, with its remarks on the dresses worn by the queen and Elizabeth of York suggests an eye-witness; so too, and even more strongly, is a similar description of court ceremonies of Christmas 1482, with comments on the fashionable clothes worn by Edward IV and on the beauty of his daughters, prefaced by the phrase 'you might then have seen' (*CC*, 572, 563). A similar phrase ('In the morning you might then have seen') introduces his account of the reactions in London to news of the events at Stony Stratford and Northampton in April 1483 (*CC*, 565). He seems also to have been present at the stormy council meeting in April 1483, following the death of Edward IV, with its unique description of the crucial part played by Lord Hastings, and alone among contemporaries he gives the exact date, time of day and place in the palace of Westminster at which the lords and others signed an oath of allegiance to Richard's son, Edward prince of Wales (*CC*, 564–5, 570).

unusual qualifications in a writer of English history during the Middle Ages: he was an intelligent man of affairs, possessed of inside knowledge of the workings of politics and government in his own day, about which he shows himself remarkably well-informed. Finally, he was writing within a few months of Richard's death about events within his own experience, and he therefore had no need to rely upon transmitted oral information such as reached Vergil and More from the lips of Tudor partisans. Where it can be tested, his reliability is of a high order, and his reputation for accuracy has recently emerged triumphant from a vigorous modern debate concerning the date of death of William, Lord Hastings.[77]

He is a cautious and politic author who, although he writes clearly and authoritatively, unfortunately does not always choose to tell all he knows. His judgements were often elliptically phrased and sometimes appear intentionally inscrutable, as in his comment on the nature of the malady which killed King Edward IV.[78] Although he was probably in a position to know about the fate of the princes, he states no clear opinion thereon, preferring instead to cite some verses by 'a certain poet' on the three Richards who had ruled England which clearly condemn Richard for his nephews' deaths.[79] His stated intention, however, was to set forth his material 'in as brief terms and in as unprejudiced a manner as we possibly can', and at the end he claims to have given 'a truthful recital of the facts, without knowingly intermingling therewith any untruthfulness, hatred or favour whatsoever'.[80] In general, his narrative seems to bear out this claim. Save for an excessive and unreasoning dislike of the northerners, which he shared with other southern authors, his attitude is detached and urbane, although on more than one occasion he assures us that he could have said harsher things had he chosen to do so.[81]

Given all these circumstances, the hostility of the chronicler's account towards Richard is most noticeable. In describing the usurpation he stresses

[77] For the debate, see below, pp. 83–4. For his reliability as a source for Edward IV's financial policies, see Ross, *Edward IV*, 380 ff. The chronicler clearly prided himself on his inside knowledge, and his comment on the oath-swearing ceremony mentioned above ('a new oath, drawn up by some persons to me unknown') reflects his irritation when he did not possess it (*CC*, 570).

[78] The king was not 'seised with any known kind of malady, the cure of which would not have appeared easy in the case of persons of more humble rank' (*CC*, 563–4; Ross, *op. cit.*, 414–15). He is equally elusive in his remarks on the death of Henry VI in 1471 ('Hence it is that he who perpetrated this has justly earned the title of tyrant . . .', *CC*, 556: H. T. Riley took this to refer to Edward IV, but Richard may have been meant).

[79] *CC*, 575–6.

[80] *CC*, 549, 575.

[81] *CC*, 498, and, for his dislike of northerners, see A. J. Pollard, 'The Tyranny of Richard III', 150, 157–8, 162, and further below, pp. 123–4.

the elements of deceit and dissimulation which marked Gloucester's conduct, especially as they were displayed at Northampton and Stony Stratford. In London, his public genuflections of goodwill towards the dowager queen and expressions of loyalty to the young king could not conceal 'a circumstance which caused the greatest doubts', that is, the continued detention in prison of the young king's relatives and servants. The three strongest supporters of the young king were then removed 'without judgement or justice', and since the rest of his subjects feared a like fate, the two dukes (Gloucester and Buckingham) could do just as they pleased. Once they had the king's younger brother in their control, they 'no longer acted in secret, but openly manifested their intentions'. Richard's claim was no more than 'the colour for this act of usurpation'. Rumours circulated that the petition asking Richard to assume the throne had been drawn up in the north, but 'at the same time there was not a person but what very well knew who was the sole mover in London of such seditious and disgraceful proceedings'.[82] The execution of Rivers and his friends at Pontefract is likewise condemned: 'this was the second innocent blood which was shed on occasion of this sudden change'. Richard arbitrarily prevented the execution of Edward IV's last will, by seizing the treasures set aside for that purpose, in order to satisfy his 'haughty mind'. Much is made of Richard's exactions of 'forced loans', rather deliberately twisted into 'benevolences', a form of taxation which Richard himself had condemned in parliament: with exaggeration the chronicler claims that the king's wholly unscrupulous agents extracted immense sums from all the king's subjects. Then, he continues, obviously suggesting that he knew far more than he was prepared to tell, 'Oh God! why should we any longer dwell on this subject, multiplying our recital of things so distasteful . . . and so pernicious in their example that we ought not so much as to suggest them to the minds of the perfidious. So, too, with other things which are not written in this book, and of which I grieve to speak. . . .' Richard's public denial of his supposed intention to marry his niece, saying 'that such a thing had never entered his mind', simply arouses the chronicler's scepticism, for, he says, speaking of a council meeting at which he was clearly present himself, 'there were many persons present . . . who very well knew the contrary'.[83]

What conclusions can safely be drawn from this lengthy but necessary survey of our principal narrative and literary sources? Certain broad points seem clear. We have strong *contemporary* evidence that Richard

---

[82] H. T. Riley (trans., 489) took this remark to apply to the duke of Buckingham; it is much more likely that Richard himself was meant.

[83] For the above paragraph, *CC*, 486–99, *passim*.

was disliked and mistrusted in his own time. Whatever their differences in emphasis and interpretation, two independent authors, each writing within a few months after the events he describes, agree in their overall hostility to Richard. Their views are supported by the vernacular chronicles, so far as these can be trusted. To reject their opinions, and to suggest that they were deliberate liars (as some of Richard's defenders would have us do) is to take refuge in a rosy cocoon of wish-fulfilment. They may have their prejudices, and they may make mistakes, but to admit such faults is not to undermine their essential reliability.

We have to consider these writers in part as reporters and not only as interpreters. What they themselves believed may be of less importance than what they have to tell us about what other men believed. It would be difficult not to infer from their combined evidence that a great many men in England during Richard's reign suspected that he had disposed of his nephews by violent means. Equally, we can be confident that he was widely regarded as a usurper by his own subjects, since his claim to the throne never commanded any general credence. Like Richard II in his last years, the third Richard was highly vulnerable to the circulation of malicious and seditious rumours which both found difficult to control, and other evidence shows that not only was Richard regarded as an unlawful king but was also thought capable of poisoning his own queen in order to marry his niece.[84] It is unlikely that Richard killed his queen – no contemporary source specifically says so – but his evident alarm at the thought that such a story might gain credence even among his faithful northerners clearly shows how fragile he felt his reputation to be in the eyes of his own subjects.

The circulation of rumours hostile to Richard III within a few months after his death is a strong indication that they derived from similar stories of a date before August 1485. Such rumours were current on the continent as well as in England. For instance, a Spanish correspondent of the Catholic kings of Spain, writing from near Cadiz on 1 March 1486, saw Richard's fall as divine judgement on a wicked ruler who was already known to them as the murderer of his nephews. Some of his information derived from Spanish merchants who had left England as early as January 1486. The letter-writer, Diego de Valera, had no motive for distortion. That a belief in Richard's wickedness was strongly held by people in England and Spain within six months after his death is an indication that it can scarcely have been disseminated by the then little-known Henry

[84] On this point, see Ross, 'Rumour, Propaganda and Popular Opinion during the Wars of the Roses', in R. A. Griffiths, ed., *Patronage, the Crown and the Provinces*, 15–32, esp. 20–2.

Tudor.[85] It is possible to argue that even the poisonous and self-interested exaggerations of men like Rous and André would have lacked any plausibility had they not rested on some earlier foundation, especially since Henry VII himself showed no official disposition to blacken the reputation of his predecessor – perhaps because he had no need to do so.

Finally, it is a gross distortion of the available evidence to contend that the Tudor writers *invented* the wickedness of Richard III. The historian can rarely hope for certainty, or, as Richard's defenders seem to demand, for the sort of proof which would stand up in a court of law. It is only too often the historian's task to balance probability against improbability. On this issue all the probabilities point to the fact that the Tudor writers were building upon a foundation of antagonism to Richard III which antedated his death at Bosworth.

One final caveat must be entered. All the information considered above comes from writers associated with *southern* England, especially the capital. This was a region which conspicuously failed to support Richard in his hour of need. A different view might have been obtained from many of Richard's noblemen and from his subjects in the north of England, perhaps even in the midlands. Unfortunately, their views are not recorded in words. Their attitudes have to be inferred from their actions.[86]

The fluctuating fortunes of Richard's reputation since Bosworth may be disposed of more succinctly, since they have been the subject of an admirable recent survey.[87] The first snowdrop of a new pro-Ricardian tradition comes in the year after Shakespeare's death, 1617, with an essay by Sir William Cornwallis, *The Encomium of Richard III*,[88] which has been described as 'an exercise in rhetoric to defend the indefensible'. A far more comprehensive defence was written about the same time by the Elizabethan courtier, Sir George Buck (d. 1622), who became Master of the Revels to James I and in this capacity licensed several of Shakespeare's later plays. Until recently, historians have had to rely upon a much truncated and spoilt version of his work published by his nephew, George

---

[85] A. Goodman and A. Mackay, 'A Castilian Report on English Affairs, 1486', *EHR*, lxxxviii (1973), 92–9. The letter is printed in translation in E. M. Nokes and G. Wheeler, 'A Spanish Account of the Battle of Bosworth', *The Ricardian*, no. 36 (1972), 1–5.

[86] But cf. Pollard, 'Tyranny of Richard III', 153–6; Hanham, 60–4 ('Richard's Relations with the City of York').

[87] A. R. Myers, 'Richard III and Historical Tradition', 181–202, on which much of the next few paragraphs, including quotations, is based, except where otherwise acknowledged. See also P. M. Kendall's review of 'Richard's Reputation' (*Richard III*, 418–34), where the emphasis is very different.

[88] Ed. A. N. Kincaid (1977).

Buck, in 1646. Now, thanks to the literary detective work of the modern editor of the original version,[89] the elder Buck emerges as a more serious defender of Richard's reputation than had hitherto been thought, more careful in his use of sources and less haphazard in his method. Buck's connections with a number of founder-members of the Society of Antiquaries, like Sir Robert Cotton and the records-oriented Camden and Stowe, turned his attention to the value of records as a source of material, and he had the advantage of being able to consult the original manuscripts of the Croyland Chronicle in Cotton's famous library. Although he remains an irritating author in some ways, crabbed in style, diffuse and prolix, and given to immensely long if often learned digressions, his defence of Richard is not without its merits. The one significant addition to the Ricardian story (if we can accept it) is that, far from rejecting a match with her uncle, the young Elizabeth of York was willing and impatient for it to be accomplished. The evidence is a letter written by her to John Howard, duke of Norfolk (while Queen Anne was still alive), which, Buck tells us, he was allowed to see by the graciousness of the Howard earl of Arundel of his own time: the earl 'keepeth that princely letter in his rich and magnificent cabinet, among precious jewels and rare monuments'.[90] Given the greater conscientiousness of documentation we now know to have been shown by the elder Buck in contrast with his nephew, it is hard to brush aside this circumstantial statement. Yet, since the letter has not been seen since, it is equally difficult to accept it.

The eighteenth century brought with it a certain growth of scepticism about the Tudor Saga, pioneered by Rapin de Thoyras, followed by the historian of York, Francis Drake, and the scholarly Thomas Carte, and opposed only by David Hume who, though a great philosopher, deserves only a low rating as an historian. The best-known defence of Richard came, however, from that society luminary and man of letters Horace Walpole, whose *Historic Doubts on the Life and Reign of Richard III* were published in 1767. His approach had all the off-hand grace of the dilettante: 'The attempt was mere matter of curiosity and speculation. If any man, as idle as myself, should take the trouble to review and canvass my arguments, I am ready to yield so indifferent a point to better reasons.'[91] However, he cared sufficiently to recant his views in a *Postscript* published in 1792. His horror at the events of the French Revolution and its Reign of Terror led him to believe that 'any atrocity may have been attempted or practised by an ambitious prince of the blood aiming at the

[89] Sir George Buck, *The History of King Richard III*, ed. A. N. Kincaid (1979).

[90] Buck, ed. Kincaid, 190–1.

[91] Walpole's Preface, and Myers, *op. cit.*, 194, for the recantation mentioned below.

Crown in the fifteenth century'. In any event, his *Historic Doubts* were not based on any new scrutiny of the evidence, and he was therefore forced to break down the tradition by 'rational, forensic methods', along the line that it was not reasonable for a man of Richard's usual character to behave as the Tudors had supposed him to have done.

The first half of the nineteenth century saw two significant developments. The age of the Romantic Revival brought with it an increased admiration for the Middle Ages, and a more sustained effort to understand them by industrious investigation. Thus an influential historian like Sharon Turner[92] was in a much better position to explain Richard's usurpation, while his Evangelical principles prevented him from condoning it. There was also an increased interest in the value of records as historical sources and as correctives to narrative material. An interesting example of this is the two-volume work of Caroline Halsted, appropriately enough the wife of a rector of Middleham.[93] As a child of the Romantic age she wrote in affecting, indeed, melting prose. But there was also some whalebone behind the outer garment of sensibility. Her work contains 82 appendices covering 128 pages drawn from record sources, including the important manuscript known as Harleian 433.

The later part of the nineteenth century saw another and much more important development in the entire study of the history of medieval England, with the emergence of the professional historian, armed with a more critical, often sceptical approach to accepted interpretations and much more closely reliant on original sources, especially record materials. Fifteenth-century history, in particular, benefited from the labours of James Gairdner, a formidable and prolific scholar, whose main achievement lay in his impressive work as an editor. To his unflagging industry we owe the publication of many volumes of chronicles, letters and record material, among them two volumes of *Letters and Papers Illustrative of the Reigns of Richard III and Henry VII*.[94] These studies led him in 1878 to publish his *Life and Reign of Richard the Third,* which in turn influenced the views of most of the leading historians of his day, including J. R. Green, Sir James Ramsay and Bishop Stubbs. Gairdner has rightly been criticised for his excessive reliance on the value of tradition, in this case the Tudor tradition, and especially the work of Thomas More. The result was an interpretation of Richard III much more hostile in tone than that adopted by nearly all writers of the century before him.

Gairdner's work, however, produced a most violent reaction in the

[92] S. Turner, *The History of England during the Middle Ages*, 3 vols (3rd edn, 1830); Myers, *op. cit.*, 194–6.

[93] C. A. Halsted, *Richard III as Duke of Gloucester and King of England* (1844).

[94] Rolls Series (1861, 1863).

work of a most colourful figure, Sir Clements Markham, sailor, civil
servant and administrator, geographer and author, whose output included
three historical romances and eighteen biographies. He publicly clashed
head-on with Gairdner in the pages of the *English Historical Review* for
1891, and their debate was continued in Gairdner's revised edition of his
*Life* (1898) and Markham's own book, *Richard III: His Life and
Character* (1906), the most out-and-out defence of Richard ever written.
Markham's method was simple: the complete reverse of the Tudor tradition was expounded in terms as black and white as it had originally been
set forth in the sixteenth century. Henry VII becomes the odious villain,
his principal aide being an impossibly ubiquitous and malign Cardinal
Morton, whose main activity seems to have lain in working out his obses-
sional desire to blacken Richard's reputation. For Markham, Richard is
a Galahad, 'a young hero' and an outstanding example of 'British pluck',
who can be exonerated of each and every one of the crimes laid at his
door by the early-Tudor propaganda machine. As A. R. Myers observed,
Markham's extremism worked against his credibility: 'it is as impossible
to believe in his crowned angel as in Shakespeare's crowned fiend'.

There developed about this time an unfortunate divide between the
specialist and the popular views of Richard, which is almost the same as
saying between the amateur and the professional. Markham was the philo-
progenitive ancestor of Richard's modern defenders. His offspring have
included an Oxford professor of English law, a headmaster of Eton, several
peers of the realm and a number of historical novelists and writers of
detective stories. Apart from some with serious pretensions to be writing
history, notably the late Paul Murray Kendall[95] (himself an American
professor of English literature), the writers of fiction are the most prominent, among them Philip Lindsay, whose zeal for Richard matched that
of Markham himself, Josephine Tey, whose best-selling *Daughter of Time*
(1951) concerning the fate of the princes was described by that fount of
historical authority, the *Daily Mail*, as 'a serious contribution to historical
knowledge', Rosemary Hawley Jarman, author of *Speak No Treason*,
and a number of others, nearly all women writers, for whom the rehabili-
tation of the reputation of a long-dead king holds a strange and unex-
plained fascination. A permanent forum for the continued defence of
Richard's name came with the foundation in England in 1924 of the

---

[95] Kendall's widely-read biography (1955) is the only substantial life of Richard
to have been published since Gairdner wrote. Although the author admits that at
times he goes beyond the facts and 'reconstructs' (as in his blow-by-blow account of
Bosworth), and in spite of an empurpled prose style which tends to enhance his
partisanship, the book is soundly based on a wide range of primary sources, for which
it shows a proper respect. See the review by S. B. Chrimes in *History*, xli (1956),
213–14.

Richard III Society, originally known as the Fellowship of the White Boar. This was to be followed by a similar organization in America, where it is known as The Friends of Richard III Incorporated, and which included among its founder-members the film actresses Helen Hayes and Tallulah Bankhead, and by other branches in other continents, numbering some 2,000 members between them. The aims of these societies are sufficiently summarized by those of the English branch: 'In the belief that many features of the traditional accounts of the character and career of Richard III are neither supported by sufficient evidence nor reasonably tenable, the Society aims to promote in every possible way research . . . to secure a re-assessment'. But it is only fair to add that, in recent years at least, the English Society, as evidenced in the pages of its journal, *The Ricardian*, has played a much more objective and constructive role in Ricardian studies. Its sponsorship of a four-volume edition of the one great unpublished source for the reign, B.L. Harleian MS 433, which is still in progress, is a good example.[96]

Apart from an extraordinary sensitivity to any criticism of their eponymous hero, it has been a persistent weakness of the more extreme 'revisionists' to regard anything written about Richard III after 1485 as *ipso facto* discredited and prejudiced, except when it happens to suit their case. For example, Polydore Vergil, as a Tudor author corrupted by Morton, cannot be relied upon, and yet becomes an acceptable authority when he reports a general belief that the princes were still alive and had been spirited away abroad. Similarly, the story that Elizabeth Woodville, about to leave sanctuary, wrote to her son the marquess of Dorset urging him to return to England, rests solely on the testimony of Vergil, but is nevertheless reputable because it shows that Elizabeth had no reason to mistrust Richard, for, the argument runs, if he had killed her sons by her second marriage, why should she risk her son by her first marriage?[97] Far too much of the pro-Ricardian stance rests on hypothesis and speculation, on a series of connected 'ifs' and 'buts', on the 'may have been', or even worse – the unacceptable historical imperative – the 'must have been'.

This has been accompanied at times by an unpleasant animus against academic historians, in spite of the fact that they have largely come to adopt a 'moderate' stance. Dr A. L. Rowse stands almost alone in maintaining a 'traditionalist' stance, based, it would seem, on a rooted belief in the value of Shakespeare's view of the fifteenth century but using only Shakespeare's sources to prove it.[98] Professional historical attitudes have been conditioned by two complementary lines of inquiry, first, a fuller

[96] Ed. Rosemary Horrox and P. W. Hammond, 2 vols to date (1979, 1980).
[97] Williamson, *Mystery of the Princes*, 94, 116.
[98] *Bosworth Field and the Wars of the Roses* (1966).

understanding of the reasons behind the development of the Tudor tradition, and second, a much wider knowledge of politics and society in fifteenth-century England as a whole. The first has led to a more critical appreciation of the value of the Tudor tradition and a certain unwillingness to throw the whole bodily out of the window, especially when it can be confirmed by contemporary evidence. The second line of inquiry, conducted without the 'constitutional' preconceptions and moral prejudices of nineteenth-century historians, has had even more important consequences. Although not without its constructive side, the later fifteenth century in England is now seen as a ruthless and violent age as concerns the upper ranks of society, full of private feuds, intimidation, land-hunger and litigiousness, and consideration of Richard's life and career against this background has tended to remove him from the lonely pinnacle of Villainy Incarnate on which Shakespeare had placed him. Like most men, he was conditioned by the standards of his age. At the same time, modern research has given us a fuller understanding of the problems facing any king who tried to rule in fifteenth-century England, and, in particular, we now have the knowledge to compare the problems facing Richard with those of other usurpers: Henry IV, Edward IV and Henry VII. It can be argued that Richard's difficulties were perhaps insuperable from the start, and the manner in which he usurped the throne merely made them more acute. It may well be that his failure to retain his throne was due more to his own political (and military) mistakes than his reputation for moral ruthlessness. The reader may judge.

# PART ONE

# THE DUKE OF GLOUCESTER

Chapter 1

# FORTUNES OF A YOUNGER SON, 1452–1471

At the time of his birth on 2 October 1452, no man could plausibly have predicted for Richard Plantagenet the high and troubled destiny which was to lead him to the throne of England thirty-one years later. True, his father, Richard duke of York, was one of the great magnates of England, and a member of that small group of 'princes of the blood royal' (as they were already being called in 1450), whose high birth set them apart from the rest of the peerage. Like others of the group, he had a claim to the throne of England then occupied by the third king of the House of Lancaster, Henry VI, and there are signs that Duke Richard was actively coveting the crown for himself from the early 1450s, although he advanced no formal claim until after the renewed outbreak of civil war in 1459.[1] Richard himself, however, was only the seventh-born son in the inordinately large family which his mother, Duchess Cecily of York, provided for her husband, although three of his elder brothers had died in infancy, leaving Richard as the fourth surviving son. Thus he was no more than a junior cadet of a great aristocratic family.

The ducal household of York had been peripatetic. Richard's eldest sister, Anne (later duchess of Exeter), had been born as long ago as 1439, at one of her mother's favourite residences, Fotheringhay in Northamptonshire, where Duke Richard had established a collegiate church in the then fashionable mode of aristocratic piety. The duke's eldest son, Henry, who died young, had been born at Hatfield; two of Richard's surviving elder brothers, Edward (later Edward IV) and Edmund earl of Rutland, at Rouen while the duke was Henry VI's lieutenant-general in France. Another sister, Margaret, who was later to become duchess of Burgundy, entered her cradle at Fotheringhay; another son, John (who died young), at Westminster; and George, later duke of Clarence, at Dublin, where Duke Richard was king's lieutenant in Ireland in 1449. Thereafter, Cecily seems to have taken a brief rest from the exhausting business of childbearing until she produced Richard himself at Fotheringhay in 1452. Richard was therefore too young to enjoy the sort of separate establish-

[1] For a reassessment of the political significance of York's dynastic position, see R. A. Griffiths, 'The Sense of Dynasty in the Reign of Henry VI', in *Patronage, Pedigree and Power in Late Medieval England,* ed. Charles Ross, 13–36.

ment with household governors and tutors which Duke Richard provided for his two eldest sons, Edward of March and Edmund of Rutland, at Ludlow Castle in the heartland of the York family estates in the Welsh Marches. As a small boy he was probably brought up, along with George, at Fotheringhay under the direct care of a mother renowned for her unostentatious piety.[2]

By the time Richard had reached the tender age of seven, disaster had overtaken his family. The duke of York's pretensions to a controlling place in the government led to his being driven into exile in Ireland in 1459. Edward of March fled with York's leading supporters, the earls of Salisbury and Warwick, to the English stronghold at Calais. Their estates, and those of many of their followers, were confiscated to the crown in the packed and partisan parliament held at Coventry in November 1459. York and his friends were subjected to the dreaded sentence of attainder, by which they were proclaimed rebels, traitors and outlaws. The duchess of York remained in England, perhaps because she was still in Fotheringhay when her husband had to flee from Ludlow. According to one contemporary chronicle, she made her way to King Henry VI and submitted herself to his grace, interceding successfully at the same time for many of the duke's people, who thereby escaped the severest penalties of the law. The duchess of York herself was placed under the protective custody of her sister, Anne Nevill, duchess of Buckingham, whose husband was one of Henry's principal supporters. Where Cecily and her younger children spent the next few months is not known, but she was probably treated with concern and dignity as befitted Buckingham's sister-in-law.[3]

There followed a sudden and dramatic reversal of political fortune. In June 1460, the Nevill earls, Salisbury and Warwick, together with Edward of March, launched a successful invasion of England from Calais. After occupying London, they defeated the king's forces at Northampton on 10 July 1460 (where the duke of Buckingham was killed), and captured Henry VI. This enabled them to establish a Yorkist-controlled government run technically in the name, and with the authority, of their royal prisoner.

[2] C. A. J. Armstrong, 'The Piety of Cecily, Duchess of York: A Study in Later Medieval Culture', in *For Hilaire Belloc*, ed. D. Woodruff (1942).

[3] Scofield, *Edward IV*, I, 37 and n. 2. One strongly pro-Yorkist chronicler, however, asserts that the duchess had been badly treated by the Lancastrians while still at Ludlow (*English Chronicle*, ed. J. S. Davies, 83). See Kendall, 37, 440 n., for the suggestion that her sons were placed in the care of Archbishop Bourchier during the summer and autumn of 1460: cf. below, pp. 6–7. But in September 1460, following her husband's landing in England, the duchess was temporarily residing at the London house of John Paston, together with the boys and their sister, Margaret. In October the duchess went to join her husband at Hereford, leaving the children behind her at Paston's house, where they were visited daily by their elder brother, Edward earl of March (*PL*, III, 233).

Duchess Cecily and her younger children then probably took up residence in the London inn of the duke of York, Baynard's Castle beside the Thames. The duke himself lingered in Ireland until September 1460 when he landed in North Wales. It was immediately obvious that he intended to claim the throne for himself. The assembled lords of parliament, however, rejected this claim, and would go no further than to admit that he should succeed Henry VI when that king had reached the end of his natural life, thereby disinheriting Henry's son by Queen Margaret of Anjou, Edward prince of Wales. This arrangement, however, soon ceased to correspond with political reality. The Lancastrians, led by Queen Margaret, quickly mobilized their forces in the north of England. Richard of York, his second son, Edmund earl of Rutland, and the earl of Salisbury were defeated and killed at the battle of Wakefield on 30 December 1460. Queen Margaret's victorious troops advanced south and defeated the Yorkist forces commanded by the earl of Warwick at the second battle of St Albans (17 February 1461). The enemy now stood at the gates of London.

In this dangerous situation, Duchess Cecily thought it prudent to send her younger sons to safety abroad. She entrusted them to the care of Duke Philip the Good of Burgundy, head of a family with which York had already sought marriage alliances. As lord of a virtually independent state, whose resources fell not far short of those of the kingdom of France itself, Duke Philip was also master of the most extravagant and fashionable court in Europe. Its modes and attitudes were soon to exercise a powerful influence on the ceremony and culture of the Yorkist court in England.[4] The duke received the two boys with courtesy and respect. On 17 April, when they were at Sluys, the duke's emissaries waited upon them to carry them to the ducal palace at Bruges: among the escort provided was no less a person than the papal legate himself. At Bruges the duke visited, feasted and entertained them in person, but what impression the lavish splendour of the court of Burgundy left upon an eleven-year-old and an eight-year-old is unfortunately not recorded. Their stay, however, was short. By early June 1461 they were at Calais, there to take ship for England.[5]

For by now the political situation at home had again changed dramatically. Edward of March had defeated the Welsh Lancastrians at the

[4] C. A. J. Armstrong, L'échange culturel entre les cours d'Angleterre et de Bourgogne à l'epoque de Charles le Téméraire', in Cinq-Centième Anniversaire de la Bataille de Nancy (Nancy 1979), 37–49.

[5] Scofield, Edward IV, I, 178; M. A. Hicks, 'The Career of George Plantagenet, Duke of Clarence, 1449–1478' (unpublished Oxford D. Phil. thesis, 1974), 7–8, and references cited there. The deference shown to the boys in the later stages of their visit reflects their change of status, after Edward of March had become king and proved the victor at Towton (29 March).

battle of Mortimer's Cross (2 or 3 February 1461), marched upon London, and there, on 4 March 1461, he was proclaimed king as Edward IV. On 29 March he decisively overwhelmed the main Lancastrian army at the hard-fought battle of Towton. As he slowly returned to London to prepare for his coronation on 28 June, he judged it safe enough to send for his younger brothers. George and Richard therefore returned to England, about 12 June 1461, now as the nearest kinsmen of a reigning king, himself still only eighteen years old. Not surprisingly, they played a prominent part in the elaborate ceremonial of Edward's coronation. On 26 June they were among the twenty-eight knights of the Bath whom he created that evening. On the following day, dressed in blue gowns with white trimmings, they rode before him in the solemn procession to Westminster. On 28 June George was created duke of Clarence and was soon after elected a Knight of the Garter. Richard had to wait until 1 November 1461 before he was made duke of Gloucester and probably longer still before he was admitted to the Order of the Garter. This preferential treatment of the elder brother was to continue throughout the first eight years of Edward's reign.[6]

Comparatively little is known of Richard of Gloucester's upbringing, or even of his whereabouts, in the years of his adolescence. Contrary to the belief of P. M. Kendall, it is unlikely that he entered the household of his mighty cousin, the earl of Warwick, at Middleham Castle in Yorkshire as early as the closing months of 1461. There is some evidence that, with his brother Clarence and his unmarried sister Margaret, he was kept under the general eye of the royal household, which supplied them with money, clothes and transport. They did not necessarily follow the king about on his extensive travels, but may have had some small establishment of their own in the royal palace at Greenwich.[7] Perhaps also both boys were temporarily in the custody of their kinsman, Thomas Bourchier, archbishop of Canterbury, who was much later (in December 1471) rewarded by Edward IV because he had 'at the king's request . . . supported the king's

---

[6] Scofield, *op. cit.*, 182, 216 and *n.*; cf. *CP*, II, 542; V, 738, for Richard's not being nominated Knight of the Garter until 4 February 1466. Kendall's statements (pp. 50–2) that 'Richard reaped a richer harvest' of lands than his brother Clarence (cf. below, pp. 9–10), that 'Edward made no attempt to disguise the greater trust he reposed in Richard than George', and, that by 1464, Richard 'had already won first place' in the king's confidence are totally misleading, and a product of wishful thinking, not historical fact.

[7] Hicks, 'Clarence', 10–13. Nothing is known of Richard's education at either this or any later stage, but as princes of the blood royal both he and Clarence probably received much the same form of education later prescribed by Edward IV for his son, Prince Edward of Wales (Ross, *Edward IV*, 7–9; and see also K. B. McFarlane, *The Nobility of Later Medieval England*, 228–47, for aristocratic education in general).

brothers . . . for a long time at great charges', and both dukes visited Canterbury in the archbishop's company in August 1463, when the youthful Clarence behaved with an arrogance which was to become habitual.[8]

By 1464 the paths of the two dukes had begun to diverge. Clarence was made steward of England at the coronation of Edward's queen, Elizabeth Woodville, in May 1465, and in the following year, when he reached sixteen, he was declared of full age. Late in 1465 Richard had been placed in the custody of Richard Nevill, earl of Warwick. There he probably remained at least until 1468, when he too reached the age of sixteen, or even into the following year.[9]

Richard's sojourn in the household of Warwick 'the Kingmaker' probably had a powerful influence on his later development, though we possess no corroborative details. Warwick was then by far the mightiest magnate in England. From his paternal Nevill forebears he had inherited great estates in the north of England, particularly in Yorkshire, with their administrative centres in the two great strongholds of Middleham in the North Riding and Sheriff Hutton a few miles north of York. He was also powerful in the north-western counties, where he was warden of the west march towards Scotland, with his base at Carlisle. Through his mother, the dowager countess of Salisbury, Richard inherited the estates of the Montagu earldom of Salisbury, lying mainly in south-central England. Most important of all, his own marriage to the heiress, Anne Beauchamp, daughter of Richard Beauchamp, earl of Warwick, had brought him not only his title but also the huge patrimony of the wealthiest of the English

---

[8] *CPR, 1467–77*, 295–6; Hicks, 'Clarence', 18; *Chronicle of John Stone*, ed. W. G. Searle (Cambridge Antiq. Soc. Publications, xxxiv, 1902), 28. See above, *n.* 3, for the suggestion that these expenses belong to 1460, or perhaps to 1461 (the boys' transport to Burgundy).

[9] Warwick was granted, in Michaelmas term 1465, £1,000 towards the cost of Richard's maintenance from the wardship and marriage of Lord Lovell's heir (Scofield, *op. cit.*, I, 216 and *n.*), from which both Scofield and Kendall, 45, 442, inferred that Richard had been in Warwick's household since late in 1461 or some time in 1462: cf. n. 7 above. Warwick was not formally granted the custody of the Lovell heir and the wardship of his lands until 13 November 1467 (*CPR, 1467–77*, 51). Kendall, 52–3, further believed that there was an open breach between Edward and Warwick over the king's marriage in 1464, which 'put an end to Richard's formal tutelage' in the Middleham household (a mistaken belief: cf. especially Ross, *Edward IV*, 114–16). Kendall also relied on isolated mentions of Richard as a witness to royal charters as evidence of his presence in a particular place at any one time, a most dangerous practice. Richard's appearance on a commission of oyer and terminer of 20 February 1467 for the city of York suggests that he was still in the north, as does his absence from the powerful commission to investigate the alleged treason of Sir Thomas Cook on 20 June 1468 (on which Warwick, Clarence and almost everyone else of note were appointed to serve): *CPR, 1461–7*, 530; *CPR, 1467–77*, 103.

earls, centred in the midlands and the south, but including also the lord-ship of Glamorgan in South Wales. To these great assets by birth and marriage he had added enormously from the fruits of political power. His own period of control of government during the summer and autumn of 1460, supplemented by generous grants from a grateful Edward IV, had enabled him to acquire a series of lucrative and influential offices, and large estates forfeited by Lancastrian supporters, especially north of Trent. Other members of his family received similar advancement. All this made Warwick immeasurably the greatest power in the north of England, especially since the great rivals of his family, the Percy earls of Northum-berland, had been eclipsed by the fortunes of war.[10]

His castles of Middleham and Sheriff Hutton – and it is a reasonable assumption that much of the young Richard's time was spent there – were thus the centres of patronage, influence and aristocratic social life for the counties north of Trent. It is a fair presumption that here Richard, in his formative years, made the acquaintance of his future wife, Warwick's younger daughter, Anne Nevill, and one of his closest friends and most loyal supporters in later life, Warwick's ward, Francis, Lord Lovell. No less important was Richard's introduction to the large circle of northern noblemen and gentry – Scropes, FitzHughs, Greystokes, Dacres – who revolved round the regional courts of the Nevills in these early years of Edward's reign. Richard was later to become the political heir of Warwick in the north, and his northern connection was to be of crucial importance both in his usurpation of the throne and during his short reign.[11] Much of his later success in winning committed support from the northerners derived from his marriage to Warwick's heiress and from his own promi-nence after 1471, which offered his well-wishers and servants unusual opportunities for advancement; but it may also have owed a good deal to the fact that he was not personally a stranger to this society. Northern society was tightly clannish, independent and resentful of outside control, but by 1471 Richard was in its eyes no unknown and alien southerner.[12] It is a sign of Richard's early independence of character that this close association with his overweening and overwhelming cousin of Warwick

[10] Ross, *Edward IV*, 70–1, and Appendix III (437–8). Warwick's youngest brother, John Nevill, was created Earl of Northumberland and granted almost all the Percy estates in that county in May 1464, and his other surviving brother, George Nevill, chancellor of England 1461–7, was made archbishop of York in March 1465, and received other valuable rewards (*ibid.*, 72).

[11] Below, pp. 47–51; and for some reference to his personal followers from the north before 1471, see Ross, 'Some "Servants and Lovers" of Richard III in his Youth', *The Ricardian*, iv, no. 55 (December 1976), 2–5.

[12] See below, chapter 3, *passim*.

did not persuade him to follow his brother Clarence's example of supporting Warwick's factious opposition to Edward IV.

Meanwhile, Edward himself was grappling with the problem of making
provision for the endowment of his younger brothers on a scale befitting
their royal dignity. Edward had many demands on his resources, but he
gave a high priority to the needs of Clarence, who was not only the elder
brother, but also Edward's heir apparent, at least until the birth of his first
child, the Princess Elizabeth, in February 1466. Appointed lieutenant of
Ireland on 28 February 1462 (an office which he could execute by deputy),
Clarence was endowed between then and July 1465 with very extensive
estates forfeited from the Percy family in northern England, together with
the Honour of Richmond in Yorkshire. South of the Humber he was given
wide estates, forfeited from the earl of Wiltshire and others, in the west
country and the midlands, St Briavels and the Forest of Dean on the other
side of Severn, and the lordship and county of Chester, normally part of
the appanage of the prince of Wales. The extent of his holdings is shown
by the fact that from 1466 onwards he was being appointed to commissions of the peace in no less than eighteen counties, chiefly in south-west
and south-central England. In 1467 his lands were valued at 5,000 marks
(£3,666 13s 4d) in annual income (scarcely less than the dower of the
queen herself) and even this probably underestimates their true value.[13]

In contrast, the provision made for Duke Richard was at once less
generous and notably less secure. On 12 August 1462 he was granted
extensive lands, comprising the lordships of Richmond in Yorkshire and
Pembroke in West Wales, many lands forfeited from the (De Vere) earl of
Oxford in Essex, Suffolk and Cambridge, together with certain farms and
offices, including the constableships of Gloucester and Corfe Castles, and
he was soon to be appointed (on 2 October 1462) admiral of England,
Ireland and Aquitaine.[14] But in practice this endowment proved largely
worthless. Richmond was taken from him as a result of his brother's
jealousy and given to Clarence instead; Pembroke was then, and continued to be, firmly under the control of William, Lord Herbert, who
became its earl in 1468, and by 18 January 1464 Richard had lost all the
De Vere estates when they were restored to John, 13th earl of Oxford.

[13] Ross, *Edward IV*, 117 and *n*. The valuation excludes reversions (i.e., expectations) of lands worth a further 1,000 marks *p.a.* The queen's household was
costing just over £4,500 *p.a.* in 1466-7. Hicks, 'Clarence', 22, states that the grant to
Clarence of the county of Chester (August 1464) never took effect, perhaps because
of the announcement of Edward's marriage a month later.

[14] *CPR, 1461-7*, 197, 214. In the grant of 12 August, he is described as 'admiral
of the sea', but this probably relates to his constableship of Corfe Castle, which, by
custom, carried admiralty jurisdiction in Somerset and Dorset with it, especially
over the Isle of Purbeck.

Edward attempted to compensate Richard for the loss of Richmond by giving him instead, on 9 September 1462, all the forfeited estates of Robert, Lord Hungerford and Moleyns, chiefly in Berkshire and Wilt-shire, together with the lordship of Chirk in the Welsh Marches. But this grant in turn was cancelled by the oral order of the king to the chancellor on 30 March 1463.[15] Rather tardily the king endeavoured to make further provision by granting Richard the newly-forfeited estates of Henry Beau-fort, duke of Somerset, on 20 December 1463, but for all their high dignity and political importance the Beauforts had been only poorly endowed with land, most of their revenue coming from annuities paid by the royal exchequer, and such estates as there were were heavily en-cumbered with the life interests of two Beaufort dowager duchesses, both of whom had many years to live.[16] Not until 25 October 1468 did he once again receive a grant of the Hungerford estates. This should have repre-sented the inheritance of a comparatively wealthy baron, valued at some £800 yearly in 1436, even before the marriage of Robert, Lord Hunger-ford to the affluent heiress of the Moleyns family. By 1468, however, they were worth comparatively little to Duke Richard, perhaps some £500 of yearly income.[17] Nevertheless, they seem to have been his main source of revenue before 1469. Thus Gloucester's endowment was literally no more than a tithe of the vast revenues provided for his elder brother, even mak-ing suitable allowance for Clarence's position as Edward IV's heir male apparent. In fact, the king made less provision for his younger brother than for many royal supporters who were not members of the family. If his lack of an appanage suitable to a royal prince could be taken as legi-timate cause for grievance, then Richard had far more reason to turn against Edward in 1469 than had his factious brother Clarence.

Nor can Richard's comparative youth be taken as an explanation for his apparent lack of resentment at his second-rate treatment by his royal brother. In the summer of 1469, when Clarence joined Warwick in rebel-

---

[15] CPR, 1461–7, 212–13 (Richmond to Clarence); CP, X, 240 (restoration to Oxford); CPR, 1461–7, 228 (Hungerford grant and cancellation).

[16] Ibid., 292; CP, XII, 47, 53. The lordship of Pembroke had been granted in tail male to William, Lord Herbert on 3 February 1462 (CPR, 1461–7, 114).

[17] Many Hungerford lands had been granted to trustees to repay the great debts incurred in the ransom of Robert, Lord Hungerford (d. 1464) from the French; others were given to his son, Thomas, or to other persons by Edward IV himself; and there were two dowagers, Margaret Botreaux (d. 1478) and Eleanor Moleyns (d. 1476). Both were considerable heiresses in their own right (e.g., Lady Eleanor Moleyns's lands were valued at £473 p.a. in 1461), but their inheritances did not form part of the estates granted to Duke Richard, either in 1462 or in 1468. (CP, VI, 617–20; W. Dugdale, The Baronage of England, II, 209–11; CPR, 1461–7, 181, 183, 284, 333, 359; T. B. Pugh and C. D. Ross, 'The English Baronage and the Income Tax of 1436', BIHR, xxvi (1953), 19–20).

1(a). Edward IV, by an unknown artist, but attributed to the Netherlands School and based on a portrait datable before 1472.

1(b). Elizabeth Woodville. Panel portrait, probably contemporary, from Queens' College, Cambridge.

2(a). The unfinished castle of William, Lord Hastings at Kirby Muxloe, Leicester-shire. Work was abandoned there within days of his death on 13 June 1483.

2(b). Warwick Castle, showing some of the building attributed to Richard III.

lion against Edward IV, he was nearing seventeen years of age, and, like Clarence himself, could reasonably expect to have been declared of full age and fit to manage his own affairs as soon as he reached sixteen. In the Middle Ages, boys quickly became men, especially if they were of high birth. Henry VI was just sixteen in 1437 when he asserted his royal prerogative and declared an end to his minority (and indeed he had been displaying a precocious wilfulness three years earlier); Edward IV was only eighteen when he usurped the throne, and no one, except perhaps Warwick, doubted that he was an effective king, with a mind of his own. Duke George of Clarence was only thirteen in 1462 when his jealousy of Richard apparently caused King Edward to revoke the grant of the honour of Richmond to his younger brother and secure it for himself instead. The tendency of nineteenth– and early twentieth-century English society (recently partially modified) to prolong a man's adolescence to the age of twenty-one was alien to the Middle Ages when politics were involved, just as the rules of canon law relating to marriage and divorce could be more readily bent or broken for kings and their families than for lesser mortals. In these circumstances Duke Richard's conspicuous loyalty to his elder brother in the crises of 1469–71 is the more remarkable, although it is true that being less prominent at court than Clarence he had not been subject to the same frustrations and pressures which made his brother turn traitor to Edward IV in 1469.

Richard of Gloucester first began to play an independent role in English politics in the summer of 1469, when the hostility between Edward IV and the earl of Warwick finally exploded into violence. Well-informed contemporaries believed with some justice that the origins of the breach between the king and his powerful cousin lay in differences over foreign policy: Edward resolutely refused to accept Warwick's desire for an alliance with Louis XI of France and instead preferred a close connection with Burgundy, symbolized in the marriage of Richard's sister, Margaret, to Duke Charles of Burgundy in 1468. Warwick's wrath over his failure to prevail in this matter was intensified by the steady decline of his influence at court and the frustration of his family ambitions. Here the underlying cause was Edward IV's secret marriage in May 1464 to Elizabeth Woodville, the impoverished widow of a Lancastrian, John Grey (Lord Ferrers), who had been killed at St Albans. This unsuitable match might in itself have been accepted, once the initial shock and dismay felt by the English nobility had subsided, but it was the wider political consequences of the marriage which led to rancour. For Elizabeth Woodville had a large family, including two sons by her first marriage, five brothers and seven unmarried sisters, for all of whom her new husband had to make provision suitable to the dignity of a queen's relatives. Edward had not the resources to endow them lavishly with land, but he could lend his active assistance in providing them with well-connected and well-endowed husbands or wives, often by rather unscrupulous means which are said to have given particular offence to Warwick.[18] More important for the earl of Warwick, however, was that, in cornering the marriage market for his wife's kinsmen, Edward had effectively deprived Warwick of suitable husbands for his own heirs, his two daughters, Isabel (born in 1451) and Anne (born in 1456), unless they were to be allowed to marry the king's brothers, George and Richard. This Edward resolutely refused to permit. Moreover, the appearance of the numerous and jealous Woodville clan at court, where they soon seemed to possess an overweening influence with the king, led to a natural alliance between the queen's kin and those members of the aristocracy who had been raised to power by Edward himself, several of whom had married Woodvilles.[19] The most prominent of these was the powerful, grasping and energetic William Herbert, who became earl of Pembroke in 1468 and whom Edward had made a virtual viceroy in Wales, but there were also others like Humphrey, Lord Stafford (created earl of Devon in 1469) and John, Lord Audley, later to be denounced as grasping favourites in Warwick's manifesto of 1469. The Woodville connections spread even into older-established aristocratic groups, such as the Bourchiers (Henry Bourchier, earl of Essex, brother of the Archbishop of Canterbury, had allowed his heir, William, Viscount Bourchier, to marry one of the queen's sisters). Warwick therefore faced the hostility of an increasingly powerful connection, constantly at court and close to the king, which challenged the formerly dominant Nevill interest, and the abrupt dismissal of the earl's brother, Archbishop George Nevill, from the chancellorship of England on 8 June 1467, was a clear sign that Edward no longer intended to accept the earl's political tutelage. This the arrogant earl refused to accept. Dignity, continuing royal favour, an honourable and respected position at court and in council were for him no compensation for effective power. From 1468 at the latest Warwick was actively planning and plotting to recover his former dominance, by force if necessary. His principal ally, and the means to power, was Richard's elder brother.[20]

[18] Ross, *Edward IV*, 92 ff.; J. R. Lander, 'Marriage and Politics in the Fifteenth Century: The Nevills and the Wydevilles', *BIHR*, xxxvi (1963), 135–43 (reprinted in Lander, *Crown and Nobility, 1450–1509*, 94–126). Much important new material on this theme has been assembled in M. A. Hicks, 'The Changing Role of the Wydevilles in Yorkist Politics to 1483', in *Patronage, Pedigree and Power in Late Medieval England*, ed. C. Ross, 60–86. For the marriages, see Table 4; in addition, the queen's father, Richard Woodville, Lord Rivers, was created Earl Rivers, appointed treasurer of England and also Constable of England.

[19] Ross, *op. cit.*, 94, 130.

[20] For this, and what follows, in general, see Ross, *Edward IV*, 104–25.

George duke of Clarence had his own reasons for discontent, not dissimilar from those of Warwick. Although the potential succession of a woman to the throne of England raised its own problems, Clarence was no longer exclusively heir apparent to Edward's crown after the birth of Elizabeth of York in February 1466. The fertile queen and her no less vigorous husband could reasonably expect to produce a male heir given time: two more daughters, Mary and Cecily, were born to them in August 1467 and March 1469, and the first son, Edward prince of Wales, arrived in November 1470. If his position could never be quite the same again after Elizabeth's birth, Clarence, as the king's nearest brother, could still expect a special place at court and an advantageous marriage. This latter the king either could not, or would not, provide. In 1466, during the negotiations with Burgundy, a double marriage was proposed, Margaret of York to Duke Charles, Clarence to Charles's infant heir by a previous marriage, Mary of Burgundy. The Burgundians proved unwilling to pursue this notion. At the same time, Warwick's negotiations with King Louis XI for an Anglo-French alliance offered hopes of a good continental marriage for Clarence, combined with the prospect of becoming lord of Holland, Zeeland and Brabant if an Anglo-French attack should succeed in dismembering the Duchy of Burgundy.[21] This somewhat speculative proposal foundered on the rocks of Edward's refusal to consider an alliance with France, and neither would he sanction Clarence's marriage to Warwick's elder daughter, Isabel. At the same time, Clarence's self-esteem, and to some extent his material interests, were threatened by the rise of the Woodville faction and its 'new Yorkist' allies. The Italian observer, Dominic Mancini, writing years later, tells us that Clarence was openly hostile to the queen and her family. The queen in her turn feared for the succession of her offspring if Clarence were not removed, especially since he was comely, charming and eloquent. These remarks related to the circumstances of Clarence's fall in 1478, and it would be rash to read too much into them in connection with the events of 1468–9. Yet they fit both with what we know of Clarence's petulant and jealous character and the single-mindedness with which the queen promoted the interests of her family.[22] Clarence, therefore, actively lent his support to the earl's plan to procure his marriage with Isabel Nevill in spite of the king's opposition. He may even have believed, as one

[21] Rymer, *Foedera*, XI, 565; Scofield, *op. cit.*, 405. Kendall, 60, mistakenly accepted the garbled and inaccurate report of the Milanese ambassadors to the Court of France that Holland, Zeeland and Brabant were intended for Richard of Gloucester, together with a French bride, since Clarence was already married; but Clarence was not married in 1467 (the date of the report), and Louis's proposal was meant to win over Clarence, not Gloucester (*Calendar of State Papers, Milan*, I, 118–20).

[22] Mancini, 63.

continental chronicler suggested, that Warwick intended to make him king in place of his brother.[23]

From all this intrigue Duke Richard carefully kept aloof.[24] When trouble came, he emerged as one of Edward IV's closest and most loyal supporters. He had been with Edward at Salisbury in February 1469 for the trial of the alleged traitors Henry Courtenay and Thomas Hungerford, and the records of the hearings show that he actually served as the leading member of the commission of oyer and terminer which condemned them to death: both Clarence and Warwick were conspicuously absent.[25] He was probably present at the important Garter ceremony at Windsor on 13 May 1469, when the order was conferred on Duke Charles of Burgundy, and was certainly with the king in June, when Edward set out, along with Earl Rivers, Lord Scales and other Woodvilles, on a pilgrimage to Bury St Edmunds and Walsingham. It was here that the king heard, on or about 18 June, that Warwick and Clarence had now declared their hand. The earl and the duke crossed to Calais, where Clarence was married to Isabel Nevill on 4 July by Warwick's brother, the archbishop of York. More immediately threatening, however, was the major rebellion, led by one Robin of Redesdale, which the Nevills had fomented in the north of England. In response, the king moved to Nottingham, where he awaited the arrival of the troops which he had commanded Humphrey Stafford, earl of Devon and William Herbert, earl of Pembroke to raise in the west country and in Wales. This royalist army clashed with the rebels at the battle of Edgecote, near Banbury, on 26 July 1469, and Redesdale's northerners triumphed after a hard-fought engagement. Pembroke and his brother, Sir Richard Herbert, were taken captive, and summarily executed by the earl of Warwick at Northampton; Devon suffered a like fate at Bridgwater, and soon after Earl Rivers and one of his younger sons, John Woodville, were rounded up and equally abruptly executed on Warwick's orders, without any semblance of a trial. Here Gloucester's former guardian offered him a prime example of the ruthless and unlawful elimination of political opponents, who could not be regarded as traitors, for they had not been in arms against their king. Gloucester himself was to follow this precedent in 1483.

Gloucester's whereabouts during this episode are not known, but it is unlikely that he was still with the king when the latter, now almost alone and deserted by his men, fell into Nevill hands a few days after the battle,

---

[23] Calmette and Perinelle, *Louis XI et l'Angleterre,* 108, and Pièce Justificative, no. 30; Ross, *Edward IV,* 133 ff.

[24] Kendall, 61, 444, rightly dimisses the rumour that Richard was actively involved in the scheme to marry Clarence to Isabel Nevill; and, for what follows in general, Ross, *op. cit.,* 122 ff.

[25] P.R.O., K.B. 9/320; Ross, *op. cit.,* 123 and *n.*

and was sent off as a prisoner first to Warwick Castle and then to Middleham. There followed an uneasy period during which the earl of Warwick, himself based on Middleham, attempted to rule the country in the name of the captive king, following the pattern which had been successful in 1460. The earl communicated with the king's council in London by a series of writs and letters, nominally backed by Edward. Since Gloucester was not yet a member of the council,[26] he had no direct hand in this interim government. But when, early in September, Warwick found that his regime lacked authority, and in particular could not keep effective order in the realm, he was forced to release the king, who seems to have been at liberty and his own master when he appeared at York soon after 10 September. He then summoned his lords, Gloucester prominent amongst them, to join him in the north, whence he arrived in state in London in mid-October 1469.[27]

Even then Edward's problems were far from solved. A strong group of moderates amongst the nobility prevented him from resorting to extremes against Warwick and Clarence, and an uneasy peace between the king and his two most powerful subjects concealed their mutual animosity. But there was an urgent need for Edward to repair and rebuild the power-base of 'king's men' which had been badly damaged by the events of 1469, and, amongst other problems, he had to make immediate provision for the vacuum which had been left in the government of Wales and the Marches by the death of William Herbert, earl of Pembroke. Many of the major offices which Herbert had held had been granted to him in tail male, and should therefore have descended to his son, William Herbert, later 2nd earl of Pembroke; but this son was a minor, not yet of age to assume his father's role; moreover, the earl of Warwick had awarded some of these offices, such as the chief justiceship of South Wales, to himself in August 1469. This situation clearly could not be allowed to continue. Edward now deliberately decided to make use of his younger brother in a mature political role. On 17 October 1469 he was created Constable of England, an office formerly held by Richard, Earl Rivers, and for the better maintenance of his estate was granted two Duchy of Lancaster honours, Clitheroe and Halton in Lancashire and Cheshire, and in November the castle and lordship of Sudeley in Gloucestershire, which Edward IV had forcibly extracted from its ageing lord, Ralph Butler, Lord Sudeley, father of his former mistress, Eleanor Butler.[28] Edward thus made some amends

---

[26] Richard first appears in official council records as a councillor on 5 February 1472 (Lander, *Crown and Nobility*, 309), but the records are far from complete, and it is unlikely that he was not a councillor at least by May 1471.

[27] Ross, *op. cit.*, 135.

[28] *CPR, 1467–77*, 178; Somerville, *op. cit*:, 409, 510; *CCR, 1468–76*, 102–3 (Sudeley).

for the rather shabby treatment his brother had received in terms of landed endowment. But the duke's main sphere of operations was meant to be in Wales. On 7 November 1469 he replaced Lord Hastings as chief justice of North Wales. Ten days later he was appointed chief steward of all the Duchy of Lancaster lordships in South Wales, and on 30 November received similar offices in the principality of Wales and the earldom of March. Finally, on 7 February 1470, he displaced Warwick as chief steward and chamberlain of South Wales. Thereby he became the principal representative of the royal authority in Wales and the Marches. These appointments can scarcely have endeared him to his former mentor, Warwick, who had hoped during the brief period of control he enjoyed in the summer of 1469 to retrieve his plans for the aggrandizement of the Nevills in South Wales (where he was already Lord of Glamorgan). These had been already frustrated by Edward IV's preference for William, Lord Herbert, as deputy of the king in this region, but the extent of Warwick's concern for his objective is shown by the fact that he tried yet again to re-establish himself in South Wales during the short-lived Readeption of Henry VI in 1470–1.[29]

The young duke was not to be left without experienced advice and assistance. Lesser offices in Wales were given to Walter Devereux, Lord Ferrers of Chartley, a former servant of the duke of York, who was later to die fighting for Richard III at Bosworth; to Sir Roger Vaughan of Tretower Court near Brecon, a kinsman and associate of William Herbert, 1st earl of Pembroke; and to the well-tried civil servant, John Donne, who was given special responsibilities in West Wales.[30] But it was also intended that Richard should depart for Wales at once, for much of the country, especially its western parts, had fallen out of royal control. On 19 October 1469 Gloucester was to be paid £100 at once; on 6 November he had 500 marks towards the expenses of his household 'and other charges by him to be borne according to our ordinance and commandment', and a further £100 on 10 November for such stuff for his household 'as he must nedley have ere he depart hence'. Richard was still in London when he formed part of the distinguished company assembled in the palace of Westminster to watch Henry Percy, heir to the earldom of Northumberland (and soon to be restored to it), but he probably departed for the Marches soon after, armed with a commission of array (29 October) to raise the men of the English border counties, followed by another order empowering him to reduce the castles of Carmarthen and Cardigan, which were being held by rebels against the king.[31] For the next few months he

[29] *CPR, 1461–71*, 293, 295; Ross, *op. cit.*, 156 (Warwick); *CPR, 1467–77*, 178–80 (Richard's offices).
[30] *CPR, 1467–77*, 173, 183, 185.
[31] *CCR, 1468–76*, 100; *CPR, 1467–77*, 180–1, 195.

was apparently busily engaged in Wales, enforcing a measure of order and reasserting the crown in this lawless and disaffected part of the realm.

For this reason he played little part in the crucial stages of the next crisis to confront Edward IV. Later in February 1470, rebellion occurred, this time in Lincolnshire, and the complicity of Warwick and Clarence soon became apparent. Edward reacted with vigour and urgency. Moving north with his chief supporters – Gloucester was not among them[32] – he caught and dispersed the rebels at 'Lose-Cote Field' (12 March) before they could effect a rendezvous with the forces of the earl and the duke. The king then set off in pursuit of Clarence and Warwick, now proclaimed to be 'his great rebels', reaching York on 20 March. Some time during these events Edward probably ordered Richard to join him with such forces as he could raise in Wales and the Marches. Marching up through the border counties, he seems to have clashed in Lancashire with the retainers of Thomas, Lord Stanley, the most powerful lord of that region. Stanley – as Richard later discovered to his extreme cost – was the quintessential trimmer, shifty, self-seeking and unreliable. But he was also Warwick's brother-in-law, and may have intended to support him, as he did later in October 1470 when Edward was in exile, and Warwick once again triumphant: Warwick certainly hoped for his support, for he and Clarence crossed from Chesterfield in Derbyshire to Manchester to enlist his aid. Stanley may also have resented the grants of the previous autumn to Richard of the honours of Halton and Clitheroe, where he held the principal offices: the intrusion of a royal duke into his own special sphere of influence was probably unwelcome to him. Richard's armed presence in Lancashire may have been one factor in deciding Stanley not to succour the rebels, who now fled south with the king in pursuit.[33] Gloucester was ordered (on 26 March) to array the men of Gloucestershire and Hereford to assist in the pursuit of the rebels, and was probably with the king at Exeter when he received a further commission of array against the rebels in Cornwall and Devon on 17 April.[34] Clarence and Warwick, however, had now taken ship from Devon and, after various misadventures, reached a safe haven in France about the beginning of May. Soon after, Richard of Gloucester returned to Wales, where he presided over the great sessions at Carmarthen on 18 June 1470.[35] However, Gloucester's active connection with the government of Wales soon came to an end. The evidence of

[32] R. Flenley, *Six Town Chronicles*, 164. For the events described in the next two paragraphs, the best contemporary account is in *Chronicle of the Rebellion in Lincolnshire, 1470*, ed. J. G. Nichols, *passim*, and for a modern account and analysis, see Ross, *op.cit.*, 137–45.

[33] Kendall, 83–4, 448 *n.*, followed by Ross, *op. cit.*, 143–4.

[34] *CPR, 1467–77*, 290.

[35] R. A. Griffiths, *The Principality of Wales in the Later Middle Ages*, I, 158.

commissions suggests that in July 1470 he accompanied the king to the north, where Edward went to suppress a rising in Yorkshire led by Warwick's brother-in-law, Lord FitzHugh of Ravensworth.[36] Moreover, on 26 August 1470, Richard was appointed warden of the west marches towards Scotland. This appointment foreshadows his future career in the north, but it also linked his fortunes more closely than ever with his royal brother, for it represented his intrusion into an office which was traditionally a preserve of the Nevill family, and which had been held by them almost without a break since 1399, and for the previous seventeen years by Warwick himself.[37] Richard was now enjoying the fruits of Warwick's downfall, an offence not likely to be forgiven if fortunes changed – as soon they did, rapidly and disastrously for Edward and his supporters. In his French exile, Warwick had lost no time in agreeing to King Louis XI's proposal that he should come to terms with his former enemy, the ex-queen Margaret of Anjou, now herself a refugee in France. With French assistance, Warwick was to invade England and restore the imprisoned Henry VI to the throne. This compact was sealed by the marriage of Henry VI's heir, the seventeen-year-old Edward of Lancaster, prince of Wales, to Warwick's younger daughter, Anne Nevill (who was now also seventeen); the formal betrothal of the young couple took place in Angers Cathedral on 25 July 1470. In return for French assistance – for this was to be Louis XI's diplomatic master-stroke – the restored government of Henry VI would join France in declaring war on Louis's arch-enemy, Charles duke of Burgundy: together they would overwhelm and dismember the powerful Burgundian state.[38] In early September, Warwick and Clarence, in company with John de Vere, earl of Oxford, one of Warwick's brothers-in-law, and Jasper Tudor, the Lancastrian earl of Pembroke and half-brother to Henry VI, set sail from La Hogue in Normandy and landed safely in Devonshire some four days later.

There ensued a dramatic collapse of Edward's authority. Warwick was soon joined by the earl of Shrewsbury and Lord Stanley with large retinues, and together they marched on Coventry. Edward, still loitering in the north of England, suddenly found himself virtually isolated, chiefly because of the defection of Warwick's brother, John Nevill, who had recently been deprived of his title of Earl of Northumberland, and the lands which accompanied it, in favour of Henry Percy, restored to his hereditary earldom on 25 March 1470. The desertion of the hitherto loyal Montagu proved fatal to Edward's chances of raising an army in the

[36] CPR, 1467–77, 221.

[37] R. L. Storey, 'The Wardens of the Marches of England towards Scotland', EHR, lxxii (1957), 607.

[38] Scofield, op. cit., 527–34; Calmette and Périnelle, op. cit., 109, 120.

north, and, as in 1469, he was soon deserted by all his men. He still had in his company his brother Richard, his brother-in-law Anthony Woodville, Earl Rivers and William, Lord Hastings, but none of them could hope for any mercy from Warwick, whose ruthlessness towards his enemies had been so amply demonstrated in 1469. For them at least a hasty flight was clearly the better part of valour. There was no good reason to suppose that Clarence's brittle sense of family affection would preserve them from the execution-block or a long, cold imprisonment in the Tower, even supposing he had the influence to protect them.[39] A hasty dash across Lincolnshire and the Wash brought the refugees to King's Lynn, where Earl Rivers's local influence secured them ships. On 2 October 1470 they set sail for the Low Countries. Edward himself seems to have landed in the roads of the island of Texel at Marsdiep, but Gloucester and Rivers, in another ship, came ashore much further south, in the Weilingen in Zeeland. So hasty had been their flight that they were entirely without funds. Edward is said to have been reduced to rewarding the master of his ship with a fine furred gown, and there is evidence among the records of the town of Veere (in Zeeland) that Gloucester had been able to borrow £3 2s 2d from the town's bailiff.[40] Fortunately, the exiles soon came under the care of Louis of Bruges, lord of Gruthuse, Duke Charles's governor of Holland, who had also been his ambassador to England and knew the king personally. They were well entertained throughout the autumn at his house in The Hague, where Gruthuse, a noted bibliophile, had amassed a splendid library of illuminated manuscripts. Acquaintance with this collection later had a powerful influence on King Edward's book-buying habits, and books of history and chivalrous romance, similar to those owned by Gruthuse, specially commissioned and decorated in Bruges, came to form an important part of his royal library. William, Lord Hastings copied his master's tastes, but they do not appear to have attracted Duke Richard, to judge from what is known of his rather meagre collection of books.[41] If Gruthuse's hospitality was warm and generous, in other respects the prospects before the exiles were gloomy indeed. Anxious to give no offence to the new government in England, the duke of Burgundy was not prepared officially to recognize the presence of his brother-in-law within his dominions. Not until Louis XI declared war on Burgundy, and put pressure on England to follow suit, did Duke Charles abandon his professions of friendship for the House of Lancaster and turn instead to Edward of York. Thereafter Charles gave rather grudging backing to the small expedition of some 36 ships (many lent by

[39] Ross, *op. cit.*, 150–3, 156–7.

[40] Maaike Lulofs, 'King Edward in Exile', *The Ricardian*, iv, no. 44 (1974), 9–11.

[41] For Edward's library and literary tastes, see Ross, *op. cit.*, 264–6, and the references there given; for Richard's books, see below, pp. 128–9.

the Hansard merchants or hired by Edward) and 1,200 men with which Edward planned to invade England. They finally set sail from Flushing on 11 March 1471.

Their venture was highly perilous. Hoping to land in East Anglia, where they might expect support from sympathisers like the duke of Norfolk, and from the tenants and followers of Earl Rivers in Norfolk, they found the country held against them, and were forced northwards towards the still more hostile coast of Yorkshire. Their little squadron was hit by storms and scattered, but they eventually made a landfall in the peninsula of Holderness, south-east of Hull, and on the following day (15 March) made contact with each other. Large bands of armed men lay in wait for Edward; the nearest town, Hull, refused to admit him; and to gain entry into York he was reduced to adopting the tactic used long before by another invader, Henry of Bolingbroke, of claiming that he had returned merely to recover his Duchy of York, not the throne itself.[42] After these first uneasy days, the fortunes of the small invasion army began to improve, largely because the newly-restored Henry Percy, earl of Northumberland, with whom Edward had been in contact during his exile, prevented his men from taking up arms against the king, and also effectively immobilized Marquis Montagu. As Edward's army moved south without direct challenge, his supporters began to declare themselves, particularly the great midland following of William, Lord Hastings, which brought in some 3,000 men, and it was therefore at the head of a growing and substantial force that he moved on to challenge the earl of Warwick at Coventry. At this point a great deal depended upon the attitude of the duke of Clarence, now moving up from the west country with a substantial force of men. From exile Edward had persistently worked, through all the contacts at his disposal, upon the fears and suspicions of his brother. The duke had little to gain and a great deal to lose if the restored government of Henry VI were to continue in power; a decline in influence and prestige, and the loss of many of his estates, mainly taken from former Lancastrians, was the most likely prospect before him. Edward's olive branch – a promise of forgiveness for his recent treacheries and a restoration to favour – therefore held many attractions for Clarence, especially since many of his supporters were showing reluctance to commit themselves to his – and Warwick's – cause. According to the contemporary official account of King Edward's 'Recoverie of England', Gloucester was in Edward's company when the three brothers met outside the town of Warwick, and Clarence then made the final decision to defect to the Yorkist cause; but in the version written much later by Polydore Vergil,

[42] For a fuller account of the events of March to May 1471, described in the pages which follow, see Ross, op. cit., 161–77, and the references there given.

Gloucester was the chosen negotiator, 'as though he had been appointed arbiter of all controversy', who first conferred secretly with the duke, and then prevailed upon the king to accept his brother's submission. 'Finally,' Vergii adds, 'not war but peace was in every man's mouth; then, armour and weapons laid apart upon both sides, the brothers gladly embraced one another.'[43] Clarence's adherence made it possible for Edward to risk leaving Warwick mewed up in Coventry, in his rear, and march directly on his capital. There he arrived on 11 April 1471, to be reunited with his queen, and to greet for the first time the son she had borne to him in the sanctuary of Westminster on 2 November 1470.

In the next six weeks Edward IV undertook the swift and vigorous campaign which finally secured his position on the throne. At Barnet on 14 April he overwhelmed the forces of Warwick and his allies, Warwick and his brother Montagu being left dead on the field, although the earl of Oxford made good his escape and survived to trouble both Edward IV and Richard III in later years. At Tewkesbury on 4 May Edward achieved an equally decisive victory over Queen Margaret's Lancastrian army. Her son, Edward prince of Wales, was killed in the battle, and Margaret herself was later taken prisoner. On 21 May Edward returned to London, which had successfully resisted an assault led by Warwick's kinsman, the Bastard of Fauconberg, and a force of rebels from Kent and Essex. On the very night of Edward's triumphal entry into the capital, the captive king, Henry VI, died in the Tower of London.

In these events Gloucester, rather than Clarence, whose treason had been too recent to inspire much confidence, may have been Edward's principal lieutenant. At Barnet Richard is said to have commanded the Yorkist vanguard, a statement which elicited from Paul Murray Kendall six pages of highly-charged imaginative prose:[44]

> The slight and youthful duke of Gloucester tersely gave his captains the word to advance banner. . . . Richard was in the thick of the conflict wielding a heavy battle axe. . . . Edward, in his turn, sensed that victory depended upon his reserve. . . . If his brother Richard could hold out – messengers came and went through the mist : Richard would hold, without reinforcements. . . . Out of the mist loomed the great sun banner of the House of York. A giant figure strode forward. Pushing his visor up, Richard saw that the King was smiling at him in brotherly pride. . . .

The incautious reader might be forgiven for thinking that the author himself was present at the battle. In fact, no contemporary source (not even a letter written by Richard's sister, Duchess Margaret of Burgundy,

[43] *Historie of the Arrivall of Edward IV in England*, ed. J. Bruce, 11; PV, 141.
[44] Kendall, 93–9.

within the same month as the battle), mentions his commanding a division (although the idea is not inherently implausible), still less that the issue of the battle depended on his fortitude.[45] However, the impersonal evidence of a record source certainly reveals that Richard was in the thick of the fighting, for members of his entourage were slain fighting at his side.[46] For the battle of Tewkesbury, however, we have specific evidence that Gloucester was entrusted with the vanguard of the king's army.[47] After the battle, as Constable of England, he sat in judgement on Edmund Beaufort, duke of Somerset and other Lancastrians who had sought sanctuary in Tewkesbury Abbey and were removed thence by force, all being condemned to death and summarily executed in the market-place. There was nothing especially savage in this sentence. All the accused were irreconcilable opponents of the Yorkist regime, and many had abused pardons granted to them by Edward IV in earlier years.

The death of the Lancastrian prince of Wales at Tewkesbury, followed by that of his father, Henry VI, in the Tower of London, were later to be regarded as murders, and added to the list of Gloucester's many crimes in the 'Tudor Saga', although quite unrelated to the mundane facts of historical evidence. No shred of blame can fall on Richard for Prince Edward's fate,[48] although an element of suspicion regarding his involvement in the death of Henry VI perhaps remains, given the typically enigmatic statement of the Croyland Chronicler that 'he who perpetrated this has justly earned the title of tyrant', a remark which might be applied to Edward IV, whom the chronicler elsewhere accuses of arbitrary tendencies.[49] At most, however, he may have been the agent, not the director of King Henry's murder, since, as Gairdner long ago pointed out, the decision to murder another king would only have been made by the king personally.[50] It is a serious weakness in the case for Richard's defence that his counsel are prepared to accept this argument in relation to Henry VI,

[45] *Historie of the Arrivall*, 18–21 (which mentions no divisional commanders on either side); *Chronicle of John Warkworth*, 15–17; and, for Duchess Margaret's letter, Waurin, *Anchiennes Cronicques d'Engleterre*, ed. Dupont, 210–15.

[46] Ross, 'Some "Servants and Lovers" of Richard in his Youth', *The Ricardian*, iv. no. 55 (1976), 2–4 (statutes of Queens' College, Cambridge, commanding prayers to be said for those slain in Richard's service at Barnet and elsewhere, including several named persons: this was done no doubt on Richard's own instructions, in the course of making bequests to the college).

[47] *Historie of the Arrivall*, 29–30 (the only detailed contemporary account of the battle).

[48] Above, p. xlv, n. 78.

[49] *CC*, 556. For discussions of the evidence, see Kendall, 451–2; Gairdner, *Richard III*, 16–19.

[50] Gairdner, *op. cit.*, 16–19.

but not for a similar situation in 1483 in connection with the death of Edward IV's sons.

At no time between his birth and 1471 was Richard of Gloucester a dominant figure on the stage of English politics. The space here devoted to his childhood, adolescence and early manhood can be justified in defining the mental climate which dominated his upbringing. Richard would have been at once insensitive and unintelligent (and there is no evidence that he was either) if he had not reflected on these early experiences. His father had unsuccessfully claimed the throne of England against an accepted and consecrated king, backed by the threat of force. His brother had used force more effectively to seize the throne: his claim in law was largely irrelevant to pragmatic political reality. His guardian, the earl of Warwick, had been even more ruthless in eliminating his political rivals – especially the Woodvilles – without due process of law, and had, incidentally, demonstrated the power of a great northern connection in national politics. Weakness in the face of a factional threat might have dire consequences: Richard had shared Edward's exile in Burgundy. The experience of another decade of English politics did nothing to demolish the impact of such lessons.

# Chapter 2

# GLOUCESTER, CLARENCE AND THE COURT, 1471–1483

Edward IV was by nature a generous man. Certainly, he proved anxious to reward those who had helped him during 'the time of his great necessity', his younger brother being conspicuous among them. Richard was the principal beneficiary from the political resettlement which followed Edward's restoration to the throne.[1] What may have begun from a spirit of gratitude soon became linked to a conscious policy of making Richard heir to the offices, estates and influence formerly enjoyed by Warwick in the north of England. Resuming his offices of Constable and Admiral of England, he was also appointed, on 18 May 1471, Great Chamberlain of England, an office made vacant by Warwick's death, but which had earlier been held by Clarence. On 4 July he became, again in place of Warwick, chief steward of the Duchy of Lancaster in the north parts, and further took over from Lord Stanley, now paying the price for his support of Warwick, as chief steward of the Duchy within the county palatine of Lancashire. Then, on 14 July 1471, he was given a grant in tail of all Warwick's estates north of Trent, including the lordships of Middleham and Sheriff Hutton in Yorkshire and Penrith in Cumberland, which had descended to the earl from his father.[2] Resuming the office of warden of the west march which had been granted to him in 1470, he was also made keeper of all the royal forests north of Trent (18 May 1472), an office taken from Henry Percy, earl of Northumberland.[3] From the summer of 1471 onwards Richard appears regularly on a long series of north-country commissions, but to enable him to devote proper attention to his responsibilities in that region, he had been relieved of his offices in Wales, now divided between William Herbert, 2nd earl of Pembroke and John Talbot, 3rd earl of Shrewsbury.[4] Finally, in this immediate post-restoration period,

---

[1] Ross, *Edward IV*, 185–7.

[2] *CPR, 1467–77*, 260, 262, 266; Somerville, *History of the Duchy of Lancaster*, I, 422, 493. The grant to Gloucester of the Nevill estates, which had been entailed, ignored the rights of the legitimate male heir, Warwick's nephew, son of his brother John Nevill, George Nevill, duke of Bedford.

[3] *CPR, 1467–77*, 338; R. L. Storey, 'Wardens of the Marches of England towards Scotland', *EHR*, lxxii (1957), 607–8, 615. During the brief restoration of Henry VI, Warwick had presumably taken over the wardenship of the west marches, which he had held from 1461 until Gloucester's appointment in August 1470.

[4] Ross, *Edward IV*, 195; and for the commissions, *CPR, 1467–77*.

his endowment was substantially increased in December 1471, when he was given all the forfeited estates of the recalcitrant Lancastrian John de Vere, 13th earl of Oxford, and of the leaders of the Lincolnshire rebellion in 1470. These, lying chiefly in the eastern counties of England, especially Essex, amounted to the very considerable total of some eighty manors in all, worth well in excess of £1,000 yearly.[5]

The grants of 1471–2 formed the foundation of Gloucester's might in the north, but much more was to come. Gloucester became sheriff of Cumberland for life in February 1475, and in June he was given the castle and lordship of Skipton in Craven in the Pennine region of West Yorkshire, the principal estate of the Lancastrian family of Clifford. Shortly before that (in September 1474), he negotiated an exchange of lands with the king, surrendering lands of his wife's inheritance in the counties of Derby and Hertfordshire for the exceptionally wealthy manor of Cottingham near Hull (worth nearly £270 yearly earlier in the century) and the castle and lordship of Scarborough on the east coast of Yorkshire.[6] In March 1478 a similar surrender of southern properties (Corfe in Dorset, Farleigh Hungerford in Wiltshire and Sudeley in Gloucestershire) brought him in exchange the castle of Richmond in North Yorkshire, with the fee-farm of its town, and the reversion of the castle and lordship of Helmsley and two dependent manors, also in North Yorkshire, upon the demise of Marjorie, Lady Roos (she conveniently died a few days later).[7] In February 1480 his commission as warden of the west march towards Scotland was renewed for ten years, although at a reduced salary of £1,000 in wartime and £800 in time of truce, and on 12 May 1480, as England's relations with Scotland deteriorated, he was appointed king's lieutenant-general in the north, which gave him authority to call out all the king's lieges in the marcher counties, and hence a general supervisory authority along the border.[8] Finally, in the parliament of January 1483, Edward created for his brother a great hereditary palatine lordship comprising the counties of Cumberland and Westmorland, together with any parts of south-western Scotland which he might afterwards conquer.[9] This remarkable grant had

[5] *Ibid.*, 297. To this Richard later added the dower interests of Oxford's mother, the dowager countess Elizabeth Howard (see below, p. 31).

[6] *RP*, VI, 125–6; *CPR, 1467–77*, 485, 507, 549, 556; *Inquisitions Post Mortem . . . Henry IV and Henry V*, ed. W. P. Baildon and J. W. Clay (Yorks. Archaeological Society, Record Series, lix, 1918), 79–80.

[7] *CPR*, 90.

[8] Storey, 'Wardens of the Marches', 608, 615; *CPR*, 205; Rymer, *Foedera*, XII, 115–16. His appointment as lieutenant-general, which was renewed in 1482, gave him power 'to call out all the king's lieges in the marches towards Scotland and the adjacent counties'.

[9] *RP*, VI, 204–5.

two unique features. It was the first (and also the last) time since the creation of a palatine county in Lancashire in 1351 that any English shire had been made into a palatinate: this meant in practice that the king's writ did not run within the shire and its lord had full control of all its affairs.[10] Secondly, Richard and his heirs were to hold the office of warden of the west march towards Scotland along with the palatinate. Thus, for the first time, a major military command under the crown passed out of direct royal control and became instead an hereditary private possession. This final act may represent some slackening of grasp on affairs by Edward IV, who was to die from an unknown illness only three months later, or the pressure which Richard could now bring to bear on his royal brother. This apart, it is hard not to see in the steady consolidation of Gloucester's power in the north over more than a decade the working of a conscious policy by Edward IV. Despite his experience with Warwick before 1470, Edward chose to rely upon the authority of a single man north of Trent, instead of seeking some conciliar solution (such as he adopted in Wales and the Marches). The result was to create an over-mighty subject even more powerful in the north than Warwick had ever been.[11]

Following the death of Clarence in 1478, Richard of Gloucester had become probably the wealthiest lay landowner in England. Modern research has suggested that, at the height of his power, Clarence had probably enjoyed an income of some £7,000 yearly from land.[12] Gloucester could scarcely have enjoyed less in the later years of Edward's reign, for, in addition to all the lands and offices which he held by royal grant, he had also come to enjoy his wife's share of the great Beauchamp-Despenser estates formerly held by Richard Nevill, earl of Warwick. These were worth something of the order of £3,500 yearly.

The great quarrel between his brothers provided Edward IV with his most difficult domestic problem in the second decade of his reign. In essence, it sprang from the wish of the duke of Clarence to keep complete control of all the inheritance of his mother-in-law, Anne Beauchamp, countess of Warwick, to which his own wife, Isabel, was co-heiress. This

---

[10] For the Lancaster precedent of 1351, see Somerville, *op. cit.*, 40–5. Lancashire was to have the privileges of the ancient palatinate of Chester; Richard was specifically given the no less ancient privileges of the palatinate of Durham.

[11] Storey, 'Wardens of the Marches', 608; Ross, *Edward IV*, 193 ff. It should be noted, however, that the 'conciliar solution' in Wales turned out to be for the benefit of the Woodville family: see further below, pp. 35, 181–2.

[12] As calculated by Hicks, 'Clarence', 342, for the year 1473. By 1478, following Clarence's loss of lands given to him by royal grant, it had probably been reduced to some £4,600 (Hicks, 342).

could only be achieved at the expense of her younger sister, Anne (and, of course, the countess of Warwick herself). Clarence's possessiveness was matched by Gloucester's desire to marry Anne Nevill and thereby to secure her share of the Warwick lands for himself. In the process of their argument, Clarence proved the more petulant and unaccommodating of the two, but both brothers showed a greed and ruthlessness and a disregard for the rights of those who could not protect themselves which shed an unpleasant light on their characters. Edward IV – the man in the middle – appears scarcely less favourably, although he might have pleaded his duty to keep the peace of the realm even if he achieved his purpose by somewhat dubious legal methods.[13]

In spite of his treacherous record, Clarence had been treated with extraordinary generosity following Edward's recovery of power. The king had every right to claim (when he indicted Clarence of treason in 1478) that he (Edward) 'gave him so large portion of possessions, that no memory is of, or seldom hath been seen, that any King of England heretofore within his realm gave so largely to any of his brothers'.[14] In 1471 Clarence had been restored to his former estates, except those Percy lands given back to the earl of Northumberland, for which he had been amply recompensed with lands formerly belonging to the Courtenay family in Devon and Cornwall.[15] More important, he was allowed to take possession of all the Beauchamp-Despenser lands formerly enjoyed by Warwick in right of his wife. From the beginning this was an act of dubious legality. Warwick was never formally attainted in parliament, but he had been indicted of treason under the common law.[16] Any resultant forfeiture for treason, however, could apply only to the estates Warwick had inherited from the Nevills in the north (granted, as we have seen, to Richard of Gloucester, at the expense of the heir male in law) and the lands of the Montagu earldom of Salisbury. It could not have extended to the inheritance he held in right of his wife, Anne countess of Warwick. In spite of the obvious injustices involved, however, in March 1472 Edward promised Clarence that he should have secure possession of all the estates of the earl and countess of Warwick, save those already granted to Gloucester: neither by act of parliament nor by any other means would they be taken from him and his heirs.[17] In spite of this indulgent treatment, Clarence showed

---

[13] For a general survey of the dispute, Ross, *Edward IV*, 187–93.

[14] *RP*, VI, 193.

[15] *CPR, 1467–77*, 279–80, 330.

[16] P.R.O., K.B. 9/41, mm. 38 ff. This was a *posthumous indictment* for treason brought against Warwick and Montagu before special commissions in Hertfordshire and Middlesex in May 1472.

[17] *CPR, 1467–77*, 330.

himself intensely jealous of the favours shown to Gloucester. His influence with Edward was enough for him to secure the revocation of the grant to Gloucester of the office of chamberlain of England, which was given instead to Clarence on 20 May 1472.[18] His reaction to the news that Gloucester wished to marry the younger Warwick heiress was even more violent.

Duke Richard had been given little reason to love or respect his brother Clarence. He had every reason to disregard Clarence's selfish sensitivities. In terms both of birth and wealth, Anne Nevill was the obvious bride for Gloucester (just as Isabel had been for Clarence). No one had seriously suggested that he might marry abroad. Nor need we follow the romantic imaginings of Caroline Halsted in 1844 or Paul Murray Kendall in 1955 in supposing the marriage to have been a love-match from the start.[19] Medieval marriages of the upper-class variety had much more to do with lawyers than with love, liking or lust. Material advantage or occasionally social aspiration were always the primary considerations. From the bride's standpoint also there was much to be said for the match. Only Gloucester possessed the political muscle to wrest her from the grasp of Clarence, and force him to disgorge her share of the Warwick inheritance, although even this would be at the expense of her unfortunate mother. Probably, therefore, she willingly consented to her abduction by Duke Richard from Clarence's care (there is a colourful but not wholly improbable story that Clarence had attempted to conceal her from Richard's agents by disguising her as a kitchen-maid in London).[20] From sanctuary at St Martin's, she was probably taken home to Middleham Castle. In law, their marriage could only be valid with the aid of a papal dispensation, since they were related within the prohibited degrees. Political urgency, however, demanded that the marriage should take place as soon as possible without Rome's affidavit, but worldly cynicism inspired the insertion of a clause into later formal acts, guaranteeing Gloucester's title in Anne's estates should the marriage later end in divorce because of its technical illegality.[21] The precise date of the marriage is unknown.

---

[18] *Ibid.*, 344. On the preceding 16 March he had been re-appointed to his office of lieutenant of Ireland for a term of twenty years (*ibid.*, 335–6).

[19] C. A. Halsted, *Richard III*, I, 264–6; Kendall, 105–9. Halsted's account of the return of Richard and Anne to the north of England must be recommended to all devotees of Victorian Romantic Sensibility.

[20] *CC*, 557. Since it comes from this source, the story may deserve credence.

[21] *RP*, VI, 100–1. With the proviso that Gloucester should remain unmarried. Otherwise he was to enjoy Anne's estates for life. Thus not only the mother (Countess Anne) but also the wife, Duchess Anne, might be deprived of the inheritance to the benefit of Gloucester himself.

Decided upon by 17 February 1472, it probably did not take place until after Easter 1472, for marriages were prohibited during Lent.[22]

The royal brothers' quarrel over Anne Nevill soon became a matter of public knowledge, and the king was compelled to intervene. At a council meeting in the palace of Sheen in February 1472, the two dukes personally presented their respective arguments. Even the lawyers present were impressed by the skill with which they argued: as one contemporary ruefully – and with hindsight – remarked: 'these three brothers, the king and the two dukes, were possessed of such surpassing talents, that, if only they had been able to live without dissensions, such a threefold cord could never have been broken without the utmost difficulty'.[23] Clarence's position was that Gloucester might have the lady, but not her lands. Later, under heavy royal pressure (perhaps the threat that the lands he held by royal grant might be taken from him), Clarence climbed down and agreed to a partition of the estates, although he was meanwhile confirmed in possession of all the estates he already held except those previously released to Gloucester. His creation as earl of Warwick and Salisbury on 25 March 1472 seemed to give formal acknowledgement to his prior status in the affair.[24] The principle of partition was not translated into practice, largely because of Clarence's continued opposition to the whole scheme. In any event, there were formidable legal difficulties involved. Neither duke wished to hold his share by royal grant, since grants could be revoked under the authority of a parliamentary act of resumption, as Clarence discovered to his cost in 1473. Each wished to hold by inheritance, and this meant extinguishing the claims of the widowed countess of Warwick. From her sanctuary at Beaulieu in Hampshire, where she had remained since her landing with Margaret of Anjou in 1471, the countess bombarded the king, the royal family and parliament with pathetic pleas that justice should be done to her. It may have been no more than a tactical ploy in a sordid contest, but in June 1473 Duke Richard persuaded his mother-in-law to leave Beaulieu, and had her conveyed north to Middleham under the care of an already trusted confidential servant, Sir James

---

[22] The statement that they were married on 12 July 1472 (*CP*, VI, 741; *Handbook of British Chronology*, 38) rests on no contemporary authority. Cf. T. B. Pugh, *Glamorgan County History*, III, 687, for the suggestion that they were married before 18 March 1472. The first dated reference to their being married belongs to May 1474 (*RP*, VI, 100–1). Kendall's statement that their only child, Edward of Middleham, later prince of Wales, was born in 1473 (Kendall, 110) also lacks authority. In fact, he was probably not born until 1476 (Pugh, *op. cit.*, 687–8; P. W. Hammond, *Edward of Middleham, Prince of Wales*, 12, 35–6).

[23] *CC*, 557.

[24] *PL*, V, 135–6; *CP*, XII (pt. ii), 394.

Tyrell. Soon after, rumours began to circulate that King Edward intended to restore her to her estates and that she, in turn, would grant them to her new protector.[25] The tension between the dukes continued, with increasing irritation on all sides. In November 1473 Sir John Paston claimed that 'Clarence maketh him as big as he can, showing as he would but deal with the duke of Gloucester', but the king intended to 'be as big as they both, and to be a stifler between them'. A less reliable source reported in the following February that Gloucester 'was constantly preparing for war with the duke of Clarence'.[26]

Finally, the king himself took stringent action to bring the insubordinate Clarence to heel. In November 1473 parliament approved another act of resumption, the fourth of the reign. Its most striking feature was that Clarence was given no clause of exemption, and, at a single stroke, was deprived of all the very valuable lands he held by royal grant.[27] This uncompromising assertion of the royal will led to a further act of parliament, in May 1474, settling all the Warwick estates upon Clarence and Gloucester in right of their respective wives. The dowager countess's claims were extinguished by declaring her legally dead.[28] A further act of parliament, in February 1475, vested all rights to the Nevill lands in the north in Richard of Gloucester and his heirs male, on the ground of the treasons committed by Warwick's immediate heir male, John Nevill, Marquis Montagu, although no formal act of attainder was passed against him. This effectively demolished the claims of John Nevill's son, George Nevill, duke of Bedford, and, in the parliament of 1478, George Nevill, who was then about to become of age, was degraded from his dukedom on the simple-seeming but false grounds that he no longer possessed a suitable estate to support such a high dignity.[29] The parliamentary act of 1474 relating to all the former Warwick lands had already led to a formal partition of the inheritance which left Gloucester the richer by the pos-

---

[25] Scofield, *Edward IV*, II, 27; *PL*, V, 188–9; *Historical Manuscripts Commission, 11th Report*, App. VII, 95.

[26] *PL*, V, 195; *Calendar of State Papers, Milan*, I, 178.

[27] *RP*, VI, 71–98; Wolffe, *Royal Demesne in English History*, 153–6, 158.

[28] *RP*, VI, 100–1.

[29] *RP*, VI, 124–5, 173. George Nevill should have inherited half the estates of his maternal grandfather, Sir Edmund Ingoldsthorpe, and his maternal grandmother, Joan, sister and heiress of John Tiptoft, earl of Worcester (d. 1470), *CP*, IX, 92–3; XII (pt. ii), 846. Since the act of 1475 had vested the Nevill inheritance in Gloucester and his heirs so long as any heir male of John Nevill survived, Gloucester took care of his own interests by securing the custody and marriage of George Nevill on 9 March 1480 (*CPR*, 192).

session of lands (including the lordship of Glamorgan) worth, perhaps, in excess of £3,000 yearly.[30]

Richard of Gloucester cannot be seen as other than an active participant in this ruthless carve-up of the estates of others. In the process he gained an insight, through Edward's actions, into how acts pushed through docile parliaments could be used to give high authority to support claims which were untenable in any court of common law. Not only the parliaments of 1472–5 and 1478 but also Edward's last parliament of 1483 provided abundant examples of the illicit exercise of a sovereign's will.[31] Richard's success in establishing his wife's claims to a half-share of her inheritance does not stand alone in marking him out as a typical member of a land-hungry and ruthless upper aristocracy, prepared, if all else failed, to use might and influence to support their demands. In 1471 he had been granted the estates of John de Vere, earl of Oxford, in which his future supporter, John Howard, 1st (Howard) duke of Norfolk, was to become his principal deputy.[32] The dowager-countess, Elizabeth Howard, had her one-third interest in these lands, but she was also an heiress in her own right. In 1473, presumably again with the king's backing, Gloucester forced her to surrender her entire estate to him. Her son and his friends later complained that this had been achieved 'by heinous menace of loss of life and imprisonment'. They spoke of the 'duke's inordinate covetise and ungodly disposition', and, not without some justification, argued that the countess's deprivation was 'against all reason and good conscience'. Their petition was brought before the first parliament of Richard's successor (it was both *ex parte* and *ex post facto*) but there seems little doubt that a cruel advantage had been taken by Richard of a defenceless widow, whose son, John earl of Oxford, was at the time menacing the shores of Cornwall.[33] Nor did Duke Richard show any willingness to right an injustice already perpetrated by his father-in-law, Richard Nevill, against one of his own family. In law, Warwick's daughters, Isabel and Anne,

---

[30] For the partition, B.L. Cotton. MSS, Julius B XII, fos. 136–8; PRO, Duchy of Lancaster, D.L. 26/69; *RP*, VI, 124–5. Clarence retained most of the lands of the Beauchamp-Despenser-Salisbury inheritance in the west midlands and south-central and south-western England. Gloucester had all the entailed lands of the Nevills in the north (which he held already), with the addition of the former Beauchamp lordship of Barnard Castle in Co. Durham, and a group of Welsh marcher lordships, Glamorgan, Abergavenny, Pains Castle, Elvell, and Welsh Bicknor, with scattered lands in eastern England, especially in the county of Buckingham.

[31] Below, pp. 35–6.

[32] *CPR, 1467–77*, 297, 545 (Howard's appointment as steward of the De Vere lands, Suffolk and Essex, 26 August 1475).

[33] *RP*, VI, 282, 473–4; *CCR, 1468–76*, 334–5; B.L. Cotton. MSS, Julius B XII, fos. 230–2; *RP*, VI, 282, 473–4; *Calendar of Chancery Proceedings, Richard II to Elizabeth* (Record Commission), I, xc, xci.

were heiresses to the lands of the Beauchamp earldom of Warwick, if the tenuous rights of their aunts of the half-blood were excluded. But the estates of their grandmother, Isabel Despenser, countess of Warwick, should have been divided between the heirs of her two marriages. In spite of royal licences empowering George Nevill, Lord of Abergavenny, the heir male of Isabel's first marriage, to enter upon his inheritance (which included Abergavenny and Glamorgan), he had been prevented by Warwick's power and disregard for law from doing so. Another licence of January 1477 was equally ignored by Richard of Gloucester, who continued to treat the lordships as his own, both as duke and later as king.[34] Much of the unscrupulous greed which was so much a hallmark of the junior line of the house of Nevill in the fifteenth century seems to have been passed on by Warwick to his younger son-in-law.

How far Richard of Gloucester was an active accomplice in the overthrow and eventual murder of his brother Clarence must remain a matter of argument. No one can seriously deny that the king bore the ultimate responsibility. It was he who launched the charge of impeachment for treason against Clarence in the parliament of 1478. It was Edward also who spoke against Clarence, in a record alive with his overwhelming irritation at his brother's behaviour, and it was he who gave final agreement to the demand from a deputation from the commons that, since Clarence had been found guilty, then the mandatory death sentence should be carried out. All this led to the private execution of Clarence in the Tower of London on 18 February 1478, perhaps by drowning in that notorious butt of malmsey wine.[35] Recent research, however, strongly suggests that there is much evidence to support Mancini's stated belief that, at least behind the scenes, the queen and her Woodville relatives provided the main driving-force in bringing about the duke's overthrow.[36] No contemporary source implicates Gloucester himself. The Croyland Chronicler, and indeed Polydore Vergil (who claimed to have got his information from questions to Edward's surviving councillors), lay the blame firmly on the king and do not mention Richard at all. (Polydore's silence on this point is perhaps of particular significance.) Mancini went so far as to say that Richard was overwhelmed with grief at his brother's

---

[34] *CPR, 1452–61*, 358; *ibid., 1461–7*, 119; *CPR*, 12; R. L. Storey, *End of the House of Lancaster*, 231–41 (Appendix VI, 'The Warwick Inheritance'); Pugh, *Glamorgan County History*, III, 200–3 and notes, 611 ff. Richard's continued occupation of Glamorgan can be illustrated by two of his charters as lord, in 1477 and 1484 (G. T. Clark, *Cartae et alia munimenta . . . de Glamorgancia*, II, 216–8, 225–7, with reproductions of his seal). For similar evidence regarding Abergavenny, see below, p. 162.

[35] Ross, *Edward IV*, 187–93, for a general account of the dispute.

[36] Hicks, 'Clarence', 123 ff.; Mancini, 63, 69.

death, and vowed to avenge it.[37] More reported the opinion of 'some wise men' that Richard was privately not dissatisfied with the execution of his difficult and jealous brother, and may have welcomed it as removing one barrier between himself and the throne he was already planning to usurp. But, More added cautiously, 'of all this point there is no certainty, and whoso divineth upon conjectures, may as well shoot too far as too short'.[38]

Yet it is unlikely that Gloucester was not at least an assenting partner in the overthrow of Clarence. Not even the influence of the Woodvilles would have persuaded Edward to take action against Duke George if Richard had actively opposed it, and Gloucester had already shown (on the French campaign of 1475) that he was capable of taking an independent line.[39] He had been present at the council meetings in 1477 at which the assault upon Clarence had obviously been decided; he played a prominent part in the Woodville-dominated ceremonies for the marriage of the king's younger son, Richard duke of York, to Anne Mowbray in January 1478; and he had lent his aid to the systematic packing of the parliament of 1478 (at least five of his retainers being members of the house) which eventually left Clarence isolated before a docile house of commons.[40]

Nor were Richard's gains from the fall of Clarence by any means negligible. On 15 February 1478, three days *before* Clarence's murder, Richard's small son Edward was created earl of Salisbury, which had been one of Clarence's titles. Six days later, Richard was re-appointed Great Chamberlain of England, an office he had been forced to surrender to

[37] *CC*, 562–3; *PV*, 167–8; Mancini, 63. There is an echo of Mancini's belief in a letter which Richard sent in September 1484 containing instructions for Gerald FitzGerald, 8th earl of Desmond, whose father had been murdered, it was alleged, by the earl of Worcester on the instructions of Queen Elizabeth Woodville, but the text of the letter (Gairdner, *L & P*, I, 67–9, from Harl. 433, f. 265) does not support the interpretation put upon it by Kendall (255, 444) that Richard blamed the Woodvilles for the deaths of Desmond's father and his own brother, Clarence. The letter refers in regretful terms to Desmond's murder, but continues 'notwithstanding that the semblable [similar] chance was and happened sithen [since] within this realm of England, as well of his brother, the duke of Clarence as other his nigh kinsmen and great friends', yet Richard gives permission to Desmond to seek by all lawful means the punishment of his father's murderer. At best this letter seems tongue-in-cheek: who were the other 'nigh kinsmen and great friends' of Richard allegedly murdered (unless by himself?).

[38] More, 8–9.

[39] Ross, *Edward IV*, 233.

[40] The MPs were Sir William Parr (Cumberland), Sir William Redman (Westmorland), Sir John Pilkington (Yorkshire), Edward Redman (Carlisle) and Miles Metcalfe (York city) – an indication of Gloucester's influence in the north. (Hicks, 'Clarence', 186–7; Ross, *Edward IV*, 343–4, for the packing of this parliament in general.)

Duke George in 1472.[41] Three parliamentary acts in Richard's favour provide a further indication of the price – or the reward – for his support in 1478. One allowed him to alienate portions of the Warwick inheritance which had been forbidden both to him and Clarence by the act of 1474. A second approved an exchange of lands between the king and himself which enabled him to give up his marcher lordship of Elvell in return for the Duchy of Lancaster lordship of Ogmore, conveniently placed beside his estates in Glamorgan. The third deprived George Nevill, duke of Bedford from his dukedom and disabled him, thereby, from having an effective voice in parliament.[42] Nor does the often repeated claim that the inclusion of Clarence among those for whose souls prayers were to be said in Richard's proposed foundation of a chantry college at Barnard Castle in Co. Durham represents some sort of conscience payment on his part rest on any foundation of evidence.[43] On balance, therefore, it seems quite inconsistent with what we know of Richard's character, and of his past relations with Clarence, that he had not condoned – to say the least – the carefully orchestrated overthrow of his brother in 1478.

After February 1478, Gloucester appears to have been less and less at court. Any overt breach between himself and the Woodvilles seems to belong to the last five years of Edward's reign, and was certainly not inspired by any difference of opinion arising from Clarence's death. In the years between 1471 and 1478 he had frequently been present at meetings of the royal council in London.[44] In 1475 he had accompanied Edward on his invasion of France, commanding the largest personal retinue in the entire army, exceeding even Clarence's 120 men-at-arms and 1,200 archers. He is said to have disapproved of Edward IV's intention to use the campaign to seek diplomatic and financial advantages rather than military glory. Certainly, he was conspicuously absent (given his high rank) from the meeting on the bridge at Picquigny between Edward IV and Louis XI which led to the signing of an Anglo-French peace treaty. Later, however, accepting the *fait accompli*, he visited the king of France at Amiens and accepted from him handsome presents of

---

[41] *CPR*, 67–8. On 5 March 1478 he also acquired (by way of exchange) the castle of Richmond and other northern properties (*ibid.*, 90).

[42] *RP*, VI, 170–3.

[43] Below, p. 130.

[44] Lists of those present at council meetings are notably deficient for these years, but Gloucester's presence at court on a number of occasions is suggested by the frequency with which he attests royal charters (PRO, C. 53/195–8 *passim*). The attestation of a royal charter cannot be taken to mean that he was present on a particular occasion, but a regular recurrence of a name on a witness list suggests that its owner was about the court.

horses and plate.[45] Richard also played his proper part in the major family ceremonies of the 1470s, such as the solemn reburial of his father, Richard duke of York, and Edmund earl of Rutland, his brother, at Fotheringhay in 1476, the great official banquet given by Edward prince of Wales on 9 November 1477 and the marriage of Richard duke of York to Anne Mowbray in January 1478. From the occasion of Prince Edward's feast, there survives what, in hindsight at least, seems an ironic account of Gloucester's coming to pay homage to Richard duke of York for all the lands he held from him as of the Duchy of Norfolk. The prince, then aged four-and-a-half, had been placed upon a bed-seat beside the cloth of estate. Gloucester knelt before him, and placing his hands between the prince's, did formal homage. York, in response, 'thanked him for that it liked him to do it so humbly'.[46] This may have been the first meeting between the two Duke Richards: it was almost certainly the last.

After this we hear little of Richard of Gloucester at the centre of government save in connection with the affairs of Scotland. His increasing responsibilities in the north of England, and still more the coming of war with Scotland in the early 1480s, in which Richard was to play the commanding role, may provide a considerable part of the explanation for his apparent withdrawal from Westminster and the life of the Yorkist court in these later years of Edward IV's reign.[47] It is, however, beyond question that this estrangement was based upon less obvious and certainly less well-documented developments which were of an essentially political nature.

Edward IV's achievements had been many and substantial. Yet at the highest level of politics his legacy was not a happy one. His actions during the later years of his reign sowed the seeds of discord within the Yorkist political establishment, as was most painfully revealed by the events of the three months following his death. His major error lay in allowing to the ambitions of the queen and her family an even greater freedom of action in the second decade of his rule than he had done in the first. This made it possible for them 'to establish a regional hegemony and a powerful and committed retinue, thus becoming more than a court party'.[48] That end was achieved by the king's indulgence in permitting them to take over and use for their own ends the patronage and resources vested in the two princes, Edward prince of Wales within Wales and the Marches and in the prince's Duchy of Cornwall, and Richard duke of York as heir to the inheritance of the Mowbray dukes of Norfolk, and, to a lesser degree, by the favour he showed to the queen's elder son by her first marriage,

[45] Commynes, *Mémoires*, II, 67; Scofield, *Edward IV*, II, 135–6, 140, 147.
[46] B.L. Additional MSS 6113, f. 74; Scofield, *op. cit.*, II, 167–8.
[47] Below, pp. 44–8.
[48] M. A. Hicks, 'The Changing Role of the Wydevilles', 82.

Thomas Grey, marquis of Dorset. In the process he made a frontal assault
on the ark of the covenant of any landowning society – the law of inheritance. To extend the power of Prince Edward in Wales, William Herbert,
2nd earl of Pembroke, was forced in 1479 to give up his earldom (accepting that of Huntingdon instead) together with all his family's power and
its entailed offices in West and South Wales.[49] In law, Duke Richard of
York could not retain the inheritance of his child-wife, Anne Mowbray,
unless he had issue by her, an unlikely event since she died at the age of
eight in 1481, when the duke was even younger. Acts of parliament, in
1478 and 1483, were used to vest the Mowbray estates in the duke of
York, some for life, others to him and his heirs male, thereby giving a
colour of legality to a situation which violated the rules of landed inheritance.[50] Even less should the infant heir of Thomas Grey, marquis of
Dorset, have been allowed to inherit all the estates of the Hollands, dukes
of Exeter, except for those settled, by an even more arbitrary endowment,
on his younger brother, Richard Grey, for whom no previous provision
had been made.[51] Once again an act of parliament (on the model of that
which had disinherited Anne countess of Warwick in 1474) was used to
provide the authority of the supreme court of the realm for an essentially
illegal act.[52]

All this was accomplished only by giving offence to a number of powerful private individuals, quite apart from its effects upon the sentiments of
the landowning class in general; and we cannot altogether discount the
cumulative impact of Edward's arbitrary acts upon their attitudes, to
which Richard's disinheritance of the princes added a further and major

---

[49] J. Beverley Smith and T. B. Pugh, 'The Lordship of Gower and Kilvey', in
*Glamorgan County History*, III (ed. Pugh), esp. 261–3; D. E. Lowe, 'The Council of
the Prince of Wales and the Decline of the Herbert Family during the second reign
of Edward IV (1471–1483)', *Bulletin of the Board of Celtic Studies*, xxvii (1977),
278–97. Examples of the exploitation by the Woodvilles of the princes' patronage
may be seen in the appointments of Earl Rivers as receiver-general of the Duchy of
Cornwall (1473), of Sir Richard Grey, the queen's younger son, as constable of
Chester (1479), and, after the confiscation of Herbert's earldom of Pembroke, of her
kinsmen Richard Haute to various offices in West Wales, and of Richard Haute the
younger to be constable of Swansea and steward of Gower (a lordship taken from
Herbert in the name of Richard duke of York). For Woodville interference in parliamentary elections in areas controlled by the princes, e.g. Cornwall, see K.
Houghton, 'Theory and Practice in Borough Elections to Parliament during the
Later Fifteenth Century', *BIHR*, xxxix (1966), 130–40; E. W. Ives, 'Andrew Dymmock and the Papers of Antony, Earl Rivers, 1482–3', *BIHR*, xli (1968), 216–25.

[50] *RP*, VI, 169–70, 205–7.

[51] *Ibid.*, 215–18; *CP*, V, 212–15; Ross, *Edward IV*, 336–7.

[52] Cf. Richard III's use of an act of parliament to legalize the disinheritance of
his nephews, Edward of Wales and Richard of York, which could not have been
achieved by the laws of inheritance (below, p. 175 and Appendix).

violation. If the highest in the land could be so treated, then what chance did any lesser person stand when confronted by a ruthless king? (There is here an obvious parallel, not sufficiently noticed, between the declaration of 1483 that the princes were bastards, and Richard II's arbitrary confiscation of the inheritance of John of Gaunt, duke of Lancaster, in 1399, to the disadvantage of his heir, Henry Bolingbroke.) William Herbert, 2nd earl of Pembroke, may have been (as is often suggested) a man of limited ability, and was quite certainly not the man his able father had been, but he had every reason to feel aggrieved at the shabby treatment he had received at the hands of Edward IV and the Woodvilles. Degraded from his family's high position in Wales, deeply impoverished as a result, he was a natural supporter of any political action which would overthrow the Woodvilles.[53]

More important were the co-heirs of the Mowbray dukedom of Norfolk, William, Lord Berkeley and John, Lord Howard, especially the latter. William Berkeley was a high eccentric by fifteenth-century standards. Without children of his own, he sought to use his claim to great estates to gain social advancement during his own lifetime. When the Mowbray heiress married Duke Richard of York, he agreed to surrender his share of the reversion of her estates if she died without male issue, with Edward IV as reversionary heir. This was allegedly because he owed the crown debts of £34,000, which Edward IV undertook to repay, but his real reward was his creation as Viscount Berkeley on 21 April 1483. When Richard of Gloucester extinguished the rights of Edward IV's heirs male by declaring them bastards before his accession, Berkeley recovered his rights at law to one-half of the Mowbray inheritance. His support was readily bought by his creation as earl of Nottingham (one of the Mowbray titles) on 28 June 1483, although later he proved anxious to surrender all these lands to the king once more, perhaps in pursuit of the title of Marquis Berkeley which he eventually achieved under Henry VII.[54] If Berkeley was an aberration from the norm – and not, in any event, of great political importance – John, Lord Howard was not. A highly successful and loyal servant of Edward IV, he had built up a position of considerable influence in East Anglia, and was a powerful and experienced member of the king's council. His support was worth having. How he had reacted to his being deprived of his share of the Mowbray titles and estates is not known. He continued loyal to Edward until the king's death, but he would have been less than realistic if he had not felt a certain chagrin at the king's disregard of his rights in law. A Woodville-dominated minority – the immediate prospect in April 1483 – offered Howard no hope of making good his

[53] D. E. Lowe, 'The Council of the Prince of Wales...'.
[54] RP, VI, 205–7; J. Smyth, Lives of the Berkeleys, II, 117–29; CP, II, 133–5.

claims. His creation as duke of Norfolk on 28 June 1483, and his being allowed to enter on his share of the Mowbray inheritance may have been his reward for supporting Richard of Gloucester's bid to make himself king. In any event, they offered a tempting bait to a man who was later to prove as loyal to Richard III as he had been to Edward IV.[55] Herbert, Berkeley and Howard may not have been the only members of the aristocracy who may have felt a sense of grievance at Edward IV's attitudes towards the laws of inheritance.[56]

These rather indigestible matters of inheritance were the stuff of which much of fifteenth-century politics were made. Divisions within the high Yorkist establishment were not, however, concerned only with such matters. Two other powerful men had rather different reasons for disliking any prolongation of Woodville power. The young Henry Stafford, duke of Buckingham, was head of the wealthiest and most long-established of the English magnate families: if his ducal title stretched back only so far as his father's creation in 1444, his Stafford earldom derived from the mid-fourteenth century. His career under Richard of Gloucester proved that he was grasping and ambitious to a degree. He had been denied his claim to enjoy the other half of the inheritance of the De Bohun family, formerly earls of Hereford, Essex and Northampton, which he regarded as his own when the male line of the house of Lancaster was extinguished in 1471 – a claim later to be conceded by Richard III.[57] He had been shown some favours soon after Edward IV's recovery of power in 1471, being allowed (in 1473) entry to his inheritance while still only sixteen years of age, and, being married to a Woodville, had played his part in the court ceremonies surrounding the marriage of Richard of York and Anne Mowbray in January 1478. He had also been associated in the attack upon Clarence, through his appointment as steward of England for the duke's trial a month later. Thereafter he had been cold-shouldered by king and court. Denied all the offices and responsibilities which a magnate of his rank might expect, he had even been excluded from all commissions of the peace except in the county of Stafford. The grants made to him by Richard of Gloucester during the Protectorate clearly reveal his desire to exercise power and influence in Wales and the Marches, but this too had been denied him while Edward IV lived, since his aspira-

[55] Ross, *Edward IV*, 248–9, 324–5, 336; Anne Crawford, 'The Career of John Howard, Duke of Norfolk, 1420–1485' (unpublished M. Phil. thesis, University of London, 1975), 191–5; and below, pp. 78, 95.

[56] T. B. Pugh, 'The Magnates, Knights and Gentry' in *Fifteenth-Century England, 1399–1509*, ed. S. B. Chrimes, C. D Ross and R. A. Griffiths, 111–12; Ross, *Edward IV*, 336–7.

[57] Somerville, *History of the Duchy of Lancaster*, I, 178–82, 230 (for the Bohun inheritance), and below, p. 114.

tions ran counter to those of the Woodvilles to dominate in Wales through their control of the prince's person. This, indeed, was probably the main reason for Buckingham's being placed in a political limbo during Edward's later years.[58]

William, Lord Hastings was the most powerful and prominent of the non-royal nobility who owed his advancement entirely to the favour of Edward IV himself. A life-long friend of the king, with an outstanding record of loyalty to his master, he occupied the influential office of king's chamberlain throughout the reign. This position controlled access to the king's person, and was therefore of key importance in the competition for royal patronage. Despite his considerable worldly success, he enjoyed the respect of his contemporaries as an upright and honourable man. At the same time he commanded considerable power through his great estates and large retinue in the midlands and through his office as captain of Calais, which gave him control of the largest standing garrison maintained by the English crown. Hastings was quite strong enough to protect his own interests, but he too was on bad terms with the Woodville group. According to More, the queen hated him because she resented his influence with Edward, and thought him 'secretly familiar with the king in wanton company', although he seems to have shared this dubious distinction with her sons, Thomas and Richard Grey, and with one of her brothers, Sir Edward Woodville, who were described as the principal 'promoters and companions of his [the king's] vices'.[59] (The licentious behaviour of the younger members of the queen's family was later to make them an obvious target for Richard's moralistic propaganda.)[60] Earl Rivers seems neither to have forgotten nor forgiven Hastings for having supplanted him in the office of captain of Calais in 1471, and as late as 1482 was busy spreading slanders about him, including the charge that Hastings might betray Calais to the French. By this date Hastings also had a well-attested feud with Thomas Grey, marquis of Dorset, with whom he had quarrelled 'over the mistresses whom they had abducted, or attempted to entice from one another': they too were suborning informers and incriminating each other.[61] Edward IV was sufficiently worried by the strife

---

[58] C. Rawcliffe, *The Staffords, Earls of Stafford and Dukes of Buckingham, 1394–1521*, 125–6; D. A. L. Morgan, 'The King's Affinity in the Polity of Yorkist England', *Trans. Royal Historical Society*, 5th series, xxiii (1973), 18 and *n.*; Hicks, 'Changing Role of the Wydevilles', 81. Royal favours to Buckingham cease abruptly after the trial of Clarence, at which time the king acted as godfather for the son (named Edward) born on 3 February 1478 to Duke Henry and his wife, Katherine Woodville.

[59] More, 10–11; Mancini, 69.

[60] Rymer, *Foedera*, XII, 204–5, and below, pp. 136–7.

[61] Mancini, 69; More, 11; Ives, *op cit.*, 221–2.

between Hastings and Dorset to attempt a reconciliation between them in the last days of his life, at least according to More, whose imaginative reconstruction of the scene was later developed by Shakespeare.[62]

Whatever the influence of his great northern affinity, Richard of Gloucester's takeover of power in 1483 would not have been possible unless such deep divisions had existed among the ruling Yorkist nobility. For this Edward IV was largely responsible, especially through his promotion of the interests of the highly unpopular and unattractive queen. The reputation of the entire family was such that in 1484 Richard did not even need to identify by name 'the persons insolent, vicious and of inordinate avarice' who had drawn Edward IV from the paths of virtuous government through their adulation and flattery and the temptations of sensuality and concupiscence. This was an official propaganda statement, but the Croyland Chronicler believed that, even among those loyal to Edward IV and the succession of his son, the 'more prudent members' felt that until he (Edward V) 'reached the age of maturity, the boy's maternal uncles and brothers must at all costs be excluded from any controlling positions about him'.[63] This is the main reason for the stark contrast between the violent events which followed Edward's death and the very different solution to a similar situation in 1422, when a united aristocracy combined to secure the peaceful succession of a nine-month-old baby, despite the prospect of the longest minority the country had ever faced, and rejected the pretensions of another duke of Gloucester, Henry V's younger brother, Humphrey, to a position of power.

Edward IV compounded the difficulties of the succession problem by his own lack of foresight. Thomas More observed that while he was still alive he was irked by the quarrels among his friends: 'yet in his good health he somewhat less regarded it, because he thought whatsoever business should fall between them, himself should always be able to rule both the parties'.[64] What he had not counted upon, or provided for, was his own premature death while his heir was still a minor. He could scarcely have been unaware of the unpopularity of the Grey-Woodville connection, yet he had entrenched their power and placed the princes under their control, a position from which they could only be dislodged by force. On the other hand, as the only adult surviving male of the House of York, Richard of Gloucester was the natural and inevitable choice to be given the custody of the young king, and to act as Protector during his minority. Edward IV's last will, and the codicils which he added to it upon his deathbed, have not survived, but it seems reasonably certain that

[62] More, 11–13; Shakespeare, *Richard III*, II, i.

[63] *RP*, VI, 240; *CC*, 564 ('brothers' here equals 'half-brothers', i.e. Thomas and Richard Grey). For the general background, Ross, *Edward IV*, 99–103, 425–6.

[64] More, 10.

he intended to place these responsibilities upon Duke Richard until Edward came of age.[65] Not to have appointed him, given his power and proximity of blood, would have been a recipe for trouble, since neither he nor many others wished to accept a Woodville-dominated minority. Equally, the Woodvilles could be expected to resist all attempts to deprive them of their control of the princes, on which their power in the future rested, and this, if successful, would expose them to the revenge of the many who hated them. The dilemma could not be solved by any last-minute effort on Edward IV's part: it was the unavoidable consequence of the contradictions of his policies over the previous decade.

Nor was it likely that the problems of a minority could be resolved by agreed action on the part of the Yorkist establishment. It was unfortunate for Edward V that, in an aristocracy reduced in numbers by deaths in civil war and executions, there existed no strong middle party, uncommitted to one faction or the other and capable of imposing a policy of moderation and balance.[66] The senior statesman among the Yorkist nobility, the experienced and respected Henry Bourchier, earl of Essex, had died on 4 April 1483, only a few days before the death of Edward IV himself. His heir was his grandson, a boy of some ten or eleven years. His demise left only one duke and six earls of full age, if we exclude Gloucester and his immediate ally, Buckingham, on the one hand, and Earl Rivers and his nephew, Dorset, on the other. Of these magnates, John de la Pole, 2nd duke of Suffolk, husband of Elizabeth Plantagenet, Edward IV's and Richard III's sister, seems to have been something of a political lightweight. Edward IV had never thought sufficiently of his ability to appoint him a member of the king's council, and, despite his high rank, he even had to wait until 1473 before Edward chose to secure his election to the Order of the Garter. Three of the six earls, Westmorland, Arundel and Kent, were now old men, no longer very active politically, although Arundel seems to have been trusted by Richard III.[67] Two more, Huntingdon for certain and Northumberland probably, had their own reasons for supporting Richard of Gloucester in any conflict for power with the Woodvilles.[68] The last, the twenty-one-year-old John de la Pole,

---

[65] *CC*, 564; Mancini, 60, 107–8; PV, 173; Bernard André, *Vita Henrici VII*, 23. For the question of the personal custody of the young king, see below, pp. 66–7.

[66] Pugh, 'Magnates, Knights and Gentry', 113.

[67] For his grants and appearances on commissions of oyer and terminer and array, *CPR*, 349, 358, 397, 465, 492, 545.

[68] For Huntingdon, see below, p. 158. Northumberland may have hoped that Richard's removal to the south would restore his family's position of unchallenged power in the north (in which he was to be disappointed, below, pp. 168–9). Pugh, *op. cit.*, 113; cf. M. A. Hicks, 'Dynastic Change and Northern Society: The Career of the Fourth Earl of Northumberland, 1470–89', *Northern History*, xiv (1978), 78–107, esp. 81–9.

earl of Lincoln (Suffolk's son and heir), soon emerged as a strong supporter of Gloucester, and, after the death of Richard's son, became a
principal claimant to the Yorkist throne.[69] Among the rank and file of the
nobility were several men who had been long-time servants of Edward
IV, members of his council, and indebted for office, land or title to his
patronage, such as John, Lord Dinham, Walter Devereux, Lord Ferrers
of Chartley and John, Lord Audley.[70] They might have been expected to
support the succession of Edward V, but in the event proved to have no
qualms about taking service under Richard III. The key person in the
attitude of men like this who might be counted in a 'loyalist group' was
William, Lord Hastings, but, initially at least, he too was a supporter of
Duke Richard – against the Woodvilles.

In 1422 it had been a prominent churchman, Henry Beaufort, bishop
of Winchester, who led the opposition to Duke Humphrey of Gloucester's
aspirations to power.[71] In 1483 no such leadership came from the septu-
agenarian archbishop of Canterbury, Thomas Bourchier, who neither
encouraged nor resisted Gloucester's coup d'état, although he was said to
have been reluctant to officiate at Richard's coronation.[72] Thomas
Rotherham, archbishop of York (who had links with the queen), and John
Morton, bishop of Ely, were clearly regarded as untrustworthy by Richard,
perhaps because they were prepared to support Hastings in a bid to
secure the succession of Edward V. Both were arrested, along with
Hastings, in the Tower on 13 June 1483. Later, two more bishops, Lionel
Woodville of Salisbury and Peter Courtenay of Exeter, took leading parts
in Buckingham's rebellion of 1483, and were attainted for their treason.
But in general the English episcopate of 1483 had much less coherence
and independence of mind than its counterpart in 1422. Its subservience
was a direct product of Edward IV's policy of promoting careerist civil
servants to the episcopal bench. Most bishops accepted Richard's new

---

[69] See further below, pp. 158–9.

[70] All three had joined the Yorkists before Towton, and Dinham (1467) and
Ferrers of Chartley (1461) had been raised to the peerage by Edward IV. For their
rewards, see Ross, *Edward IV*, 80–1, 137. Dinham was in actual command of Calais
(*vice* Lord Hastings) when Richard assumed the throne in June 1483 (Gairdner,
*L & P*, I, 11–16) and was appointed captain there by him. For their loyalty to
Richard III, see below, pp. 160–1. Others in the Calais command (e.g. Mountjoy)
readily took service under Richard (Gairdner, *op. cit.*, 14–15). Ferrers of Chartley,
however, had strong connections with the Herberts and Vaughans, and, therefore,
with the earl of Huntingdon.

[71] J. S. Roskell, *The Commons in the Parliament of 1422*, 99.

[72] Mancini, 101; *Registrum Thome Bourgchier*, ed. F. R. H. du Boulay, xxii–
xxiii.

3. The remains of the Great Hall at Middleham Castle, Yorkshire, built by
Richard as duke of Gloucester.

4(a). The supposed tomb of Edward of Middleham, prince of Wales, son of Richard III, at Sheriff Hutton church, Yorkshire.

4(b). The ruins of Sheriff Hutton Castle.

regime without apparent qualm; one or two supported it from the start.[73]

Had he lived even a few years more, enough to achieve the modest age of fifty, Edward IV might reasonably have hoped that his adult male heir would have been accepted as king without too much discord. Given the deep political tensions his own policies had helped to create, his premature death at the age of forty provided an invitation to dynastic disaster.

[73] R. J. Knecht, 'The Episcopate and the Wars of the Roses', *University of Birmingham Historical Journal*, vi (1958), 108–31, esp. 120–5. It is worth noting that active support for Richard came from two bishops with northern connections, William Dudley, bishop of Durham, and Richard Redman of St Asaph's, who was a member of the Westmorland family of that name much patronized by Richard.

Chapter 3

# THE HEIR OF NEVILL: RICHARD DUKE OF GLOUCESTER AND THE NORTH OF ENGLAND

Richard III is unique among medieval English kings in the extent of his connections with the north of England. By 1483 he had come to know the region and its people more thoroughly than any of his predecessors. He is also entirely exceptional in the degree to which his power base was very largely north-country.[1] Some of his formative years had been spent in the north at Middleham Castle. His wife and future queen, Anne Nevill, was heiress to the great northern connections of her family, stretching back for more than a century, and her marriage was an important factor in winning for her husband the loyalty of the men of her native region.[2] Further, Edward IV had made Richard heir to the Nevill affinity through the systematic grants to him of land and office formerly held by Warwick. By 1483 he had become the dominant figure in England north of Trent. His pre-eminence is especially reflected in the fact that he was to become England's principal commander in the wars with Scotland which marked the later years of Edward IV.

Full accounts of the Anglo-Scottish war of 1481–3 already exist in print, so no more than a summary is needed here.[3] Edward IV himself was largely accountable for the war, perhaps as an angry response to the attempts of the king of France to engage Scotland against England on what might be described as his outer right flank. Fears of a Scots invasion of northern England are reflected in Gloucester's appointment – the first of its kind – as lieutenant-general of the north on 12 May 1480, which gave him power to call out the levies of the borders and adjacent counties, followed by the issue of commissions of array for Yorkshire, Cumberland and Northumberland. In the event, the threat from the Scots turned out to be no more than a large-scale and destructive raid led by the earl of Angus, which ended in the burning of Bamborough, twenty miles inside

[1] Henry Bolingbroke in 1399 had a powerful following from the northern estates of the Duchy of Lancaster and backing from major northern lords, like the earl of Westmorland and the earl of Northumberland, but the very extensive duchy lands in the midlands and the south were scarcely less important as a support for the new Lancastrian regime.

[2] It was seriously suggested in 1485 that he might lose northern support if he were thought to have poisoned his queen (CC, 572).

[3] R. Nicholson, *Scotland: The Later Middle Ages*, 490–507; Ross, *Edward IV*, 278–83, 287–90; Scofield, *Edward IV*, II, 276–9, 294, 305–6, 314–23, 333–49.

English territory: Gloucester and Northumberland led their retainers and the county levies from the north on a counter raid late in the summer of 1480. The formal decision to mount an invasion of Scotland was taken by king and council at Westminster in November 1480, and large-scale preparations were put in hand for the following summer. Duke Richard's appointment as lieutenant-general was not renewed, since the intention was that King Edward should lead the English army in person. Although considerable sums of money were spent (Gloucester himself received £10,000 for the wages of his men in the north), and the English fleet under John, Lord Howard achieved a damaging raid on the Firth of Forth, the land invasion never materialized, largely because of King Edward's delays, and his final decision not to take command in person, made only very late in the campaigning season. Intermittent warfare continued along the borders in the winter of 1481–2, and the English laid siege to the well-defended fortress of Berwick-upon-Tweed (which had been surrendered to the Scots by Queen Margaret of Anjou in 1460), but without result.

In 1482 the English renewed their efforts, this time under Gloucester's control. A new prospect opened in the spring of that year with the arrival in England of a pretender to the throne of Scotland, Alexander duke of Albany, brother of King James III. Richard was present at Fotheringhay Castle on 3 June 1482 when a treaty was signed with Albany, the English promising to support his claim to the throne in return for a number of territorial and diplomatic concessions. Edward then decided not to lead the invasion in person (perhaps for reasons of ill-health), and Gloucester's commission as lieutenant-general was renewed on 12 June, which meant that he became the effective commander-in-chief of the invasion. An imposing force had been assembled by the middle of July, numbering perhaps 20,000 men. Although the army included the marquis of Dorset, Sir Edward Woodville and others from the south, it was essentially a northern army, with Northumberland and Stanley as Gloucester's principal lieutenants (as is illustrated by the large number of bannerets and knights created by these three in the course of the campaign, Gloucester's being the most numerous).[4] Faced by this impressive force, the town of

---

[4] According to the list given in W. C. Metcalfe, *A Book of Knights Banneret, Knights of the Bath and Knights Bachelor* (1885), 5–7, in 1481 Gloucester dubbed 5 knights (all lords: Lovell, FitzHugh, Scrope of Masham, Lumley and Greystoke) and appointed 20 bannerets, all northerners; the earl of Northumberland dubbed 18 knights, again northerners. In 1482, on 24 July, Gloucester made knights or bannerets of 49 men, Northumberland dubbed knights, as did Lord Stanley. With the exceptions of Sir Edward Woodville, Sir Walter Herbert, Sir John Elrington and Sir James Tyrell, all those so appointed by Richard in 1482 were northerners, as were (so far as they can readily be identified) those appointed by Stanley and Northumberland. The vast majority of the men promoted by Richard in 1481 and 1482 were later active in his service as king.

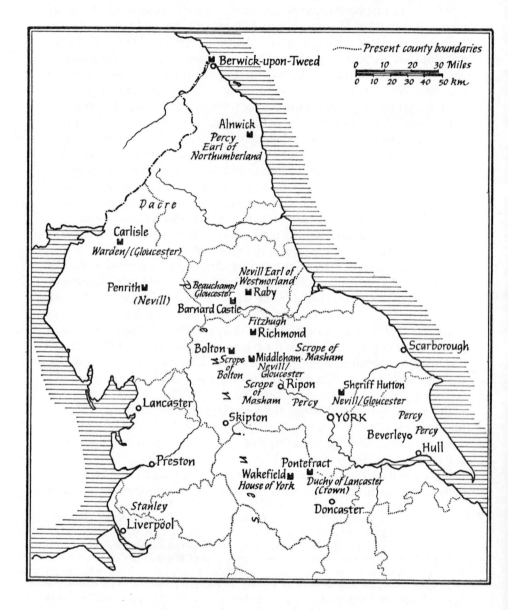

Berwick-upon-Tweed

Alnwick
*Percy*
*Earl of*
*Northumberland*

*Dacre*

Carlisle
*Warden/(Gloucester)*

Penrith
*(Nevill)*

*Nevill Earl of*
*Westmorland*
*Beauchamp/* Raby
*Gloucester*
Barnard Castle

*Fitzhugh*
Richmond

Bolton                    *Scrope of*
*Scrope* Middleham  *Masham*
*of*     *Nevill/*
*Bolton* *Gloucester*
*Scrope*        Ripon
*of*            Sheriff Hutton
Lancaster *Masham*  *Nevill/Gloucester*
*Percy*
Skipton          YORK
*Percy*
Beverley
*Percy*
Preston            Hull

Pontefract
Wakefield
*House of York*  *Duchy of Lancaster*
*(Crown)*
*Stanley*           Doncaster
Liverpool

Scarborough

Berwick opened its gates to the English. The garrison of the castle held out, however, and it was left invested while the English army moved forward, pillaging and devastating as it went, towards Edinburgh.

The purpose of the expedition, it must be remembered, was essentially political, to install Albany as a complacent puppet of a Yorkist king of England. Certainly, there was little prospect of military glory, for the Scots had already defeated themselves. Aristocratic discontent with the rule of James III and his 'familiars' erupted even as the English crossed the border. On 22 July 1482, James III himself was seized by the opposition, and many of his courtiers were hanged at the Bridge of Lauder. James was taken back a prisoner to Edinburgh Castle. There was, therefore, no organized opposition to the English advance.

Arrived at Edinburgh, Gloucester found himself in something of a quandary, for the mercurial Albany (himself in an awkward circumstance) decided to accept the promise of a restoration of his lands and the prospect of being made lieutenant-general of the realm of Scotland rather than pressing his claim to the throne.[5] Duke Richard, who might easily have sacked and burnt Edinburgh, did not do so. Instead, he contented himself with a written assurance from Albany that he would remain true to the treaty of Fotheringhay, and a guarantee from the citizens of Edinburgh that any moneys paid by the English for a proposed royal marriage alliance (between the duke of Rothesay, James III's heir, and Edward IV's daughter, Cecily) would be reimbursed. The English army marched back to Berwick, where, on 11 August 1482, all but some 1,700 men of the army were disbanded and sent home: the staunch defenders of the castle, however, had no hope of relief from the Scots government and duly surrendered on 24 August. The recovery of Berwick was the sole positive outcome of the campaign of 1482, and, as the Croyland Chronicler sourly observed, it proved highly expensive to maintain in English control.[6] In no sense can the invasion of Scotland be cited in evidence to support the oft-repeated claims by Richard's defenders that he was possessed of outstanding military qualities. Further, any hopes founded upon the duke of Albany of obtaining an effective English ally in Scotland proved to be a magpie's nest, although this was a fault of Edward IV's diplomacy, not Richard's.[7]

Richard of Gloucester's acquisition of the lands and offices held in the north of England by the earl of Warwick, and before him by his father Richard Nevill, earl of Salisbury, and his grandfather, Ralph Nevill, earl

[5] Nicholson, *op. cit.*, 506–7.

[6] *CC*, 563.

[7] Nicholson, 507–14, and below, pp. 192–3.

of Westmorland, combined with his marriage to Warwick's daughter, were to prove of supreme importance in gaining him admission to the fiercely independent and clannish landed society of the northern counties. With some exception for Yorkshire, the shires north of Trent were neither populous nor wealthy. Nevertheless, they were – and had been over a century or more – significant as a great reservoir of armed men, a role they were to retain during Richard's own usurpation and subsequent reign.[8] Their loyalties, however, were not lightly given to an outsider, as both Henry VII and Henry VIII were to discover. Richard's position as heir to the Nevill interest gave him a powerful lien on their support, which his own familiarity with the north and the very powerful patronage he could dispense merely served to strengthen.

Both the nobility and the gentry of the northern counties were tightly linked by blood, marriage and traditional associations, as well as by mere neighbourhood.[9] In north Yorkshire, for example, there were strong links with the Nevills. Richard, Lord FitzHugh, whose principal base at Ravensworth lay only a few miles from Middleham Castle, was a cousin of Duke Richard of Gloucester: his mother, Alice Nevill, was daughter to Richard Nevill, earl of Salisbury, who, in turn, was the elder brother of Richard of Gloucester's own mother, Cecily Nevill.[10] Lord FitzHugh himself married a daughter of Edward IV's master of the horse, Sir Thomas Burgh of Gainsborough in Lincolnshire, which is perhaps the reason why Burgh is one of the few household servants of King Edward to become a supporter of Richard III. Another near neighbour of the lord of Middleham was John, Lord Scrope of Bolton, some miles up the dale, whose first wife had been a FitzHugh. His second wife was Elizabeth, the widow of William, Lord Zouche of Harringworth in Northamptonshire, which again may explain why her son John, Lord Zouche was a strong supporter of Richard III. Both Scrope and Zouche had close associations with a rising young Northamptonshire lawyer, William Catesby, who married Elizabeth Zouche's daughter, Margaret, and it may have been Catesby's associations with these lords which first brought him to Richard's attention (for otherwise Richard had few confidants without north-

[8] R. L. Storey, 'The north of England', in *Fifteenth-Century England, 1399–1509*, ed. Chrimes, Ross and Griffiths, 129–44.

[9] For the gentry in north Yorkshire in relation to these themes, see the valuable papers by A. J. Pollard: 'The northern retainers of Richard Nevill, Earl of Salisbury', *Northern History*, xi (1976 for 1975), 52–69; 'Richard Clervaux of Croft: A North Riding Squire in the Fifteenth Century', *Yorkshire Archaeological Journal*, L (1978), 151–69; 'The Richmondshire Community of Gentry during the Wars of the Roses', in *Patronage, Pedigree and Power in Late Medieval England*, ed. Ross, 37–56.

[10] See Tables 2 and 3.

country associations). The FitzHughs were also linked by marriage with the barons Greystoke, who had lands in Yorkshire and Cumberland, and with the lords Dacre of Gilsland in Cumberland (as Table 2 shows). Both Greystokes and Dacres had ties by marriage with each other and with the other baronial family of Scrope, that of Masham (near Middleham).

Such interconnections could be multiplied, and were not necessarily decisive in determining political allegiance: the long rivalry between the senior line of the Nevills, represented by the earls of Westmorland, and the junior line, represented by Salisbury and Warwick, is a case in point. Nevertheless, John, Lord Scrope of Bolton, and Ralph, Lord Greystoke seem to have been members of Richard of Gloucester's council as early as 1475. Greystoke, FitzHugh, Scrope of Masham and the Durham baron, Thomas, Lord Lumley were all knighted by Duke Richard on the Scottish campaigns. Dacre and the two Scrope barons later became councillors of Richard as king. None of these noblemen had benefited much from Edward IV during his second reign, whereas service to Richard proved very rewarding, especially for Dacre, since Richard's removal to the south enabled him to win control of the west march towards Scotland, a coveted prize which was to prove the foundation of the Dacre fortunes under the Tudor kings.[11]

One of Richard's closest friends, Francis Lovell, was, like Richard himself, another accepted outsider in northern society. His principal family estates lay in the counties of Oxford (Minster Lovell), Northampton and Shropshire, but in 1474 he had become heir through his grandmother to the northern baronies of Deincourt and Grey of Rotherfield, which brought him wide estates in Yorkshire and Lincolnshire and helped to make him one of the wealthiest barons below the rank of earl. Made a ward of Richard Nevill, earl of Warwick, and brought up at Middleham, he was married in 1466 to Anne, daughter of Henry, Lord FitzHugh. His earliest public services were performed in the north, and he served under Duke Richard in the Scottish campaigns of the early 1480s. Their joint sojourn at Middleham in the period of their youth seems to have resulted in a lasting friendship between Richard of Gloucester and Lord Lovell. It may have been Richard's influence with Edward IV which led to Lovell's promotion to a viscountcy in January 1483: one of his 'sponsors' was their joint cousin, and Lovell's brother-in-law, Richard, Lord FitzHugh. But their friendship was to be more fully expressed later by Francis's promotion to the Order of the Garter, and his appointment as chamberlain of the household, an office which implied constant personal contact with the

[11] R. Davies, *Municipal Records of the City of York*, 41, 72; above, n; Lander, *Crown and Nobility*, 318; Storey, 'Wardens of the Marches', 615.

king.[12] Of his ability we know nothing. Of his loyalty there can be no question, and it persisted after Richard's death, shown in his rising of 1486 and his part in the Lambert Simnel affair of 1487, which ended at the Battle of Stoke in June. The circumstances of his death are even more mysterious than those of the princes in the Tower.[13]

Connections among the northern gentry were scarcely less important to Richard than those with the nobility, especially in Yorkshire, for they were to provide him with many of his most trusted servants, and, ultimately, his lieutenants in the south of England. Here again, to be the heir of Nevill was of importance, for the great majority of Warwick's former servants in Yorkshire transferred to Duke Richard in 1471. For example, of thirty-six men receiving fees charged upon the Middleham lordship in 1473–4, no fewer than twenty-two had been in Warwick's service some ten years before: many, either in their own persons or their fathers', had previously served Warwick's father, Salisbury, in the 1450s.[14] Some of the more prominent came from families whose homes lay close to Middleham. Thus Sir John Conyers of nearby Hornby Castle was head of a family with a long record of service to the Nevills. His brother William was the 'Robin of Redesdale' who led the Nevill-inspired rebellion of 1469 against Edward IV. John had been Warwick's steward of Richmondshire with a fee of £13 6s 8d. Richard continued him in this office with an increased fee of £20, and he was almost certainly a member of the duke's council. On Richard's accession he became a knight of the body to the king, was given an annuity of 200 marks and substantial grants of land in Yorkshire, where he was active on local commissions. Other members of the family (it was a very large one, for John's father had had twenty-five children) also served Richard both as duke and king.[15] Another prolific family which greatly improved its hitherto very modest fortunes in Richard's employ was that of Metcalfe of Nappa, five miles up the dale from Middleham. James Metcalfe was the youngest son of a family which had no less than nine members on Warwick's pay-roll in the 1460s. In 1471 he was retained by Gloucester at the inconspicuous fee of £6 13s 4d, but in 1483 found himself suddenly elevated to the influential and profitable office of chan-

---

[12] *CP*, IV, 128–30; VIII, 223–4; Dugdale, *Baronage of England*, I, 560–1; *CPR*, 213, and above, *n*; J. Enoch Powell and Keith Wallis, *The House of Lords in the Middle Ages*, 524–6 (where FitzHugh is wrongly said to be Lovell's father-in-law).

[13] *CP*, VIII, 225 and *n*. A prevailing legend is that he was walled-up in a room in his own house at Minster Lovell in Oxfordshire.

[14] G. M. Coles, 'The Lordship of Middleham, especially in Yorkist and early Tudor times' (unpublished M.A. thesis, Liverpool, 1961), esp. Appendix B; Pollard, 'Northern Retainers of Richard Nevill', 57 ff.

[15] *CPR*, 391, 393–4, 401, 425, 492; Harl. 433, fos. 287, 287v; Coles, *op. cit.*, 121 ff.; Pollard, 'Richmondshire Community of Gentry', 38, 50–1.

cellor of the Duchy of Lancaster, and in 1484 was further rewarded with lands in Bedfordshire to the annual value of 100 marks.[16] His brother Miles, a trained lawyer who had been Warwick's attorney-general in the 1460s, later became a member of Duke Richard's council, was appointed recorder of the city of York on the duke's recommendation to the city authorities, acted as his deputy chief steward in the Duchy of Lancaster and, during the Protectorate, was made a justice in the county palatine of Lancaster on 26 May 1483.[17] This was one of several appointments of north-country men made within the first few days of Richard's arrival in the capital, and underlines his trust and confidence in them during the struggle for control which was to follow.[18]

Former Nevill servants were, however, not the only element in Duke Richard's swollen northern affinity. Some of its more prominent members were drawn from families with a tradition of service to the House of York itself. Sir John Saville was head of a substantial West Riding family, with lands at Thornhill near Sandal Castle, and his forebears had been in the Yorks' service since before 1399, commonly as constables of Sandal. His association with Richard was to almost double his income when he was appointed constable of the Isle of Wight, with a fee of £200, in 1484.[19] Others again had risen in the service of Edward IV. For example, Sir James Harrington of Hornby in Lancashire, whose family also held extensive estates in Yorkshire, had been a servant of Warwick (as had his father, Thomas, of Warwick's father), deserted Warwick in 1471, and moved into the royal household as a knight of the body. But he also had connections with Duke Richard (who may have supported him in his private feud with Lord Stanley), as did his brother, Sir Robert Harrington, who was made a banneret in Scotland by Richard in 1482 and whose services to Richard as king were to be rewarded with very substantial grants of land to the value of £326 12s yearly.[20] One or two others were weaned from the service of Henry Percy, earl of Northumberland (such as Sir Hugh Hastings of Fenwick in the East Riding of Yorkshire, a kinsman of the

[16] B.L. MS Harl. 433, f. 285; *CPR, 1476–85*, 380; Coles, *op. cit.*; Somerville, *Duchy of Lancaster*, I, 391–2.

[17] Coles, *op. cit.*; Somerville, *op. cit*, 426; *Grants*, 61. James, father of Thomas and Miles, was made master forester of Wensleydale, and two other brothers, Richard and Brian, were given annuities by Richard after he had achieved the throne (*CPR*, 455–6, 517).

[18] E.g., Guy Fairfax, another ducal councillor, chief justice of Lancashire, also on 26 May (*Grants*, 61).

[19] He was also granted lands in the same area worth £66 13s 4d *p.a.* (*CPR*, 410; B.L. MS Harl. 433, f. 289).

[20] J. C. Wedgwood, *History of Parliament, 1439–1509, Biographies*, 423–7; Coles, *op. cit.*, App. B; Somerville, *op. cit.*, 514; B.L. MS Harl. 433, f. 288; Pollard, 'Northern Retainers of Richard Nevill', 57.

earl who was in Gloucester's retinue in Scotland in 1482), but the real erosion of the Percy following in the north took place only after Richard's accession to the throne.[21]

Others again seem to have no known connection with the families of Nevill, York or Percy, but were simply attracted into Richard's service by reason of the influential patronage he commanded or by mere geographical proximity to the centres of his power. One example was Sir Thomas Gower, a member of a relatively obscure family whose estates lay at Sheriff Hutton and Stittenham nearby. Knighted by Gloucester on the 1482 campaign, he was sufficiently trusted by him to be given charge of Earl Rivers after his arrest in April 1483, and later became a knight of the king's body with substantial annuities.[22] Several members of the Mauleverer family of Allerton Mauleverer in the West Riding of Yorkshire, some twenty-five miles from Middleham, achieved a brief and unexpected prominence in the sunlight of Richard's patronage: one succeeded another as Richard's sheriffs of Devon, a third was to be escheator in Kent and Middlesex in 1483.[23] Two other relatively obscure men who blossomed similarly were Sir Thomas Markenfield of Markenfield near Ripon, and yet another Yorkshireman, Sir Thomas Everingham, a professional soldier with a record of service going back to the last campaign of the Hundred Years' War, but more recently as a commander of English forces in the service of the duke of Burgundy. Markenfield became a knight of the body, with an annuity of 100 marks and lands in Somerset worth £100 yearly, while Everingham was appointed lieutenant of the fortress of Ruysbank in the march of Calais and was rewarded with a lavish grant of lands in Devon, Somerset and elsewhere worth no less than £200 a year.[24] All these men are of interest, for they illustrate Richard's tendency to rely upon men who might reasonably be considered upstarts by the standards of the day (Ratcliffe is another, as we shall see): none of them was of sufficient importance to be appointed to his local commissions of the peace – the mark of a substantial gentleman – in his own right. The generosity of the rewards they received is no less interesting. The £200 a

[21] Wedgwood, *op. cit.*, 432–3; B.L. MS Harl. 433, f. 285v; *CPR*, 490, and on Northumberland's relations with Richard generally, see Hicks, 'Dynastic Change and Northern Society: Henry Percy', *passim*, esp. pp. 91–2.

[22] Wedgwood, *op. cit.*, 386; B.L. MS Harl. 433, f. 118v; *CPR*, 424, 482. The annuities were worth £100 a year, but his own estates only £58.

[23] *Calendar of Fine Rolls, 1471–85*, 276–7, 300, and for their rewards, B.L. MS Harl. 433, f. 283v, 289v.

[24] B.L. MS Harl. 433, f. 282; *CPR*, 299, 398, 429, 460, 470, 572; Scofield, *Edward IV*, II, 267n., 290–1, 296.

year which Everingham and Markenfield each received from a grateful king was more than all except some two hundred men below the rank of baron in the entire realm possessed by way of landed income.[25]

Across the border from Yorkshire, Richard's influence gradually penetrated into the palatine county of Durham, where he acquired, through his marriage, the lordship of Barnard Castle. Along with Middleham, Sheriff Hutton, Sandal near Wakefield and Penrith, this was one of the many residences which he embellished during his period of residence in the north between 1471 and 1483, and later as king.[26] The duchess of Gloucester was admitted to the sisterhood of Durham cathedral priory in 1476, and in 1484, as king, Richard visited the cathedral, where he was later regarded as a notable benefactor: amongst other things he presented the monks of Durham with his 'parliament robe of blue velvet wrought with great lions of pure gold'.[27] His main achievement was to end the long-standing feud between the junior and senior Nevill lines (the latter having dominated the county for some time) and win over the ageing earl of Westmorland and his nephew Ralph, Lord Nevill (who succeeded to the title in 1484), as well as securing the support of Sir George Lumley, heir of the other Durham magnate, Lord Lumley, and the goodwill of the bishop of Durham, William Dudley (1476–83).[28]

Richard's other main area of influence lay in the north-west of England, in Cumberland and Westmorland. Here the pattern in the structure of the duke's affinity was similar to that in Yorkshire. In this area the once powerful Percy influence had been overtaken by the intrusion of the Nevills as wardens of the west march in the 1440s and 1450s and by the eclipse of Percy fortunes during Edward IV's first decade. Many of the leading families of the region moved into the Nevill orbit – Parrs, Huddlestons, Musgraves – and chose to continue in the service of Duke Richard. For example, Sir John Huddleston of Millom in Cumberland was a

[25] J. P. Cooper, 'The Social Distribution of Land and Men in England, 1436–1700', *Economic History Review*, 2nd series, xx (1967), 419–21.

[26] R. Allen Brown, H. M. Colvin and A. J. Taylor, *The History of the King's Works*, II, 558, 600. At Sandal he commissioned the building of a new tower, and later, when the castle became the headquarters of the council of the north, a new bakehouse and brewhouse: Harl. 433, f. 175v, 183v, 191v. For his great hall at Middleham, see Pl. 3.

[27] Hicks, 'Dynastic Change and Northern Society: Henry Percy', 85–6; Mary O'Regan, 'Richard III and the Monks of Durham', *The Ricardian*, no. 4 (1978), 19–22.

[28] Hicks, *op. cit.*, 86.

trustee of the duke's in the Middleham estates and in the lands of the countess of Oxford in East Anglia by 1479; he was later to become sheriff of Cambridge during Richard's reign. His second son, John, became an esquire of the king's body, was granted lands in Worcestershire and Gloucestershire, and either he or his brother Thomas was sheriff of Gloucester in 1483–4. Sir John's elder brother, Sir Richard Huddleston, was already an established ducal servant when, during the Protectorate, he was made keeper of the north-western lands of the marquis of Dorset. By 28 November 1483 he had been made a knight of the body, constable of Beaumaris Castle, sheriff of Anglesey and master forester of Snowdon in North Wales.[29] John Musgrave from Cumberland was yet another northerner who became an esquire of the body, received lands in Wiltshire worth £102 yearly, became sheriff of that county and was M.P. for Salisbury in Richard's parliament, while his kinsmen Richard and William Musgrave continued to serve the king in the north. Similar rewards and employments in the south came the way of the Redman or Redmayne family of Levens Hall in Westmorland and Harewood in Yorkshire.[30] Few of these families are prominent in the records of royal administration before 1483. Sir William Redman, for example, although M.P. for Westmorland in 1478, with Gloucester's backing, does not even appear on the commissions of the peace under Edward IV.

The most remarkable and certainly the most meteorically successful of these men from the north-west was the first member of the notorious trio of the Rat, the Cat, and Lovell the Dog. Richard Ratcliffe was a younger son of a lesser gentry family with lands around Derwentwater in the Lake District, none of whose members was important enough to achieve the office of Justice of the Peace until Sir Richard's promotion under Richard III. Before 1483 he had become a ducal councillor, one of Richard's trustees in the lordship of Richmond and steward of Barnard Castle, and he was created knight and banneret by Richard on the Scottish campaigns. He was to remain one of the king's most trusted confidants. Knight of the Garter, royal councillor, sheriff of Westmorland for life, he also received

[29] Wedgwood, op. cit., s.n.; CPR, 363, 369, 372, 379, 393, 395, 396, 398, 400, 434, 488, 505–6, 556, 570; CCR, 1476–85, 189; Calendar of Fine Rolls, 1471–85, 276. For Nevill influence in the north-west, see R. L. Storey, The End of the House of Lancaster, 105–23; P. Jalland, 'The Influence of the Aristocracy on Shire Elections, 1450–70', Speculum, xlvii (1972), 495–501; and see also Hicks, op. cit., 85; 'four of the ten known knights of the shire for Cumberland and Westmorland in 1472–83 were his men'.

[30] Wedgwood, op. cit., s.n.; Harl. 433, fos. 283, 284v; CPR, 397, 492, 545, 577.

rewards from forfeited lands on a scale exceptionally lavish even by Richard's own generous standards.[31]

Thus Richard made his bid for power in 1483 as the leader of an exceptionally large and powerful northern affinity. It was important for the future that his pre-eminence in the north had been achieved without unduly alienating the other two great magnates of the region, Northumberland and Stanley. His predominance is reflected in the large number of private disputes which were referred to his arbitration. Thereby he (and his council) helped to keep the peace in an otherwise lawless region, where recourse to the ordinary courts of law was less usual than a resort to violence. He is even to be found – and this is most unusual, and a reflection of his extraordinary influence – adjudicating in disputes of an essentially ecclesiastical nature, where, ordinarily, one might have expected the archbishop of York or an appropriate body of learned canon lawyers to have been consulted.[32] Equally, his power is shown in the influence he exerted on appointments to the bench of justices of the peace, to the office of sheriff and in parliamentary elections during the period 1471–83. But this rested upon a condominium, a sharing of regional power, with Northumberland and Stanley. The earl was allowed to retain his commanding influence in Yorkshire's East Riding and in the county of Northumberland proper, while the duke was dominant in the North Riding of Yorkshire and in Cumberland and Westmorland. Where their interests overlapped, there seems to have been a general cooperation between them (for example, of nine sheriffs of Yorkshire between 1474 and 1483, four served the duke and three the earl); they compromised in allowing each other's followers to be returned to parliament; and they can be found acting as joint arbiters in disputes between their respective retainers.[33] Meanwhile, the Stanley family had used its connections with Edward IV and the prince of Wales's council to retain control of Cheshire and Lancashire, and to extend its power into North Wales. This was an area of influence in which Richard

[31] Harl. 433, fos. 284, 285; Davies. *York Records*, 148; Atthill, *Church of Middleham*, 84–5; *CPR*, 472, 512; *Dictionary of National Biography*, xlvii, 134–5 (which states that in addition to the other rewards mentioned above, he was also steward of the York lordship of Wakefield, but without citing authority). See further below, p. 121.

[32] For his arbitrating a dispute between the abbot and convent of Selby, Yorkshire, and the parishioners of Snaith in 1481, see *The Register of Thomas Rotherham, Archbishop of York*, ed. E. E. Barker (Canterbury and York Society, LXIX, 1976), I, 194–5. I am indebted to Professor R. B. Dobson for his advice on the unusual nature of this action.

[33] Hicks, 'Dynastic Change and Northern Society: Henry Percy', 87–9; Ross, *Edward IV*, 199–203; *Plumpton Correspondence*, lxxxviii, and *CCR, 1468–76*, 365 (for joint arbitrations).

never interfered. The relative harmony between the three magnates can be seen on the Scottish expeditions when all three commanders, not Richard alone, were allowed to create knights and appoint bannerets. Northumberland, at least, proved a not unwilling partner in Richard's bid for power. Thomas Stanley was a somewhat different matter. The Stanleys, as always, had their eye on the main chance, but at least Thomas accepted Richard's usurpation and supported him against the duke of Buckingham (and his own wife, Margaret Beaufort) during the rebellion of 1483, for which he received very substantial rewards.[34]

Harsh political realities ultimately forced Richard, as king, to rely upon his northern supporters to a greater degree than he might have wished – his reign proved to be an experiment (never to be repeated) in the government of the realm by the head of a great northern connection. But its political importance was certainly increased by the very marked and continued affection and preference which he showed towards its members, particularly those who had been close to him as duke of Gloucester. It was a loyalty which went beyond, and cannot be simply explained solely in terms of, political necessity. Despite his determined but ultimately vain effort to win over Edward IV's household men, it was natural enough that, during the queasy weeks of his takeover of power in the capital and his occupation of the throne, he should turn to his trusted northern friends in all tasks of political delicacy. Within a few days of his arrival in London, he decided to seize the estates of Earl Rivers, newly arrested solely on Richard's personal authority. The task was given to two Yorkshiremen, Sir Thomas Wortley and William Mauleverer, esquire, this being one of the first recorded acts of Richard's Protectorate.[35] It was another Yorkshireman, John Nesfield, who was appointed to guard the sanctuary of Westminster Abbey to prevent the escape of the dowager queen, Elizabeth Woodville, and her daughters.[36] The messenger chosen to go north and organize the army which the Protector might need to overawe parliament in support of his claim to the throne was Sir Richard Ratcliffe himself, and, according to one authority, it was upon Ratcliffe's direct command that Earl Rivers and his associates were later executed at Pontefract without due form of trial.[37] When, on 13 June 1483, Richard decided to eliminate Lord Hastings, two more Yorkshiremen, Robert Harrington and Charles Pilkington, shared command with the earl of Surrey of the

---

[34] For the Stanleys, M. A. Hicks, 'Changing Role of the Wydevilles', 78–9; D. A. L. Morgan, 'The King's Affinity in the Polity of Yorkist England', *TRHS*, 5th series, xxiii (1973), 18–19, and for Stanley and Northumberland during the usurpation, below, pp. 78, 88, 121.

[35] *Grants of Edward V*, 3.

[36] *CC*, 567.

[37] *York Civic Records*, I, 73; *CC*, 489.

armed assassins placed behind the arras in the council room in the Tower of London.[38]

More significant, if less immediate, was the steady occupation by men from the north of many of the important offices which involved close and regular personal contacts with the new king. Francis, Lord Lovell became chamberlain of the household; its controller was Sir Robert Percy from Yorkshire; John Kendal, Richard's new secretary, came from York; John Harington, who had been a member of the ducal council, became clerk of the king's council in December 1483, and Richard's influence secured his appointment as a non-resident clerk of the council to York city.[39] Of thirty-two men described as knights of the king's body in the Patent Rolls of the reign, no fewer than fifteen came from the four counties of Yorkshire, Lancashire, Cumberland and Westmorland, and the same is true of thirteen of the thirty-four esquires of the body mentioned in that record. Northerners soon made an appearance on the king's council to an unusual degree. The records are defective, but of fifteen barons known to have been councillors, eight came from the north.[40] Amongst the twenty-three non-noble lay members of the council whose names have been recorded, five were northerners, and there is some evidence that others who do not occur in official records were also councillors.[41]

More significant still were the elections to the Order of the Garter, always a mark of the sovereign's high personal favour. Only seven vacancies occurred during Richard's brief reign. Six were filled by northerners, if we may include Francis Lovell: the others were Lord Stanley, and the knights Thomas Burgh, Richard Tunstall, John Conyers and the inevi-

[38] At least according to the original MS version of Polydore Vergil's English History, printed as an appendix to D. Hay, *Polydore Vergil*, 204–5.

[39] *CPR*, 434; *York Civic Records*, I, 79, 81, 93, 103 (which reflect York's estimate of the influence with the king of Harington and Kendal); *VCH, Yorkshire, City of York*, 74; *CP*, VIII, 224. There were, of course, some important southerners also in the king's immediate circle, notably Thomas Howard, earl of Surrey, steward of the royal household, Sir James Tyrell, master of the henchmen in the household and then master of the horse, and Sir Thomas Montgomery, who seems, from the tasks entrusted to him and the rewards he received (lands worth £412 *p.a.*), to have enjoyed Richard's close confidence. All had lands and connections in Suffolk and Essex, and seem to have formed an association with Richard as duke through his control of the De Vere estates in that region after 1471.

[40] *CPR, passim*. J. R. Lander, *Crown and Nobility 1450–1509*, 318–19, lists the names of councillors known from official records. The eight barons were Northumberland, Dacre, the two Scropes, Stanley and his son Strange, FitzHugh and Lovell.

[41] Brackenbury, Burgh, Ratcliffe, Sir Richard Tunstall and Richard Salkeld. The well-informed author of the 'Ballad of Bosworth Field' (for which see below, App. 2), who had a first-hand knowledge of the northern gentry, claims that Sir Marmaduke Constable 'of King Richard's councell hee was nye'.

table Richard Ratcliffe.[42] The same consideration applies to Richard's ecclesiastical preferments, which reflect his enduring affection for northerners. Only three episcopal vacancies occurred during his brief reign. Two (in succession) went to Thomas Langton from Westmorland; the other (Durham) to John Shirwood, son of a town clerk of York. But several of Richard's clerical servants from his time as duke also enjoyed his patronage as king. For example, William Beverley, rector of Middleham church and the first dean of his new college there, became dean of the prestigious college of St George's, Windsor, in 1483, and was also made precentor of York Minster. Thomas Barowe, whose name and early career strongly suggest that he too was a northerner, and who had certainly been the duke's chancellor before 1483, became master of the rolls in September 1483 and keeper of the Great Seal in August 1485, as well as being rewarded with a canonry at Westminster and the archdeaconry of Colchester.[43] Towns were politically less important than nobles, bishops or gentry, but here too Richard's northern preferences stand out. He was exceptionally generous to the city of York. It seems to have been his clear intention to release the town from the whole of the annual fee-farm it owed to the crown, although in practice this intention was frustrated by the stubborn conservatism of the exchequer, and it is not surprising that York mourned his demise.[44] But Hull, Beverley and Newcastle also received financial concessions from him; Pontefract was made a borough; and Scarborough in Yorkshire, of which he had been lord, was (astonishingly for its size and importance) made into a shire incorporate, a dignity only previously enjoyed by such major towns as London, Bristol and Norwich.[45]

There was, of course, nothing unusual in a new king promoting his own servants and adherents, and, in the natural course of things, this was especially true of usurpers like Henry IV, Edward IV and Richard himself. What is exceptional is the degree to which so many of Richard's followers came from north of Trent, and of his continuing loyalty to his former servants as duke. His attempts as king to broaden the geographical

---

[42] G. F. Beltz, *Memorials of the Most Noble Order of the Garter*, clxvi–vii. The odd man out is Thomas Howard, earl of Surrey.

[43] A. B. Emden, *Biographical Register of the University of Cambridge, s.n.*; *CCR, 1476–85*, 432–3.

[44] *York Civic Records*, I, 101 ff. For the information about the remission of the fee-farm, I am indebted to the researches of Lorraine Attreed, of the University of York, into 'The Relations between the Royal Government and the City of York, 1377–1451' (unpublished M.A. thesis).

[45] *CPR*, 415, 455, 484, 509; *Cal. Charter Rolls, 1427–1516*, 262–5; Somerville, *History of the Duchy of Lancaster*, I, 149; Wedgwood, *History of Parliament, Register*, 719. Not surprisingly, Scarborough lost its unlikely status as a county as soon as Henry VII became king.

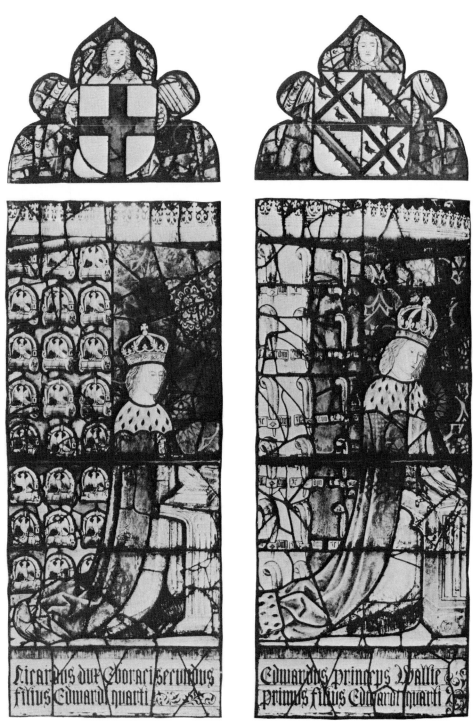

5. The princes in the Tower: Richard duke of York (*left*), and Edward prince of Wales (*right*), the sons of Edward IV. From a stained-glass window in Canterbury Cathedral.

6(a). The White Tower in the Tower of London. The princes were last seen withdrawn behind the windows.

6(b). The initial letter of the Register of Robert Stillington, bishop of Bath and Wells 1466–91, who produced the story that the marriage of Edward IV and Elizabeth Woodville was invalid and that the princes were therefore bastards. His name appears immediately below the initial.

7. Crosby Hall, now in Chelsea, where Richard III lodged on his arrival in London in May 1483.

8. A seventeenth-century print of a public sermon being delivered from St Paul's Cross, London, from where Dr Shaw delivered his sermon proclaiming Richard III king of England.

bases of his support were, at least in part, frustrated by such obstinate personal preferences. It is important to realize that in southern England men from the north were still regarded with fear and mistrust, as wild, warlike, lawless and licentious. The advance of a northern army upon London in 1461 had produced something approaching a state of panic, and at least one major chronicler of the period displayed something amounting to a hatred of men from the north.[46] At best they were aliens, men largely unfamiliar with court and capital. Certainly, they were intruders into the comfortably southern Yorkist establishment of Edward IV's time. As such, they were to prove a political disadvantage to Richard, especially when he was more or less forced to introduce them into the administration of the southern shires.[47]

[46] A. J. Pollard, 'The Tyranny of Richard III', *Journal of Medieval History*, iii (1977), 147–65, esp. pp. 162–3, for a discussion of this point.
[47] See below, pp. 119–24.

# PART TWO
# THE USURPATION AND ITS AFTERMATH

# Chapter 4

# THE ROAD TO THE THRONE: THE EVENTS OF APRIL TO JUNE 1483

The brief months of Edward V's unhappy reign provide a period of violent political drama with few close parallels in English history. Within four weeks of his father's death, the person of the young king was violently seized by his paternal uncle of Gloucester. His maternal uncle, Earl Rivers, together with other Woodville kinsmen and connections of Edward V, were arrested, sent to prison in Pontefract, and there were soon to be executed without any due form of trial. Six weeks later, other opponents of Duke Richard, notably William, Lord Hastings, were similarly arrested, and either executed or imprisoned. Edward V himself had been lodged in the Tower, and was soon joined there by his younger brother, Duke Richard of York, extricated under duress from the sanctuary at Westminster. Thence neither ever emerged. Both were declared bastards, and unfit to inherit the throne. Richard himself became king in Edward's place on 26 June 1483.

If these events provided Shakespeare with ready material for an immortal drama, for the historian their interpretation is beset by acute problems. By definition, this was a period of a struggle for power, carried on in an atmosphere of rumour, suspicion, propaganda exercises, plot and counter-plot. Only those at the centre could be fully aware of what was going on, certainly not contemporary or later chroniclers, with the possible exception of the Croyland writer, who, however, chose not to reveal all he may have known. Consequently, the evidence is continuously conflicting and uncertain, often scanty in relation to major events. These difficulties have not been diminished by the very different methods of approach adopted by different historians.[1]

Yet how we interpret these events has an important bearing on our estimate of Richard's motives, character and abilities. Thus the hostile Tudor writers saw in Richard's violent actions nothing other than the natural expression of his innate ambition and wickedness. Confident and ruthless, he was pre-determined 'to wade through slaughter to a throne',

---

[1] Whereas the Tudor writers tended to use their overall estimate of Richard as tyrant and villain to colour their accounts of the events of the Protectorate, modern historians have tended to infer his character and motives from a close scrutiny of the events themselves without preconceptions. On this point generally, see above pp. xxiv–xxx, liii.

as Thomas Gray's *Elegy* expressed it. In essence, though with substantial modifications, this tradition still commanded respect as late as the end of the nineteenth century, and was accepted by such considerable scholars as Stubbs, Ramsay and Gairdner. More modern scholars have reacted sharply in the other direction. Richard did not dictate events: rather he was their prisoner, if not their victim, with the somewhat curious result that, instead of ruthlessness linked with ability, we have diminished responsibility but also reduced political abilities. For A. R. Myers, presenting a moderate modern view, Richard was 'probably an anxious and nervous man rather than a cruel and merciless one': it was only 'the responsibilities and perils of an unexpected royal minority [which] aroused in his nature the elements of fear, ambition and impulsive ruthlessness which led him further and further along the path of political expediency at the expense of duty and honour'.[2] The most recent and extreme version of this modern revision presents Richard as not merely uncertain of his intentions, but deeply incompetent in their execution. He was a 'man of limited political perceptions', and his actions were 'more those of a foolish man than a calculating one'. When, very late in the day, he decided to seek the throne for himself, his seizure of power was carried through in a 'hasty, sloppy and poorly explained manner'.[3] It is worth noticing, in passing, that this modern revision of the events of the Protectorate sits somewhat askance with the opinion of well-informed contemporaries much closer to the events than we can possibly be. For the Croyland Chronicler, Richard was a man who carried out all his schemes 'swiftly and with the utmost vigilance' and Polydore Vergil attributed to him qualities of 'circumspection and celerity' – and these were the judgements of writers who were in no way concerned to defend Richard. Mancini, perhaps with more bias, saw him as an ambitious man, who nurtured well-defined plans under a cloak of deceit and dissimulation.[4]

The extraordinary problems of the evidence are highlighted by the difficulty which historians have always found in providing a convincing answer to one vital question: when, and why, did Richard decide to seek the throne for himself? We need not take seriously the Tudor back-projection, that he was planning to make himself king before the death of Edward IV, for he could not have anticipated that his vigorous, if debauched, brother would die at the age of forty. Was the violent seizure of Edward V at Stony Stratford a planned step on the way to the throne? Few historians have dared to claim this with any certainty, although

[2] Myers, 'Character of Richard III', 131, whose views are followed by B. P. Wolffe, 'When and why did Hastings lose his head?', *EHR*, lxxxix (1974), 842.

[3] Charles T. Wood, 'The Deposition of Edward V', *Traditio*, xxxi (1975), 264.

[4] *CC*, 568; PV, 200; Mancini, 80–3.

contemporary sources strongly suggest that some people at least already suspected Richard's ultimate intentions in the weeks immediately following the seizure of the young king.[5] Most scholars now tend to connect his final decision with the execution of Hastings on 13 June, 'the first overt act . . . which seems to reveal to us his intention to usurp'.[6] But even this is not without its difficulties. Was the violent action against Hastings and his supporters an essential move in a pre-conceived plan, or did he decide only later, in the realization that his action was irreversible, and that having gone so far, he could only go further? Had he made up his mind even then? It has recently been argued that only as late as 20 June, two days before he claimed the throne, did he finally admit to himself that 'the spectre of continuing crises and conflicts' could only be dispelled by eliminating 'the one common bond among his enemies, loyalty to Edward V'.[7] However difficult it may be to find an answer to these questions, they need to be kept well in mind.

The first moves in the struggle for power were initiated by the Woodville group in London during the days immediately following King Edward's death on 9 April 1483. They evidently planned to maintain their position by force if necessary, by seizing the royal treasure in the Tower, putting a fleet to sea under Woodville command, arranging for an early coronation of the young king, bringing him to London at the head of an army controlled by Earl Rivers and his friends, and devising a form of interim government from which the duke of Gloucester would be largely excluded. Much depended on their ability to control the royal council. During the week of 9–16 April, while the dead king's body lay in state in Westminster Abbey, many notables, both lay and ecclesiastical, joined those already assembled in London for the very elaborate funeral ceremonies of Edward IV, which took place between 17 and 20 April. No less than nineteen peers and ten bishops took part in the obsequies, together with a conspicuous gathering of Edward IV's former household officials and servants.[8] There were few notable absentees, apart from the northern magnates (Gloucester himself, Northumberland and the aged earl of Westmorland) and other barons from the far north who could not be expected to reach London in time; Rivers and his friends in the Welsh Marches, for whom again

[5] *CC*, 566; Mancini, 80–3.

[6] Chrimes, *Lancastrians, Yorkists and Henry VII*, 131. More recently, Richard's decision that a usurpation attempt might succeed has been directly linked with the dispatch of a letter on 10–11 June to summon an army from the north (J. A. F. Thomson, 'Richard III and Lord Hastings'. *BIHR*, xlviii (1975), 30).

[7] Wood, 'Deposition', 268.

[8] Gairdner, *L & P*, I, 3–10, for a contemporary account of the funeral.

distance was an obstacle; the duke of Buckingham, whose whereabouts are not known; and, conspicuous among the prelates, the now venerable Thomas Bourchier, archbishop of Canterbury. Other aged noblemen, like the duke of Suffolk and the earl of Arundel, were represented by their sons, the earl of Lincoln and Lord Maltravers. Many of these men, including eight lords and nine bishops, had been councillors of the dead king. It was, therefore, a substantial body of councillors which met at Westminster either before or, more probably, soon after Edward's final internment at Windsor.[9] Although in some ways divided among themselves, perhaps their strongest common bond was loyalty to the heir of the king whom they had served for years, and who had helped to make their fame and fortune.[10]

It is quite incorrect to say that this council which 'the Woodvilles had called into being' was 'as unlawful as their own pretentions'.[11] As with previous royal minorities, in 1377 and 1422, the available lords, spiritual and temporal, assumed that the royal authority had devolved upon them by reason of the death of the king and the minority of his heir.[12] Immediate practical decisions were needed to keep the administration running. As in 1422, the appointments of the judges of king's bench and common pleas were renewed, and measures were agreed upon for the defence of the realm against the activities of Louis XI's admiral, Philippe de Crèvecoeur, known to the English as Lord Cordes, who had been vigorously prosecuting an undeclared war at sea.[13] But the authority of the council by no means ended there. The wishes of a dead king, even one so powerful as Henry V had been, had no binding force in law, and, in 1422, his councillors had effectively combined to defeat the pretensions of another duke of Gloucester to a form of regency and had established themselves, with parliamentary backing, as the true government of the realm during the

[9] For a list of Edward's councillors, see J. R. Lander, *Crown and Nobility, 1450–1509*, 308–20.

[10] As suggested by *CC*, 564–5. Among the 'loyalists' we can probably include all the bishops and Hastings and the marquis of Dorset of the lay lords, but there were also probably present several lay lords who afterwards emerged as strong supporters of Richard III, such as Howard, Audley and Ferrers, whose attitude may have been anti-Woodville from the start.

[11] Kendall, 168.

[12] J. S. Roskell, 'The Office and Dignity of Protector of England, with special reference to its origins', *EHR*, lxviii (1953), 193–233, especially 196: 'They must act, pending the appointment of a sworn council of the regular kind, not only as the king's advisers but as virtually constituting the executive.' This important and scholarly discussion, although cited in Kendall's footnotes, seems to have been largely ignored by him.

[13] Mancini, 80–1, 118–19.

long minority of Henry VI.[14] Even the wishes of Henry VIII for the government of the realm during the minority of his son could be largely ignored after his death. The council of regency came to be dominated by Edward VI's uncle, the duke of Somerset, with far greater powers than had been enjoyed by Gloucester in 1422; and this was achieved through Somerset's exploitation of the nominal authority of the nine-year-old king, and in violation of statute.[15] Who was to control the person of the king in 1483 was not clear. Henry VI had been careful to separate the *tutela* (or wardship) of the inheritance which he intended for Humphrey duke of Gloucester from the custody of the person of his heir, which he placed in other hands. There is some evidence that Edward had intended to place both functions in the hands of Duke Richard, but in his last years he had certainly done nothing to disturb Earl Rivers's tenure of his position as Edward V's governor, and in some ways seems to have entrenched him in his control.[16] Whatever his intentions may have been – and we cannot know for certain – it was quite possible for the council to overrule them and make other arrangements.

This discussion serves to illustrate certain very important points. First, uncertainty about what the council might decide explains why Gloucester thought it vital to seize the person of the young king at an early stage, and made it his first positive move. Control of the person of the king – a lively adolescent much influenced by his mother and her family – was of far greater political importance in the circumstances than had been that of a nine-month-old baby in 1422. Second, it shows why control of the council was so important to the Woodville group, for, properly handled, it could be used to defeat Gloucester's claim to power in the minority government. If it could be persuaded to endorse a Woodville-dominated minority before either Gloucester or the young king reached London, then the Woodville battle was largely won. This was the essential subject of the discussions in the council in late April 1483, and this also is what the Woodvilles could not achieve, although they came close to their objective. Their influence was clearly considerable, for on 27 April commissions were appointed to levy the tax on aliens which had been voted by parliament in January, on which Rivers and Dorset figure prominently alongside Hastings and many of Edward IV's household men, but from which both Gloucester and

[14] Roskell, *op. cit.*, *passim*.

[15] Mortimer Levine, *Tudor Dynastic Problems, 1460–1571*, 76–7; Roskell, *op. cit.*, 229. In March 1547 Somerset was formally appointed 'governor of the person of the king and protector of our kingdoms, lordships and subjects'.

[16] For Rivers, see below, p. 70. Roskell, *op. cit.*, 205–6, 227–8. The evidence that Richard was to have control both of the king's person and of the realm comes from Bishop Russell's draft sermon for the opening of the parliament of June 1483 (*Grants*, xlviii), and on this point see further below, p. 75.

Buckingham were conspicuously missing.[17] The council also agreed to the fixing of a very early coronation date – Sunday 4 May – and (at least according to Mancini) voted against the notion of a full regency for Gloucester, as Edward IV in his will had directed, in favour of a regency council of which the duke would be the chief member. This was done, he says, because of the danger that 'if the entire government were committed to one man he might easily usurp the sovereignty', and in spite of a letter from Gloucester to the council, setting forth his merits and good intentions: this was carefully circulated in the city of London and won him some popular support.[18] Woodville influence seems to have been strong enough to override the doubts of those who felt that important arrangements should not be made so hurriedly, and without consulting the likely Protector. Indeed, the marquis of Dorset was confident enough to say in public that 'we are so important, that even without the king's uncle we can make and enforce these decisions'.[19] The Croyland Chronicler, with a more informed knowledge of English politics, and almost certainly writing from a seat within the council, gives a rather different version of events. For him the main factor was the feeling among 'the more prudent members of the council' that a Woodville-dominated minority would be both undesirable and politically dangerous. To prevent a Woodville take-over by force, they vetoed the queen's suggestion that the young king should come to London with a substantial army at his back: instead he

[17] *CPR*, 353–5, for the commissions. Dorset, 'uterine brother to the king', was appointed in 5 counties, Rivers, 'uterine uncle', in 3, Hastings in 7.

[18] Mancini, 71–3. Although not very familiar with English constitutional arrangements, Mancini clearly contrasts the notion of a full regency with the more limited power of a protector. Rather confusingly, the Croyland Chronicle suggests the opposite: according to this source, Richard was given (when appointed Protector, see below, p. 75) 'power to order and forbid in every matter, just like another king, and according as the necessity of the case should demand' (*CC*, 566). But since the Chronicler specifically cites the precedent of Duke Humphrey of Gloucester in 1422, and equally specifically states that such powers might be exercised only with 'the consent and goodwill of all the lords', it is clear that he, also, is thinking of a limited power resting on the approval of the council. When in 1427, Duke Humphrey of Gloucester had sought a definition of his powers, the lords in parliament declared that he had agreed to exercise a position as 'chief of the king's other councillors, not the name of tutor, lieutenant, governor, nor regent, *nor any name that would imply authority of governance of the land* [my italics], but the name of protector and defender, which signifies a personal duty of attendance to the actual defence of the land. ...' (Myers, *English Historical Documents*, IV, 464). On balance, it seems clear that in 1483 the lords in council were acting on the most obvious and immediate precedent for action during the minority of a king – that of 1422, although they could also have turned to that of 1377.

[19] Mancini, 73–5.

was to bring no more than 2,000 men.[20] This decision was partly the consequence of a violent intervention by Lord Hastings, who especially feared Woodville vengeance if that party achieved supreme power, and threatened to flee to his Calais stronghold unless it were accepted that the king should come only with a moderate retinue. When the queen accepted 2,000 as a compromise figure, Hastings agreed, confident in the knowledge that Gloucester and Buckingham could be relied upon to bring at least as many. Thus far the council had acted with moderation, resisting extremists on both sides. No formal authority had yet been given to Gloucester, but precautions had also been taken against a Woodville coup d'état, 'it being the most ardent desire of all who were present that the prince should succeed his father in all his glory'.[21] In London, therefore, matters stood nicely balanced when, on 30 April, the startling news arrived that Duke Richard had seized the young king, had arrested Rivers and the Woodville group from Ludlow, and had dismissed Prince Edward's intimates and attendants, and, presumably, all the troops who had followed him from the Marches of Wales.

In the provinces matters moved more slowly, and, given the political tensions of the day, with a surprising lack of urgency. News of Edward IV's death did not apparently reach his son at Ludlow until 14 April. Two days later he wrote to the borough of Lynn, where his governor, Earl Rivers, had close connections, informing the people that he was going to London for his crowning 'with all convenient haste'. Even so, he did not leave Ludlow until 24 April and reached Stony Stratford on 29 April.[22] Perhaps the long delay is explained by the time needed for Rivers to assemble the large army which the council feared he would bring. But it is also possible that at this stage Rivers had no good reason to suspect that evil was afoot, or that Gloucester was planning a violent stroke to secure his own position.

For it was no inexperienced or gullible man who was taken by surprise at Northampton on 29–30 April. Anthony Woodville, 2nd Earl Rivers, has come down to us as a versatile and engaging personality. Experienced as a soldier, sailor and diplomat, he was also an accomplished courtier and the most renowned jouster and knight-errant of the England of his day. He combined with these qualities a strong streak of religious asceticism, which took him on frequent pilgrimages and caused him to wear a hair-

---

[20] The figure of 2,000 must be taken as a chronicler's estimate of a moderate force. In fact, by the standards of the time, it constituted a small army. According to the Black Book of Edward IV's household, the retinue of a duke (for example) was no more than 240 (Myers, *The Household of Edward IV*, 96).

[21] *CC*, 564–5.

[22] *Historical Manuscripts Commission*, 11th Report, Appendix III, 170.

shirt beneath the furred and silken garments of a nobleman. His poems, and his translations from the French which Caxton published under his patronage, show serious intellectual and literary interests which set him apart from the somewhat raffish and hedonistic society of the Yorkist court, typified by his nephew, the marquis of Dorset. His *gravitas* was sufficiently esteemed by Edward IV for him to have been made governor to the heir to the throne. Traditionally, he has been regarded as something of a political lightweight, a chivalrous humanist dilettante, but the recent discovery of some of his business papers suggests that, on the contrary, he was politically highly aware, constantly in search of the latest information from his agent in London, seeking to use the electoral patronage of his royal charge, the prince of Wales, and carefully entrenching himself as controller of the prince's person and as effective ruler of Wales in Prince Edward's name. Sir Thomas More believed that he was 'an honourable man, as valiant of hand as politic in council', and Mancini says that he 'was always considered a kind, serious and just man, and one tested by every vicissitude of life. Whatever his prosperity, he had injured nobody.'[23]

This was the man who accepted the suggestion of Gloucester and Buckingham that they should meet the young king on the way to London, and help escort him into the capital.[24] Perhaps Rivers was over-confident, buoyed up by news from London that his kinsmen had things firmly under control, and secure in the support of the substantial force of Welsh men-at-arms which had followed him from Ludlow. Perhaps he believed that Duke Richard's previous record gave no firm reason to fear for the safety of the young king. Certainly, he can have had no suspicion as to the violent outcome of his meeting with the dukes, or he would surely have made straight for London without deviating by way of Northampton and Stony Stratford. Against this background of comparative trust and good-will – at least on Rivers's part – the premeditated *volte-face* of 30 April was totally sudden and unexpected.

Up to this point, however, Richard's behaviour had been impeccable. Reassuring letters had been sent by him to the queen and council, expressing his good and honourable intentions, and he had caused the nobility and gentry of Yorkshire to assemble in York to swear a solemn oath of fealty

[23] *Excerpta Historica*, 171–3, 240–5; John Rous, *Historia Regum Angliae*, 213; W. B. Crotch, *The Prologues and Epilogues of William Caxton*, 18–19; E. W. Ives, 'Andrew Dymmock and the papers of Antony, earl Rivers, 1482–3', *BIHR*, xli (1968), 216–28; More, 14; Mancini, 66–9.

[24] Mancini, 74–5. The Croyland Chronicle, 565, mentions no pre-arranged meeting, but says that when the dukes reached Northampton, Rivers and his friends were sent there by the young king to pay his respects, and to submit everything to the will and discretion of his uncle Gloucester.

to Edward V.[25] Richard himself had led the way. Only on 20 April had he begun to move slowly south towards Northampton. He too may have been delayed by the time taken to assemble a suitable following from the ranks of his northern supporters (although he did not have a retinue large enough to overawe the Londoners), and also by the lapse of time necessary for news of the deteriorating situation in London – from his point of view – to reach him in Yorkshire. If Hastings was his informant, then the dangers must have been clearly set forth – the way in which important decisions were being taken without consulting him, the confidently arrogant behaviour of the Woodvilles, and the plans for a very early coronation, which would put an end to his position as Protector and expose him to the savage mercies of the queen's family. No one knew better than he that the precedent for the judicial murder of a royal duke was no more than five years old.

Nor could he count upon the goodwill of the young king. Mancini says that Edward V had charm, dignity and an educational attainment in advance of his years, and this judgement was echoed by Bishop Russell, soon to become Chancellor of England, when he spoke of Edward's 'gentle wit and ripe understanding, far passing the nature of his youth'.[26] But this attractive if precocious youth – a true son of his father – had inevitably absorbed his political attitudes from his mother and her family, and he knew little of an uncle whom he had met only occasionally and ceremonially. For Richard to gamble his political future, and perhaps his life, on the temperamental disposition of this young king, who, if Woodville plans succeeded, could come to exercise full royal power under their control within a matter of a fortnight, was indeed a risk. His decision to take control of the king by force is understandable. Unless we are to assume that the idea was put into his mind fully-formed by the ambitious, volatile and persuasive Buckingham when they met at Northampton (which is not impossible), he had already determined upon some such plan of action during the leisurely spring days of his march south towards London. This does not mean, however, that he already had plans to seize the throne for himself, for which the capture of Edward V was an essential and calculated preliminary. He still had one viable alternative course of action before him.[27]

Less understandable and less reassuring to the nervous politicians of the day were the elements of deceit and dissimulation with which the coup d'état was accomplished. Contemporary as well as Tudor sources stress that Rivers was lulled into a false security by the bonhomie and especially

---

[25] *CC*, 565.
[26] Mancini, 92–3; *Grants*, xlvii.
[27] See below, pp. 75–7.

'cheerful and joyous countenance' with which the dukes of Gloucester and Buckingham greeted Rivers over dinner at Northampton on the evening of 29 April, only to find himself abruptly arrested at dawn on the following morning by their armed retainers. The dukes then moved on to Stony Stratford, where they took control of the young king, dismissed his personal attendants and arrested his half-brother, Richard Grey, his treasurer, Sir Thomas Vaughan, and Sir Richard Haute. To justify all this, Mancini tells us, the dukes put on a mournful countenance, and first told the king that his Woodville advisers had brought about his father's death, ruining his health through involving him in their debaucheries: this is an authentic and very credible touch, marking the beginning of the virulent and puritanical propaganda campaign by which Richard sought to discredit the Woodvilles by attacking their morals.[28] They also alleged that the young king's friends and familiars had conspired Gloucester's death, and that it was common knowledge that they had sought to deprive him of the regency conferred on him by Edward IV. These were claims which Edward V, not surprisingly, found hard to accept. He bravely defended his advisers, pointing out that they had been given him by his father, in whose prudence he had every confidence, and that 'he had seen nothing evil in them and wished to keep them unless otherwise proved to be evil'. He had also, he said, full confidence both in the peers of the realm and in the queen his mother, a remark which called forth an angry retort from Buckingham, 'who loathed her race': men, not women, said the duke, should govern kingdoms, and so, if 'he cherished any confidence in her he had better relinquish it'. The young king's admirable show of spirit was to no avail, for he perceived clearly that 'although the dukes cajoled him by moderation', they were demanding rather than supplicating. He had no choice but to surrender himself to the care of his uncle. Scarcely less ruthless than Richard's arrest of Rivers and his companions was the way in which he now wished to regard them as traitors without trial, a position which the council later refused to accept on the grounds that Gloucester had no formal authority as Protector at this stage. But Rivers and the other prisoners were sent north for safe-keeping, and among the first recorded acts of the Protectorate were the appointments of trusted northern supporters of the duke to seize the estates of Rivers and the marquis of Dorset, as though they had already been forfeited.[29]

The *volte-face* at Northampton and Stony Stratford is a key event in the history of Richard's usurpation, since for the first time the Woodville group was now deprived of the initiative. But it was very far from solving

[28] For the propaganda, see below, pp. 136–8; for the meetings at Northampton and Stony Stratford, Mancini, 74–7; *CC*, 565.

[29] Mancini, 76–9; and for the appointments mentioned below, *Grants*, 3.

Richard's problems. When the news reached London on the night of 30 April–1 May, it produced consternation. The queen, taking her younger son, Richard of York, and her daughters with her, at once withdrew to sanctuary in Westminster Abbey, a clear indication of how little confidence she had in Richard's good faith. The Woodville group contemplated raising an army to recover the king by force, only to find it did not command enough support.[30] The effect of the news on Lord Hastings is more difficult to determine. Polydore Vergil believed that he had not expected such violence, and now regretted having given his support to Richard. This appears rather unlikely, since he seems to have been urging precisely this kind of action on Richard in order to frustrate the Woodvilles, and More tells us that the queen's party was defeated in London because Hastings persuaded the council that Richard's action would prove to be justifiable when legally examined. We also have the weighty authority of the Croyland Chronicle for the idea that two armed parties formed in London: 'some collected their forces at Westminster in the queen's name, others at London under the shadow of the Lord Hastings'.[31] But if Hastings still believed in the sincerity of Duke Richard's intentions, others did not. According to Mancini, Richard took sufficiently seriously rumours that he had 'brought his nephew not under his care, but into his power, so as to gain the crown for himself', that he wrote both to the council and the mayor of London to deny them: he had rescued the king and the realm from perdition, and the deed had been necessary for his own safety and to provide for that of the king and kingdom. His detractors were not convinced. This episode (admittedly described by a rather hostile source and perhaps distorted by hindsight) underlines both Gloucester's sharp awareness of the need to influence public opinion and his very limited success in doing so. The atmosphere remained one of unease, rumour and suspicion.[32]

The failure of the Woodvilles to win firm and united support in the capital led to the collapse of their cause, and the dispersal of their leaders, for they had few illusions as to what would become of them if they fell into the hands of Gloucester and Buckingham. Sir Edward Woodville put to sea with the fleet, and a part of Edward IV's treasure from London. The rest had been divided between the queen herself and the marquis of Dorset, who, after first joining her in sanctuary, later escaped to stir up opposition to the new regime.[33] Yet, if dislike of the Woodvilles had

[30] Mancini, 78–9.
[31] PV, 175; More, 23; *CC*, 566.
[32] See below, pp. 78–9.
[33] Mancini, 78–81, and Armstrong's note, p. 117.

prevented any concerted resistance to the actions of the two dukes, Gloucester and Buckingham, they were far from having things all their own
way.

The events of the next three weeks are somewhat meagrely recorded in
the chronicles – perhaps because no one knew much, or cared to say much,
about the political jockeying which went on behind the scenes, but our
knowledge of the struggle for power is now supplemented by the more
impersonal but more reliable evidence of records (the register of government grants and warrants begins in earnest on 10 May).[34] On 4 May, the
date originally appointed for his coronation, the young king, accompanied
by Gloucester and Buckingham with a retinue of no more than 500 men,
made his formal entry into London. He was met outside the city, in the
meadows of Hornsey, by the mayor and aldermen in scarlet, and some
500 citizens, all clad in violet, in contrast with the sombre black apparel
of Gloucester and his men. Prominently displayed before the eyes of the
Londoners were four cart-loads of weapons and armour bearing Woodville devices, which, Gloucester made it known, were clear proof that his
enemies had intended to slay him as he came from the country. On
entering London, the duke immediately endeavoured once more to
reassure the many who still doubted his good intentions by causing all the
lords spiritual and temporal and the mayor and aldermen of London to
swear fealty to the new king.[35] Furthermore, at a council meeting on 10
May, a new date was fixed for Edward V's coronation, which appears to
have been Tuesday 24 June, later modified to Sunday 22 June.[36]

This same council meeting formally appointed Gloucester as Protector
of England. Since, however, he had only now become Protector, the
council refused to listen to Gloucester's demands that Rivers and his
friends should be condemned as traitors, because the alleged ambushes

[34] *Grants*, 1–45, for the period 5–21 May.

[35] Mancini, 80–3; *CC*, 566; *GC*, 230.

[36] 24 June is the date specifically given by *CC*, 566, accepted by Armstrong
(Mancini, 123–4) and Kendall, 184–5. But that the date finally intended was 22 June
is clear from the general writs of 20 May fixing 18 June as the date on which those
who wished to be knighted at the coronation should present themselves in London,
amplified by the fifty personal summonses sent out on 5 June which refer to the
coronation on 22 June, which repeat that would-be knights should present themselves four days in advance. C. T. Wood, 'Deposition', 255, is therefore clearly mistaken in saying that 'no official document mentions the coronation or its date before
June 5', and his argument that Richard faced a dilemma on this issue cannot be
sustained. Nor can the statement in Simon Stallworth's letter of 9 June (*Stonor
Letters*, II, 159–60) – 'There is great business against the coronation, which shall be
this day fortnight, as we say' – reasonably be interpreted as evidence that he had
only just heard of it (cf. Hanham, 'Historians', 10; Wood, 'Deposition', 255 *n*.). The
phrase 'as we say' in this context clearly implies a previous letter which has not
survived.

9(a). A fifteenth-century window in the Guildhall of London, where Richard's claim to the throne was pronounced.

9(b). Baynard's Castle, the London palace of Cecily Nevill, mother of Richard III. Engraving by Claes Jansz Visscher from his long view of London, *c.* 1625, before its destruction in the Great Fire.

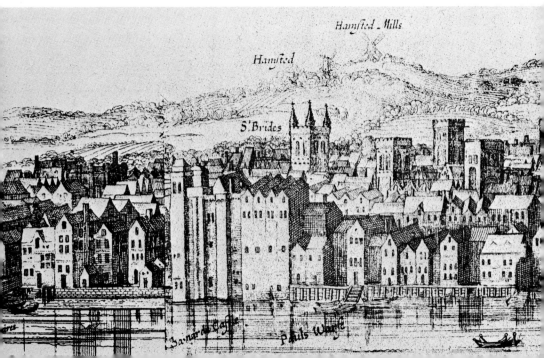

10(a). The Angel Inn, Grantham, Lincolnshire, where Richard III stayed on the eve of the rebellion of 1483.

10(b). Letter from Richard III sent from Lincoln on 12 October 1483 to the Chancellor, Bishop Russell, demanding delivery to him at Grantham of the Great Seal of England, with his own autograph footnote denouncing the treachery of the duke of Buckingham.

prepared for him by Rivers at Stony Stratford were not then directed against the person of a protector. These were clear signs that the council was prepared to back Gloucester only so long as he was seen to be promoting the succession of Edward V, and preserved a proper legality in his actions. Moreover, the all-important question of how long he should retain his position as Protector seems not to have been discussed. The most recent and relevant precedent available to the council in 1483 was the position of Duke Humphrey of Gloucester in 1422. His Protectorate had been formally ended in November 1429 when Henry VI, then nine years old, had been crowned, and authority had passed into the hands of a council ruling in the king's name until Henry was declared of age in November 1437, although provision had been made at the time for the king to terminate the Protectorate before his coronation if he so pleased.[37] This precedent explains why the Woodville group was so anxious to arrange an early coronation. Even as things stood, with the coronation now planned for 22 June, Gloucester's tenure of power, limited as it was in terms of real authority, could last only for a few weeks. In these difficult circumstances, Richard's likely plan of action seems to have been to break with precedent and extend the Protectorate beyond the coronation until the king came of age. This becomes clear to us from the draft sermon prepared by the new chancellor, Bishop Russell of Lincoln, for the opening of the parliament which had been summoned on 13 May to meet on 25 June: the chancellor's sermon was then the equivalent of a modern speech from the throne, and may be regarded as official government policy. Turning, as was usual, to the example of the ancients, Russell cited the admirable precedent of Marcus Emilius Lepidus, who, after the death of Ptolemy, had been given – by the Senate – both the custody of the heir and of his realm. Both had benefited from Marcus's tutelage by the time the heir came of age. So, too, it should be with Richard, said Russell, who referred to his 'martial cunning, felicity and experience'. 'In the meantime,' he continued, 'till ripeness of years and personal rule be, as by God's grace they must once be, concurrent together, the power and authority of my lord protector is so behoveful and of reason to be assented and established by the authority of this high court, that amongst all the causes of the assembling of parliament at this time of year, this is the greatest and most necessary first to be affirmed.' Finally, the young king was made to express his consent, through Russell, to this arrangement.[38] Politically, to put this plan into practice meant obtaining the support of the strong moderate anti-Woodville group in the council, and later the assent of parliament when it met in late June. During the many upheavals of the

[37] *RP*, VI, 326–7.
[38] *Grants*, xlvii–xlix.

previous thirty years, parliament had shown little disposition to do other than approve the actions of the current regime and had reversed the actions of its predecessors with equanimity. To win support within the council proved, however, to be much more of a problem.

Meanwhile, and in the short term, the recognition of Gloucester as Protector put in his hands the powers of appointment and patronage vested in the crown. His take-over of control is marked in the records by a series of writs and warrants issued in the king's name 'by the advice of our dearest uncle, the duke of Gloucester, Protector of this our realm during our young age', although occasionally they were issued by Gloucester himself, rather grandiloquently, as 'brother and uncle of kings, protector and defensor, Great Chamberlain, Constable and Admiral of England'.[39] He proceeded at once to replace the great officers of state. On 10 May Bishop John Russell of Lincoln succeeded Archbishop Rotherham of York as chancellor of England, thereby removing a long-term and much trusted servant of Edward IV, who had already shown an undue sympathy with the queen dowager by releasing the Great Seal of England into her hands.[40] John Russell's vacant place as keeper of the privy seal was taken by John Gunthorpe, dean of Wells and a former dean of the chapel in the household. Both appointments are of interest, for they provide early evidence of Richard's marked preference for men of learning in his patronage of the clergy.[41] The new treasurer of England, appointed to succeed the old earl of Essex, who had died on 4 April 1483, was the under-treasurer, Sir John Wood. Speaker of the Commons in the last parliament of Edward IV (January 1483), Wood very probably already enjoyed Gloucester's confidence.[42] Also at the centre of government Richard seems to have made a serious, although ultimately unsuccessful, effort to win the support of King Edward IV's household men. He was obviously concerned to oust Woodvilles and their sympathizers from key positions. For example, with Edward Woodville's fleet at sea and threatening the south coast of England, control of the castles of Carisbrooke in the Isle of Wight and Pochester in Hampshire, the one held by Rivers's son-in-law, Robert Poyntz, the other by Edward Woodville himself, became vital: the new captains were two local members of Edward IV's former household, William Berkeley and William Ovedale. Of some seventy recorded grants of the

[39] E.g., *ibid.*, 12, 17.

[40] According to More, 22, Rotherham had surrendered the Great Seal to her on the night she entered sanctuary at Westminster, but on second thoughts had recovered it from her. By 7 May it seems to have been in the possession of Thomas Bourchier, archbishop of Canterbury (Mancini, 121: Armstrong's note).

[41] On this point, see further below, pp. 132–4.

[42] Roskell, *The Commons and their Speakers in English Parliament, 1376–1523*, 291–3; Wedgwood, *History of Parliament, Biographies*, 955–6.

period of the Protectorate, only five of the sixty-four recipients had had
definite links with Richard before this date; another four were northerners
whose grants may be presumed to derive from some earlier connection with
Duke Richard. No less than fifteen of these grants went to men who had
been in Edward IV's household, including its controller and his chaplain.[43]
We are ill-informed about the chronology of changes in the royal household, but it seems likely, on balance, that many of Edward's men retained
their former positions. Their replacement by northerners seems to have
come later, after Richard had taken the throne. Their loyalty, in any
event, was to Edward V rather than to Richard himself: many were later
to rebel against him for this reason. Tentatively, however, he held their
support, so long as they thought his intentions honourable: their acceptance of Duke Richard is one good reason for doubting Mancini's hindsight
assertions that there was any kind of general belief – at this stage – that
Richard's mind was set upon the throne.

Politically, even more important than his dispositions at Westminster,
was Richard's need to bind his chief supporters' allegiance to him, and to
establish, through them, an effective control of the provinces. The grants
to Duke Henry of Buckingham are especially revealing, both of Richard's
need of his support and of his own greed and ambition. Long excluded
from power, Duke Henry now received from Richard a most spectacular
delegation of royal authority, entirely without precedent in the entire
annals of the medieval English monarchy – and which was never to be
repeated. Appointed chief justice and chamberlain in both North and
South Wales for life on 10 May, he was at the same time given the supervision and governance of all the king's subjects there, and was made
constable and steward of all the castles and lordships in Wales and the
Marches at the disposal of the crown, some fifty-three in all. The effect was
to make him virtually viceroy in Wales, with a power far exceeding that
considerable authority wielded by William Herbert, 1st earl of Pembroke,
in the early years of Edward IV's reign. Buckingham was also promised
all other senior posts along the Welsh March as they fell vacant, which
clearly increased his already vast powers of patronage. Nor was this all.
He was given supervision of the king's subjects in the English counties of
Shropshire, Hereford, Somerset, Dorset and Wiltshire, with power to raise
armed levies and keep back royal revenues for appropriate uses in those
areas.[44] Perhaps nothing better reveals Richard's sense of his own
insecurity in May 1483 than these remarkable grants to Duke Henry.

Other men's support was secured less dangerously and expensively than

---

[43] Horrox, 'Patronage', 29–30.
[44] *Grants*, 5–7, 8–11; *CPR*, 349; Rawcliffe, *The Staffords, Earls of Stafford and Dukes of Buckingham, 1394–1521*, 31.

was that of Buckingham. Certainly, no one else received benefits on anything like the same scale. John, Lord Howard was made chief steward of the Duchy of Lancaster south of Trent (useful for the patronage it entailed), but otherwise he had to wait for more substantial rewards until Richard became king – the rewards only a king and not a mere protector could give – although he may have been privately promised the dukedom of Norfolk he was soon to receive.[45] Northumberland, the other great satrap, was not ignored: on 10 May (the same day as the grants to Buckingham), he was confirmed in his position as warden of the east march towards Scotland, and ten days later was appointed captain of Berwick-upon-Tweed, with the very substantial and costly garrison of 600 men, for a period of five months.[46] Northumberland's support of Richard, however, may well have been based upon his expectations of greater influence in the north, rather than these specific appointments, which were the least he could have relied upon.[47] There were appointments also for a few special confidants, among them William Catesby and some northerners.[48] Finally, no special favour was shown to William, Lord Hastings. He merely retained the offices he already held, and not until 20 May was he confirmed in the lucrative position of Master of the Mint which he had enjoyed throughout Edward IV's reign.[49]

Contemporary writers seem to have been in little doubt that by the end of May the Protector was planning to usurp the throne for himself. The Croyland Chronicler tells us that in spite of his officially loyal gestures – the oaths of fealty to the young king and the setting of a date for the coronation – 'a circumstance which caused the greatest doubts was the detention of the king's relatives and servants in prison; besides the fact that the Protector did not, with a sufficient degree of consideration, take measures for the preservation of the dignity and safety of the queen'. Mancini is more specific. Relating the reading of Gloucester's letters 'in the council chamber and to the populace', he then reports: 'all praised the duke of Gloucester for his dutifulness towards his nephews and for his intention to punish their enemies. Some, however, who understood his

---

[45] *Grants*, 4–5. Howard was certainly on close terms with Richard by this time. On 15 May, the day after he received the Lancaster stewardship, he presented Richard with a valuable covered cup, weighing no less than 65 ounces of gold (*Household Books of John, Duke of Norfolk and Thomas, Earl of Surrey, 1481–1490,* ed. J. Payne Collier, 399). For a less materialist view of Howard's actions, see Anne Crawford, 'The Career of John Howard, Duke of Norfolk, 1420–1485' (unpublished M. Phil. thesis, University of London, 1975), 191–5, and Kendall, 193–6.

[46] *Grants*, 19–20.
[47] On this point, see further below, pp. 167–9.
[48] E.g., Catesby to be chancellor of the earldom of March, 14 May (*Grants*, 3–4).
[49] *CPR*, 348.

ambition and deceit, always suspected whither his enterprises might lead.'[50] Neither authority can be regarded as wholly impartial, especially here the Croyland Chronicler. If he were Bishop Russell, we have good contemporary evidence that he was somewhat reluctant to accept office from Duke Richard, and that, therefore, he felt himself especially deceived when Richard went on to claim the throne for himself and, in Croyland's view, to murder his nephew.[51] Yet unless the modern historian is to take an unjustifiably benevolent view of Richard's character, he must, of necessity, pay some credence to these primary authorities. If Richard had not decided to take the throne for himself by the end of May, he was soon to do so.

To say this of Richard is not to make him the unnatural and inhuman villain of the Tudor tradition. He had, after all, convincing reasons for seeking a violent solution to his problems. His continued tenure of the Protectorate was of brief duration, to say the least, even if council and parliament approved his plan to extend his authority beyond the coronation. Henry VI, for political reasons, was declared of age on 12 November 1437 when he was still fifteen years of age.[52] Richard II, not a direct precedent in this context, since there was no official minority, had come to exercise direct royal power at least by 1384, when he was seventeen. Edward V was twelve years old in the summer of 1483. If precedent were followed, Gloucester could hope for no more than three years of power before the king came of age and, meanwhile, Edward's consent was needed for Gloucester to rule, although it seems unlikely that he could have asserted his will against his uncle without some powerful political backing. Richard's seizure of Rivers and his friends, his capture of the king's person, and his known desire to get Richard duke of York under his control had aroused suspicions which all his assurances had failed to dispel. Moreover, he must be seen in the context of his own age and, more particularly, of the record of his own family. This last scarcely suggested any turning of the cheek in the face of one's enemy. Richard duke of

---

[50] *CC*, 566; Mancini, 80–3. There is some conflict between the two accounts because *CC* dates the execution of Hastings (correctly) *before* the delivery of the duke of York from sanctuary, Mancini *after* it, and as a consequence.

[51] Russell's unease about taking the chancellorship is mentioned in Simon Stallworth's letter of 21 June 1483 (*Stonor Letters*, II, 161). The fact that he was dismissed from his office on 29 July 1485 suggests that there was no great confidence between the king and his servant. The general point that contemporaries, as well as Tudor historians, regarded Richard as ruthless and calculating is well made by Hanham, *Richard III and his Early Historians*, 126, 191–2.

[52] I owe to Dr R. A. Griffiths the suggestion that he was declared of age during a period of temporary ascendency by Humphrey of Gloucester and his supporters, who hoped to use the king's authority for their own purposes, although he had begun to take a positive part in government at least a year before that.

York, his father, had not hesitated to use violence in pursuit of his political ambitions. His brother, Edward IV, himself a usurper, had not stopped short of fratricide in his judicial murder of Clarence, and had shown himself notably arbitrary in promoting the interests of his immediate relatives in defiance of the laws of inheritance. Given this family tradition, why should Richard have not thought in similar terms? Yorkist attitudes on these matters had been neither gentle nor genteel. For Richard, the practical problems involved in deposing his nephew may have exercised his mind more than any ethical considerations. The deposition of Edward V did not necessarily involve his murder – Edward IV had kept Henry VI alive for ten years after his usurpation of Henry's throne; and, if Richard did not seize power for himself, he could expect little mercy from his enemies. No one familiar with the Woodvilles could have looked forward to gentle forgiveness. Richard had been born into an age of extreme political ruthlessness. He was a man of his times; and the times were sadly out of joint.

The main stumbling-block in Richard's path to the throne at the end of May was the continued and stubborn refusal of the queen-dowager to emerge from sanctuary or to release Richard duke of York into his custody. Although Gloucester still apparently possessed the backing of the council, negotiations with the queen on this issue had already broken down by 9 June.[53] It was clearly unsuitable to stage the coronation of Edward V while his younger brother, and heir apparent, was so blatantly withheld from public view, an argument which must have been convincing to those on the council who still believed in Richard's good intentions. Equally, if by now Richard planned to make himself king, it was essential that he should control the persons of both of Edward IV's sons. Action to remove the young king could not succeed for long if the next legitimate heir were not already in his grasp.

Before the delivery of the duke of York from sanctuary had been achieved, however, Richard had already taken violent action to rid himself of those most likely to oppose any plan to depose Edward V or even to extend the period of the Protectorate until his official coming-of-age. These people included the leading 'loyalists', William, Lord Hastings, Archbishop Rotherham and the supple and wily Bishop John Morton of Ely. They may have enjoyed the support of Thomas, Lord Stanley.[54] Were Hastings and his friends by now involved in a conspiracy with the Woodvilles to overthrow the Protector, as Richard himself alleged? Was

---

[53] Wood, 'Deposition', 263.

[54] For Stanley, see below, p. 86. Lesser persons arrested and imprisoned included Oliver King, a former secretary of Edward IV and later bishop of Exeter and Bath and Wells, and Mistress 'Jane' Shore.

the story of a conspiracy merely invented by Richard to justify his ruthless removal of his political opponents? Had Hastings now fallen out with Richard because of the overweening favour shown to Buckingham, or was he merely opposed to Richard's plan to extend the Protectorate, having apparently already agreed to it? Was the removal of Hastings a pre-emptive bid (like the coup at Stony Stratford) to forestall resistance to Richard's claim to the throne? To none of these questions can one give an entirely firm or ready answer, and recent historians have been deeply divided on the whole issue.[55]

The evidence for any conspiracy between Hastings and the Woodvilles, especially with Mistress Shore – the former mistress of Edward IV and now the mistress of Lord Hastings – as go-between, is slight indeed, and rests entirely on Richard's own allegations. These took two forms. The first was contained in one of two surviving letters (probably part of a series) which he despatched, by the hand of Sir Richard Ratcliffe, to the north on 10 and 11 June, commanding his northern supporters to come to his aid.[56] In the letter to the city of York, a reason was given for the summons, couched in Richard's usual extravagant style of propaganda:

> to aid and assist us against the queen, her blood adherents and affinity, which have intended and daily doeth intend, to murder and utterly destroy us and our cousin, the duke of Buckingham, and the old royal blood of this realm, and . . . by their damnable ways . . . the final destruction and disherison of you and all other inheritors and men of honour, as well of the north parties as other countries, that belongen us. . . .

An extravagant claim indeed, and a fine appeal to regional sentiment, but unsupported by any evidence, except such as 'our trusty servant, this bearer [Ratcliffe] shall more at large show unto you'. Richard's second set of charges for the first time specifically linked Hastings with the queen in treasonable conspiracy. For these we are wholly dependent on the elaborate accounts of the dramatic scene in the council chamber on the morning

[55] The case for a conspiracy was argued at length by Kendall, especially pp. 204–8, but has received some support from Myers, 'Character of Richard III', 127; Wood, 'Deposition', 256–8, 267–8; M. H. Keen, *England in the Later Middle Ages*, 484. It has been vigorously rejected by Hanham, *EHR* (1972), 242, and by Wolffe, *EHR* (1974), 842, who says correctly (providing we exclude Richard's own statements) that 'contemporary evidence for a conspiracy between Hastings and the queen dowager is not extant and it is most unlikely that it will ever be discovered'. Some historians, while implicitly rejecting any conspiracy theory, have taken up More's suggestion that Hastings was sounded out by Catesby as to his attitude to Richard's own claim to the throne, but got no favourable response (e.g., Chrimes, *Lancastrians, Yorkists and Henry VII*, 132; Thomson, *BIHR* (1975), 30).

[56] *YCR*, I, 73–4 (the letter to the city of York); *PL*, VI, 71–2 (letter to Ralph, Lord Nevill).

of 13 June given by Polydore Vergil and Thomas More, when Richard charged the queen and Jane Shore with sorcery, and involved Hastings therein. Both accounts may have a common source in Bishop Morton, who was present then.[57] Polydore, with his usual supple reasonableness, says merely that the sorcery had produced in Richard a deep bodily feebleness, since he had been unable to rest, drink or eat over the past few days. More, by contrast, adds dramatic embellishments, such as appealed to Shakespeare, like his baring of his newly-withered arm, and his sending out for a 'mess of strawberries' from the Bishop of Ely's nearby garden – here perhaps an authentic note of reminiscence from Bishop Morton himself.[58] But both writers make it perfectly clear that they thought Richard's suggestions of a conspiracy to be no more than his own invention. More, for example, reports that the lords in council were astonished by the Protector's suggestions, and especially by the idea of a plot:

> For well they wist, that the queen was too wise to go about any such folly. And also if she would, yet would she of all folk least make Shore's wife of counsel, whom of all women she most hated, as that concubine whom the king her husband had most loved.

The idea that in what he may have regarded as a critical situation, Hastings, full of suspicion about Richard's intentions, may have turned to the Woodvilles for help (such as they could give), is not implausible. The rivalry between Hastings and Dorset is well-attested; there had been a clash between him and the Woodvilles in 1482; but there had been also less well-advertised examples of cooperation, or at least of agreeable co-existence.[59] If, as a member of the inner circle of councillors, his suspicions had been aroused by knowledge of Richard's summons to the northerners, he may well have wondered about its implications. For what reason did the Protector wish to bring these troops to London? It can be argued that they were intended merely to overawe the forthcoming parliament into accepting an extension of Richard's powers as Protector. Yet this was

[57] PV, 179–81; More, 47–9.

[58] Strawberries are possible in England by 13 June, in a good summer, and especially in a walled garden, as Morton's no doubt was.

[59] Hastings appears to have made no objection to the marriage of his wealthy step-daughter, Cecily Bonville, to the queen's son by her first marriage, Thomas Grey, marquis of Dorset, although he was certainly powerful enough to have done so if he wished; and the records of the Mercers' Company do not suggest any antagonism between Hastings and the queen in Edward IV's later years (Ross, *Edward IV*, 336; *Acts of Court of the Mercers' Company*, 118–27).

something to which Hastings had already, apparently, agreed. What had happened to change his mind? It is unlikely that he was sufficiently moved by the favour shown to Buckingham and others to shift his ground, nor had he good reason to do so. He seems to have retained his offices as captain of Calais and chamberlain of the household, and had been confirmed as master of the mint. If not much rewarded, he had not been rebuffed.[60]

All this leaves two alternatives. Either Hastings had become suspicious of Richard's ultimate objectives, and had to be removed because of his known and unshakeable loyalty to the young king, a point on which all contemporary and early Tudor sources insist, or Richard, knowing in advance that Hastings would not support his own claim to the throne, took surprise action to disarm the most dangerous source of opposition. Hastings's strength lay in his position as leader of the moderate loyalist elements in the council, and a council which had only recently refused to endorse Richard's charges of treason against Rivers and his friends was scarcely even now under the Protector's thumb. The latter alternative was strongly suggested by both immediately contemporary sources. The Croyland Chronicler speaks of Hastings's elation at the success of the dukes in their take-over of power: and remarked on the fact that the transfer of power 'had been effected without any slaughter. . . . In the course, however, of a very few days after the utterance of these words, his extreme joy turned into sadness.' The 'deluded' satisfaction of Hastings as expressed by Croyland finds a clear echo in Mancini: 'Thus fell Hastings, killed not by those enemies he had always feared, but by a friend whom he had never doubted.'[61] Either way, it is difficult to avoid the conclusion that Hastings and his friends had to be removed because Richard now planned to usurp the throne for himself. Whether or not they already had well-formed suspicions as to his intentions, they would oppose his scheme to the last.

At all events, Gloucester and Buckingham achieved the same element of complete surprise which they had done at Stony Stratford. Their coup d'état was planned for 13 June, and recent attempts to prove that Hastings's death took place a week later on Friday 20 June, which would, if accepted, have crucial consequences for any interpretation of Richard's

---

[60] The idea that Hastings turned away from Richard because of the rise of Buckingham, and the favour shown to men like Northumberland, Howard and Lovell was suggested by Kendall, 190–6 and Myers, 'Character of Richard III', 127. This, however, at best is a speculation for which there is little direct evidence, and it ignores the specific statements of contemporaries about the reasons for his removal (below, n. 61).

[61] CC, 566; Mancini, 90–1.

usurpation, must now, after extensive controversy, be decisively rejected.[62] We need not suppose that Hastings and his friends were so politically naive as to walk into the lion's den, for even if Hastings were guileless (as the Croyland Chronicler and More rather implausibly suggest), Bishop Morton certainly was not. It was probably to conceal his plans to the very end that Richard arranged for two innocent-seeming meetings of the council for 13 June, one at Westminster under the chancellor, with a brief to discuss arrangements for the coronation, the other at the Tower of London – to which Hastings and his supporters were summoned – perhaps officially to discuss more urgent political problems.[63] Perhaps, on the other hand, this circumstance should have given them warning, but they clearly did not expect that Richard would use violence in the comparatively sacred context of a council meeting. Before the councillors arrived, Richard had previously placed a number of armed men in ambush in a nearby chamber, under the charge of John Howard's son, Thomas Howard, and

---

[62] The debate was begun by Dr Alison Hanham largely on the basis of her discovery in the records of the London Mercers' Company (now in the form of a sixteenth-century copy) of an entry which appeared to show that Hastings was still alive on Friday 20 June. Her critics, especially Dr B. P. Wolffe, have been able to show that the dating of this entry is unreliable, that the revised chronology involved not only a strained interpretation of other evidence, but also the rejection of much circumstantial evidence to the contrary, including the specific statement of the Croyland Chronicle, and required acceptance of an unlikely and large-scale official conspiracy to falsify government records months after the event. As Dr J. A. F. Thomson observed, 'the historian must guard against forcing events into a pattern where their own inherent logic is allowed precedence over important evidence'. For the debate, see Hanham, 'Richard III, Lord Hastings and the Historians', *EHR*, lxxxvii (1972), 235–48; Wolffe, 'When and why did Hastings lose his head?', *EHR*, lxxxix (1974), 835–44; J. A. F. Thomson, 'Richard III and Lord Hastings – a problematical case reviewed', *BIHR*, xlviii (1975), 22–30; Hanham, 'Hastings Redivivus', *EHR*, xc (1975), 821–7, and her *Richard III and his Early Historians* (1975), 24–9; Isolde Wigram, 'The Death of Hastings', *The Ricardian*, no. 50 (1975), 27–9; Wolffe, 'Hastings Reinterred', *EHR*, xci (1976), 813–24; C. H. D. Coleman, 'The Execution of Hastings: a neglected source', *BIHR*, liii (1980), 244–7. The consequences of adopting the revised dating (and the attractions of doing so) emerge clearly from the account of the usurpation in Wood, 'Deposition', especially pp. 264–8, who accepted Hanham's early arguments. If Hastings was still alive on 20 June, *after* the duke of York had come under Richard's control, and after the issue on 17 June of writs of *supersedeas* cancelling the meeting of parliament summoned for 25 June, he would have had far greater reason to suspect Richard's ultimate intentions. This in turn makes the theory of a Hastings–Woodville conspiracy altogether more plausible, and hence a more obvious reason for Richard to take violent action to rid himself of Hastings. Professor Wood has now revised his views in a forthcoming article.

[63] *CC*, 566; PV, 180.

two of his reliable northerners, Charles Pilkington and Robert Harrington.[64]

The result was the dramatic scene, familiar to all readers of Shakespeare, in which Richard accused Hastings of plotting treason in concert with the queen. Without Hastings having been given a chance to reply, armed men rushed into the council chamber, at a signal from the Protector, seized Hastings and cut off his head forthwith on Tower Hill without any semblance of trial. The two prelates were arrested and confined to the Tower; so too was Lord Stanley, who seems to have been slightly wounded in the affray.[65] Hastings's death was universally regretted, for, in spite of his great wealth and power, he had been much respected as an upright, loyal and honourable man, and his liberality had made him popular. A typical comment on his death was that of the *Great Chronicle of London*: 'And thus was this noble man murdered for his troth and fidelity which he bare until his master [Edward V].'[66] The unpopularity of Richard's latest move is shown by the fear, dismay and consternation which it immediately produced in the capital, as the news of Hastings's summary end spread through the city. There was general uproar and commotion. Men began to rush to arms, to be quietened only by speedy action from the mayor, and soothing official reassurances that a plot had been discovered against the person of the king, and Hastings, its originator, had paid the penalty. According to Mancini, many people suspected that 'the plot had been feigned by the duke so as to escape the odium of such a crime'. But the dangers of a rising in London were also held in check by reports that many thousands of Richard's northerners and the duke of Buckingham's men were now approaching the capital.[67]

[64] These names come from the original MS version of Polydore's *English History*, later omitted in the printed text (D. Hay, *Polydore Vergil*, 204–5). The presence of the two northerners is entirely plausible, and Howard's role in the affair receives some support from Edward Hall, *Chronicle*, 361, who identifies Howard as the 'mesne knight' acting as Hasting's escort to the Tower mentioned by More, 51. More probably refrained from naming Howard because he was alive and powerful at the time of his writing.

[65] Rous, *Historia Regum Angliae*, 216; More, 49. His arrest and imprisonment are described by PV, 181–2, who explains his early release to Richard's fear that his son, Lord Strange, might stir up trouble for him in the north-west.

[66] GC, 231; and PV, 179, 'bountifulness and liberality, much beloved of the common people, bearing great sway among all sorts of men and persons of great reputation', and More, 52 ('a good knight and a gentle . . . a loving man and passing well beloved. Very faithful, and trusty enough, trusting too much.')

[67] Mancini, 90–1; *Acts of Court of the Mercers' Company*, ed. Lyell, 155; and (for the troops), Simon Stallworth's letter of 21 June (*Stonor Letters*, II, 161). Estimated at 20,000, the size of the force was grossly exaggerated, but it reflects the fears of the Londoners. CC, 566, also speaks of 'vast numbers' and 'multitudes of people . . . under the special conduct and guidance of Sir Richard Ratcliffe'. These exaggerations echo the fears of London and the south for northern aggression felt in 1461, which emerge so strongly in the political poems of that period.

Hastings's overthrow also had significant consequences at a higher political level. Together with the arrest and imprisonment of Rotherham, Morton and Stanley (although the latter was soon released), it seriously weakened the position of the moderates on the council by depriving them of the leadership of the one great surviving magnate who could oppose Richard with any chance of success. Although, when Richard made his next move, to secure the person of the duke of York, he is said still to have had the council's backing, it was probably now a somewhat chastened body of men. Fear, rather than genuine approval, may well have dictated its consent.[68] The death of Hastings also removed the natural leader of the still influential body of Edward IV's household men, the core of the county establishment of the southern shires, who, as their later rebellion shows, could well have been mobilized in support of Edward V's continued occupation of the throne, although Hastings's own retainers, according to one rather unsubstantiated report, now switched their allegiance to the duke of Buckingham.[69] Finally, the strength of the hostile reaction to Richard's coup, the suspicions which it had aroused, and the continuance of opposition to his authority, can only have hardened Richard's conviction that only the authority of a king could ensure his political survival. If he had not decided before to seek the throne for himself, he surely did so now. The overthrow of Hastings and his supporters was an irreversible step on the road to the throne.[70]

Events now moved swiftly towards the climax which many men had feared. An overawed council accepted Richard's officially plausible argument that the coronation of Edward V could not properly nor decently take place whilst his only brother and next heir, Richard of York, was still withheld in sanctuary: the mere fact of his continued presence in Westminster Abbey pointed a glaring finger of suspicion at the intentions of the Protector's regime, especially with preparations for the coronation now far advanced. The council agreed that a new initiative should be made to procure his release. On Monday 16 June the ageing cardinal of Canterbury was sent to Westminster to persuade the queen to release York into his custody. He appears to have acted in good faith and he promised that the boy should be returned to her care after the coronation. Whether reluctantly or not – for accounts differ – the queen complied with the

---

[68] *CC*, 488: 'The three strongest supporters of the new king being thus removed without judgement or justice, and all the rest of his faithful subjects *fearing the like treatment*, the two dukes did henceforth just as they pleased' (*my italics*).

[69] *Stonor Letters*, II, 161 (Stallworth's letter of 21 June): 'my Lord Chamberlain's men have become my Lord of Buckingham's men'.

[70] For the ingenious, if rather perverse argument that even now Richard had not decided to usurp the throne, but intended merely to seek a continuation of his Protectorate, see Wood, 'Deposition', 263–5.

archbishop's request, but it is worth noticing that she was not prepared to leave sanctuary herself or to release her daughters (who were of no political importance at this stage).[71] As regards Richard of York, she had little choice. Persuasion was backed by force. The sanctuary had been surrounded by numbers of armed men, and it is scarcely possible to doubt that, if the queen had not listened to official reason, Richard would have risked the moral obloquy of forcing the sanctuary. Here again he had violent family precedents to guide him: in 1454 his father, Duke Richard of York, had broken into this same sanctuary to secure the person of the duke of Exeter, and in 1471 his brother, Edward IV, had forced the sanctuary of Tewkesbury Abbey to seize the duke of Somerset and other defeated rebels, whom he then promptly executed.[72]

With the younger prince now safely in his grasp, Richard moved with speed and efficiency towards establishing his own claim to the throne. On the day following York's delivery from the sanctuary at Westminster, and his despatch to join Edward V in the Tower of London, writs of *supersedeas* were issued cancelling the meeting of parliament summoned for 25 June, although, in fact, many of these writs arrived too late to prevent the arrival in London of those elected members who had already left their homes.[73] About the same time, preparations for the crowning of Edward V were abandoned, although no official record of its cancellation has survived.[74] Orders were sent north for the execution of Earl Rivers,

[71] Mancini, 88–9, says that Bourchier suspected no guile, but adds that he agreed to the task in order to prevent a violation of sanctuary, and perhaps by his personal guarantee 'to mitigate the fierce resolve of the duke'. The Croyland Chronicle, 566, says that he was *compelled* by the dukes, surrounded by their troops, to enter the sanctuary ('cogentes Dominum Cardinalem'), and appeal to the good feelings of the queen. PV, 178, makes him only the leader of a deputation which included Buckingham, Howard and 'sundry other grave men'.

[72] For 1454, *Chronicles of London*, ed. Kingsford, 164; for 1471, Ross, *Edward IV*, 172. Both Mancini and Croyland stress the threat of force; see previous note.

[73] Only two of these writs appear to have survived, to York and the borough of New Romney (*YCR*, I, 75; *Historical MSS Comm., 5th Report*, 547), discussed by Wood, 'Deposition', 259–62, and Hanham, 'Historians', 32–3, 38–40 (in the light of Hanham's proposed revision of the date of Hasting's death).

[74] The York entry contains no reference to the coronation; the expense accounts of the New Romney burgesses contain a countermanding of both coronation and parliament (Hanham, 'Historians', 32–3, citing MSS in the Kent County Record Office), which is undated. Despite general assumptions to the contrary, coronation and parliament did not always and necessarily go together. During the reigns of the three Lancastrian kings, parliament had been summoned for the time of the coronations, but Richard II had been crowned in July 1377, and his first parliament did not meet until October; Edward IV had been crowned in June 1461, but his first parliament (postponed) did not meet until November; Richard's own accession to the throne took place in the context of a quasi-parliamentary assembly, but not his coronation (below, p. 83). His first parliament was assembled in January 1484, some six months after his coronation.

Richard Grey, Vaughan and Sir William Haute, a command which only someone who meant to be king could have risked despatching. They were duly beheaded on 25 June 1483 at Pontefract. Most sources say they had no form of trial, but one suggests that some form of tribunal sat upon them before the earl of Northumberland, whom Richard may well have wished to implicate directly in the circumstances of his usurpation.[75] Observers in London thought it no less sinister that within days of Richard of York's being lodged in the Tower, the attendants who had hitherto waited upon the young king were now withdrawn from him, including his physician, Dr John Argentine, an Italianate doctor and astrologer who later became Provost of King's College, Cambridge. Edward V and Richard of York were withdrawn into the inner apartments of the Tower, where they were seen more and more rarely, until at length they ceased to appear altogether.[76] Finally, to eliminate any possible rival within the York family, the Protector caused Clarence's son, the unfortunate Edward earl of Warwick (who was to spend almost all his life in the Tower) to be brought to London, where he was placed in charge of his aunt, Anne duchess of Gloucester.[77]

On Sunday 22 June 1483, an interval of only nine days after the execution of Hastings, and six days since the seizure of York, a Cambridge doctor of theology, Ralph Shaw, was commissioned to preach a public sermon from St Paul's Cross in London, the recognized rostrum for 'official spokesmen' in late-medieval England. Therein he set forth Richard of Gloucester's claim to the throne of England. This claim was again advanced in an eloquent speech to the mayor and aldermen of London by Duke Henry of Buckingham on Tuesday 24 June, and again in his address to an assembly of lords and gentry on the following day.[78]

Precisely on what grounds Richard justified his claim to the throne in June 1483 has been the subject of lengthy debate. According to the circumstantial account given by Dominic Mancini, the most nearly contemporary observer, he initially alleged that Edward IV had been a bastard, and therefore unfit to rule: *a fortiori*, his sons could not be legitimate kings of England.[79]

> Edward, said they, was conceived in adultery and in every way was unlike the late duke of York, whose son he was falsely said to be, but Richard

---

[75] Mancini, 126 (Armstrong's note); *GC*, 567, which makes Ratcliffe responsible; Rous, *Historia Regum Angliae*, 213, for Northumberland's role in this affair.

[76] For Argentine, see the note by Armstrong in Mancini, 127, and the references cited there. As a fellow Italian scholar, he may well have been one of Mancini's direct informants.

[77] Mancini, 88–9.

[78] Mancini, 94–7; *GC*, 231–2.

[79] Mancini, 94–5. The same point is made by *GC*, 232.

duke of Gloucester, who altogether resembled his father, was to come to the throne as his legitimate successor.

If this were true, it represented a ruthless and calculated assault upon the virtue of Richard's own mother, Cecily duchess of York, a lady renowned for her piety. Indeed, Polydore Vergil, picking up the theme later on, remarked that she afterwards complained bitterly 'in sundry places to right many noble men, whereof some yet live' of the great injury which her son Richard had done to her.[80]

Other sources, however, stress the allegation that Edward's *sons* were bastards, and hence unfit to rule. According to the Croyland Chronicler, who seems to be quoting (in hindsight) from the petition to parliament in 1484, the grounds for this accusation were that Edward IV's marriage was invalid in canon law, because when he married Elizabeth Woodville in 1464 he was already pre-contracted to Lady Eleanor Butler.[81] This alleged pre-contract, which has attracted so much attention from Richard's defenders, is said to have come to light through extraordinarily timely and convenient revelations from Bishop Stillington of Bath and Wells, a careerist political prelate whom Commynes described as 'ce mauvais évêque'.[82]

While it is not impossible that both versions of Richard's claim were in circulation in June 1483, each was inherently weak and implausible.[83] Doubts about the paternity of Edward IV had been raised by the earl of Warwick in 1469 and again by Clarence shortly before his downfall in 1478, but no shred of evidence was ever offered to support them. Kings born outside England, like Edward IV – 'The Rose of Rouen' – were

---

[80] PV, 186–7. That the same story has been around earlier is reported by Mancini, 61–2, who says that the duchess of York 'fell into such a frenzy, that she offered to submit to a public inquiry, and asserted that Edward was not the offspring of her husband the duke of York, but was conceived in adultery, and therefore in no wise worthy of the honour of kingship'. If this were true, it is curious that Richard launched his assault on the throne from his mother's London home at Baynard's Castle; that later he wrote to her in friendly and filial terms (B.L. Harl. MS 433 f. 2v); and that it was never mentioned again. The official *Titulus Regis* of 1484 contains no explicit reference to the issue.

[81] *CC*, 567.

[82] Commynes, *Mémoires*, ed. Calmette, II, 64–5.

[83] There is some reason to believe that Stillington's revelations were made known only much later (Mortimer Levine, 'Richard III: Usurper or Lawful King?', *Speculum*, XXXIV (1959), 391–401, esp. 392–3; Wood, 'Deposition', 258–9, 283–4). A very different version of the pre-contract story seems to have been in circulation in 1483 (i.e. that Edward had gone through a form of proxy marriage with a French princess), if Mancini can be believed (pp. 96–7).

vulnerable to such unsubstantiated and chauvinistic charges.[84] Nor will the pre-contract story stand up to serious scrutiny. Apart from the fact that there was little sense in Richard's well-known wish to marry his niece, Elizabeth of York, in 1485, if she were indeed the bastard he had proclaimed her to be, the pre-contract formed only one, and not the most important item, in the petition brought before the parliament of 1484 which ratified his title to the throne. The text of this petition, as entered on the parliament roll, provides us with our fullest knowledge of Richard's claim in its considered and developed form.[85]

This document is a mixture of the specious moralizing and deliberate deceit which characterize Richard's propagandist effusions. It begins with an immoderate attack on Edward IV's government as influenced by the Woodvilles – 'such as had the rule and governance of this land, delighting in adulation and flattery, and led by sensuality and concupiscence, followed the counsel of persons insolent, vicious and of inordinate avarice, despising the counsel of good, virtuous and prudent persons'. Hence the prosperity of the realm had been decreased, felicity turned into misery, and 'the order of policy, and of the Law of God and Man, confounded'. The laws of the church had been broken and justice set aside, with a consequent growth of murders, extortions and oppressions, so that no man was sure of his life, land and livelihood, nor of his wife, daughter or servant, 'every good maiden and woman standing in dread to be ravished and defouled'. There had also been inward discords and battles, and destruction of the noble blood of this land. The petition then turned to impugn the validity of Edward IV's marriage on three counts. First, it had been done without the assent of the lords of this land, and through the practice of sorcery and witchcraft by Elizabeth herself and her mother, Jacquetta duchess of Bedford. Secondly, the marriage took place in 'a private chamber, a profane place', rather than publicly in a church, according to 'the laudable custom of the Church of England'. Thirdly, as a kind of afterthought, the pre-contract story is introduced. Edward and Elizabeth had been living in adultery, and it followed that all their children had been bastards. Finally, the children of George duke of Clarence were debarred from any claim to the throne by reason of their father's attainder in 1478.

All this led to the conclusion that Richard duke of Gloucester was the undoubted son and heir of Richard duke of York (and moreover had been born in this land, a passing reference to Edward IV's supposed bastardy),

---

[84] Armstrong's note in Mancini, 109–10. The fact that Richard himself had been born in England was stressed in his own claim to the throne in 1484 (*RP*, VI, 241).

[85] *RP*, VI, 240–2. For the pre-contract, see below, p. 91.

and he was, therefore, the 'very inheritor of the said Crown and Dignity Royal, and as in right King of England, by way of inheritance'. His claim was further justified because of his personal qualities, his 'great wit, prudence, justice, princely courage, and the memorable and laudable acts in divers battles' which he had performed.

This highly tendentious piece of propaganda failed to carry conviction at the time and has not stood up under modern scrutiny. There was just sufficient plausibility in the charges of sensuality at court, Woodville greed and the difficulty of obtaining impartial justice in Edward IV's time to make it worth attempting to grind some political capital from them, but as a general comment on the government of Richard's brother it amounted to a piece of gross misrepresentation. As to the invalidity of Edward IV's marriage, it was not made invalid because the lords had not assented, nor by the fact that it had been celebrated privately, and no evidence was produced to support the far-fetched charge of sorcery and witchcraft. The pre-contract story is equally unconvincing.[86] Again no evidence was produced to prove it; its sudden appearance, apparently on the unsupported statement of Bishop Stillington, is suspicious in itself, and, if it were true, it is curious that the issue had never been mentioned by any of Edward IV's declared enemies, notably Warwick and Clarence, during his lifetime. If the marriage were invalid, this was a matter for the ecclesiastical courts, not for parliament, which had no jurisdiction over matters of morals. Again, if a pre-contract existed, making the marriage of 1464 invalid, there was nothing to prevent Edward and Elizabeth going through another ceremony of marriage after the death of Eleanor Butler in 1468; the two sons of the marriage, Edward and Richard, were born after that date, in 1470 and 1473 respectively, and the only child of the king and queen who might have been regarded as a bastard was their eldest daughter, Elizabeth, born in 1466. Finally, it had been regarded as a valid marriage for twenty years both by church and state, although many people might have been interested in attacking it.

Nor did the charge that Clarence's heirs were debarred from succession to the throne because of his attainder command much plausibility. His son Edward had been allowed to assume the title of earl of Warwick which descended to him from his mother, and to inherit at least part of her estates; and the sentence of attainder against the duke seems to have extended only to his ducal title and the lands which he held by royal grant. Not only were there precedents for attainted persons assuming the throne, but, at least according to one source, Richard himself recognized Edward

[86] Mortimer Levine, 'Richard III: Usurper or Lawful King?', 391–401, and his *Tudor Dynastic Problems, 1460–1571*, 28–31. For a defence, Kendall, 257–61, 552–6.

of Warwick as heir to the throne, following the death of his own son, Edward prince of Wales, in April 1484.[87]

Richard of Gloucester has recently been castigated by a modern commentator for his failure to produce a more convincing claim to the throne.[88] Yet it is hard to see how he could have done better. His position was quite different from that of Henry IV in 1399, who could convincingly accuse Richard II of acts of tyranny and constitutional irregularity, or of Edward IV, who had a genuine if arguable legitimist claim to rule, as well as a case against Henry VI's failure to be an effective king. Edward V's youth and the shortness of his reign made it impossible for Richard to demonstrate that he was unfit for his royal office. Richard's claim inevitably lacked conviction, since no firm evidence, as distinct from innuendo, could be produced in support of his allegations. Certainly it wholly failed to win acceptance from his subjects either then or later. Mancini described Shaw's sermon as 'contrary to all decency and religion', and tells us that even before it was made the people of London were cursing Richard 'with a fate worthy of his crimes, since no one now doubted at what he was aiming'. The Croyland Chronicler brands Richard's manoeuvres as 'seditious and disgraceful proceedings'. The accounts given by the London Chronicles, which appear to incorporate eye-witness testimony, of the events of 22–25 June are even more specific. Shaw's sermon, according to the *Great Chronicle*, was so ill-received that this formerly popular preacher was afterwards held in little repute, and it attributes his death in the following year to chagrin and remorse. Buckingham's speech in the Guildhall was eloquent and well-delivered, made 'without any impediment of spitting or other countenance', but that too met with little favour: only a small number of the Londoners present said 'yea, yea', and these 'more for fear than for love'.[89] Mancini also says that the assembly of lords which on 25 June decided to accept Richard as king did so largely out of fear. Having been told not to enter London with large retinues, because of the citizens' dislike of large numbers of armed men within the walls – yet another example of Richard's plausibility and skill in tactical manoeuvre – they now found themselves overawed by the two dukes, 'whose power, supported by a multitude of troops, would be hazardous and difficult to

[87] Rous, *Historia Regum Angliae*, 217–18; Hanham, *op. cit.*, 123. Henry VI was still under sentence of attainder (1461) when he resumed the throne in 1470; Edward IV had been attainted in 1470 before he resumed the throne in 1471.

[88] Wood, *op. cit.*, 264 ff.: 'Wretchedly conceived ... hasty, sloppy, and poorly explained'. This section of Professor Wood's article contains a valuable discussion of the constitutional issues involved. See also W. H. Dunham Jr and Charles T. Wood, 'The Right to Rule in England, Depositions and the Kingdom's Authority, 1327–1485', *American Historical Review*, lxxxi (1976), 738–61.

[89] Mancini, 94–5; *CC*, 567; *GC*, 232; Fabyan, 669.

resist'; with the fate of Hastings fresh in their minds, and probably also for lack of an effective leader, they decided that docility was preferable to valour.[90] The outbreak, only four months later, of a strongly supported rebellion in southern England, which was initially intended to secure the release of Edward IV's sons from the Tower, is further evidence that a great many Englishmen could not easily reconcile themselves to Richard's illegal deposition of his nephew.[91]

But Richard was now too far committed to be deterred by the lukewarm or openly hostile reception accorded to his claims. The task of stage-managing his assumption of the throne was left to Henry duke of Buckingham. It would appear – there is some confusion about the dating of these events – that on Wednesday 25 June there was an assembly of lords and notables who had come to London for the coronation and the meeting of parliament under Buckingham's chairmanship. It was not, of course, a true parliament, since apart from the writs of cancellation which had been issued on 17 June, it had been summoned in the name of a king who was now declared not to be a king, but this did not prevent Richard from claiming, three days later, that he had been ordained king 'by the concord assent of the Lords and Commons of this Royaume'.[92] This gathering drew up a petition requesting Richard to assume the throne. On the following day, 26 June, the assembly came together once more, and with the mayor and aldermen and other leading London citizens, waited upon the Protector in his mother's London town-house at Baynard's Castle, and there Buckingham presented the petition. After a token hesitation, Richard agreed to their requests, and, forthwith, 'attended by well near all the lords spiritual and temporal of this realm', he rode to Westminster Hall, and there took his seat upon the marble chair – the King's Bench – in indication of his formal assumption of the throne.[93] The date of his coronation was fixed for Sunday 6 July.

The usurpation of Richard III was made possible in the first instance by the deep divisions which existed among those who had held power at the

---

[90] Mancini, 94–7.

[91] Below, pp. 112–13.

[92] Writ to the captain of Calais, 28 June 1483; B.L. Harl. MS 433, f. 238, quoted in full by Wood, 'Deposition', 269–70. Kendall's suggestion (pp. 231–2) that this was a truly parliamentary gathering ('a joint session of Lords and Commons') must be resisted: he was probably misled by Mancini, 96–7, who thought it a genuine parliament. The Parliament Roll of 1484 specifically states that 'neither the said three estates, neither the said persons ... were assembled in form of parliament' (RP, VI, 240).

[93] Writ to Calais of 28 June, as above. B.L. Harl. 433, f. 238; CC, 566. For the dating, see Gairdner, 93–4; Kendall, 222–3; Jacob, Fifteenth Century, 620; Armstrong's note to Mancini, 131.

court of Edward IV, and especially by the rift which separated the grasping and unpopular Woodville group and those who, like Hastings, were otherwise loyal to the succession of Edward's legitimate heir. The chances of preserving an unchallenged succession were further weakened by the estrangement of many of the rank-and-file nobility from the dangerous game of high politics, which was partly a consequence of the Wars of the Roses and partly of Edward IV's own policies. There is a most striking contrast between the unanimity and coherence with which the nobility acted in 1422 to confirm the position of Henry V's infant heir and to defeat Humphrey of Gloucester's claim to real power, and the confusion and uncertainty which attended every stage of aristocratic reaction to the political manoeuvres of Edward V's reign. Nor can we discount Richard's own forceful character. Richard, unlike Humphrey of Gloucester, took recourse to violence to establish his position. On the two occasions when it mattered – the seizure of Edward V on 30 April and the arrest of Hastings on 13 June – he achieved surprise and advantage by ruthless means, and, even if the throne were not his original objective, these moves seem to have been the product of calculation rather than impulse or fear. Behind him, too, loomed the ominous threat of hordes of armed men from the north, of whom southerners had an illogical and extravagant fear – a significant element in the development of the idea that Richard was a tyrant, since all surviving chronicle sources are of southern origin.[94] In the event, these troops did not arrive in London until after Richard had assumed the throne (they were mustered in Finsbury Fields on 1 July), but their continued presence outside London helped to ensure that no last-minute opposition to the new king would have much chance of success. Scarcely less important was the backing which Richard enjoyed from a small group of very powerful men who supported him for a variety of reasons – self-interest, personal friendship, dislike of the Woodvilles, resentment against the policies of Edward IV or the hope of personal gain.

The arbitrary methods by which Richard achieved the throne, combined with the patent weakness of his claim and the growing suspicion, in the months immediately following his accession, that he had murdered his nephews, undoubtedly cost Richard the sympathy and affection of many of his subjects in the south of England. But his unpopularity with ordinary folk, or even gentry, in these regions did not matter a great deal so long as he could retain the support of the great magnates and by a skilful use of patronage win over the rest of the uncommitted baronage to his cause.[95] The difficulties which confronted him in balancing the rival claims and jealousies of his supporters were already apparent in the

[94] Pollard, 'Tyranny', 150, 162.
[95] See below, pp. 158 ff.

deliberately elaborate and expensive ceremonies of his coronation on 6 July. When he had assumed the throne on 26 June, John, Lord Howard had stood at the right hand of the marble chair in Westminster Hall. Now newly created duke of Norfolk and earl marshal of England, he had been specifically appointed steward of England for the coronation ceremonies.[96] But Buckingham sharply indicated his pre-eminence by enforcing his claim to be master of ceremonies at the crowning, and it was he who had 'the chief rule and devising' and bore the white wand of high steward at Westminster. His duchess, born Katherine Woodville, was the most conspicuous absentee from the celebrations.

[96] *CPR*, 358–60; 'Observations on the Wardrobe Account for the year 1483', *Archaeologia*, I (1770), 374. A contemporary narrative of the coronation ceremonies is in *Excerpta Historica*, 379–84.

Chapter 5

# THE FATE OF EDWARD IV's SONS

Indeed, no fact stands forth more unchallengeable than that the over-whelming majority of the nation was convinced that Richard had used his power as Protector to usurp the crown and that the princes had dis-appeared in the Tower. It will take many ingenious books to raise this issue to the dignity of a historical controversy.

So thought a great English statesman, who was also a realist politician and no mean historian.[1] Were it not for the continued appearance of 'ingenious books' (and articles) concerning the fate of the princes in the Tower,[2] it would not be necessary to commit pen to paper. Quantities of ink and passion have already been expended, over several centuries, upon this, the most celebrated of English murder mysteries, so beloved of the English-speaking peoples. Yet it is perhaps worth venturing cautiously into this minefield if only to suggest two points: first, that the problem has generally been approached in false terms, and secondly, that much more important than any mere detective-story solution to the mystery is the apparent belief of Richard's own contemporaries that he was guilty of his nephews' deaths. In any evaluation of his reign, it is the implications of this fact which are of consequence, whether he was innocent or guilty in fact.

Defenders of Richard III have been very anxious to believe that he could not have been convicted of murder in a modern court of law, although modern professional historians have displayed no such unlikely

---

[1] Winston S. Churchill, *A History of the English-Speaking Peoples*, I (1956), 383–4.

[2] Elizabeth Jenkins, *The Princes in the Tower* (1978), a sober account, summing up against Richard III; Audrey Williamson, *The Mystery of the Princes* (1978), a fanatical and often purblind defence of Richard III; Jack Lezlau, 'Did the Sons of Edward IV outlive Henry VII?', *The Ricardian*, iv (1978), 2–14 (based upon sup-posed 'hidden messages' in the paintings of Holbein the Younger), and other articles in *The Ricardian* (under similar titles), v (1979), 55–60, 24–7; Nigel Balchin, 'Richard III', *British History Illustrated*, i (no. 4, Oct. 1974). These are only some recent examples. For fresh air, see the healthy scepticism of Charles T. Wood, 'Who Killed the Little Princes in the Tower?', *Harvard Magazine* (January-February 1978), 35–40.

scruples.[3] It is inherently improbable that, almost five hundred years after the event, evidence for an alleged murder, conducted in secrecy, could convince a modern court, even allowing for the fallibilities of such tribunals in twentieth-century English murder trials. Nor can anything too positive be derived from a discussion of the physical evidence. This takes the form of two sets of human bones. The one still in existence, found in 1674, was declared to be the bones of Edward V and his brother, and was thus ceremonially re-interred in Westminster Abbey on the orders of King Charles II (who had a certain interest in this matter of deposition). The second set, it is alleged, was discovered in 1647 in a walled-up room in the Tower, where two young victims, apparently boys, had been left to die. The evidence, as distinct from the plausibility that this is how the princes met their deaths, is, however, desperately thin. It involves accepting a statement by a certain Mr Johnson about a report by a John or Jonathan Webb concerning some bones found in the Tower some thirty years before, while, it was said, Sir Walter Raleigh and Lord Grey of Wilton were prisoners there, which provides a date of between 1603 and 1614. At the time of their discovery, the bones were 'supposed by the company then present' to be those of the princes, even though they appeared to be appropriate to children aged six and eight, whereas the princes (in 1483) were aged eleven and thirteen. The bones were never medically examined, even by the uncertain standards of seventeenth-century doctors, and have never been seen since.[4] So the now non-existent bones of 1647 may safely be disregarded, on decent grounds of lack of evidence as distinct from speculation.

The remains now at Westminster are much more plausible. The tomb at Westminster was opened in 1933, and an examination was conducted by Dr Tanner, an archivist, and Professor Wright, an anatomist. Their

[3] To quote only a selection of recent professional opinions deciding against Richard III: V. H. H. Green, *The Later Plantagenets* (1955), 361; E. F. Jacob, *The Fifteenth Century* (1961), 623–5; G. A. Holmes, *The Later Middle Ages, 1272–1485* (1962), 225; A. R. Myers, 'Character of Richard III', 123–5, and his article on Richard III in *Encyclopaedia Britannica* (1964 edn); S. B. Chrimes, in *History*, xlviii (1963), 23, and in *Lancastrians, Yorkists and Henry VII* (1964); B. Wilkinson, *Constitutional History of England in the Fifteenth Century* (1964), 165; J. R. Lander, *The Wars of the Roses* (1965), 246–7, and in *Government and Community: England 1450–1509* (1980), 318–19; M. M. Keen, *England in the Late Middle Ages* (1973), 485.

[4] The walled-up room theory was accepted as plausible by S. B. Chrimes (*History*, xlviii, 1963), partly because it fits with the suggestion made by the contemporary French chronicler, Molinet, as to the manner in which the princes met their death. There is, however, no evidence that the fifteenth century practised this particular form of cruelty. The report of the discovery is contained in an appendix to Tanner and Wright's article: see following note. On the whole question of the bones, see **Appendix I.**

findings led to the conclusion that the bones were indeed likely to have been those of the princes. Access to the remains has since been denied, and the partial disagreements of modern medical experts as to the validity of this conclusion can only rest upon the report published by Tanner and Wright.[5] Nevertheless, the medical evidence, especially as concerns the teeth (the best means of dating the age of a skeleton) seems, on balance, to confirm the findings of Tanner and Wright.[6] Moreover, even if the medical evidence can be impeached, there remains a problem for Richard's defenders. If the bones now in the Abbey are not those of the princes, then whose were they? Even in the violent history of the Tower of London, the secret burial of the remains of two young persons, of approximately contiguous age, was scarcely a regular occurrence, and certainly not a recorded occurrence, for we know the fate of almost all those for whom imprisonment in the Tower eventually brought death. Probability points strongly towards the bones found in 1674 being those of Edward IV's sons. Speculations that they were not (as, for instance, in a recent notion that the bones were those of Roman children buried on the site before the Tower was built) seem unrewarding.

The historian must rely upon a convergence of probabilities in such matters, especially upon what can be learned about the fate of other imprisoned royal personages in the previous two centuries of political strife. In this harsh climate, to keep alive a politically dangerous person, and especially a deposed king, was an act of folly. Now, all that we know about the deaths of such persons whose position compares with that of the princes in 1483 suggests very strongly that they met their ends on the orders of the reigning king or the government of the day. It has been shown beyond all serious doubt that Edward II was nastily put to death in Berkeley Castle on the instructions of his supplanters, Queen Isabella and her paramour, Roger Mortimer. Richard II does not seem to have hesitated in arranging the murder of his disliked uncle, Thomas duke of Gloucester, when he decided to rid himself of those surviving appellants who had humiliated him and his friends in 1386–8. Some lingering doubts may remain about the manner of death of Richard II himself in Pontefract Castle in 1400, since it is possible that he died of neglect or melancholy rather than direct assassination, but it is highly unlikely, in any case, that he would have been allowed to remain alive for long once the supposition that he was still alive made him a focus for rebellion. His successor, Henry IV, was not by nature (except in moments of anger) a ruthless man, but to have kept Richard II alive in such circumstances was

[5] L. E. Tanner and W. Wright, 'Recent Investigations regarding the Fate of the Princes in the Tower', *Archaeologia*, lxxxiv (1934), 1–26.

[6] See Appendix I.

a dangerous luxury. Equally, there is a strong suspicion that Henry VI's politically inconvenient uncle, Duke Humphrey of Gloucester, was murdered at Bury St Edmunds in 1447 on the orders of the ruling Suffolk clique. Edward IV found it convenient to keep the now decayed Henry VI in the Tower as long as his son and heir, Edward, the Lancastrian prince of Wales, was alive and free in France. The official chronicle says that Henry VI died 'of pure displeasure and melancholy' on the very night of Edward IV's return from his mighty triumph at Tewkesbury, where Prince Edward had been killed: the coincidence of these events scarcely commands much credence on the official theory. Ultimate responsibility must rest with Edward IV for the judicial murder of his own brother, George duke of Clarence, for he regarded the duke as politically irresponsible and potentially dangerous.[7] These two latter examples (Henry VI and Clarence) were, of course, part of Richard of Gloucester's own personal experience. Why, then, should it be supposed that Richard, as king, would depart from this established pattern of *raison d'état*, especially given that his position was more insecure than that of his predecessors, and the legality of his claim seems to have been generally disbelieved?

In the light of these historical precedents, it can be argued that Richard III had both a very strong motive and obvious opportunities for finally disposing of his nephews once he became king. The idea that they were dead within some weeks of his accession to the throne seems to have been widely believed by his contemporaries. Fifteenth-century England was not a police state, in which people might disappear from view for years on end and still remain alive. It was quite possible that the boys were murdered in circumstances which no one, even at the time, was able to discover. Yet it is extremely unlikely that, so long as the princes remained alive, people with the right connections would have been unable to discover that fact. Guards, servants, even officials of the Tower were corruptible. Moreover, while the boys were alive, the fact seems to have been known. They were seen shooting and playing in the gardens of the Tower, presumably some time in July 1483, and were even again observed after they had been withdrawn into its inner apartments.[8] It was their subsequent disappearance which convinced men that they were dead.

[7] (Edward II): T. F. Tout, 'The Captivity and Death of Edward of Carnarvon', *Collected Papers*, III (1920), 145–90; M. McKisack, *The Fourteenth Century*, 94; (Thomas duke of Gloucester): A. Steel, *Richard II*, 238–9, and the articles there cited; (Richard II): Steel, *op. cit.*, 238–9; J. L. Kirby, *Henry IV of England*, 94–5; (Humphrey duke of Gloucester): B. Wilkinson, *Constitutional History of England in the Fifteenth Century*, 24–8 (as with 1483, foreign writers, who could speak more freely, are unanimous in saying the duke had been murdered); (Henry VI and Clarence): Gairdner, *Richard III*, 16–19; Kendall, 451–2; Ross, *Edward IV*, 175–6, 241–5.

[8] *GC*, 234; Mancini, 92–3.

These general presumptions can be supported by what we can learn from contemporary evidence, without any reliance upon Tudor sources. They may be briefly summarized, since its context has already been discussed in the Introduction.[9] The Croyland Chronicler, the best-informed source, states that a general belief in the fact of the princes' deaths was a factor in the rebellion of 1483, and, elsewhere, if obliquely, he makes clear his own belief that Richard was guilty. Mancini leaves little doubt that, in general opinion, the princes were dead before he left London in July 1483, or as to who was responsible, although he admits he does not know how they died. The various London Chronicles, in so far as they may be regarded as contemporary, are specific in their charges against Richard III and, moreover, imply a date for the princes' deaths some time in 1483.[10] Continental authors were unanimous in their belief in Richard's guilt. Certainly, we cannot disregard the statement made to the States-General of France at Tours in January 1484 by the Chancellor of France, Guillaume de Rochefort. This has been described as 'an amazing outburst for an official allocution', and very unlikely to have been made by de Rochefort, otherwise 'a learned and rather staid personality', unless he possessed special intelligence. He specifically accuses Richard III as guilty of his nephews' deaths.[11] All this lends support to the notion, generally held not only at home but abroad, that the princes died some time before the end of 1483, and that Richard was responsible.

Reasonable inferences from the behaviour of those closely concerned add a further element of support to this argument. We may begin with the queen-mother, Elizabeth Woodville. She was clearly implicated in the plan of autumn 1483 to place Henry Tudor on the throne, on condition that he married her eldest daughter, Elizabeth of York. It totally passes belief that she would have been willing to support a plan which would automatically disinherit her sons by Edward IV unless she had excellent reasons to believe them already dead (and she was well able to find out). It has been objected, by Richard's defenders, that on 1 March 1484 she proved willing to emerge from her year-long stay in sanctuary at Westminster and deliver not only herself but her daughters into the hands of the man supposed to have done her sons to death only a few months earlier. This argument ignores both the practical realities of her situation and the nature of Richard's public promises to her regarding her own and her daughter's welfare. By the spring of 1484 the rebellion of Yorkist

[9] Above, pp. xli–xlvi.

[10] Even in the *Great Chronicle*, the marginal notes, 'Innocents', and 'Death of the Innocents', were written in the hand of the chronicler who wrote the portion ending in 1496 (*GC*, 234, 236, and intro. xxii).

[11] Mancini (Armstrong's introduction), 22–3.

loyalists had been crushed without much difficulty, Henry Tudor's invasion had proved abortive and there was little prospect that Henry Tudor, or anyone else, could effectively challenge Richard's position on the throne. Nor was she even secure in sanctuary at Westminster, for rights of sanctuary had been broken before when political necessity demanded, and Richard had already shown a good deal of patience in allowing her to remain there for so long.[12] Even so, she left sanctuary only in return for the most solemn and public promise Richard could contrive. Placing his hands on the relics of the Holy Evangelists, and pledging the word of a king, he took an oath, in the presence of the lords spiritual and temporal of England and of the mayor and aldermen of London, that he would fully protect her and her daughters and make suitable provision for their marriages.[13] The entire document reeks of the queen-dowager's suspicion, while spelling out her pragmatic acceptance of the likelihood that in the foreseeable future there would be no king of England other than Richard III. Such arrangements were not without parallel. In just such a mood, and in the hope of securing her son's future, another ex-queen, Margaret of Anjou, had made a deal in 1470 with Warwick the Kingmaker, who had done so much to bring about her husband's deposition and the deaths of many of her friends and kinsmen. Her permitting her son's marriage to Warwick's daughter was an act of cynical realism which surprised even a hardened contemporary like Philippe de Commynes.[14]

Similar deductions may be made from the behaviour of Henry Stafford, duke of Buckingham, in the autumn of 1483. To secure general support for his scheme to replace Richard III by Henry Tudor, it was necessary for people to believe that the princes were already dead, which the rebels in the south appear to have done readily enough. Even if we regard Buckingham and his allies as unprincipled, and quite capable of pretending that the princes were dead to suit their own ends, can we also regard them as wholly foolish? Who, among the many Yorkist loyalists supporting the rebellion, would have accepted Henry Tudor as king had the princes been produced alive and unharmed – something which Richard signally failed to do? The rebels of 1483 included a number of men with

---

[12] The house of York had set precedents in this respect. Henry duke of Exeter had been forcibly taken fom sanctuary at Westminster in 1454 by Richard's own father, Richard, duke of York, and the defeated Lancastrians were similarly removed from Tewkesbury Abbey in 1471 by his brother, Edward IV. For the issue in general, see I. D. Thornley, 'The destruction of sanctuary', in *Tudor Studies presented to A. F. Pollard*, ed. R. W. Seton-Watson (1924).

[13] Harl. 433, f. 308, printed by Gairdner, 165–6.

[14] Commynes, *Mémoires*, ed. J. Calmette and G. Durville, I, 198.

close connections with the court and its personnel.[15] It is hard to believe that they would have been duped into supporting Henry Tudor's claim to the throne unless they had established to their own satisfaction that the rightful king, Edward V, was already dead. A body of practical and experienced men, with much to lose by backing a rebellion, would have been unlikely to act on mere rumour. Not all of them were likely to have been mistaken.

Finally, Richard's own behaviour appears to suggest his guilt in the deaths of his nephews, and it is worth returning to this point. The rebellion of 1483 began as a movement to restore Edward V to his rightful throne. For Richard to have produced Edward V and his brother as alive and well at this stage would have been no advantage to him. Once the rebellion turned into a rising which assumed that the princes were dead, Richard's failure to prove that they were alive seems very striking. He was, in fact, in a cleft stick. The princes alive were dangerous. The princes dead were a source of opprobrium and the belief that they were dead fuelled the fire of any other claimant to the throne. Even the stoutest of Richard's modern defenders admitted, after setting out the evidence on his behalf, that 'the most powerful indictment of Richard is the plain and massive fact that the princes disappeared from view after he assumed the throne and were never again reported to have been seen alive. This fact . . . weighs heavily against the indications of his innocence.'[16]

For this reason, it has become a matter of urgency for Richard's defenders to find an alternative executioner. This is an almost impossible task, since, as A. R. Myers observed, 'for alternative explanations no evidence (as distinct from speculation) has ever been offered'.[17] Three candidates have been suggested. The case against John Howard, duke of Norfolk was never much more than a *jeu d'esprit*, rests upon a variety of misunderstandings and has recently been effectively dismissed in print.[18] The arguments that Duke Henry of Buckingham (the late P. M. Kendall's front-runner) was guilty of the princes' murder are superficially more plausible, yet they involve extraordinary convolutions and are ultimately unconvincing. A very recent discovery of new evidence suggests that the princes were put to death in 1483 on the advice or instigation of Duke

[15] See below, Chapter 6.

[16] Kendall, 410.

[17] A. R. Myers, in *Encyclopaedia Britannica* (1964).

[18] The case against Howard was put forward in a variety of public lectures (although not in print) by S. T. Bindoff, and by Melvin J. Tucker, *The Life of Thomas Howard, 1443–1524*. For the dismissal, see Anne Crawford, 'John Howard, Duke of Norfolk; A Possible Murderer of the Princes?', *The Ricardian*, v (1980), 230–4.

Henry, and indeed this may well have been true.[19] But this scarcely exonerates King Richard, and, in any event, the notion that any subject of the king, however powerful and eminent, would take the initiative and the responsibility in murdering a deposed king deserves to be treated with full scepticism. Just as it is inherently unlikely that Richard himself could have put Henry VI to death in 1471 without the knowledge or consent and probably the express orders of King Edward IV, so it is quite improbable that Buckingham, who was then so close to Richard (and if he were the murderer, then the deed must have been done in the summer of 1483), would have ventured to act independently on such a vital issue. No one supposes that Richard disposed of his nephews by his own hand, but it is equally little short of fantasy to suppose that anyone else did so except on his direct command. The risks were far too great. The murder of that turbulent priest, Thomas Becket, by four knights 'of low intelligence' in the hope of gaining favour with the king appears to be the only example in English medieval history of a political murder, except during rebellions, not sanctioned by the reigning king.[20]

For Sir Clements Markham and his followers, Henry VII himself was the hottest candidate for the position of child-murderer. This notion never had anything to commend it, is unsupported by any shred of direct evidence, runs counter to the medical evidence and has nowadays been abandoned by all but the most unregenerate of Richard's admirers. It has been very plausibly argued (by S. B. Chrimes) that Henry was himself ignorant of the precise circumstances of the princes' deaths, and rested content with a general charge, set forth in the act of attainder of 1485, about the shedding of the blood of innocents, directed against Richard without further specification. Only many years later when (as Chrimes put it) 'he reached a point in his fortunes at which the laying of as many Yorkist ghosts as possible had become a matter of urgency', did he produce, via the arrest of Sir James Tyrell, a suitable but not very convincing confession which laid the blame on Richard III, and, as A. R. Myers has observed, it is inherently unlikely that he could not have produced a clearer and firmer story of the princes' murder by Richard III if he had also been efficient enough to suppress every report of their being still alive in 1485 and their *subsequent* murder.[21]

In the final analysis, Richard III remains the most likely candidate by far to have murdered his own nephews. It is scarcely possible to doubt

[19] To be developed by Professor Richard Green in a forthcoming article in *English Historical Review*.

[20] W. L. Warren, *Henry II* (1973), 508–10.

[21] S. B. Chrimes, *Lancastrians, Yorkists and Henry VII*, 136–7, 161–2; Myers, 'Character of Richard III', 124–5.

that they met their deaths by violence during the summer of 1483. He had by far the strongest motive, as well as the most obvious opportunity. Nothing of what we know of his character in general, and the conditions of his upbringing in particular, makes his having committed such an act at all unlikely.

What matters more, in the context of Richard's own political survival, are the consequences of what many of his subjects believed to have been a peculiarly atrocious crime, even by the rather tarnished standards of the fifteenth century. The dynamics of Richard's violent usurpation, and the evident dubiety of his title to the throne, may have dictated that the princes should be rid out of this world, and knowledge of this fact could not be confined within the walls of the Tower. As we shall see, the general acceptance in the southern and western counties of England of the idea that the king had disposed of his innocent nephews played a large part in promoting support for the rebellion of 1483, although, even for the rebels, it may have represented no more than the crowning act in a series of judicial murders and acts of political ruthlessness which offended contemporary opinion. The London Chronicles, reflecting early-Tudor popular opinion, make particular play with the resentment felt against the supposed murder of the princes, and their deposition also. On the other hand, the rest of the country seems to have been untroubled by such sentiments. The loyalty of Richard's northerners was in no way shaken. Nor did any belief that Richard had disposed of his nephews prevent his securing the support of many members of the nobility of his realm. Even in the shires which supported the rebellion of 1483, the final alienation of gentry sympathy probably owed more to his policies following the revolt, especially his increased and perhaps excessive dependence upon his northerners. It was his mistakes upon the battlefield of Bosworth, rather than any supposed guilt in the death of his nephews, which ultimately was to cost Richard his throne.

Chapter 6

# THE REBELLION OF 1483 AND ITS CONSEQUENCES

The series of associated risings which broke out in the southern and western counties of England in the autumn of 1483 proved to be a key event in Richard's political fortunes. Yet the label commonly applied to them – 'the Duke of Buckingham's rebellion' – is singularly misleading. For the risings were planned before Buckingham's adherence became known. Very few of the rebels had any known connection with the duke, and, in the event, his failure to raise an effective force in Wales and the Marches did nothing to assist and much to discourage a potentially powerful rebellion in England.

Who, then, rebelled against Richard in 1483, and why? The names of the rebels, as known to us through successive government proclamations and the subsequent act of attainder, show clearly that it was essentially a rising of the substantial gentry of the counties from Kent to Cornwall, south of a line from the Thames to the Severn. P. M. Kendall advanced the unlikely claim that 'It was the Woodvilles . . . who dominated the movement, provided most of its strength, and directed its energies'. Even less plausible is his suggestion that a significant element in the revolt were 'old Lancastrians, like the Courtenays . . . eagerly sniffing the air of unrest'.[1] On the contrary, although Woodville influences and connections were not unimportant, an analysis of the movement reveals a very different picture. The strongest link among the rebels lay in the fact that most were loyal former servants of Edward IV, and amongst these some of the most influential had had close connections with his household.

There were three main centres of rebellion. First, there was the south-east which drew support from Kent, a traditionally rebellious county, but also from Surrey and Sussex. Here the leaders were essentially Edward IV's former household servants, although some, not surprisingly, also had connections with the households of the queen and the princess.[2] Sir George

---

[1] *Richard III*, 260–1.

[2] Except where otherwise stated, the biographical details which follow are derived from Wedgwood, *Hist. Parl., Biog.*, supplemented by material from the Calendars of Patent Rolls. For the south-east, see also A. E. Conway, 'The Maidstone Sector of Buckingham's Rebellion, October 18, 1483', *Archaelogia Cantiana*, xxxvii (1925), 106–14.

Brown of Betchworth in Surrey is a good example. Although his father, Sir Thomas, had been put to death by the earl of Warwick in 1460 for his share in the defence of the Tower of London, he soon entered the Yorkist service, probably under the influence of his new stepfather, Sir Thomas Vaughan, who became Edward's treasurer of the chamber and was later one of the victims of Gloucester's coup d'état. Thereafter Brown's career shows that mixture of service in the royal household and in the shires which was characteristic of the gentry servants of Edward IV. Sheriff of Kent in 1480-1 and a regular commissioner in the county, M.P. for Guildford in 1472 and for Surrey in 1478, he was also a knight of the body much in Edward's confidence, and carried the banner of St George at the king's funeral.[3] The wealthy Sir John Fogge, of Ashford in Kent, had been one of Edward's longest-serving followers who had joined the Yorkists when they first landed in England in 1460. He became treasurer of the king's household (1461-8) and was a royal councillor throughout the reign. Like Brown, he was one of the work-horses of the regime in Kent and represented the shire in parliament in 1478. Through his first wife, Alice Haute (who had died as long ago as 1462), he had Woodville connections and had been associated with the queen-dowager's father and mother in the attacks upon Sir Thomas Cook in 1468. But the dominant fact in his career was his service to Edward, and this long-term connection is probably the main reason for his joining the rebellion. He also had close associations with the young Edward prince of Wales as one of his councillors since 1473, and he had been active in the administration of the prince's lands, especially in the Duchy of Cornwall.[4] Another man who had connections with both king and queen was Nicholas Gaynesford, of Carshalton in Surrey, who had been the first Yorkist sheriff of that county, and had served in the king's chamber before transferring into the queen's household in 1475. He was obviously on terms of personal friendship with both Edward and Elizabeth, who stayed at his house on hunting trips soon after their marriage, and he kept a special stock of wine there for their refreshment on such occasions.[5] Sir Thomas Bourchier of Barnes, a younger son of Lord Berners, had been one of Edward's knights of the body and constable of Windsor Castle. Thomas Fiennes of Herstmonceux in Sussex was the second son of Richard Fiennes, Lord Dacre of the South, Queen Elizabeth Woodville's chamberlain; but Thomas likewise

[3] Gairdner, *L & P*, I, 5. In 1479 the Paston family sought his good offices as one of those 'which wayre most upon the Kyng, and lye nyghtly in hys chamber': *PL*, VI, 29.

[4] *CPR, 1467-77*, 283; and for his influence in Cornwall, see K. N. Houghton, 'Theory and Practice in Borough Elections during the Later Fifteenth Century', *BIHR*, xxxix (1966), 137-8.

[5] Scofield, I, 286-7.

11(a). Autographed letter of Francis, Viscount Lovell, written from Lincoln on 11 October 1483 to Sir William Stonor commanding his support against the rebels. Stonor had in fact already joined the rebellion.

11(b). Part of the Act of Attainder against the rebels of 1483, from the Parliament Roll of 1484. This portion relates to the attainder of John Morton, bishop of Ely. (The original sewing of the Parliament Roll is seen at the top.)

12(a). Anthony Woodville, Earl Rivers, with Caxton beside him, kneels before Edward IV, his sister Queen Elizabeth and Edward prince of Wales to present the printed copy by Caxton of the *Dictes des Philosophes* in 1477. The standing figure, centre background, may be Richard duke of Gloucester. (Lambeth Palace Library MS 265.)

12(b). Bishop Russell's tomb in his chantry in Lincoln Cathedral.

had been an esquire of the body to King Edward and was sheriff of Surrey and Sussex in 1480-1.[6]

Among the few rebels in this area whose connections were essentially with the Woodvilles was Sir William Haute, a ringleader in the Kentish rising, for whose seizure Richard offered a reward of 300 marks or £10 *per annum* of land in December 1483. Through his mother he was a first cousin of Queen Elizabeth Woodville; his brother, Sir Richard Haute, had been a councillor of the prince of Wales and was one of those seized at Stony Stratford and executed along with Earl Rivers; and his nephew, Richard Haute, esquire (son of Sir Richard), who also rebelled in 1483, had been associated with the household of the younger of the two princes, Richard duke of York. He had been prominent in the jousting at the Woodville-dominated wedding celebrations of Richard of York and Anne Mowbray in 1478, and was afterwards appointed constable of Swansea and steward of the Gower lordship acquired by Duke Richard in right of his wife.[7] But Sir William Haute had also been a prominent servant of King Edward in Kent, and was serving his third term as sheriff when the reign came to a close. Although the duke of Buckingham had estates at Tonbridge in Kent, only one of the local rebels had any discoverable connection with him. This was John Pympe, esquire, of Nettlestead in Kent, who had been a ward of Humphrey Stafford, 1st duke of Buckingham, and afterwards of his duchess; but through his mother, Philippa St Leger, he had links with Sir Thomas St Leger and the marquis of Dorset, and through his wife, Elizabeth Cheyne, with the prominent Wiltshire rebel, Sir John Cheyne.

Apart from the five yeomen of the crown (whose presence underlines the household element in the rebellion) afterwards attainted for their treason, such men were the natural leaders of society in the south-east, an area where magnate or baronial influences were significantly less strong than in most parts of England. As such they could expect to command a considerable personal and popular following. They also belonged to a society tightly connected by intermarriage, and for the most part they were able to call upon the support of their kinsmen when they chose to rebel. Nicholas Gaynesford was joined by his son, John, of Allington in Kent, and Richard Guildford, esquire, rose with his father, Sir John. Richard himself had married Anne Pympe, sister of the rebel John Pympe, and Richard's father married John's mother, Philippa St Leger. Another rebel, John Darell of Calehill, was Richard Guildford's first cousin, and another, Edward Poynings, Henry VII's future deputy in Ireland, was Sir George Brown's stepson. Occasionally families were divided in their

[6] *CPR, 1467–77*, 588; *CPR, 1476–85*, 180, 261; *CFR, 1471–85*, 207.
[7] *CPR, 1476–85*, 288; Scofield, II, 205; *Glamorgan County History*, III, 263.

allegiance: for example, James Haute, brother of Sir William and uncle of the rebel William Haute, remained loyal and, in reward for his good services against the rebels, obtained a grant in March 1484 of William's forfeited lordship of Ightam Mote in Kent and other lands. For the most part, however, they clung together, and rose in rebellion.

The second centre of rebellion lay in south-central England, where assemblies were planned at Salisbury in Wiltshire and Newbury in Berkshire. Its support came not only from these shires, but also from Hampshire, Dorset and Somerset, and from one or two men whose estates lay outside the area, such as Sir Richard Woodville, younger brother of Anthony, and later himself third Earl Rivers. Here too the pattern was much the same, save that several leading rebels had been connected in the past with Duke George of Clarence, like Sir Roger Tocotes of Bromham in Wiltshire, who had been steward of the duke's lands in Hampshire and had rebelled with him in 1470. John Harcourt, of Stanton Harcourt in Oxfordshire, was formerly Clarence's receiver in the south-west, Sir William Norris of Yattendon had been his steward of Caversham, and the Somerset knight, Sir John St Loo, had been one of his fee'd retainers.[8] Most of them, however, had also been in the service of King Edward. Sir William Norris, for example, had become a knight of the body by 1474. Others again were essentially king's men. Thus Sir William Berkeley, of Beverstone in Gloucestershire, had been an esquire of the body, constable of Southampton and Winchester, and along with other household men had played a prominent role in the recent royal funeral celebrations. Sir John Cheyne, of Falston Cheyne in Wiltshire, one of the ringleaders hereabouts, was yet another prominent servant of King Edward, a former esquire of the body and master of the king's horse from 1479–83, who had been, along with Lord Howard, one of the hostages left behind in France in 1475 as guarantee for the speedy evacuation of the English invasion army. Sir Giles Daubeney, of Barrington and South Petherton in Somerset, a former esquire and knight of the body, had served Edward as sheriff in Somerset, Dorset and Devon and had recently been appointed by him constable of Bridgwater. Sir William Stonor, of Stonor in Oxfordshire, who had been M.P. for that shire in 1478, was another former knight of the body, but seems also to have had links with the queen (who in 1481 made a present of a doe to 'our trusty and well-beloved William'), and also with the marquis of Dorset.[9]

Here again family ties probably played a part in spreading support for the rebellion. John Harcourt, for instance, was a brother-in-law of Sir William Norris and also of John Norris of Bray who rebelled in Devon;

[8] I am indebted to Dr M. A. Hicks for this information on Clarence's servants.
[9] *Stonor Letters*, II, 70, 122–4.

Sir Richard Beauchamp (styled Lord St Amand) was a stepson of Sir Roger Tocotes; and the rebellion of Sir John Cheyne brought in his brothers (or younger sons) Humphrey and Robert. As in the south-east, Lancastrian sympathies and connections are noticeably absent. Sir Walter Hungerford, of Heytesbury in Wiltshire and Farleigh Hungerford in Somerset, may have had little cause to like the House of York, for his father, Robert, Lord Hungerford, had been executed by the victorious Yorkists after the battle of Hexham in 1464, and his elder brother, Thomas, had been beheaded at Salisbury in 1469 on charges of treason. Yet Sir Walter himself carefully stayed aloof from the upheavals of 1469–71 and had prospered in the service of Edward IV: he had been lieutenant of Dover, sheriff of Wiltshire in 1478–9 and M.P. for the county in 1478, and in 1483 he was one of the esquires of the body who had carried the dead king's corpse to Westminster Abbey.[10] It would therefore be rash to suggest that his disloyalty in 1483 sprang from latent Lancastrian sympathies. Resentment at his treatment by Edward IV may have influenced the behaviour of another former Lancastrian, Sir Nicholas Latimer, who had fought for Henry VI at Wakefield, Towton and in the north in 1462. He had experienced great difficulty in recovering his inheritance, and this led him to join the duke of Clarence in rebellion in 1469–70. Thereafter, he seems to have prospered in Clarence's service, whom he followed in France in 1475, and he was sufficiently re-established in county society to sit in parliament as knight of the shire for Dorset in 1472–5.[11] Finally, it is possible that some of the rebels in this region were in the service of the young bishop of Salisbury, Lionel Woodville, the dowager-queen's brother, whose motives for rebellion need no further comment.

In the south-west, where the rebels were to gather at Exeter on 18 October, leadership of the rising lay with two men who had close ties with each other, and equally strong motives for disaffection. One of these was Thomas Grey, marquis of Dorset, the other Sir Thomas St Leger. The latter was first and foremost a servant of King Edward throughout his reign: he had been controller of the royal mint from 1461 onwards, and esquire and then a knight of the body, and master of the king's harthounds from 1478 to 1483. But after his marriage (about 1472) to Edward's sister, Anne duchess of Exeter, he had tied his fortunes to the Woodville group, and especially to Dorset, whose son was now contracted in marriage to St Leger's daughter by Duchess Anne, so that together they might inherit the Exeter estates, which lay chiefly in the west country.[12] He had everything

[10] Gairdner, *L & P*, I, 5.
[11] Lander, 'Attainder and Forfeiture, 1453 to 1509', *Historical Journal*, iv (1961), 139–40.
[12] Above, p. 36; Ross, *Edward IV*, 336–7.

to lose if Richard remained on the throne. With them rose Sir Robert Willoughby of Broke in Wiltshire, who had been steadily employed in local administration in the west country since 1470 and had served as sheriff of Cornwall in 1478–9 and of Devon in 1480–1: his father, Sir John, had been an equally reliable royal servant in Somerset and Wilt-shire. Sir Thomas Arundel, of Lanherne in Cornwall, resembled him in belonging to a family which had served the crown in the south-west, but had no discoverable household connections, as did another Cornishman, Richard Nanfan, who had been sheriff there in 1479–80.

Of the many adult male members of the Courtenay family in south-western England, only three chose to rebel in 1483.[13] One of these, Sir Edward Courtenay of Boconnoc, had obvious motives for disaffection. His father, Sir Hugh, had been executed after Tewkesbury, and he was also direct heir to the former Lancastrian earldom of Devon, which he was to recover immediately after Henry VII's accession to the throne. By contrast, the younger branch of the family, the fecund Courtenays of Powderham, were divided in their loyalties, but most remained loyal to Richard III. Of the seven sons of Sir Philip (d. 1463), the eldest, Sir William, was rewarded for his loyalty with an annuity of £20, while his younger brother, Philip (a former servant of Clarence), was given one of £40, and the youngest brother, John, one of 40 marks. Two of the brothers made a different choice. The successful clerk, Peter Courtenay, although he had supported the Readeption of Henry VI in 1470–1, had served Edward IV as his secretary and councillor and in various secular capacities, and was rewarded by promotion to the bishopric of Exeter in 1478. His motive for revolt remains a matter of mere conjecture, as does that of Sir Philip's fourth son, Walter, a rather obscure figure who had received no public employment since 1472.[14] The remaining thirteen named rebels in the south-west were lesser figures, who are difficult to identify.[15]

It is clear, therefore, that if we exclude the marquis of Dorset and his Woodville kinsmen Sir Richard and Bishop Lionel of Salisbury, and one

[13] For what follows, see J. A. F. Thomson, 'The Courtenay Family in the Yorkist Period', *BIHR*, xlv (1972), 233–46.

[14] *Ibid.*, 240–2; R. J. Knecht, 'The Episcopate and the Wars of the Roses', *Univ. of Birmingham Historical Journal*, vi (1958), 122. He was present at Baynard's Castle on 27 June, had walked beside Queen Anne at the coronation and had been appointed to a commission as late as 28 August 1483.

[15] They include John Trevelyan, son of a former prominent household servant of Henry VI; Thomas Pyne of Exeter, gentleman, who had been Edward IV's last escheator in Devon and was re-appointed by Richard III (*CFR, 1471–85*, 698, 734, 768); and one yeoman of the crown.

or two others, like St Leger, who had close links with them,[16] this was essentially a rebellion of former servants of Edward IV, many of them of long standing and some prominence, and of whom a significant number had been employed in his court and household. Why did these men reject the new king? It would be rash to deny the force of self-interest as a motive for rebellion in that harshly competitive and acquisitive age. The household element in particular had just lost their natural leader through the death of William, Lord Hastings and may (although it is unlikely) have turned instead to the newly all-powerful Buckingham for protection, but this would hardly explain their raising a rebellion which was already well under way before Buckingham's defection from King Richard became known.[17] They may have feared for the loss of their positions at court now that they were dependent on the goodwill of a king whose own following was largely different in personnel from his brother's. These positions they might have expected to retain if Edward V had remained king, or to recover if he were restored. But there are several reasons why this hypothesis lacks conviction. First, we know little of the chronology of the changeover in household positions, save for the most senior offices, and therefore we cannot tell whether many of these men had been ousted from court in the few weeks between the end of the Protectorate and the first indications of gathering rebellion.[18] Secondly, those of Edward's household men who chose to remain loyal seem to have had no difficulty in keeping their places in the new king's service, and these include some of Edward's longest-serving and most trusted officials, such as Sir Thomas Burgh, Sir Thomas Montgomery and Sir John Scott, all three of whom continued to be king's councillors as they had been under Richard's

[16] A small group of men was separately attained for plotting treason with Buckingham at Brecon Castle. Apart from John Morton, bishop of Ely, they include Sir William Knyvett of Buckenham in Norfolk, a kinsman of Buckingham's, for whom see Wedgwood, op. cit., a London merchant, and a necromancer (RP, VI, 245).

[17] For the chronology of the rebellion, see below, pp. 115-17. The suggestion that Hastings's former household associates turned to Buckingham rests on a highly ambiguous statement by Simon Stallworth in a letter of 21 June 1483 to Sir William Stonor (Excerpta Historica, 17; Stonor Letters, II, 161): 'All the lord Chamberleyne mene be come my lordys of Bokyngham mene.' This may, however, have been meant to apply to Hastings's large indentured retinue (for whom see W. H. Dunham, Lord Hastings' Indentured Retainers, passim). If so, Stallworth was sadly misled. For of Hastings's former retainers, only John Harcourt of Stanton Harcourt joined the rebellion of 1483.

[18] Above, pp. 76-7. A contemporary account of Richard's coronation names 'Sir Thomas Percy', an error for Robert, as the new controller, and Sir William Hampton, an error for Hopton, as the new treasurer (Excerpta Historica, 382; cf. Myers, Household of Edward IV, 288-9). Sir John Cheyne is usually said to have lost his office as master of the horse to Sir James Tyrell. For a similar policy of dispensing with household men, but without victimization, after Henry IV's usurpation, see A. L. Brown, 'The Reign of Henry IV', in Fifteenth-Century England, 22-3.

brother. Thirdly, Richard seems to have gone out of his way to try to win over the goodwill and support of some of those who later rebelled. Although, according to Sir Thomas More, he was personally on bad terms with Sir John Fogge, perhaps because of Fogge's connections with the Woodvilles and with Edward V, he had him brought from the sanctuary where he had fled for fear, and ostentatiously shook him by the hand as a gesture of pardon and reconciliation.[19] Sir Thomas Lewkenor, of Trotton in Sussex, had been created a Knight of the Bath at Richard's coronation, as had Sir William Berkeley and Sir Thomas Arundell. Berkeley was made governor of the Isle of Wight on 9 May and confirmed on 27 July 1483. Sir William Knyvett had been made constable of Castle Rising on 18 July.[20] Richard would naturally have been unwilling to lose the services of such influential and experienced men in the running of the shires, and it is therefore even more unlikely that he would have risked alienating them by depriving them of their local offices or of such fees and annuities as they had enjoyed of Edward's gift.[21] A change in the winds of patronage is scarcely a convincing reason for the defection of so large a number of substantial gentry.

It is much more likely that the rebellion was a direct result of the outrage and resentment felt by Edward's loyal servants of Richard's treatment of his heirs. This is precisely what is suggested by the Croyland Chronicler, the only informed contemporary account of the rising. He tells us that the people of a number of counties – all accurately named – began to form meetings and confederacies to secure the release of the princes from the Tower, and further to take King Edward's daughters from sanctuary and send them overseas

> in order that, if any fatal mishap should befall [the princes] the kingdom might still in consequence of the safety of the daughters some day fall again into the hands of the rightful heirs.[22]

[19] More, 81.

[20] *Excerpta Historica*, 384; Berkeley's temporary appointment to the Isle of Wight is among the earliest recorded acts of the Protectorate, 9 May 1483 (*Grants*, 1–2); formal appointment, *CPR, 1476–85*, 461; for Knyvett, *ibid.*, 362.

[21] Very few of the grants made by Richard as Protector or as king up to the end of August 1483 were made at the expense of those who later became rebel leaders. They were mainly of offices which came to Richard through the death of Hastings or on the lands of Edward prince of Wales: e.g., Hastings was replaced as receiver-general of the Duchy of Cornwall by John Sapcote, an esquire of the body to Edward IV and brother-in-law of John, Lord Dinham, the new steward of the Duchy (*Grants*, 16; *CPR, 1476–85*, 430).

[22] *CC*, 567–8; *CPR, 1476–85*, 465–6 (for the commissions of oyer and terminer). A period of at least some weeks must be allowed for the elaborate intrigues leading up to the rebellion in its final form on 18 October, since this involved not only Reginald Bray's recruitment of the rebels to accept Buckingham's scheme, but also communications across the Channel between Margaret Beaufort and the queen-dowager in England and Henry Tudor in Brittany.

Their determination to 'avenge their grievances' was in no way checked when rumours spread that the princes had died a violent death. This intelligence merely made them receptive to the later scheme proposed by Buckingham and Queen Elizabeth Woodville that Richard should be replaced by Henry Tudor, earl of Richmond, on condition that he married Elizabeth of York, now King Edward's rightful heir. Much the same is reported by one of the more reliable of the London Chronicles:[23]

> In this year many knights and gentlemen, of Kent and other places, gathered them together to have gone toward the duke of Buckingham . . . which intended to have subdued King Richard; for anon as the said King Richard had put to death the lord chamberlain and other gentlemen, as before is said, he also put to death the two children of King Edward, for which cause he lost the hearts of the people. And thereupon many gentlemen intended his destruction.

The continued hatred and mistrust which these men felt for Richard is shown in their reluctance to accept pardons from him; even those who did so could not be depended upon, and like Sir Walter Hungerford and Sir Thomas Bourchier, turned against him on the eve of Bosworth.[24]

What converted this original movement of Yorkist loyalists into a plan to place Henry Tudor on the throne was the proffered leadership of Duke Henry of Buckingham to achieve that end and the appeal to Yorkist sentiment contained in Henry's promise to marry Elizabeth of York. This scheme arose from intrigues between Buckingham himself, the queen-dowager, Henry Tudor in Brittany, and Henry's mother, Margaret Beaufort, countess of Richmond: the master-mind behind the entire plan may well have been the wily John Morton, bishop of Ely.[25] The duke's motives for turning against his master were a mystery both to his own contemporaries and to early Tudor writers who knew the people involved.

---

[23] Vitellius A XVI, in Kingsford, *Chronicles of London*, 191: this is the only London Chronicle which correctly places the rebellion in 1483 rather than 1484.

[24] PV, 219–20. A number of others were bound over in large sums to be 'of good and true bearing' towards the king, and had to accept other conditions: e.g., Thomas Lewkenor had to abide with Sir John Wood, treasurer of England, until the king's pleasure was known, whilst Nicholas and John Gaynesford were prohibited from entering the county of Kent without royal licence (*CCR, 1476–85*, 365, 366, 369; see also below, pp. 180–1).

[25] The accounts of these conspiracies given by Polydore and More differ widely. The most recent modern survey of the evidence, largely following Polydore's version, is by S. B. Chrimes, *Henry VII*, 20–6.

They are always likely to remain so. For this reason any detailed discussion of the often contradictory reasons advanced for his rebellion is largely inconclusive. Polydore Vergil claimed that Buckingham quarrelled with Richard over the king's refusal to grant him the second moiety of the Bohun earldom of Hereford, but this notion was rejected by Sir Thomas More as politically implausible.[26] In any event, Buckingham's demand had not been refused, for on 13 July 1483 Richard solemnly promised that, so soon as parliament met, he would forthwith procure an act to reverse the arrangement made in parliament by Henry V, which had vested that king's share of the Bohun inheritance in the House of Lancaster as a private heritage.[27] Meanwhile, the duke was to be allowed to take all the revenues from the king's portion as from the previous Easter. This pledge was made in letters issued under the king's signet.[28] What more could Richard have done? Gairdner's view that in some way he defaulted on his promise because these signet letters were never reissued under the Great Seal and therefore not enrolled on the Patent Roll means nothing in the context of Richard's administrative practice, for he used his signet extensively instead of the Great Seal but with the same force and effect, and there are hundreds of acts under the signet in Harleian MS 433 which certainly took effect but never passed the Great Seal.[29]

Perhaps Buckingham really hoped to win the throne for himself, using Henry Tudor as a pawn in the game. Polydore Vergil dismissed as unreliable the common rumour that he had encouraged Richard to usurp the throne 'by means of so many mischievous deeds' in the hope that the subsequent wave of reaction against a ruler 'being hated both of God and man' would sweep the duke himself into power.[30] Buckingham seems to have been both a grasping and ambitious man. He had a claim of his own to the royal title. Through his mother, Margaret, daughter of Edmund Beaufort, duke of Somerset (d. 1455), Buckingham's claim was inferior to that of Henry Tudor, who was descended from Edmund's elder brother, John duke of Somerset (d. 1444), although both had a common ancestor in John of Gaunt, duke of Lancaster. If, however, any doubts remained about the ability of any descendant of John of Gaunt's bastard children

[26] PV, 192–4; More, 90.

[27] For the history of the Bohun inheritance, Somerville, *Hist. Duchy of Lancaster*, I, 177–81; for Henry V's act, *RP*, IV, 46 ff., 135 ff.

[28] Harl. 433, f. 107v; printed, from the Stafford archives, in Dugdale, *Baronage of England*, II, 168–9.

[29] Cf. Gairdner, 105–6.

[30] PV, 195. For the most recent discussion of the view that Buckingham's ultimate ambition was the throne itself, see C. Rawcliffe, *The Staffords, Earls of Stafford and Dukes of Buckingham*, 29 ff.

to inherit the throne,[31] Buckingham could also advance a respectable claim through Thomas of Woodstock (d. 1397), youngest son of Edward III, whose only child, Anne, had married his great-grandfather, Edmund earl of Stafford (d. 1403). In February 1474 he had procured an heraldic decree allowing him to wear the arms of Thomas of Woodstock undifferenced, 'a coate neire to the king and of his royall bloude', a development which may partly explain the evident coolness of his relations with Edward IV.[32]

Yet if he were moved by such vaulting ambition, why then did he abandon it in favour of supporting Henry Tudor's candidature? Richard had already given the duke as much as any subject could hope for, and he could scarcely have expected more from Henry Tudor, who was still a largely unknown and unpredictable personality. It is quite possible that he was moved primarily by fear for himself, as he observed the mounting movement of resentment against Richard's seizure of power. This wave of feeling became intensified as men came to believe that Richard had procured the princes' deaths, although we cannot wholly discount the notion that, once determined upon rebellion, Buckingham himself had helped to spread the rumour. If Richard's position seemed already insecure, the duke was likely, as his principal supporter, to be an immediate casualty of his overthrow. These fears may well have been exploited, as Sir Thomas More believed, by Bishop Morton, who persuaded the duke that his safest bet was to back a Henry Tudor married to Elizabeth of York, a combination which could usefully unite Lancastrian die-hards and Yorkist dissidents.[33]

The scene was thus set for a concerted movement by Richard's enemies. Perhaps with the deliberate intention of making it difficult for Richard to know where to strike first, the rebels in the south-east were to seize London; those of the counties further west were to join Henry Tudor when he landed on the south coast with such force as he could muster abroad; and Buckingham was to raise a force in Wales and cross the Severn into England at the same time as the gentry risings broke out in England. The scheme failed for a variety of reasons.

Good fortune was not on the side of the rebels. The Kentish rising went off prematurely, some ten days too soon; and it so happened that John

---

[31] For a discussion of this point, see *Excerpta Historica*, 152–4; Gairdner, 107–8. It is very doubtful whether Henry IV's insertion into a later exemplification of an act of parliament of Richard II legitimizing the Beauforts of a clause prohibiting them from inheriting the royal dignity was of sufficient authority to set aside the original act, which contained no such limitation.

[32] See Genealogical Tables. For the decree, Morgan, 'The King's Affinity', 18 and *n*.

[33] More, 91.

Howard, duke of Norfolk, was then touring his newly-acquired Mowbray estates in Surrey and Sussex, and learnt that 'the Kentishmen be up in the Weald'.[34] This early information enabled him to seize the Thames crossings at Gravesend to prevent any move across the river, to send for his fee'd men to protect London, and to notify his master at Lincoln of what was afoot. According to the Croyland Chronicler, Richard's spy service, which already had Buckingham under observation, itself provided the king with intelligence of the rising even before he received Howard's warning. Nevertheless, the bitter tone of Richard's letter to Chancellor Russell on 12 October suggests that the news of Buckingham's defection came as both a surprise and a shock: the king, it said, was deeply hurt by 'the malice of him that had best cause to be true . . . the most untrue creature living'.[35] Norfolk's prompt action in the London area, however, enabled the king to concentrate his forces against the threat from the duke in Wales, and as early as 11 October he and his lords were sending out directions to their supporters as far afield as York and Lancashire, where George Stanley assembled a sizeable force, with orders to muster at Leicester on 20 or 21 October.[36]

Even more disastrous for the rebel cause was Buckingham's failure in Wales. The Staffords were disliked as harsh and grinding landlords, and such troops as the duke could raise seem to have been reluctant and disaffected recruits.[37] The duke's rebellion gave opportunity for the expression of active hostility by some of his Welsh retainers. Sir Thomas Vaughan of Tretower and his brothers dealt a fatal blow to Buckingham's local prestige by capturing and plundering the duke's own castle at Brecon.[38] At the same time Sir Humphrey Stafford of Grafton in Worcestershire (no kinsman of the duke's) blocked the immediate exits across the upper Severn from Wales, destroying the bridges. Finally, the eternally uncertain English weather took a hand. On or about 15 October a storm of unusual violence broke over western England, causing the rivers, including the Severn, to flood, and preventing Buckingham and his men from cross-

---

[34] *PL*, VI, 73 (Howard's letter to John Paston, 10 October, summoning him and 'six tall fellows in harness' to join him in London); *Household Books of John, duke of Norfolk, and Thomas, earl of Surrey, 1481–90*, 453–79, for Howard's tour in Surrey and Sussex, and his sending men to Gravesend on 11 October.

[35] *CC*, 568; Ellis, *Original Letters*, 2nd ser., I, 159–60.

[36] *Stonor Letters*, II, 162–3; *Plumpton Correspondence*, 44–5; *YCR*, 84.

[37] PV, 199; T. B. Pugh, *The Marcher Lordships of South Wales, 1415–1536*, 240–1, where it is pointed out that none of the men later attainted for rebellion were Welshmen. Richard afterwards granted annuities to 25 Welshmen for their good services against the rebels (Harl. 433, f., 30, printed by Gairdner, 341–2).

[38] *CC*, 568; Rawcliffe, *op. cit.*, 33–4; Pugh, *op. cit.*, 241. Vaughan's hostility may have been the result of a feud with the Tudors, for Sir Thomas's father, Roger, had been executed by Jasper Tudor at Pembroke in 1471.

ing. Alone and unattended, the duke made his way to Shropshire and took refuge with one of his servants, Ralph Banaster, who lived at Wem.[39] Whether from fear or greed, Banaster soon betrayed him and he was delivered to the king at Salisbury.[40] Denied any hearing by Richard, he was executed the following day (2 November).

The news of Buckingham's capture, combined with that of the king's advance at the head of an army, took the heart out of the English rebels, who had already been waiting for days on end for news either of Buckingham's advance or the landing of Henry Tudor. (At least in English experience, delay has always proved fatal to the morale of a rebel army.) As Richard moved rapidly south to the Dorset coast at Bridport, and then on west to Exeter, where he arrived about 8 November, most of the rebel leaders took flight for France. Of the leaders in the south-west only Sir Thomas St Leger fell into the king's hands; he was executed in Exeter on 13 November. Meanwhile, Henry Tudor's little fleet from Brittany was scattered by the severe autumn gales, and only one or two ships eventually anchored off the English coast, either near Poole in Dorset or at Plymouth. By this time, it would appear, the king was already in the area and the coast was guarded: Henry prudently withdrew to France.[41] Only in the south-east was there any armed resistance. There Bodiam Castle held out for a while until reduced by Thomas Howard, earl of Surrey, Lord Cobham and others. Even here few paid for their treason with their lives. Sir George Brown, William Clifford and four yeomen of the crown were put to death in London, but most of the leaders either fled abroad or, like Sir John Fogge, were later able to secure pardons from a conciliatory king. By 25 November the king was back in London, less than six weeks since he had first heard news of the rebellion.[42]

Richard's easy and almost bloodless triumph should not be allowed to obscure the fact that the rising of 1483 had very serious consequences for the future of his regime. Richard might have taken some comfort from the failure of other members of the nobility to join Buckingham and Dorset in arms. Equally they had not noticeably taken up the sword on Richard's behalf, save for members of his immediate circle, such as Norfolk and his son Surrey, Francis, Viscount Lovell, who had been

[39] Gairdner, 138–9.

[40] He was rewarded for his services on 14 December 1483 with a grant of Buckingham's manor of Yalding, Kent, to the value of £50 p.a., Harl. 433, f. 133. He was one of those to whom lands were granted before the act of attainder of January 1484, for which see below, p. 119, and the grant was not enrolled on the Patent Roll until 15 August 1484 (CPR, 1476–85, 482).

[41] Gairdner, 139–43; Chrimes, Henry VII, 25–7.

[42] CPR, 1476–85, 370 (Bodiam); GC, 235 (executions); Kendall, 275 (Richard in London).

given a general commission of array to resist the rebels on 23 October, John, Lord Scrope of Bolton, and John, Lord Zouche, who headed commissions to arrest rebels in Devon, Cornwall, Dorset and Somerset on 13 November, and were, therefore, probably with the king on his march to the south-west.[43] Nor had the midlands counties shown any disposition to rebel, despite the presence there of many former retainers of the murdered Hastings and the servants and tenants of Buckingham himself.

Nevertheless, even in its failure, the rebellion created difficult problems. The flight of so many leading rebels now gave Henry Tudor the backing not only of Dorset and the three bishops of Ely, Salisbury and Exeter, but also of a strong group of gentry whose local influence and connections enabled them to maintain contacts with, and to stir up disaffection in the southern and western counties; and their links of blood and marriage with other rebels who remained behind and accepted pardons made these in turn unreliable. From being something of an irrelevance in English politics, Henry Tudor was converted by the rebellion into an ever-present and growing danger to Richard's security. Moreover, among these new exiles were a number of men of experience and unusual abilities, who were later to become the core of Henry VII's personal establishment. Sir John Cheyne, Sir Giles Daubeney and Sir Robert Willoughby were among the very few men whom Henry chose to elevate to the peerage; Daubeney and Richard Guildford were among his most trusted and hard-worked councillors; Daubeney and Sir Roger Tocotes served him as controllers of the royal household; Edward Poynings became his deputy in Ireland; and several of the group were not only knights of the body but were also elected knights of the Garter, a mark of the sovereign's high personal favour.[44]

The flight of these men, the natural leaders and administrators of their shires, and the political unreliability of others like them who remained in England and suffered a sentence of attainder and the loss of their lands, created a political vacuum in the counties which had supported the rebellion. A total of 104 named persons were later attainted for their treason in the parliament of January 1484. Of these about a third were afterwards pardoned, and recovered at least a part of their lands. But scarcely any afterwards received any public employment under Richard III and they could no longer be regarded as dependable as long as the threat of Henry

---

[43] *CPR 1476–85*, 370–1. William Herbert, earl of Huntingdon, was commissioned along with Sir James Tyrell, to resist the rebels in Wales on 5 November (*ibid.*, 370).

[44] See their biographies in Wedgwood, *Hist. Parl., Biog.;* and for Henry's peerage creations and use of the Garter, Chrimes, *Henry VII*, 137–40. Of the 29 non-royal persons created knights of the Garter by Henry, seven had taken part in the 1483 rebellion.

Tudor's invasion persisted.[45] None of the men pardoned in 1484 and 1485 was ever restored to the commissions of the peace in his native county. This critical defection of the southern gentry from Richard's cause forced him into greatly increased dependence on his trusted northerners, together with a few other members of his intimate circle, like Sir James Tyrell and William Catesby. The months following the rebellion saw nothing less than a veritable invasion of northerners into the landed society and administration of the southern shires, as well as into many positions of political and military importance there. Richard's concern to secure their commitment to their new responsibilities is shown by his willingness to flout both law and customary practice in making grants of rebel lands to them even before the act of attainder provided him with legal warrant. It was usual for kings to appoint to offices – stewardships, receiverships, the constableships of castles and the like – on the estates of rebels as soon as they came into royal hands, but no previous monarch had ventured to dispose of *lands* before they had been declared forfeit to the crown by a formal parliamentary act of attainder.[46] Even before he left Exeter he granted Buckingham's lordship of Thornbury, Gloucestershire, to Sir William Stanley (12 November). On his return to London at the end of November he gave various lands of Sir John Fogge, Sir George Brown and other rebels to the new vice-constable of England, Sir Ralph Ashton (12 December); Edward Ratcliffe was given Sir Robert Willoughby's manors of Broke and Southwick in Wiltshire on 14 December; and many others benefited in the same way.[47] Inevitably, such grants were made not only without legal warrant but without the taking of proper inquisitions to determine title and to establish the rights of widows or other innocent persons who had lawful claims on the estates, and parliament was afterwards persuaded to legalize such arbitrary procedures in defiance of earlier statutes requiring a proper inquisitorial procedure.[48] The illegality of these grants was very much in line with his equally arbitrary appropriation of the estates of Rivers, Dorset and the Exeter duchy during the early days of the Protectorate, and, as Dr Wolffe

[45] *RP*, VI, 244–51, and for a convenient analysis of the attainders, Chrimes, *op. cit.*, 328–9; and for the pardons, Gairdner, 159, and *CPR, 1476–85*, 435, 478, 504, 507, 532, 534.

[46] A survey of the Patent Rolls for 1459–60 and for 1461–2 shows quite clearly that only *offices* on rebel estates were granted away before the acts of attainder of November 1459 and December 1461.

[47] Harl. 433, fos. 122v, 24, 132, 132v, 133, 133v. The earliest grant was made on 2 November, the day of Buckingham's execution, to Thomas, Lord Stanley of the duke's lordship of Kimbolton (f. 120v): this, however, was merely of 'the rule, guidance, and governance' of the estate; the others cited above were in the form 'given and granted for the good service he has done and shall do'.

[48] Wolffe, *Royal Demesne*, 192–3; *RP*, VI, 249–50.

has rightly observed, seem to be the product of 'a calculated ruthlessness' rather than a state of panic.[49] Flagrant indifference to the established rules of law and rights of property could not be expected to endear the king to the landowning classes in general.

The northerners began to move into the southern counties, especially into the south-west, whence a higher proportion of rebels had fled, immediately after the rebellion. They were prominent on a number of commissions to arrest rebels and seize their lands and property, and others soon received grants of land.[50] When in November it became necessary to replace the local officials, it was a Yorkshireman, William Mauleverer, who became escheator in Kent, and Edward Redman, of Harewood in Yorkshire, was appointed sheriff of Somerset and Dorset. Another Mauleverer, Halnath, became sheriff of Devon, and Thomas Huddleston from Cumberland sheriff of Gloucestershire. The following year, in November 1484, Halnath Mauleverer was succeeded by his kinsman, Thomas, in Devon; the Cumberland esquire, John Musgrave, became sheriff of Wiltshire; in Somerset and Dorset another Yorkshireman, Sir Thomas Fulford, took over from Edward Redman; and in Cornwall a northerner, Sir Thomas Broughton, became the new sheriff. In Kent Robert Brackenbury from Durham was the new sheriff in November 1484. Such appointments reflect the king's unwillingness to rely upon the loyalty of the local gentry.[51]

After the act of attainder of January 1484, the stream of this northern 'plantation' widened into a flood. In the great distribution of forfeited lands which followed the act, northerners were conspicuous both in number and in the richness of their rewards. Again, they are most prominent in the south-western counties. Sir Thomas Mauleverer was given the castle and manor of Plympton in Devon to the value of £120 a year; Sir Thomas Everingham acquired the castle and town of Barnstaple and the castle and manor of Torrington in North Devon, together with four manors in Somerset which, together with a manor each in Oxfordshire and Berkshire, brought him lands worth £200 *per annum*; Ralph, Lord Nevill got the forfeited lands of Sir Giles Daubeney in Somerset, also worth £200 *per annum*; Lord Scrope of Bolton was given Bovey Tracey in Devon, Martock in Somerset and two Cornish manors among grants to the value of £206 yearly; Henry Percy, earl of Northumberland, was allowed to recover the Brienne lands to which he laid claim in Devon,

---

[49] Wolffe, *op. cit.*, 193.

[50] Harl. 433, fos. 133v-4v; *CPR, 1476-85*, 370-1.

[51] *CFR, 1471-85*, 276-7. The name of the 1484 sheriff of Cornwall is here wrongly given as William Houghton.

Somerset and Dorset.[52] Among the large rewards of Thomas, Lord Stanley was the manor of West Lydford in Somerset.[53] Most spectacular of all were the grants to Sir Richard Ratcliffe, who was given the former Courtenay earl of Devon's lands in Devon, including the manor, town and hundred of Tiverton, together with other lands in Dorset, Cornwall and Wiltshire, to the annual value of 1,000 marks (£666 13s 4d).[54] As a direct consequence of their new status as landowners in the region, men like John, Lord Scrope (who also became constable of Exeter), Sir Thomas and Halnath Mauleverer and Sir Thomas Broughton made their appearance as justices of the peace and on other local commissions for Devon, and their counterparts in other neighbouring counties.[55]

Further east from Devon and Cornwall the story is the same. For example, Lord FitzHugh received manors in Wiltshire, Dorset and Somerset worth £136 6s a year; Edward Redman had lands worth £84 in Wiltshire and Somerset; Edward Ratcliffe, brother of Sir Richard, was given the Wiltshire lands of Sir Robert Willoughby of Broke to the yearly value of £100; Sir John Saville got manors in Wiltshire, Hampshire and Devon worth £66 and took over from the rebel Sir William Berkeley as governor of the Isle of Wight; John Musgrave had four Wiltshire manors worth £102 9s 5d and was appointed constable of Old Sarum; Sir Thomas Markenfield had a grant, worth £100 yearly, of eight manors in Somerset; and John Nesfield, the Yorkshire esquire of the body who had been appointed to watch over Edward IV's daughters in sanctuary, got the Wiltshire lands of Sir Walter Hungerford, worth over £100 a year.[56] These, and other beneficiaries of the king's generosity, like John, Lord Zouche, now made their appearance, for the first and only time, on commissions of the peace and other local commissions in these counties.[57]

In the south-east the most prominent intruder was Robert Brackenbury, who was given the forfeited estates of Earl Rivers, the Cheyne family and Walter Robert in Kent, Surrey and Sussex, with others in Buckingham-

---

[52] Harl. 433, fos. 282 (Everingham), 283v (Mauleverer), 285 (Scrope of Bolton), 288 (Northumberland and Nevill).

[53] Harl. 433, f. 284.

[54] Harl. 433, f. 285.

[55] CPR, 1476–85, 370–1, 397–8, 556, 558. Scrope's appointment at Exeter (ibid., 502) included an annuity of 200 marks, and a further annuity of £126 18s 4d during the life of Lord Stanley.

[56] Harl. 433, fos. 282 (Markenfield), 283 (Redman), 284 (Ratcliffe), 284v (Musgrave), 287 (FitzHugh, a grant which included an annuity of 200 marks), 289 (Saville, and for his appointment in the Isle of Wight, CPR, 1476–85, 410); ibid., 485, and CC, 567–8, for John Nesfield.

[57] E.g., CPR, 1476–85, 398–9, 489, 572, 577.

shire, to the value of £137 annually, and was made receiver of all Buckingham's forfeited lands in Essex and Kent and constable of Tonbridge
Castle.[58] Other intruders into Kentish county society, whether by way of
land or office, included no less than six north-country knights, John
Savage, William Harrington, Marmaduke Constable, Ralph Ashton,
Edward Stanley and William Mauleverer.[59] Here and there local supporters of King Richard got their rewards from the forfeited estates, as
did John, Lord Dinham, his brother, Charles Dinham, and his brother-in-
law, John Sapcote, in the south-west, or the loyalist member of a rebel
family, Sir Richard Haute, in Kent, but these were comparatively insignificant amongst the flood of outsiders.[60]

The political objections to this policy may not be immediately clear to
modern eyes, but they were sharply obvious to contemporaries. Richard
was offending against deeply-held beliefs about what constituted 'the
community of the shire'. The notion of 'the community of the shire', as
interpreted by those who composed it, and without whom the shire could
not be governed, was still very much a reality in fifteenth-century
England, and indeed continued to be so for centuries to come, as both
Charles I and Cromwell were to discover.[61] The community consisted of
the established gentry families, tightly-knit, linked by blood, marriage
and common interest, highly insular in their outlook and resentful of the
intrusion of outsiders into the accepted circle. A telling illustration of this
exclusionist attitude is the objection made in 1455 against John Howard,
himself an East Anglian though not a Norfolk landowner, that he was
unsuitable as knight of the shire for Norfolk because he had 'no *lyvelode*
in the shire, nor *conversement*'. The writer further remarked that it would
be an evil precedent for the shire that 'a strange man' should be chosen,
and, if it happened, 'the shire shall not be called of such worship as it
hath be'.[62] A king might confer 'livelihood' within the shire, but he could
not create that aptly-named quality of '*conversement*'. If the men of

[58] Harl. 433, f. 284; *CPR, 1476–85*, 385, 435.

[59] All these appear on commissions of array and the peace, 1484–5 (*CPR, 1476–85*,
398, 490, 563).

[60] Harl. 433, f. 282v (Lord Dinham, lands in Devon and Hampshire, £133, and
Sapcote, Devon and Somerset, £170), f. 283 (Charles Dinham, Devon, £50). Dinham
had been appointed chief steward of the Duchy of Cornwall and Sapcote receiver
during the Protectorate, and these offices were later confirmed (*Grants*, 16, 24; *CPR,
1476–85*, 348, 430).

[61] For the seventeenth century, see Alan Everitt, 'The County Community', in
E. W. Ives, ed., *The English Revolution, 1600–1660*, 48–63.

[62] *PL*, III, 38–9; and see the comments of K. B. McFarlane, 'Parliament and
Bastard Feudalism', *TRHS*, 4th ser., xxvi (1944), 58–9, 64.

13. A page from Richard III's Book of Hours. (Lambeth Palace Library MS 474, f. 15v.)

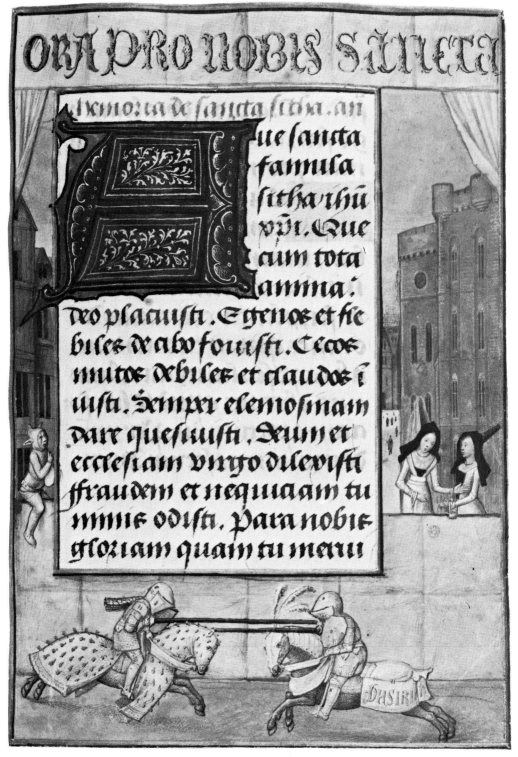

14. The Book of Hours, of Flemish origin, of William, Lord Hastings. (B.L. Additional MS 54782, f. 67v.)

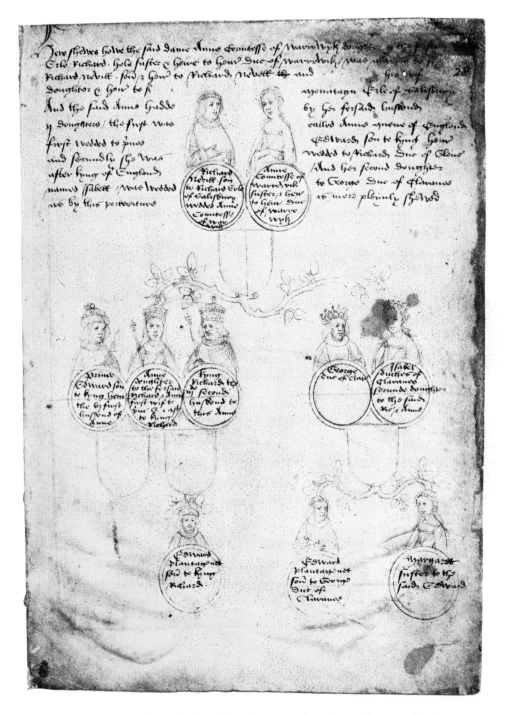

15. An illustration from the late-fifteenth-century Beauchamp Pageant, showing the descent of the Nevill family. Warwick the Kingmaker and his wife Anne stand at the top. Below on the left are Edward, son of Henry VI, his wife Anne Nevill and her second husband Richard III. On the right are George duke of Clarence and his wife Isabel Nevill. (B.L. Cottonian MS, Julius E IV, f. 28v.)

16(a). The arms of Anne Nevill, Richard's queen, from the Vegetius manuscript, *De Re Militari*. (B.L. Royal MS 18 A XII, f. 49v.)

16(b). Richard III holding Warwick Castle, from the Rous Roll by John Rous. (B.L. Additional MS 48976.)

Norfolk could so object to a Suffolk gentleman, how much more were men from north of Trent unacceptable to the gentry of Kent, Cornwall and Devon? Moreover, Richard's 'strangers' were not to be quietly assimilated into the landed society of these shires. They were intended from the first to play a dominant role, as his own words explicitly state. In a letter of 22 January 1484 addressed to all the inhabitants of the honour and town of Tonbridge, and of Penshurst and other former Buckingham lordships in Kent, the king informed them that 'for the speciall trust and confidence that we have in our trusty and welbeloved knight of our body Marmaduc Constable [of Flamborough in Yorkshire] and for other causes us moving' we 'have deputed and ordeyned him *to make his abode among you and to have the rule* within the honour and town and the lordshipps aforsaid'. The people were to be attendant upon him at all times, and to take no livery from, or be retained with, anyone else.[63] Such action struck directly at the roots of the local patronage and influence of the native gentry of the shire as well as at the control of local offices which they regarded as theirs by right and custom. It is highly likely that the 'colonization' of northerners and other outsiders on these terms finally cost King Richard the allegiance of the southern and western gentry and was equally unpopular with the inhabitants at large. For this conclusion we have the weighty authority of the Croyland Chronicler:[64]

> What immense estates and patrimonies were collected into this king's treasury in consequence of this measure [the act of attainder]! . . . all of which he distributed among his northern adherents, whom he planted in every spot throughout his dominions, to the disgrace and loudly expressed sorrow of all the people in the south, who daily longed more and more for the hoped-for return of their ancient rulers, rather than the present tyranny of these people.

Given the chronicler's well-known dislike of northerners, he may have exaggerated the importance of this 'plantation'. But there are clear signs that the successful suppression of the rebellion by no means put an end to disaffection in the south and south-east of England. There was trouble in the south-west in the summer of 1484, probably involving Richard Edgecombe, who had rebelled in 1483 and had then been pardoned, and further trouble in the shires of Hertford and Essex late in 1484. This was more serious, since it involved John Fortescue and John Risley, both

[63] Harl. 433, f. 144 (my italics).
[64] *CC*, 570.

esquires of the king's body: it was linked with disaffection in the Calais garrison and the danger of a possible invasion.[65]

In spite of – or perhaps because of – all his efforts, Richard never won or regained the loyalty of the southern gentry. Bosworth provides the final proof, for none of them thought fit to fight for Richard against Henry Tudor. Indeed, all their leaders were on the other side.

[65] I am grateful to Dr R. E. Horrox for drawing my attention to these circumstances. Evidence in support is to be found in PRO, C.81/1329/12, 15; Harl. 433, fos. 198–9, 199v. See also Dr Horrox's article in *The Ricardian*, v (1979), 87–91.

# PART THREE

# THE REIGN

Chapter 7

# THE KING IN PERSON

Past discussions of Richard's character and ability as king of England have always been bedevilled by the problem of his motivation. Confronted by the paradox between a man apparently guilty of ruthless political violence, indeed infanticide, on the one hand, and a seemingly beneficent, concerned and well-intentioned monarch on the other, Richard's critics and detractors have had no hesitation in seeking a cynical explanation. The theme was early stated by Polydore Vergil. In his view, Richard was detested by his subjects as the supposed murderer of the princes, and

> Because he could not now reform the thing that was past, he determined to abolish the note of infamy wherewith his honour was stained, and to give such hope of his good government that from henceforth no man should be able to lay any calamity that might happen to the commonwealth to his charge.

Either for this reason, or because he now genuinely repented of his former deeds, says Polydore, intent on having it both ways,

> he began to take on hand a certain new form of life, and *to give the show and countenance of a good man,* whereby he could be accounted more righteous, more mild, better affected to the commonalty ... and so might first merit pardon at God's hands.[1]

Polydore's notions have been restated in more modern times by James Gairdner, who confessedly leaned heavily on Sir Thomas More and on what he described as 'the weight of tradition', as expressed in the London Chronicles and elsewhere.[2] Gairdner's hostile account is coloured throughout by his inner conviction that Richard was at heart wicked, cruel and ruthless. He 'so suffered from the licence of unchecked power' that 'immediate expediency became his only motive'. Even his beneficent acts were seen, with some grudging reservations, as nothing more than 'a desire to appear religious in the eyes of men, so as to draw off from himself, so far as possible, the suspicion of his extraordinary wickedness'. Richard's constant harping on the vices of his enemies was 'merely cynical

---

[1] PV, 191–2 (my italics).
[2] Gairdner, x–xi, 129–30, 146, 148–9, 206.

hypocrisy'. For Richard's defenders, on the other hand, his beneficent acts as king appear as triumphant vindication of his essential goodness and virtue. They seek to cut the Gordian knot of paradox by exonerating him from all the violent crimes laid at his door. The king is the true man; the earlier Richard one much maligned by corrupt and prejudiced Tudor writers.[3] Modern professional historians, while praising Richard's abilities and good intentions as king, have tended to skirt the problem of the motives which underlay his actions, but have, on the whole, inclined to imply that his 'good deeds' sprang primarily from a concern for political advantage.[4] Yet the problem cannot be ignored, and during centuries of discussion the answer to it has formed a major element in Richard's historical reputation. How far does what we know of the king in person permit any solution to the problem?

Certain things seem clear. First, there is no good reason to doubt that Richard was a genuinely pious and religious man. A prime influence here may have been the example and precept of his mother, Duchess Cecily of York, whose life of private devotion won for her the reputation of being one of the most saintly laywomen of her generation, and whose religious interests were conspicuously shared by Richard's sister Margaret, dowager duchess of Burgundy.[5] If we had to depend solely on his public acts for evidence of his piety, a sceptic might be moved to doubt its genuineness. Fortunately, there is reliable evidence of a more intimate kind. Among the few surviving books which may safely be identified as Richard's, are several which suggest that he had a strong personal interest in the wave of pietism and mysticism which spread across Europe in the later Middle Ages, and which particularly influenced the laity. Its emphasis lay in the essentially orthodox but nevertheless very private and personal devotions of the type practised by Richard's mother, based upon a study of the famous mystical writers. One of these books was a copy of the first (non-Lollard) version of John Wycliffe's New Testament, in English,

[3] Markham, *Richard III: His Life and Character*, 133–5; Kendall, 281–5, 288–9, 306–24 (the last being a specious section in which Kendall seems not to have realized that dealing with the affairs of ordinary subjects was part of the normal concern of a king, and not something special in Richard III); H. G. Hanbury, 'The Legislation of Richard III', *American Journal of Legal History*, vi (1962), 95–113; and a number of articles in *The Ricardian*.

[4] See, for example, though different conclusions are reached, Chrimes, *Lancastrians, Yorkists and Henry VII*, 138–46; Myers, 'The Character of Richard III', esp. 119–27; Pugh, 'Magnates, Knights and Gentry', in *Fifteenth-Century England*, 110–15. There is also much of relevance to this subject in Wolffe, *The Royal Demesne in English History*, 180–94.

[5] C. A. J. Armstrong, 'The Piety of Cicely, Duchess of York: A study in Late-Medieval Culture', in *For Hilaire Belloc*, ed. D. Woodruff (1942), 73–94; P. Tudor-Craig, *Richard III*, 27.

which contains Richard's signature. Others include parts of the Old Testament, also in English, and a volume of 'The Visions of St Matilda', who had been, along with St Bridget of Sweden, one of the founders of the late-medieval movement of mystical pietism, and was one of Duchess Cecily's most admired authors. Finally, there is a Book of Hours, which includes a remarkable, if by no means unique, private prayer, full of a sense of oppression and danger. This prayer seems to have been added to the manuscript during Richard's reign and may lend support to the notion that he was in a disturbed emotional condition following the death of his only son, and under the constant threat of invasion from Richmond, as both contemporary and early-Tudor writers seem to imply.[6] The main feature of the prayer is the continuing emphasis on trials and problems: Christ is asked to 'defend me from all evil and from my evil enemy . . . and free me from all tribulations, griefs and anguishes which I face'. The impression that such works reflect the genuine religious interests of Richard and his queen is strengthened by their being in English for ease of reading, and the fact that none was an elaborate presentation copy: all were manuscripts written at a much earlier date and acquired from former owners.[7]

If the more public expressions of Richard's regard for religion and the church took conventional forms, that is no reason to suppose them any the less genuine. The most fashionable form of aristocratic piety in late-fifteenth-century England was the foundation of chantries and collegiate churches, the size of which obviously varied according to the financial resources of the founder.[8] Such foundations also had different purposes: Henry VI at Eton and King's College, Cambridge, was obviously concerned with education, whereas Edward IV's refoundation of the College of St George at Windsor was intended as a mausoleum on a grand scale for the York family and as a monument to the worldly splendour of the House of York.[9] But all contained an important element of spiritual insurance for the founder. Prayers for his good estate, and that of his wife and family, forebears and descendants, and for the safety of their souls

---

[6] *CC*, 571; PV, 191, 205 ('more doubting than trusting in his own cause . . . vexed, wrested, and tormented in mind with fear [of Henry's return] . . . whence he had a miserable life . . .').

[7] References to these works are assembled, with a useful discussion, in P. Tudor-Craig, *op. cit.*, 23, 26–9, and Appendix, 96–7, for text and translation of the private prayer.

[8] For the subject in general, A. Hamilton Thompson, *The English Clergy and their Organization in the Later Middle Ages* (1947), 132–60; J. T. Rosenthal, *The Purchase of Paradise* (1972), which perversely omits all reference to foundations by royal princes and dukes.

[9] Ross, *Edward IV*, 274–6.

after death, were a prime duty laid upon the clerks, chaplains, scholars and choristers who served these new foundations.

In this tradition Richard showed himself unusually active. But it is important to notice that many of his chief projects and foundations belong to the period before he became king, and it was unjust of Polydore Vergil to suggest that his proposed college at York was planned merely 'to appease the envy of man and to win himself goodwill'.[10] In all, he was responsible for ten chantry or collegiate foundations (apart from his patronage of Queens' College, Cambridge), a large number by any contemporary standard. It is also worth noticing that, foundations apart, Richard distributed a continuous stream of largesse to religious houses, parish churches, houses of friars and chapels and chantries. Many of his gifts were on a small scale, made locally during one or other of his royal progresses, and probably as a result of direct petition from the eventual beneficiaries. North-country establishments were conspicuous among the recipients of his charity. Some grants, however, were much more substantial, comparable with the large sums he lavished on King's and Queens' Colleges, Cambridge. In particular, he gave the vast sum of lands to the value of £241 2s 8d annually to the Benedictine nunnery of St Mary at Barking in Essex. No special explanation can be offered as to why this religious house should have attracted his patronage, unless it be his possession of the Essex lands of the De Veres, earls of Oxford, who had a close association with Barking.[11]

Not surprisingly, many of Richard's foundations, including his three most ambitious schemes, were connected with the north of England. On 21 February 1478 he procured a royal licence to establish two colleges, one at Barnard Castle in Durham and the other at Middleham in Yorkshire.[12] Since this licence was obtained within a few days of the death of his brother, Clarence, it has sometimes been assumed that Richard's plans represent his pious sorrow for his brother's cruel end. But there is no foundation for this notion. Clarence was not singled out by name as

[10] PV, 192.

[11] P. Tudor-Craig, *op. cit.*, 23, 27, credits Richard with 18 rather than 10 foundations: her mistake derives from an article by M. E. Williams, 'Richard III: Chantry Founder', *Notes and Queries,* clxviii (1934), 23–5, which does not effectively distinguish between the king's own foundations and those for which he gave licence or for which a private founder wished to associate the king and queen in the statutory prayers. For Richard's foundations other than those mentioned below, see *CPR*, 34, 372, 375, 377, 422, 473, 496. They include chantries in the nunnery of Wilberfoss, Yorkshire, the chapel of St George, Southampton, in the College of Arms, London, at Easton in Wem, Salop, at St George, Wolverley, Worcestershire, and in Carlisle Cathedral.

[12] *CPR*, 67, printed in full for Middleham in W. Atthill, *Documents Relating to the Collegiate Church of Middleham* (Camden Society), 60–3; *VCH, Durham*, II, 129–30.

a beneficiary of the regular prayers to be said in the new colleges on behalf of the king and queen, Richard's brothers and sisters, his father, his wife and his son; and it is likely that Richard had planned his establishments some time before the impeachment and trial of Clarence.[13] The expense of establishing two such colleges, both on a substantial scale, at the same time would have been considerable, and probably from the first Richard intended to proceed with only one. When he sought the sanction of parliament to allow him to alienate advowsons to his new foundation, he appears to have had Barnard Castle in mind, but in the event it was only the smaller and cheaper college at Middleham which came into being.[14]

On 4 July 1478 statutes were drawn up for the constitution and organization of the college, which reflect (as such documents often do) the personal wishes and preferences of the founder. The stalls in the collegiate church to be occupied by the dean and six chaplains (who, along with five clerks and six choristers, were to form the collegiate establishment), were named after Richard's favourite saints.[15] It is quite likely that the preamble to these statutes was composed by Richard himself, or at least under his direction.[16] The emphasis on the trials and tribulations which man faces in the secular world harks back to the themes of the private prayer already mentioned, and the references to the mutability of human fortune and the unworthiness of the individual can readily be linked with several explicit strands in the fabric of fifteenth-century pietism. The phrases suggest a genuine personal devotion rather than a mere conventional formula, even if the array of titles also stresses Richard's worldly pomp:

Richard, duke of Gloucester, Great Chamberlain, Constable of England, Lord of Glamorgan, Morgannoc, Bergavenny, Richmond and Middleham, to all Christian people to whom these presents shall come, greeting in our Lord everlasting. Know yet that it hath pleased Almighty God, Creator and Redeemer of all mankind, of his most bounteous and manifold graces to enable, enhance and exalt me His most simple creature, nakedly born into this wretched world, destitute of possessions, goods and inheritaments, to the great estate, honour and dignity that he hath now called me unto, to be named, knowed, reputed and called Richard, duke of Gloucester, and

---

[13] On the length of such processes, see Hamilton Thompson, *op. cit.*, 159.

[14] *RP*, VI, 172–3 (private bill, 1478 parliament). Barnard Castle was to have 400 marks *p.a.* revenue, as against 200 marks *p.a.* for Middleham. Together these charges were almost equivalent to the yearly income of a lesser baron.

[15] The statutes are printed by J. Raine, *Archaeological Journal*, liv (1847), 161–70. The saints, apart from Our Lady, were SS. George, Catherine, Ninian, Cuthbert, Anthony and Barbara.

[16] Hamilton Thompson, *op. cit.*, 157; Rosenthal, *op. cit*, 41 ff.

of his infinite goodness not only to endow me with great possessions and of gifts of his divine grace, but also to preserve, keep and deliver me of many great jeopardies, perils and hurts, for the which and other the manifold benefits of His bounteous grace and goodness to me, without any desert or cause . . . I . . . am finally determined, unto the loving and thanking of his Deity, and in the honour of His Blessed mother our lady St Mary . . . and of the holy virgin St Alkild [the patroness of Middleham] to establish, make and found a College within my town of Middleham. . . .

Although at the same time as the drafting of the statutes, the first dean was appointed (William Beverley, one of that group of Cambridge graduates whose close connections with Richard are discussed below[17]), Richard's performance did not live up to his promises. The expected endowments were slow to arrive, and the college at Middleham remained sadly underfinanced, partly because of his premature death and partly, perhaps, because of his shift of interest, once he had become king, towards another and even grander foundation. This was his plan to establish a college within York Minster on an exceptionally grandiose scale, providing for no less than 100 priests. Some progress had been made with this new venture by the time of Richard's death, but the brevity of his reign prevented its completion.[18]

Richard's devotion to religion explains his concern, apparently genuine and personal rather than merely politically-inspired, to show himself a good friend to and protector of the church in England. This concern, combined with his patronage of learning, won for him the acclamation of the clergy assembled in the Canterbury Convocation of 1484 for 'his most noble and blessed disposition'.[19] The promotion of learned men and of education were clearly matters close to his heart. He loved to surround himself with graduate scholars, to a degree which recalls the remarkably well-educated Henry V rather than his own brother, Edward IV; and he is highly exceptional in his very marked preference for Cambridge rather than Oxford graduates. His chancellor, John Russell, bishop of Lincoln, was the only Oxford man whom he promoted to high office. As a highly experienced administrator, diplomat and former keeper of the privy seal, Russell had obvious qualifications for the most responsible clerical office in the gift of the crown, but it is perhaps no coincidence that he was also well-known for his scholarship: 'one of the best learned

---

[17] Below, pp. 133–4. Beverley was later to become dean of Windsor (October 1483) and is said to have been a royal councillor (Harl. 433, f. 152v; *CPR*, 378; Emden, *Biographical Register . . . Cambridge*, 61).

[18] *VCH, Yorkshire*, III, 90; PV, 192.

[19] Gairdner, 162; Wilkins, *Concilia*, III, 614.

men undoubtedly that England had in his time', Thomas More was later to say of him.[20] The other clerks preferred by Richard had a common bond, not only in their Cambridge background, but also in their interest in the new humanism of Italy, although there is no evidence at all that this fashionable scholarship rubbed off on their royal master. Richard's first opportunity to fill a vacant see came in May 1483 when Richard Martin, bishop of St David's, died. The Protector's choice fell on Dr Thomas Langton, a northerner from Appleby in Westmorland, who had been a student at Pembroke Hall, Cambridge, and was later to become provost of Queen's College, Oxford. He had studied extensively in Italy, both at Padua and Bologna, where he took a Doctorate in Canon Law, and was a friend of another noted English humanist, William Selling, Prior of Christ Church, Canterbury. Langton's obvious ability is shown not only in his further advancement at Richard's hands to the see of Salisbury in February 1485, but by his later promotion to Winchester, and finally to Canterbury, under the patronage of Henry VII, although he died of plague before he could assume office.[21]

The brevity of Richard's reign permitted him only one more vacancy on the bench of bishops, this time the rich and powerful palatine see of Durham. For this clerical plum he selected another north-countryman, John Shirwood, the son of a town clerk of York. Shirwood had been a protégé of George Nevill, archbishop of York, who had appointed him archdeacon of Richmond, a jurisdiction which included Middleham Castle, and it may have been this connection which brought him to the notice of Duke Richard. Shirwood was yet another Cambridge graduate, who had studied extensively in Italy and possessed the still rare qualification of being learned in both Greek and Latin, as Richard emphasized in letters to the pope in 1484. He had already served Edward IV as resident proctor at the papal court. Richard thought sufficiently highly of him to request a cardinalate on his behalf from the pope, and he was unquestionably one of the most distinguished and able English humanists of his age, who accumulated a remarkably varied and interesting library.[22] Similarly, John Gunthorpe, dean of Wells, who became keeper of the privy seal in May 1483, an office he retained in Richard's reign, was another noted Cambridge humanist. A former Warden of King's Hall, Cambridge, he had studied in Ferrara under the great teacher Guarino da Verona and, like Shirwood, was a considerable Greek scholar. He had

[20] More, 25.

[21] Emden, *Biographical Register* ... *Cambridge*, 352–3; Weiss, *Humanism in England during the Fifteenth Century* (1957), 153–9.

[22] Emden, *op. cit.*, 524–5; Weiss, *op. cit.*, 149–53.

already been king's almoner, clerk of parliament and dean of the chapel royal in Edward IV's reign.[23]

It may be that the promotion of such men as these depended largely on their abilities, and had little to do with their scholarly interests, although late fifteenth-century England was showing an increasing awareness of the importance of humanistic scholarship as a qualification for high office in the clerical establishment of government:[24] but it is worth noticing that Richard's liking for scholars extended also into appointments of a more personal kind. He selected as his private chaplain John Dokett (or Dogett), a scholar of Eton and King's College, Cambridge, who had also studied in Padua and then in Bologna, where he became Doctor of Canon Law. He was, amongst other things, the author of a commentary on Plato's *Phaedo*, and bequeathed to King's a collection of books on canon law and theology. It cannot be altogether a coincidence that the president of Queens' College, Cambridge, at this time was Andrew Dokett, a kinsman, perhaps a brother of John, and that this college enjoyed extensive patronage from Richard III.[25]

Quite why Richard had such close associations with this group of Cambridge humanists, comparable with the Wykehamist-New College, Oxford, group of scholars so prominent in Henry VI's reign, cannot readily be determined. It may have owed something to his north-country associations with humanist scholars orginally patronized by George Nevill, archbishop of York, and in particular to the influence of his chancellor while he was duke of Gloucester, Dr Thomas Barowe. An Etonian who went on to King's Hall, Cambridge, where he probably knew John Gunthorpe and Thomas Langton, Thomas Barowe may have benefited from George Nevill's patronage in the diocese of York, for he held several valuable benefices there in the early 1470s. These, as with Shirwood, probably brought him into contact with Duke Richard, who, as king, thought highly enough of him to appoint him Master of the Rolls (the working head of Chancery) in September 1483, and later Keeper of the Great Seal on 1 August 1485, after the dismissal of Bishop Russell. In the summer of 1483 Barowe was named by Cambridge University as the king's agent in sending it 'your large and bountiful alms', Barowe being himself described as 'to his mother the University a great and faithful lover'.[26]

On that occasion the university, normally sycophantic in its dealings

[23] Emden, 275–7; A. B. Cobban, *The King's Hall Within the University of Cambridge In the Later Middle Ages*, 287.

[24] Cobban, *op. cit.*, 287.

[25] Emden, *op. cit.*, 190; W. G. Searle, *The History of the Queens' College of St Margaret and St Bernard*, 87 ff.

[26] Emden, 40–1; Halsted, II, 121–2.

with kings and princes, evidently felt sufficiently assured of Richard's regard for Cambridge to venture to appeal successfully to him for the release from prison of Thomas Rotherham, archbishop of York, who was also Chancellor of Cambridge. But Richard's interest in Cambridge went back several years before his accession to the throne. Already in 1477 he had made provision for the education of four priests and fellows at Queens' College, Cambridge, and the foundation statutes of Middleham College a year later required that, if no suitable dean could be found from among the six priests on the foundation, then he should be selected from one of these Queens' men, who was to be 'able in cunning, disposition and policy'. Here, at least, the founder's preference for managerial ability rather than scholarship may be worth noting. If these men provided no suitable candidate, then the new dean should be a graduate, at least an M.A. or a B.C.L., of the University of Cambridge.[27]

Queens', Cambridge, continued to be a prime object of Richard's patronage, much of it dispensed in the name of his own Queen Anne. Although founded by the Lancastrian, Margaret of Anjou, and further supported by Elizabeth Woodville, Richard was prepared to lavish lands and money on the college, provided it was prepared to recognize Queen Anne as a founder of the college – as indeed she briefly was, only to be conveniently forgotten when political circumstances changed in 1485. His final benefaction to the president, Master Andrew Dokett, and the fellows of Queens', dated July 1485, was munificent indeed, consisting of lands in the counties of Buckingham, Lincoln, Suffolk and Berkshire to the value of £329 3s 8d yearly. In all this there was the element of family pride as well as spiritual insurance: the college was to celebrate daily for 'the good estate of the king and queen . . . and the souls of their fathers, Richard, late duke of York, and Richard, late earl of Warwick and Salisbury' as well as accepting that it was 'of the foundation and patronage of Queen Anne'.[28]

Such considerations did not, however, apply to Richard's scarcely less generous patronage of another Lancastrian foundation, King's College, Cambridge (and the presence of several King's men in his entourage may not be irrelevant here). King's had suffered severely from the hostility of King Edward IV. Its loss of lands and income had seriously inter-rupted the progress of its building works, especially its great chapel, until Edward relented a little towards the end of his reign. Richard gave the college a series of cash presents, culminating in a gift of £300, to continue its building programme. His generosity to King's, even then described

[27] Searle, 87–92; Raine, op. cit., 162.
[28] Harl. 433, f. 289v; CPR, 477; Searle, 97–100; VCH, Cambridgeshire, III, 409.

as 'the unparalleled ornament of all England', was singled out for special
mention in the university's thanks to him on the occasion of his visit there
in 1484, as a significant part of 'his great and royal munificence'.[29]

Richard's generosity to Henry VI's principal foundation may well have
been connected with his very public professions of tenderness and concern
for the memory of a king whom many of his subjects regarded as a saint.
It is hard not to suspect some kind of political interest in Richard's decision
to translate the remains of King Henry from the obscure resting-place at
Chertsey Abbey in which they had been interred following his sudden
death in May 1471 to the splendour of the choir of St George's Chapel,
Windsor. To this day they lie buried there in ironic juxtaposition to the
bones of Henry's destroyer, King Edward IV. However this may have
been, Cambridge rightly regarded King Richard and Queen Anne as
liberal benefactors of the university. They deserved the annual mass which
the university formally established in their honour on the morrow of their
state visit in 1484.[30]

Taken together, all this evidence suggests that Richard's interest in
religion was sincere rather than cynical. There is, however, in historical
experience, no paradox between strongly-held religious beliefs and violence
and dishonesty in political behaviour. Evil deeds have not been the exclusive preserve of the atheist or the agnostic. Richard's no less conspicuously public professions of a concern for sexual morality are, however,
far more suspect. So frequently, and with such unrestrained vehemence,
did he denounce his enemies, especially the Woodvilles and later the
supporters of Henry VII, for their vice and debauchery, that one might
be forgiven for believing that he was obsessed with the subject. Indeed,
his remarkable proclamation against the leaders of the rebellion of 1483 –
with its official heading 'Proclamation for the Reform of Morals' – reads
more like a tract against sexual licence than a condemnation of armed
treason.[31] Here he brackets his 'tender and loving disposition for the
commonweal of this his realm' with his desire 'for the putting down and
rebuking of vices' as matters of equal concern. The rewards offered for the
apprehension of the rebel leaders were said to be 'for resisting the malice
of the said traitors and punishing their great and damnable vices, so that
by their [i.e., his subjects'] true and faithful assistance virtue may be lifted
up and praised in the realm to the honour and pleasure of God, and vice

[29] Harl. 433, fos. 190, 209, 210; Halsted, II, 554–5.

[30] Halsted, 554–5; Gairdner, 191–2. According to Rous, 216, the remains of Henry
VI were found incorrupt (though not embalmed when first interred), and miracles
were already being wrought at his tomb.

[31] Rymer, Foedera, XI, 204–5.

utterly rebuked and damned . . .'. It is hard to believe that a king whose pressing concern was to suppress a dangerous rebellion should have been crucially preoccupied with the maintenance of moral virtue at that precise time.

Similarly, Richard's public persecution of the delectable Mistress Shore has all the hallmarks of an attempt to make political capital by smearing the moral reputation of those who opposed him. As a former mistress not only of King Edward IV but also of Lord Hastings (who was said to have encouraged Edward into 'vicious living and inordinate abusion of his body' with her) and later still of the marquis of Dorset, she was an obvious target to be pilloried as a bawd and adulteress, and hence to blacken by association the repute of two of Richard's declared enemies. But, if we are to believe Sir Thomas More, whose account of her penance seems to have some eye-witness basis, Richard's scheme misfired. Mistress Shore, whose real name was Elizabeth and not Jane, was a woman of charm and character, at least in More's description of her (one of the earliest and most attractive characterizations of a living woman in the English language):

> Proper she was and fair : nothing in her body that you would have changed, but if you would have wished her somewhat higher. Thus say they that knew her in her youth. . . . Yet delighted not men so much in her company, as in her pleasant behaviour. For a proper wit had she, and could both read well and write, merry in company, ready and quick of answer, neither mute nor full of babble, sometimes taunting without displeasure and not without disport. . . . For many he [Edward IV] had, but her he loved, whose favour to say truth . . . she never abused any man's hurt.

Summoned to do public penance as a harlot through the streets of London, clad only in her kirtle and carrying a lighted taper, she bore herself with such demureness and dignity that the sympathies of the spectators went out to her. Soon after, she was imprisoned, and secured her release only because the king's solicitor, Thomas Lynom, fell for her charms and offered his hand in marriage. In doing so he incurred Richard's obvious displeasure. In a letter to Bishop Russell, he wrote:

> . . . it is showed unto us that our servant and solicitor, Thomas Lynom, marvellously blinded and abused with the late [wife] of William Shore . . . hath made contract of matrimony with her, as it is said, and intendeth, to our full great marvel, to proceed to the effect of the same. We for many causes would be sorry that he should be so disposed.

But Bishop Russell's exhortations to Lynom to give up his marriage plan proved unavailing, despite the disapproval of his royal master.[32]

Richard III was the first English king to use character-assassination as a deliberate instrument of policy. His denunciation of his enemies' vices must be seen in this context. For this reason, it is possible to question the sincerity of the motives which lay behind his more general condemnation of sexual immorality contained in an open letter to the bishops in 1484.[33] Here he professes that

> amongst other our secular businesses and cures, *our principal intent and fervent desire is to see virtue and cleanness of living to be advanced, increased and multiplied,* and all other things repugnant to virtue, provoking the high indignation and fearful displeasure of God, to be repressed and annulled.

He therefore commands the bishops to take sharp action against 'all such persons as set apart virtue and promote the damnable execution of sins and vices', and he promises the assistance of the secular arm in a campaign against 'such repugnatours and interruptors of virtue'. Was this anything more than what would nowadays be called a public-relations exercise, 'full of sound and fury and signifying nothing'? It seems doubtful. Nor was Richard himself blameless in this respect. He had two *acknowledged* bastards, John and Katharine. Both were probably the product of his bachelor lusts, born before his marriage to Anne Nevill: John was old enough to be knighted during Richard's royal progress in 1483, and on 11 March 1485 (although still a minor) he was appointed captain of Calais, whilst Katharine was of an age to marry William Herbert, earl of Huntingdon, as his second wife, in 1484.[34]

There are other indications that Richard was not the dour and earnest puritan which some of his modern admirers have proclaimed him to be. Richard was unfortunate in that he did not inherit the great height and powerful build of many of his Plantagenet predecessors, often allied with

---

[32] The historical facts, and the later legend about Mistress Shore, are conveniently examined by Nicholas Barker and Robert Birley in 'Jane Shore', *Etoniana*, no. 125 (June 1972), 383–414, where proof is offered that her real name was Elizabeth (née Lambert) and that the marriage to Lynom took place (cf. Kendall, 471). For More's portrait and the public penance, see More, 54–7: other early Tudor accounts (e.g., *GC*, 233) do not report his version of public sympathy at the time of her penance. The king's letter is from Harl. 433, f. 340v, printed by Gairdner, 71–2, and Kendall, 324.

[33] Harl. 433, f. 281v, printed by Gairdner, 164–5 (my italics).

[34] Rymer, *Foedera*, XII, 265; Halsted, *Richard III*, II, 269–70. These transactions suggest that both children were at least twelve or thirteen years of age, and had, therefore, been born before Richard's marriage in 1472.

17. An extract from Richard III's register of signet letters. This illustrates a letter from Richard to his mother, Cecily duchess of York. (B.L. Harleian MS 433, f. 2v.)

18. The badges of:
(a) Richard duke of Gloucester, with his usual motto, 'Tant le desiere'.
(b) William, Lord Hastings.
(c) Richard Nevill, earl of Warwick, the Kingmaker.
(B.L. Additional MS 40742, fos. 5, 11 and 10.)

good looks, as in Edward I, Edward III, Richard II and his own brother, Edward IV, whom Commynes called the handsomest prince he had ever seen, 'a truly regal figure'.[35] Possibly the fact that he was the eleventh surviving child of his mother may account for his comparative lack of physique. Certainly, such slender literary indications about his appearance as we possess point firmly towards a man who was both small and slight in build. According to Polydore Vergil, Ralph Shaw, in his notorious sermon at St Paul's Cross in June 1483, used the resemblance between Richard and his father, Duke Richard of York, both 'very little', with short, round faces, and the lack of resemblance of York and Edward IV, who was 'high of stature' and 'large of face', as the basis for the claim that Richard was the legitimate son of York, and Edward was not.[36] John Rous, who may well have seen him during his royal progress in the summer of 1483, similarly says that he was little of stature, as does the Elizabethan antiquary John Stow, on the evidence of 'ancient men', adding that he was quite handsome. The German traveller, Von Poppelau, a guest in Richard's household at Middleham, does indeed say that the king was three fingers taller than himself, but says also that he was thinner and less thick-set, with delicate arms and legs, and 'also a great heart'.[37]

There is no reliable evidence for the popular Tudor idea that he was hunchbacked. Not even the hostile Rous, who claims that he was born with teeth and with hair down to his shoulders after the unlikely term of two years in his mother's womb, calls him a crookback: he merely says that his right shoulder was higher than his left. Modern medical inquiry has suggested that he may have suffered from a minor degree of 'Sprengel's deformity', but concluded that 'probably Richard had no great degree of bodily abnormality'.[38] Even the idea of uneven shoulders is not supported by the two earliest-known surviving portraits, that in the Society of Antiquaries of London, painted about 1505, probably in the Netherlands, which shows him with straight shoulders, and that in the Royal Collection, which may be of earlier date, and in which, under recent X-ray examination, there was an original straight shoulder-line, later painted over to give the impression of a raised right shoulder, of

[35] Commynes, *Mémoires*, II, 63–4.

[36] PV, 183–4.

[37] Rous, in Hanham, *Early Historians*, 121; Von Poppelau's account of his visit to Middleham in May 1483 is discussed by C. A. J. Armstrong in Mancini, Appendix, 136–8.

[38] Philip Rhodes, 'The Physical Deformity of Richard III', *British Medical Journal* 2, (1977), 1,650–2. 'Sprengel's Deformity' is a condition arising from underdevelopment of the scapula, resulting in insufficiently flexible muscles in the right shoulder.

which so many copies were later to be made.[39] The first specific reference
to Richard's being a hunchback comes from the records of the city of
York for the year 1491. In the course of a heated argument with a local
schoolmaster, one John Payntour was later accused of having said that
Richard had been 'an hypocrite, a crook back and buried in a ditch like
a dog'.[40] But it took the reputation and literary ability of Sir Thomas
More to stamp upon the Tudor imagination the idea that Richard was
'little of stature, ill featured of limbs, crook backed, his left shoulder much
higher than his right, hard-favoured of visage', or, as Shakespeare was
to put it, 'not made to court an amorous looking-glass'.[41] He does not
seem ugly of appearance. The more flattering of the two early portraits,
that in the Royal Collection, shows a not uncomely man, despite the
obvious lines of anxiety on his brow. The Antiquaries' painting, on the
other hand, shows a gaunt, bony, tight-lipped face, again with a suggestion of anxiety. It is noticeable that in both he is shown as being much
older than his true age.[42]

If Nature had not blessed him with the physical attributes of regality
so admired by contemporaries, at least Richard, following the example
of his brother, knew how to dress like a king and present himself in a
setting appropriate to a king, in an age which set much importance by
conspicuous display. Like Edward, he lived in high state and maintained
an impressive court. He seems to have possessed also, at least in his public
mien, a pronounced taste for personal finery. For his coronation he wore,
above a doublet of blue cloth-of-gold 'wrought with nets and pineapples',
a long gown of purple velvet, furred with ermine and enriched with no
less than 3,300 powderings of bogy-shanks, an ensemble of gaudy richness
even by fifteenth-century standards.[43] Later in the day he changed into
a long gown of purple cloth-of-gold marked with the insignia of the
Order of the Garter and with White Roses of York, and lined with white
damask. On the morrow of the coronation, the royal household supplied
him with several changes of clothes (in crimson cloth wrought with droops,
in crimson cloth checked with gold, and in purple satin and purple
velvet), together with a gift from his queen, a long gown of purple cloth-
of-gold wrought with garters and roses and lined with no less than eight

[39] P. Tudor-Craig, *Richard III*, 80, 92–3. For the dating of the Society of
Antiquaries' portrait (cut from the same oak as their portrait of Edward IV), see
Brian Fletcher, 'Tree Ring Dates for Some Paintings in England', *Burlington
Magazine*, cxvi (1974), 250–8, esp. 256.

[40] *YCR*, II, 71–3.

[41] More, 7; *Richard III*, I, i.

[42] Tudor-Craig, *op. cit.*, 80.

[43] Bogy-shanks are thin strips of fleece from the legs of lambs, to be seen on the
collar of the king's doublet in both the early portraits.

yards of white damask.[44] Among the many splendid items of display ordered for the solemn investiture of the prince of Wales at York in September 1483 were three coats of arms beaten with pure gold for the king's own personal use.[45] It was long ago pointed out that all this may represent nothing more than an awareness of the political importance of ceremonious display rather than a personal proclivity for finery, but it could equally well be that Richard shared with his brother Edward a liking for rich and fashionable clothes. Certainly, the early portrait in the Royal Collection at Windsor shows him sumptuously and expensively dressed, befurred, bogy-shanked and replete with jewelled collar and hat-badge, full of pearls and rubies, fashioned in the devices of the House of York.

Nor does what little we know of his court life suggest that it was in any way gloomy and restrained. In 1484 he entertained for several days at Middleham a foreign visitor, Nicholas von Poppelau, who was suitably impressed (as no doubt he was meant to be) by the splendours of Richard's court. Von Poppelau's account of his visit remains the only first-hand description of Richard and his queen 'at home', if ever a medieval king may be so described in this nineteenth-century phrase. He was much taken by the king's personal graciousness to him. For eight days he dined at the royal table, and on one occasion Richard gave him a golden necklace, taken from the neck of 'a certain lord'. The scene conjures up strong echoes of the splendour with which Edward IV had entertained a Bohemian aristocrat, Leo von Rozmital, in 1466, or his former benefactor, the Lord Gruthuse, in 1472.[46] Von Poppelau was also much struck by the magnificence of the music during the royal mass on 2 May 1484. Here again Richard seems to have been continuing his brother's tradition, for the Yorkist court had already won an international reputation for the quality of its music.[47] As king, Richard issued a warrant to one of the gentlemen of his chapel 'to seize for the king all singing men as he can find in all the palaces, cathedrals, colleges, chapels, houses of religion and all other places except Windsor royal chapel', and some of his musicians were identifiable composers. Not all of them, however, were solely concerned with sacred music. Richard, as duke of Gloucester, had, like other noblemen, maintained several troupes of minstrels: one of these is recorded as entertaining John Howard, later duke of Norfolk, at his home in Stoke-by-Nayland in Suffolk. These players were probably much more occupied in the performance of courtly dances, so popular at the

[44] Jeremiah Milles, 'Observations on the Wardrobe Accounts for the year 1483', *Archaeologia*, i (1779), 363–87, for these and other details of the king's wardrobe.

[45] Harl. 433, f. 128.

[46] Von Poppelau, as above, 136–8; for Rozmital, see Ross, *Edward IV*, 258–9.

[47] Ross, *op. cit.*, 257–61, 274–5; F. L. Harrison, *Music in Medieval Britain*, 20–5.

court of Edward IV, and perhaps in the performance of traditional airs, than with the high liturgical tradition of the royal chapels.[48] This fits in with the comments of the Croyland Chronicler, who, with a certain clerical disapproval, comments upon 'the goings-on' at court during the Christmas festivities in 1484. Having deplored various of Richard's practices, he adds:[49]

> There are also many other matters which are not written down in this book, because it is shameful to speak of them. All the same, it cannot be passed over in silence that at this Christmas time unseemly stress was laid upon dancing and festivity and upon the presentation of vain changes of apparel of identical shape and colour to the queen Anne and the lady Elizabeth, the eldest daughter of the late king. . . .

One of Richard's greatest admirers, Bishop Thomas Langton, struck a similar note of disapproval. In the course of a well-known letter, written in English, praising Richard's high promise as a king, he lapses into the decent obscurity of a learned language to remark, in Latin: 'Sensual pleasure holds sway to an increasing extent, but I do not consider that this detracts from what I have said.'[50] These are slender but certainly significant indications from Richard's own contemporaries, both of whom moved in high places, that Richard's court was perhaps as gay and hedonistic as Edward's had been, however much he inveighed in public against the profligacy of Westminster, Windsor, Greenwich and Sheen whilst his brother had been alive. Not all was silken dalliance, however. In spite of his slender physique, Richard was a tough, hardy and energetic man, who had a proper taste for manly pursuits. He was evidently very fond of hawking, even sending abroad for new hawks as well as combing his own realm.[51] Unlike his lazier brother, he also had an active thirst for warfare. Von Poppelau reported that he wished his kingdom lay upon the confines of Turkey: 'with my own people alone and without the help of other princes I should like to drive away not only the Turks, but all my foes' – an egocentric echo of Henry V's great dream of leading a united Christendom against the infidel.[52] Certainly, he liked to be seen in this

[48] Tudor-Craig, *op. cit.*, 23–4.

[49] *CC*, 572.

[50] Printed by Hanham, *Early Historians*, 50. I have followed her reconstruction of an almost illegible sentence.

[51] Harl. 433, f. 214; commissions of March 1485 to buy 'at price reasonable goshawks, tercells, falcons, lannerets . . .' in England and Wales, and for John Gaynes to go beyond sea to purvey hawks for the king.

[52] Von Poppelau, as above, 137.

martial image, and his founding of the College of Heralds on 2 March 1484 was a symbolic testimony to his military interests.[53]

Richard shared with Edward yet another field of conspicuous display – the financing and patronage of extensive building schemes. Even the prejudiced John Rous confessed that he was praiseworthy as a builder. Although he gave money generously to the canons of Windsor to complete their chapel of St George and, as we have seen, to King's College, Cambridge, most of his building activities, like Edward IV's, were of a secular character.[54] Even before 1483 he had carried out extensive works on his castles at Middleham and Barnard Castle, aimed at modernization and the introduction of higher standards of comfort and airiness. At Barnard Castle his cognizance of the White Boar can still be seen carved in the stonework of a finely mullioned oriel window, and at Middleham he built a new great hall above the existing keep, equally widely-windowed in the fashion of the time. It appears to be now accepted that he also built the handsomely proportioned great hall at Sudeley Castle in Gloucestershire. When he became king, he undertook extensive new works at Warwick Castle, although he visited it only once. At Nottingham Castle, one of his favourite residences and his principal military base, he completed the building of the 'modern' tower, with its roomy and comfortable state apartments, which had been begun by Edward IV. There was also considerable expenditure, if on a smaller scale, on many other royal palaces and castles.[55]

In many respects, therefore, Richard appears as very much a conventional man for his age and station. He seems to have shared to the full a taste for luxury and display common to the kings and aristocracy of the Yorkist and early Tudor periods in England; and we should not forget the supplementary side of the medal, which made such things possible,

[53] In May 1480 his letters of appointment as lieutenant-general in the north spoke of 'his proven capacity in the arts of war', and in 1484 the commons in parliament, petitioning him to accept the throne, spoke of his 'princely courage' and 'the memorable and laudable acts' he had done 'in divers battles' (Rymer, *Foedera*, XII, 115; *RP*, VI, 241).

[54] Rous, in Hanham, *op. cit.*, 121; Ross, *Edward IV*, 271 ff.

[55] Tudor-Craig, *op. cit.*, 7; R. Allen Brown, H. M. Colvin and A. J. Taylor, *History of the King's Works*, II, 558, 600, 764–5. The lesser works, presumably intended for maintenance or defence, affected the Tower of London, the Palace of Westminster, and the castles of York, Kenilworth, Tutbury and Dunbar. At the York family home of Sandal Castle (Yorkshire) he commissioned an entire new tower, and a new bakehouse and brewhouse, for the newly-established Council of the North, which made its original base there (Harl. 433, fos. 175v, 183v, 191v, 192–3, 204, 217v, 218v).

the acquisitiveness, the land-hunger, the disregard for the rights of others, where his brother Edward and his father-in-law Warwick the Kingmaker had given him a splendid lead.[56]

One of the more attractive features of Richard's character was his conspicuous loyalty to his friends and followers. We have already seen how, especially after the rebellion of 1483, he was forced to promote to positions of power many of his followers from his ducal period. But not all promotions were matters of cold political necessity. Francis Lovell's appointment to the office of chamberlain of the household, involving so much regular contact with the king, probably owed a great deal to the fact that he was Richard's personal friend, and had been since they shared a boyhood at Middleham. There were other deserving priests whom he might have appointed to the deanery of Windsor (again a post involving personal contact with the king), but his choice fell upon his old acquaintance and protégé, William Beverley, dean of Middleham. Perhaps even more indicative of his affection and concern for those who served him comes from the records of an endowment he made to Queens' College, Cambridge, in 1477. The holders of the four new fellowships he established were to pray for the king and queen and the royal family, but also for the souls of five named men 'and all other gentlemen and yeomen, servants and lovers [i.e., well-wishers] of the said duke of Gloucester, the which were slain in his service at the battles of Barnet, Tewkesbury or at any other fields or journeys . . .'. These five men, all except one of fairly humble origin, were obviously members of his personal bodyguard in the campaign of 1471, who had paid the final penalty in protecting their lord. But their memory was still fresh in Richard's mind six years later.[57]

Of his family life, apart from the religious interests he seems to have shared with his queen, we know very little. The death of their only son, the ten-year-old Edward of Middleham, about the beginning of April 1484, would have been a severe blow to any hereditary monarch, especially one so insecure upon the throne as was Richard. His queen was still not thirty years of age, and might have produced more children had she lived, but she came of a stock which over three generations had produced wealthy heiresses rather than sons. Their successive husbands, including Richard himself, had preferred the prospect of acquiring great inheritances to the risk of progenitive failure in the male line, which had proved

---

[56] Above, pp. 35–8.

[57] Ross, 'Some "Servants and Lovers" of Richard in his Youth', *The Ricardian*, iv (1976), 2–5.

the ruin of so many noble families in the later Middle Ages.[58] The Nevill family, hitherto so lavishly fecund in the production of sons, had in large part failed to meet this genetic challenge. Now the House of York, scarcely less productive in its York-Nevill alliance, failed also. After a decade of marriage in which she had produced but one sickly child, Queen Anne was unlikely to bear the king another male heir.

Both king and queen were deeply and personally affected by the death of Prince Edward, as we know from direct eye-witness testimony:[59]

> On hearing the news of this, at Nottingham, where they were then residing, you might have seen his father and mother almost bordering on madness, by reason of their sudden grief.

General awareness of the king's unhappy dynastic position soon produced a flock of rumours that he intended to marry his niece, Elizabeth of York. It is an indication of his subjects' general unease and dislike of the king that these rumours soon gained an added and even more sinister connotation – that Richard procured the death of his queen in order to marry Elizabeth, and thereby, of course, to spike the dynastic prospects of Henry Tudor. Queen Anne fell ill early in 1485, but so widespread were popular suspicions of Richard's intentions and motives following her death on 16 March 1485 that:[60]

> the king was obliged, having called a council together, to excuse himself with many words and to assert that such a thing [the marriage to Elizabeth] had never entered his mind. There were some persons, however, present at that same council, *who very well knew the contrary.* Those in especial who were unwilling that this marriage should take place, and to whose opinions the king hardly ever dared offer any opposition, were Sir Richard Ratcliffe and William Catesby, esquire of his body. For by these persons the king was told to his face that if he did not abandon his intended purpose, and that, too, before the mayor and commons of the city of London, opposition would not be offered to him merely by verbal warnings; for *all the people of the north, in whom he placed the greatest reliance, would rise in rebellion against him,* and impute to him the death of his queen, *daughter and one of the heirs of the earl of Warwick, through whom he had first gained*

---

[58] Queen Anne's grandfather, Richard Beauchamp, earl of Warwick, had married two sole heiresses. By his first wife he had three daughters and no sons, and by the second one son and one daughter. The son, Henry duke of Warwick, died young, leaving only one daughter, who died in infancy. Richard Beauchamp's daughter by his second wife, Anne's mother, herself produced only two daughters from her marriage to Warwick the Kingmaker. For the effects of failure in the male line in general, see K. B. McFarlane, *The Nobility of Later Medieval England*, 172–6.

[59] *CC*, 571.

[60] *CC*, 572 (my italics).

*his present high position,* in order that he might, to the extreme abhorrence of the Almighty, gratify an incestuous passion for his said niece.

This comment is of extreme interest. Not only does it reflect the apparent belief of Richard's own chancellor, expressed in his usual elliptic way ('some persons present, who very well knew the contrary'), that the king had serious plans to marry his niece, but it also expresses the conviction of his closest councillors that even Richard's beloved northerners believed him capable of disposing of his wife in order to protect his dynastic future. It does not prove that he murdered his queen, as later Tudor statements loudly implied, but it does very much reflect the mistrust of his subjects about his character and motives.

In the end, it is to this kind of evidence – what his contemporaries thought of him, together with reasonable or likely inferences from his political behaviour – that the honest historian must commit himself. The evidence assembled above, interesting if necessarily incomplete as it may be, provides little essential clue as to his character as a politician. The chapters which follow may help to prove that what Polydore Vergil called 'the show and countenance of a good man' was forced upon him by the circumstances of his accession. Whether he was by nature or merely perforce a well-intentioned king, the reader may judge for himself from what follows.

# Chapter 8

# THE SEARCH FOR SUPPORT

1  *The People*

The cardinal issue in Richard III's reign was his urgent need to attract support wherever and by whatever means he could find it. Never before had a king usurped the throne with so slender a base of committed support from the nobility and gentry as a whole, or with so little popular enthusiasm. Moreover, earlier usurpations had found some justification as protests against misgovernment. In 1399 Henry IV had been able to win political goodwill out of the general resentment and fear of tyranny which Richard II's rule in his later years had inspired, and it was some years before many of his subjects became disillusioned with Henry in his turn. Edward IV had benefited from the yearning for strong government and financial stability engendered by the incompetence and factional strife of Henry VI's later years. Not so Richard III, whose usurpation had been, and was nakedly seen to be, an unashamed bid for personal power. Whatever its unease may have been at the prospect of a minority, the political nation in general had no wish to see Edward IV's heir removed from a throne which was rightfully his, and the rebellion of 1483 revealed the extent of the resentment and mistrust which many men felt for the new regime. After the rebellion, the need to win support assumed the character of a race against time. Richard had to get committed backing for his government before the growing number of his enemies in exile could organize an invasion with the aid of foreign powers who had their own reasons for wishing to see him overthrown.

Thus it was desperately desirable for Richard to commend himself to his subjects in general by presenting them with the image of an upright, beneficent, merciful and well-intentioned king, a monarch responsive to the interests and grievances of the people of the realm and, for good measure, a friend to religion and the church. Even more important, if it came to a power-struggle, he had to secure the loyalty of the politically weighty elements of the community, the nobility and the gentry and, by a wise and constructive use of the patronage at his disposal, to retain the loyalty of those who had supported him initially and win over the goodwill of those who had been indifferent or even hostile to his cause. Behind almost all Richard's acts as king lies the urgent pressure of these twin necessities.

The immediacy of his need is sharply illuminated by the celerity with which he set forth on a major public progress of his realm within a fortnight of his coronation. Richard lived in a strongly hierarchical society which judged a man's – and a king's – importance by the size and splendour of his entourage. This fact of life had been lost upon Henry VI, but not on Edward IV.[1] Like his brother, Richard was acutely aware of the political advantages of ceremonious display, as we can see in the calculated splendours of the coronation, the elaborate festivities shortly to be held in York, the later royal progresses of 1484 and the impressive court festivities of 1483 and 1484.[2]

About 21 July 1483 Richard left London with a large and impressive train, including five bishops, the earls of Surrey, Huntingdon, Lincoln and Warwick, and four barons, together with Sir William Hussey, chief justice of the king's bench. Probably, if not certainly, the duke of Buckingham also formed part of the company. A similar number of noble and well-connected ladies was present to attend the queen.[3] When he reached Reading on 23 July, Richard made a notably generous grant to Hastings's widow, Katherine, who was also, as a daughter of Richard Nevill, earl of Salisbury, his own first cousin and an aunt to his queen. She was to have the marriage and wardship of Lord William's heir, Edward, all the dead lord's movable property and the custody of Hastings's estates during his son's minority; and she was allowed to retain two valuable wardships (of the sons of the earl of Shrewsbury and of Sir William Trussel) which Hastings had held at the time of his death. Since Hastings was never formally attainted, and the king therefore had no clear claim to either his movable or immovable assets, Richard's act of generosity should be considered in this context.[4] On other occasions, also, Richard was at pains

---

[1] Ross, *Edward IV*, 257 ff.

[2] Above, pp. 94–5, 140–1, and below, pp. 149–51, 176.

[3] This is the list of the great persons in Richard's retinue at the time he reached Warwick given by John Rous, *op. cit.*, 217, who was probably then present, and certainly had first-hand information about the royal progress. That Buckingham was with the king until they parted at Gloucester is stated by PV, 184, and by More, 89–90, but is rejected by Kendall, 252, 480, on the grounds that he is not included in the contemporary list of the guests entertained at Magdalen College, Oxford. Kendall, however, was anxious to have Buckingham back in London so that he might murder the princes in the Tower (*op. cit.*, 411–12).

[4] Harl. 433, fos. 108v–109; *CPR*, 496. Earlier kings had been at pains not to dispose of lands and titles until their claims had been confirmed by a parliamentary act of attainder, with the exception of Richard II's confiscation of the Lancaster inheritance in 1399 (see Ross, 'Forfeiture for Treason in the Reign of Richard II', *EHR*, lxxi (1956), 560–75). For other examples of Richard III's defiance of the laws of inheritance, see below, p. 175.

to show public generosity to the wives or the widows of his political opponents. In December 1483, for example, Florence, wife of the rebel Alexander Cheyne, was taken under the king's protection – significantly, with his usual emphasis on morality, 'for her good and virtuous disposition' – and was given the wardship of her husband's lands. By contrast, in March 1484, Margaret countess of Oxford, another kinswoman both of Richard and his queen (cousin to the one, aunt to the other), and still wife to the imprisoned Lancastrian die-hard John de Vere, earl of Oxford, was given the rather slender pension of £100 yearly, 'in consideration of her poverty'. The duke of Buckingham's widow, perhaps because she was a Woodville, was even more harshly treated. For the widow of the richest landowner in England, an annuity of a mere 200 marks was rather more an insult than an act of charity.[5]

From Reading, Richard moved on to Oxford, where he arrived on 24 July and where he was splendidly entertained at the newly-built college of Magdalen by its founder, Bishop Waynflete of Winchester, one of the very few Lancastrian bishops still occupying a see. For two days, Richard listened to scholarly disputations, although how much he understood of them is an open question. The scholars participating were rewarded with liberal gifts and Richard visited several of the colleges. He then made a brief visit to the royal hunting-lodge at nearby Woodstock, where he generously granted a petition from the local people disafforesting a tract of land which Edward IV had arbitrarily annexed to the royal forest of Wychwood.[6] Moving westwards from Oxford, Richard came to Gloucester, where, 'because it bore the ancient name of his dukedom', he conferred upon it the very remarkable privilege, for a town of its size and commercial importance, of making it a shire-incorporate (like London, York, Bristol and Coventry), with its own mayor and sheriffs.[7] Further north in the Vale of Severn, at Tewkesbury, he undertook to honour a debt for the considerable sum of £310 still owing to the abbot and convent from the estate of his brother George duke of Clarence, who lay buried in the abbey's choir. When Richard reached Worcester early in August, the town offered him a benevolence to help pay his expenses, as both London and Gloucester had already done; but all these offers Richard declined, telling the people he would rather have their hearts than their money.[8]

[5] Harl. 433, fos. 77, 126v, 135–6, 200; *CPR*, 436, 450.

[6] Rous, *op. cit.*, 216; W. D. Macray, *Register of Magdalen College, Oxford* (1894), I, 11–12; Gairdner, 111–12; Kendall, 251–2.

[7] Rous, *op. cit.*, 216, confirmed by the charter itself (M. Weinbaum, *British Borough Charters, 1307–1660*, 42).

[8] Rous, 216; Harl. 433, f. 110.

During the remainder of August the royal party moved slowly north through Warwick, Coventry and Leicester to Nottingham. The castle there, where Edward had begun a programme of modernization, in the form of a new polygonal tower, with light and airy state apartments, was to become one of Richard's favourite residences, and he carried Edward's schemes through to completion.[9] His continuing and acute concern for his public image is shown by the elaborate preparations made for his entry into Yorkshire, there to display himself to best advantage to the admiring northerners. Seventy northern knights and gentry were summoned to wait upon him at Pontefract to add to the splendour of his train.[10] Upon Richard's prompting, the king's secretary, John Kendall, wrote to the mayor and aldermen of York, telling them he was sure they were preparing a reception for their monarch better than any he could devise, yet nevertheless expressing hope that there would be pageants, displays, speeches and arras hung along the streets in order to impress the 'many southern lords and men of worship' who were with the king and queen and 'who will greatly mark your receiving their Graces'.[11] Shortly after, the wardrobe of the royal household in London was instructed to supply vast quantities of finery to the king in York, including yards of cloth of gold, golden armour, gilt spurs, a thousand pennons and the enormous number of 13,000 livery badges bearing the device of the White Boar for distribution to friends, well-wishers and perhaps anyone who would wear one. All this was in connection with the planned investiture of Richard's son, Edward, as prince of Wales.[12]

The city's reception indeed lived up to expectations, with the mayor and his brethren dressed in scarlet to greet the king, no less than three pageants, a special performance of the city's Creed Play and the provision of expensive presents for the royal couple, to which all the leading citizens had contributed. The king was to have 100 marks in a pair of basins of silver-gilt, and his consort £100 of gold in a piece of plate. There were presents also for the earl of Northumberland, and here the city was carefully looking over its shoulder at the *amour-propre* of the other great man of the region. The festivities reached their climax two days after the king's arrival. On 8 September the young prince was solemnly invested with his principality in York Minster; the king and queen processed through the streets wearing their crowns; the Spanish ambassador was knighted by the king and a gold collar placed about his neck; the king's bastard son, John,

[9] Rous, 216–17; Ross, *Edward IV*, 272.
[10] Harl. 433, f. 111v; cf. Kendall, 256.
[11] *YCR*, 78–9.
[12] Harl. 433, f. 126.

was likewise made a knight.[13] Soon after, Richard's loyal citizens received their reward for so much expense. On 17 September the king reduced the city's annual fee-farm, payable to the exchequer, from £160 to £100 (the amount should be compared with the presents just mentioned for some idea of their relative value), and the mayor of York was appointed as the king's chief serjeant-at-arms, with a fee of £18 5s yearly, chargeable against the city's fee-farm.[14]

Richard's sojourn in the north was also marked by a series of gifts and grants to local churches and religious bodies, especially those connected with the families of York and Nevill and with the royal castles and estates in Yorkshire. Coverham Abbey near Middleham was given £20 towards the rebuilding of its church; the church at Barnard Castle had similar grants of £40 and 100 marks; the priory at Pontefract, where the body of the king's father had lain for many years after his death at the battle of Wakefield and before its re-interment at Fotheringhay, was allowed to recover land taken from it by Edward IV; the people of Holmfirth, a few miles south of Wakefield, received a confirmation of an earlier grant of £2 yearly to enable them to maintain a priest in their chapel-of-ease; the nunnery of Wilberfoss, near York, 'which has come to poverty', was given lands to found a chantry to pray for the souls of the king, queen and royal family.[15]

In the euphoric atmosphere engendered by royal liberality and the warmth of the north's reception, and while the king was still at York, the bishop of St David's, Thomas Langton, was moved to write to his friend, the prior of Christ Church, Canterbury, a much-quoted letter in praise of Richard and the success of his bid for popularity:[16]

> He contents the people where he goes best that ever did prince; for many a poor man that hath suffered wrong many days have been relieved and helped by him and his commands in his progress. And in many great cities and towns were great sums of money given him which he hath refused. On my truth, I never liked the conditions of any prince so well as his. God hath sent him to us for the weal of us all.

Langton was scarcely an impartial witness. A Cumberland man who had risen in Richard's service, he had only recently been promoted to the see of St David's during the Protectorate, and was soon to receive Lionel

---

[13] *YCR*, 77–82; *CPR*, 465; Rymer, *Foedera*, XII, 200; Drake, *Eboracum*, 116; *CC*, 490.

[14] *YCR*, 82; *CPR*, 409.

[15] Harl. 433, fos. 116–116v (Coverham and Holmfirth), 119 (Barnard Castle), 121 (Pontefract); *CPR*, 375 (Wilberfoss).

[16] *Literae Cantuarienses*, ed. J. B. Sheppard, 46; Hanham, 50.

Woodville's much richer see of Salisbury when the latter fled into exile in the aftermath of the 1483 rebellion.[17] He had a natural and inbuilt interest in seeing Richard succeed. But his specific statements are supported by other evidence. That Richard turned down offers of benevolences from the towns he visited is confirmed by John Rous, one of the most hostile sources for Richard's reign, and record evidence confirms a similar statement by John Kendall, the king's secretary, that throughout his reign Richard was at pains to ensure the dispensing of speedy justice, especially in the hearing of the complaints of poor folk. In December 1483 John Harington, clerk of the council, received an annuity of £20 for 'his good service before the lords and others of the [king's] council and elsewhere and especially in the custody, registration and expedition of bills, requests and supplications of poor persons'; and that portion of the council's work which dealt with requests from the poor, later to develop into the Tudor Court of Requests, received a considerable impetus during Richard's reign.[18]

If Richard's first royal progress was to be by no means his last, it was certainly the most successful, if only because, as time wore on and funds became more scarce, he could no longer afford the financially grandiloquent gestures of refusing offers of benevolences (though no more seem to have been made) or indulge himself in the publicly satisfying but expensive gifts he made to wives, widows, churches and other sympathetic subjects of royal generosity who benefited during the progress of 1483. Bishop Langton may have been correct in his belief that the calculated largesse of 1483 brought its rewards in a halcyon period of initial popularity.

How far Richard ever became more generally and lastingly popular with his subjects is much more doubtful. In particular, it is unlikely that the early goodwill he won for himself survived the gradual spread of a general belief that he had rid himself of his nephews by violence.[19] In any event, popular support was at best a volatile and elusive phenomenon. Popular protest in the fifteenth century might be expressed in riots, unlawful gatherings, sometimes, especially in London, in mob violence; but such outbursts tended to be highly local and self-interested, like the animosity shown by native citizens in London, Southampton and elsewhere to foreign merchants and entrepreneurs. In London in 1470–1 such mindless resentment had shown itself in burning down the foreign-owned breweries which supplied the citizens with their beer.[20] Moreover, in

[17] Above, pp. 133–4.
[18] Rous, 216; *YCR*, 78; *CPR*, 413; J. F. Baldwin, *The King's Council in England during The Middle Ages*, 442–3; Chrimes, *Henry VII*, 152–3.
[19] Pp. xlvi–vii, 104, 112–13, and see also below, pp. 179–80.
[20] *GC*, 211–12.

fifteenth-century political terms, concepts like 'the nation', 'the people' and 'popular opinion' have only a very limited relevance. Beneath the surface there was often much seething unrest about taxation, the lack of justice, local disorder and the economic problems of the age, but it was rarely constructively expressed unless led by elements of the socially superior classes, the knights and gentry and above all the nobility, although it could be fanned and inflamed – perhaps more than we can realize – by the sermons and leadership of the lower clergy. Most major 'popular' rebellions of the later Middle Ages, like Cade's Rebellion of 1450, or the Kentish rebellion of 1471, depended heavily on the organization and direction given them by the propertied classes, even when there were deep economic, political or social grievances; and the same point holds true even fifty years later during the Lincolnshire Rebellion of 1536 and the Pilgrimage of Grace of the following year.[21] Otherwise, like the northern rebellion against Edward IV of 1469 or the Lincolnshire rising of 1470, they were inspired by powerful families with strong regional influence, such as the Nevills and their allies, playing upon and exploiting real or imagined grievances amongst ordinary people.[22] In this strongly hier-archical society, the 'people' could only seriously influence events if they had the backing and support of the upper ranks of society, although, perhaps, general popular resentment of a particular regime might in turn affect the latter's attitudes. It was, therefore, from these propertied and armigerous classes of the political nation that Richard needed above all to find support.

## 2   The Magnates, Knights and Gentry

In his dealings with the nobility and gentry, a medieval king enjoyed two great advantages. The first lay in his exclusive right to confer titles of nobility and to promote an existing peer to a higher rank within the nobility. Unlike Henry VI, who had created three new earls, one viscount and twenty-one barons between 1436 and 1461, or Edward IV, who made thirty-two new peers during his reign, mainly in his first decade, Richard III was noticeably sparing in his distribution of titles.[23] The two co-heirs

---

[21] For a general discussion of the point, see M. E. James, 'Obedience and Dissent in Henrician England: The Lincolnshire Rebellion 1536', *Past and Present*, 3–78, esp. 69 ff. For 1471, see C. F. Richmond, 'Fauconberg's Kentish Rising of May 1471', *EHR*, lxxxv (1970), 673–92.

[22] Ross, *Edward IV*, 127–8, 138–40.

[23] For the peerage creations of Henry VI and Edward IV, see T. B. Pugh, 'The Magnates, Knights and Gentry', in *Fifteenth-Century England*, 88–95, 116–17; Ross, *Edward IV*, 332–3; for those of Richard III (below), J. E. Powell and K. Wallis, *The House of Lords in the Middle Ages*, 527.

to the Mowbray inheritance, William, Viscount Berkeley and John, Lord Howard, were raised to higher dignities, the one to the earldom of Nottingham (a former Mowbray title), the other to the dukedom of Norfolk; and John's son, Thomas Howard, was made earl of Surrey. Edward, Lord Lisle was promoted to a viscountcy. But that was all. No effort was made to reinforce the lower ranks of the peerage, now much reduced in numbers by the natural wastage which occurred in each generation through the lack of male heirs to a barony and recurrent and frequent deaths in battle or on the scaffold during an age of civil strife. Only twenty-six barons were summoned to the parliament of 1484, compared with forty-four to that of 1453 and forty-one to Edward's first parliament of 1461. Edward IV had tried to deal with a somewhat similar situation by the immediate creation of seven new barons, and he followed this up by making six more (not to mention creating eight new earls) before 1471. It is a little curious that Richard did not make any attempt at once to attract support and to strengthen his influence with the peerage by a more lavish distribution of titles. He may have felt that there were few candidates who were both suitable and dependable, and certainly to have given baronies to some of his closest friends, especially those of comparatively humble background, like Sir Richard Ratcliffe or William Catesby, would only have added to their already considerable unpopularity. Even the less upstart and more established of his supporters among the gentry, men like Sir Thomas Burgh or Sir Marmaduke Constable, were mostly northerners, whose promotion to peerages might have caused jealousy and resentment. In his cautious approach to the creation of new peers, Richard III's policy far more closely resembled that of Henry VII than either of his two predecessors.[24]

The king's second, and much more important, resource lay in the extent of his material patronage, far greater than any subject possessed, however powerful he might be. As king, he commanded a whole series of offices of profit and influence, ranging from major military commands like the captaincy of Calais and the wardenships of the marches towards Scotland, through positions like Lieutenant of Ireland or chief justice of North and South Wales, down to a wide range of constableships of royal castles and stewardships of royal estates. But the king was also a great private landowner. As duke of Lancaster, he controlled several hundred offices of profit, the fees of which were chargeable on the local revenues of the duchy estates, quite apart from any decision he might make to divert

[24] Henry VII created nine new peers, but only three of these were genuinely new creations as opposed to revivals. Three of Henry's titles went to men who had led the rebellion of 1483 (Willoughby, Cheyne and Daubeney): S. B. Chrimes, *Henry VII*, 138–9.

such revenues to individuals in the form of annuities or pensions. The kings of the House of York could also draw upon the wide estates of their paternal inheritance, the duchy of York and the earldom of March, and to these Richard III now added the lands which he himself had held as duke of Gloucester. Moreover, he could dispose of any lands which came to him by way of forfeiture for treason under a parliamentary act of attainder, or, through his feudal prerogative, lands which had escheated for lack of heirs, together with valuable rights of wardship over lands during the minority of an heir who was a tenant-in-chief of the crown, and the marriage of the heir, which was a highly marketable commodity.

In this context Richard was exceptionally well-placed. Since he had largely eliminated the Yorkist royal family, he had few dependants for whom to provide, certainly by comparison with Edward IV. His son Edward died young, leaving the lands of the prince of Wales (valued at 10,000 marks in 1460) at Richard's disposal. Unlike most kings, he seems to have made no separate provision for his queen, who was normally provided with her own dower lands worth some £4,000 to £5,000 in yearly value. His mother, Duchess Cecily, had an interest in the estates of the Duchy of York, but much revenue which might otherwise have been diverted to fulfil the terms of Edward's will remained to Richard because the executors refused to act. His brother Clarence's estates came to his hands from Edward IV. In these highly favourable circumstances, the royal estates could be expected to produce (over and above various fees, annuities and wages) the very considerable income of between £22,000 and £25,000 yearly, that is, about twice as much as the revenue enjoyed by Edward IV from the same sources.[25]

Even more important was the fact that the great forfeitures of 1483 enabled Richard to grant away very substantial revenues, worth some £12,000 yearly, without impoverishing the crown's basic income from its own lands. His grants could be made, so to speak, from gains rather than from capital.[26] After the rebellion he could draw upon all the lands which had formerly belonged to the many substantial gentry who had led the rising in the south and west. Above all, he could command the estates of the duke of Buckingham, who, by 1483, was the wealthiest private landowner in England, as well as recovering for his own use all that plethora of valuable offices which he himself had granted Duke Henry in the preceding months.[27]

All this gave him an immense reservoir of patronage. What use did he make of it? Without doubt, he distributed largesse on a most impressive,

[25] B. P. Wolffe, *The Royal Demesne in English History*, 188–90 (and *n.* on 190); Ross, *Edward IV*, 381.

[26] Wolffe, *op. cit.*, 191–4; Pugh, *op. cit.*, 114.

[27] Pugh, *op. cit.*, 105.

but certainly not on an unprecedented scale.[28] For political reasons, much of what he had to give went to his supporters from the north.[29] But considerations of personal friendship and of the degree of trust which the king placed in them also played a part in the exceptionally generous rewards given to several of his supporters, not all of them men from the north. Sir Richard Ratcliffe's political value to Richard, especially since he was regarded as a notably unpopular upstart, could not possibly justify the enormous grants of land he received in south-western England to the value of 1,000 marks (£666 13s 4d) a year. Although never ennobled, Sir Richard thereby came to enjoy an income well in excess of that normally thought appropriate for a baron of the realm, which had been estimated at £500 in Edward IV's hierarchical definition of the ranks of society in his 'Black Book of the Household' compiled about 1472.[30] Again, William Catesby, who, as 'The Cat', was the second member in Collingbourne's notorious lampoon, was given lands chiefly in the midlands to the annual value of £323 11s 8d, which made him wealthier than most knights, no mean achievement for an aspiring private lawyer. One of the small band of Edward IV's former servants who chose to continue in the service of Richard III was the substantial Essex knight Sir Thomas Montgomery, who became a member of his council: his labours were amply rewarded with a grant of lands in Essex worth no less than £412 yearly.[31] Others, too, seem to have benefited far beyond their political worth from the king's affection and confidence. Among them were Sir William Hussey, chief justice of the king's bench, Sir Robert Harrington and Charles Pilkington, both Yorkshiremen, who had been Richard's trusted agents in the murder of Hastings, Sir James Tyrell, a confidant of Richard as duke of Gloucester, Richard and Edward Redmayne, his friends from Cumberland, and his secretary, John Kendall, a man who may not have come from the landowning class at all, but was the son of a long-term minor servant and pensioner of King Edward IV.[32]

[28] Dr Wolffe (*op. cit.*, 193) suggests that nothing like it had been seen since Richard II had disinherited his opponents in 1398. This seems to ignore the even more spectacular alienation of lands by Edward IV in the early years of his reign, for which see Ross, *Edward IV*, 64–81, 95–6. In 1401 Henry IV was spending £24,000 a year in annuities (not grants of land): Pugh, *op. cit.*, 108.

[29] Above, pp. 119–24.

[30] A. R. Myers, *The Household of Edward IV*, 103–4.

[31] Harl. 433, f. 286v (Catesby), 284v (Montgomery). Another former servant of Edward IV, Sir Thomas Burgh, had lands to the value of £200 1s (Harl. 433, f. 283v).

[32] Hussey, lands in Leicestershire, and Lincolnshire, £209 a year, Harl. 433, f. 209; Harrington, £326 12s in various counties, *ibid.*, 288v; Pilkington, lands in Warwickshire and Nottinghamshire, £80 12s 11d, *ibid.*, f. 299; Tyrell, see below; Richard and Edward Redman, above, pp. 54, 120–1; John Kendall, lands in Berkshire and Oxfordshire, £80, Harl. 433, f. 289; his presents and perquisites raised this sum to £450 a year, Kendall, 316, 487–8.

Some of these men drew their rewards less from grants of land than from appointments to lucrative offices, which benefited them not only through the fees appertaining to the offices but also from the local influence which these conferred. For example, Sir James Tyrell was already established, before the reign began, as Richard's principal lieutenant in the great Marcher lordship of Glamorgan. His position as sheriff of Glamorgan and constable of Cardiff Castle, together with other offices in the lordship, brought him fees of £110 a year, but since he was also the chief man of the region, his goodwill was worth buying, and he attracted private fees from the duke of Suffolk, Lord Dudley and several ecclesiastical landowners. Tyrell himself claimed that he was making a clear profit of £100 a year from his position as farmer of the Glamorgan estates of the Abbey of Tewkesbury. After the rebellion of 1483 he acquired the no less valuable and influential office of steward of the Duchy of Cornwall, and was also made steward of the lordship of Newport and of other confiscated possessions of the duke of Buckingham in South Wales. Finally, the parliament of 1484 accepted the rather dubious claim of his wife to the lands of Sir Thomas Arundel in Cornwall. Together with wardships of minors granted to him by Richard III, all this made Tyrell a very wealthy man. If not perhaps quite as rich as Ratcliffe, he too enjoyed an income suitable for a baron.[33]

Knights and gentry like this had an immense stake in Richard's survival. Their fortunes, especially those of the more obscure northerners, had been enormously enhanced through Richard's favour. It was precisely this kind of committed support which the king sought to attract through his distribution of patronage. He was not wholly unsuccessful, but his success, with men below the rank of baron, was essentially regional. Although a not insignificant number of the gentry members of Edward IV's court circle chose to enter Richard's service, almost without exception they were men from a line north of the Thames to the Severn. Neither before nor after the rebellion of 1483 does he seem to have won the loyalty of the established country gentry from the shires from Kent through to Cornwall.[34]

Not surprisingly, it was less easy to win the support of the nobility, none of whom owed their fortunes, like a Ratcliffe or a Tyrell, to the king's favour. Nearly all of the now much reduced group of English peers benefited from Richard's rule. But it has been suggested recently that too much of his patronage was bestowed upon a comparatively small clique of trusted followers.[35] This argument will not stand up to close examina-

[33] *CPR*, 430, 474; T. B. Pugh, in *Glamorgan County History*, III, 201.
[34] Above, chap. 6.
[35] T. B. Pugh, in *Fifteenth-Century England*, 115.

tion, and it does less than justice to Richard's political acumen. Excluding
(for the moment) the four great magnates who were the chief props of his
regime at the beginning of his reign, it seems clear that Richard had
considerable success in attracting support from the aristocracy, particularly
among the lesser nobility. Nor is it true, as Sir Thomas More claimed, and
again excluding the great magnates, that 'with large gifts he get him
unsteadfast friendship', even if, to achieve this, he 'was fain to pill and
spoil in other places, and get him steadfast hatred'.[36] Few of those who
accepted his largesse afterwards ignored their obligation. Some of them
paid for it with their lives. Most, it should be said, were northern lords
who already had connections with Richard. Yet a number of others less
initially committed were won over by his lucrative patronage, if not for
other and less material reasons, and finally rewarded him with their
loyalty.

Had it not been for the subsequent defection of one of the most powerful magnates, Richard's management of the nobility might have come to
be regarded as a model exercise of patronage. One of his easier conquests
was William Herbert, earl of Huntingdon, the most impoverished of the
English earls, who had been so badly treated by Edward IV. Lack of
funds persuaded Earl William to accept in marriage Richard's bastard
daughter, Katharine, as his second wife. His reward was something of the
order of 1,000 marks a year, which almost doubled his income. Through
his appointment after the death of Buckingham as chief justice of South
Wales, he was able to recover something of the influence which his family
had formerly enjoyed in that region. Although he seems not to have been
present at Bosworth, he was loyal during Buckingham's rebellion and in
1485 his continued loyalty denied Henry of Richmond the shortest route
into England through southern Wales and forced him instead to march
north to Milford Haven and then across mid-Wales to enter England by
way of Shrewsbury.[37] John de la Pole, earl of Lincoln, son of the aged
and ineffectual duke of Suffolk, needed no special inducement to support
his mother's brother. With the death of the infant Edward prince of
Wales, he became the nearest *adult* male heir of a now childless king,
although there is no direct evidence whatever to support the claim made
by several modern scholars that he was publicly recognized as heir to the
throne by Richard: indeed, the only contemporary source to mention the
subject states that his cousin, the ten-year-old Edward earl of Warwick,
was initially accepted by Richard as his heir, despite the fact that Richard's

---

[36] More, 8. As Wolffe pointed out (*Royal Demesne*, 191–2), the first part of More's
observation has often been quoted without quoting the second, which is of interest
as a comment on Richard's standing in southern England.

[37] Harl. 433, f. 282; *CPR*, 367, 538; and below, pp. 211–12.

own claim to the throne seemed to debar Edward on the grounds that his father had been attainted.[38] However this may be, John was well cared for, being given lands worth £333 2s 5d yearly and an annuity of £176 13s 4d from the revenues of the Duchy of Cornwall, as well as being appointed, in October 1484, king's lieutenant in Ireland, and made president – to the despite of the earl of Northumberland – of the newly-established Council of the North.[39]

Of the remaining seven adult earls in 1483, three (Arundel, Westmorland and Kent) were old men. Two were rewarded through their sons, Lords Maltravers and Nevill, the latter succeeding his father as earl of Westmorland in 1484.[40] The duke of Norfolk's son, Thomas Howard, the future victor of Flodden Field, not only owed his title of earl of Surrey to Richard III, but also the extraordinarily generous annuity of £1,100 granted him during his father's lifetime.[41] William Berkeley, earl of Nottingham, was a childless man whose governing passion was an ambition for titles: he too owed both his earldom and his share of the Mowbray estates to Richard, even though he had formally surrendered his claim to the lands in return for a viscountcy under Edward IV.[42] The aged Edmund Grey, earl of Kent, had no reward. For many years he had been politically inactive and he had no great wealth or influence. Clearly his support was not thought to be worth buying. Richard's patronage of the English earls paid off handsomely. Of the eight already mentioned, three (Lincoln, Surrey, Nottingham) fought with him at Bosworth, so too, in all probability, did Westmorland and Maltravers representing Arundel; Huntingdon was on guard in South Wales; Kent did not count. Only the earl of Northumberland, who had received larger rewards than any of the others, was later to play an equivocal, if not an actively hostile role in 1485.[43]

Of the two English viscounts, Francis Lovell was Richard's closest personal friend, a relationship (like that of William, Lord Hastings with Edward IV) enshrined in his position as chamberlain of the royal household, which involved close and regular contact with the king; and he was further rewarded with grants of land to the value of some £400 a year.

---

[38] Rous, *Historia Regum Angliae*, 218–19.

[39] Harl. 433, fos. 264v, 289; *CPR*, 388–9, 448, 477.

[40] Richard increased by 100 marks to Maltravers the annuity of 200 marks *p.a.* originally granted him by Edward IV (Harl. 433, f. 310v; *CPR*, 431). Ralph, Lord Nevill was given lands in Somerset and Berkshire to the value of £200 3s 5d, together with an annuity of £80 *p.a.* charged on the annuities of Barnard Castle during the lifetime of Lord Stanley (Harl. 433, f. 288; *CPR*, 427; *CP*, XII (ii), 551).

[41] *CPR*, 479.

[42] Above, pp. 37–8.

[43] Above, p. 78; below, pp. 166–8.

Of the later political attitude of Edward Grey, Viscount Lisle, we know nothing (though he does not seem to have been at Bosworth), but he owed both his grants of land and office to Richard's benevolence.[44]

In his patronage of the lesser nobility, Richard seems to have been no less successful. Not surprisingly, the baronial members of his northern affinity figure prominently as beneficiaries of his largesse. Lords Scrope of Bolton, FitzHugh and Zouche were all given lands in south-central and south-western England, and Scrope, in addition, was appointed constable of Exeter at a fee of 200 marks and was given an annuity of £156 apart from his salary as a king's councillor.[45] Another member of Richard's council, Humphrey, Lord Dacre of Gilsland in Cumberland, was given an annuity of £100, but he benefited principally from Richard's removal from the government of the north-west. This left him as the most important lord in the region, and in September 1484 he was appointed lieutenant of the west march towards Scotland (under the king as warden), a position which was to form the basis of his family's growing power in the Tudor period.[46] Of these, Scrope, FitzHugh and Zouche were later to fight in Richard's army at Bosworth. Lord Dacre had died just two months before the battle, otherwise he would probably have been there too; his son, Thomas Dacre, almost certainly was. With these northerners, however, it would be wise to avoid suggesting too crude a causal connection between material gains and subsequent loyalty. Regional sentiment, earlier personal associations with Richard as duke, and long-standing associations with the Nevill family may all have played a part in influencing their decisions; and it is worth noting that, although neither had received any jot or tittle of his patronage, both Lords Lumley and Greystoke were to support the king in arms in 1485.

Richard also succeeded in attracting into his service a significant number of peers who had formerly been close supporters of Edward IV, whatever they may have thought about the fate of the former king's sons. Thus William Devereux, Lord Ferrers, who had been associated with the House of York since the 1450s and was connected by marriage with the Herbert family, fought at Bosworth despite his advanced years, and was killed in the battle. His loyalty had been rewarded with lands in Hertford-shire and an annuity charged on the revenues of the earldom of March, together worth some £146 a year. John, Lord Audley, another baronial work-horse of the Edwardian regime, became a royal councillor with an

[44] Lovell was also made chief butler of England, constable of England and a king's councillor, *CP*, VIII, 223–5; *CPR*, 365; Harl. 433, fos. 286–286v; for Lisle, Harl. 433, f. 284; *CP*, VIII, 59–60.

[45] Harl. 433, f. 285; *CPR*, 501–2 (Scrope of Bolton); Harl. 433, f. 285v (Zouche) and f. 287 (FitzHugh).

[46] *CPR*, 388, 485.

annuity of £100, and in December 1484 was appointed treasurer of the exchequer: he too seems to have been at Bosworth. Another royal councillor, John Sutton, Lord Dudley, was probably the son of the veteran who had been constable of the Tower of London until 1480, rather than the old man himself (who by then would have been in his eighties). Apart from his council fee of £100 yearly, his good services against the rebels in 1483 earned him lands in the midlands worth a similar annual sum, but whether he finally supported Richard we do not know.[47] John Brooke, Lord Cobham, may have been influenced in his political attitudes by his association with John Howard, duke of Norfolk, whose retainer he was, but his good services against the rebels in 1483 brought him lands in Devon, Cornwall and Kent. Henry, Lord Grey of Codnor, was well rewarded for his loyalty with lands worth £266 13s 4d yearly in Norfolk, Suffolk and Rutland, and he too was probably at Bosworth.[48] John, Lord Dinham was the head of a family which owed its entire advancement from the squirearchy to the patronage of Edward IV. His support was of value to Richard III, for his principal estates lay in the far west of England, an area where the king was politically weak, and he had been loyal during the rebellion of 1483. In return he was given lands in Hampshire and Devon worth £133 6s 8d, his brother Charles also obtaining lands on a similar if smaller scale, and in February 1484 John was appointed to the valuable office of chief steward of the Duchy of Cornwall, although apparently superseded in this position by Sir James Tyrell in August 1484.[49] In Edward V's reign Dinham had been deputy to Lord Hastings as captain of Calais, and although never himself promoted to this office, which went first to Lord Mountjoy and then to the king's bastard son John, he remained the effective resident commander of this major strategic fortress. At a time when the castles of the Calais Pale were rife with treason, Dinham remained loyal to Richard. His position at Calais explains his absence from Bosworth. Finally, Richard Hastings, Lord Willoughby and Welles, who owed his estates to the favour of Edward IV, no doubt through the good offices of his powerful brother William, was neither employed nor rewarded by Richard III; but he also seems to have donned his armour for the king in August 1485.[50]

These sixteen noblemen represent more than half the parliamentary baronage in 1485, and all may be reckoned, with some confidence, as firm supporters of the new king, not all for materialistic reasons. The political

[47] Harl. 433, f. 285 (Devereux); *CPR*, 384, 488; *CP*, IV, 341 (Audley); Harl. 433, f. 283v; *CPR*, 422, 452 (Dudley).
[48] Harl. 433, f. 283v; *CPR*, 433; *CP*, III, 346–7 (Cobham, £126 *p.a.*); Harl. 433, f. 283v (Grey of Codnor).
[49] Harl. 433, fos. 282v, 283; *CPR*, 386, 430; *CP*, IV, 378–9.
[50] *CP*, XII (ii), 446–7.

attitudes of the remaining ten are more difficult to determine, primarily because we have no evidence as to whether they took up arms on his behalf in 1485. One or two of them were certainly trusted by Richard. John, Lord Grey of Powys, for example, came of a family with long-term Yorkist connections, and was a kinsman of both the earl of Huntingdon and Lord Audley. In June 1484 he had been appointed captain of the force of 1,000 English archers which Richard sent to Brittany, and was later a commissioner in the negotiations with the Scots.[51] John Blount, Lord Mountjoy, had been temporarily governor of Calais, and then captain of Guisnes in the Calais Pale. He was removed from that office because his brother James had permitted the escape of the earl of Oxford from the castle of Guisnes early in 1485, but he may also have been an ailing man.[52] George Nevill, Lord Abergavenny, was one of the more significant omissions from the long list of Richard's beneficiaries in Harleian MS 433. He may have been actively resentful of Richard on personal grounds, since the king, as heir of Warwick the Kingmaker, was still occupying a considerable part of what he might well regard as his proper inheritance.[53]

Speculation about the political attitudes of such men remains a pleasurable but ultimately – for lack of evidence – a fruitless pastime. It should be remembered that even in the earlier stages of the Wars of the Roses, when participation in politics and, by extension, action on the battlefield, was still regarded by the nobility as a natural and dutiful activity, there was always a significant percentage of the peerage who, for one reason or another, did not appear on the battlefield. Old age, extreme youth, illness, a genuine reluctance to become involved, even the Vicar of Bray attitude which the Stanley family usually adopted, explain their absence from the fighting. By 1485, in comparison with 1459–61, attitudes had hardened. John Blount, Lord Mountjoy, who died in 1485, advised his son that it was dangerous to be great about princes.[54] Given the deaths in battle or on the block, and the forfeitures and confiscations of the previous thirty years, it was a forgiveable and understandable attitude, and offered a lesson which many of their Tudor descendants might well have taken to

[51] *CPR*, 517; *CP*, VI, 140–1.

[52] *CPR*, 385; Gairdner, 199–200; Kendall, 302, 486.

[53] That Richard continued Warwick's unlawful (or at best legally dubious) occupation of Abergavenny is shown by a number of annuities granted by him and chargeable on the revenues of the 'king's lordship' of Abergavenny, and the appointment of royal receivers therein (*CPR*, 421, 456, 474–5, 505). Similar considerations affected Richard's retention of the entire lordship of Glamorgan. For the background to the dispute, see R. L. Storey, *End of the House of Lancaster*, 230 ff.

[54] *CP*, IX, 338.

heart. Yet in this situation, where political commitment was clearly recognised as dangerous, it must he regarded as something of a success for Richard that he induced so many noblemen to support his cause in 1485. No less impressive is the fact that, apart from those in exile, no English peer declared himself for Henry Tudor until the issue was fairly joined at Bosworth.

For the greatest men of all – Buckingham, Norfolk, Northumberland and (with essential reluctance) Stanley – there was no avoiding a political choice. In the final analysis, and to a dangerous degree, Richard's political future depended upon the attitudes and loyalties of the heads of the four great surviving magnate families. They were the more important simply because they were so few. For a major aristocratic family in the later Middle Ages, survival was itself no mean task. There was always the risk of progenitive failure in the male line, which accounted for the disappearance of about a quarter of the aristocracy in each generation, but the troubled political conditions at home combined with the war in France until 1453 had enormously expanded the dangers for the higher aristocracy. Death in battle (at home or abroad) or on the executioner's block, for treason and conspiracy, had accounted for many leading members of the nobility. Forfeiture for treason and enforced exile had temporarily eclipsed the fortunes of others. Although there was often a younger brother or son to replace casualties of war and politics, survival rates were low. Few peerage families of the later fifteenth century had occupied a similar position as far back as the reign of Edward I, and the vast majority were more recent.[55] The pace of extinction among the higher nobility rose as the Wars of the Roses continued. When the civil wars began in 1455, a number of magnates had jostled with each other for political advantage, among them the dukes of York, Buckingham and Somerset, and the earls of Warwick, Salisbury, Northumberland, Devon, Shrewsbury and Wiltshire. Other magnates came and went, like the earl of Pembroke (killed in battle in 1469), the duke of Clarence (executed in 1478) and Lord Hastings (executed in 1483). Some magnate interests, and the wealth and local influence which they possessed, were absorbed into the crown: Richard III, for example, controlled the estates of the dukedom of York and the former earldoms of Salisbury and Warwick. But it was also inevitable that the few remaining independent magnates should increase their wealth and power as a direct consequence of survival. To the normal processes of marriage and inheritance, which increased their fortunes over the generations, was likely to be added a flow of royal favour in order to secure their loyalty and goodwill. Indeed royal policy in this respect had

[55] McFarlane, *Nobility of Later Medieval England*, 143–5, 172–6.

had much to do with the creation of 'over-mighty' or at least very mighty subjects.[56]

The four major magnates of Ricardian England were no exceptions to this rule and, given Richard's need for support, they could expect to see their family fortunes still further increased provided they chose to remain loyal to the new king. All four were powerful, but there were considerable differences in degree and in the ways that their power was exercised. Henry Stafford, 2nd duke of Buckingham, belonged to a family which was old by fifteenth-century standards, having acquired an earldom as far back as 1351, and a dukedom in 1444. Like the dukes of York, who by 1450 had united in their own hands the lands of many families (Warenne, Mortimer, Clare, Burgh, Geneville, Braose and Marshal), the Staffords had prospered through a series of lucrative marriages to heiresses, particularly to Anne, daughter of the royal prince, Thomas of Woodstock, who brought with her half the great inheritance of the Bohuns, earls of Hereford, as well as her father's estates. Royal favour had added to these advantages, particularly in Henry VI's reign, and by the mid-fifteenth century the first duke of Buckingham enjoyed a net income of some £5,500 yearly. It had not been diminished by 1483, and Duke Henry possessed an income substantially in excess of that of any private landowner of his time.[57] His power was enormously increased by the vast grants of office which he had received during the Protectorate, and his wide sphere of influence was made more official by the power of supervision given to him at the same time over all the king's subjects in Wales, the Marches and the adjoining counties of the Welsh-English border.[58]

If Buckingham's rebellion and execution removed the most overweening of over-mighty subjects, his disappearance merely served to enhance the political importance of the three surviving magnates. Their support became even more essential than before, and the price of securing their loyalty even higher. Two of them, Stanley and Northumberland, benefited substantially from Buckingham's fall. The third, John Howard, had already received rewards and inducements on a most generous scale. Although he came of an old-established gentry family in East Anglia, Howard himself had only recently (in 1469) achieved peerage rank, and owed his dukedom to Richard himself. But he had always had close connections with the Mowbray dukedom of Norfolk, and was already a substantial and active figure in East Anglian society. He had no difficulty, therefore, in succeeding with effectiveness to the estates and local influence

[56] See, for example, the rewards given to Richard Nevill, earl of Warwick, William, Lord Hastings and William Herbert, earl of Pembroke, in the 1460s (Ross, *Edward IV*, 70–8).

[57] McFarlane, *op. cit.*, 201–7.

[58] *CPR*, 349–50, 356.

of the Mowbray dukes, who, by 1476, had become the oldest-established non-royal ducal family in England. His wealth and power were greatly enhanced by the death in the autumn of 1483 of the most venerable dowager in England, Katherine Neville: she was the widow of the second duke, who had died as long ago as 1432. For over fifty years she had enjoyed not only her dower-third of the Mowbray estates but also an exceptionally large jointure, to the considerable impoverishment of her son and grandson, the third and fourth dukes. Her wide estates, many of them in East Anglia, now became available for division between the Mowbray co-heirs, William Berkeley and John Howard himself. Control of East Anglia by John Howard was further strengthened by Richard's own direct action. On 25 July 1483 he granted Howard some forty-six manors, many in Berkshire, Wiltshire and Cornwall, but also the manor of Lavenham and others in Norfolk and Suffolk belonging to the patrimony of the imprisoned Lancastrian, John de Vere, earl of Oxford, which Richard had himself held before he became king. On the same day, John Howard was also given the profits of twenty-five manors seized from the newly-executed Earl Rivers, all of them in East Anglia, but mainly in Norfolk. From his principal residence at Framlingham Castle in Suffolk, the new duke of Norfolk therefore effectively came to dominate East Anglia with a strength greater than that formerly enjoyed by the Mowbrays. Moreover, as a native of the region rather than an outsider (like the northerners implanted in the southern counties), he was well placed to command the loyalties and obedience of the local people. This particular exercise in patronage by King Richard paid handsome rewards. Conspicuously a loyal servant of Edward IV, Howard proved no less trustworthy for his new master. His services were invaluable during the rebellion of 1483 and, when the issue was joined in 1485, he proved to be the most important, and certainly the most reliable prop to Richard's throne.[59]

The career of Thomas, Lord Stanley stands out in sharp contrast to that of John Howard. Stanley had practised the equivocal art of political survivorship with considerable success but without much regard to faith or loyalty. Even in 1485 he might have equivocated to the end but for the action of his more impulsive brother, Sir William Stanley. Like Howard, however, Stanley came of a gentry family of decent antiquity, which had also recently (in 1456) risen to peerage status. Steadily but gradually, the Stanleys had emerged as the most important family in Lancashire, in Cheshire and the eastern parts of North Wales, especially with the gradual

[59] For a full discussion of Howard's career and rewards, see Anne Crawford, thesis cited above, p. 38; the grants of 25 July 1483 are in *CPR*, 359, 365. The death of Duchess Katherine is recorded in Harl. 433, f. 117v (appointment of a new receiver, 23 September 1483): some of the old lady's lands may already have been seized into the king's hands.

crumbling of the once-close connection which the kings of the House of Lancaster had maintained with their own palatine county. They had come to enjoy a monopoly of the major offices in Lancashire (except when challenged, briefly, by Richard himself in 1469) and in the later years of Edward IV's reign had acquired a significant place in what Dr D. A. L. Morgan has called the king's 'territorial re-ordering' of the realm on the basis of established spheres of influence.[60] In the crisis of 1483, Stanley's acute political instincts for once failed him, and he got too close to the losing side, being temporarily placed under arrest when Hastings was executed in June. By what means he extricated himself from this difficulty is not known, but he was soon at large again and basking in the sunshine of royal favour. His loyalty during Buckingham's rebellion was handsomely rewarded with a great grant of lands, some of them in the Welsh Marches and Cheshire, others, like the duke of Buckingham's lordship and castle of Thornbury in Gloucestershire, further south, to the value of £687 yearly. His brother, Sir William, was allowed to extend the family influence to North Wales.[61]

Yet the potential of Stanley's loyalty to Richard was always at very long odds: quite apart from his earlier equivocations, he remained the husband of the active and intriguing Margaret Beaufort, mother of Henry Tudor. True, Richard had tried to win his interest, not only by the grants mentioned above, but also by allowing him to keep the profits of his wife's forfeited estates. Richard III must always have been aware of the risks involved in trusting Stanley, as his eleventh-hour action, on the eve of Bosworth, in seizing Lord Strange, Stanley's eldest son and heir, sufficiently indicates. Yet what else was he to do? He could not attempt to destroy or expropriate the most powerful man in north-western England, except by the violent, illegal and unpopular means he had used to dispose of Rivers and Hastings in the summer of 1483, and any further acts of this kind would surely have raised suspicion and fear for their own positions among his existing supporters, especially the earl of Northumberland.

This fourth great magnate of the quartet came of a family which could exceed the Staffords and rival the Mowbrays in antiquity. Already substantial landowners in the north by the time of Domesday, they had been summoned as peers to parliament since the later thirteenth century, and had achieved an earldom in 1377. The influence which their wide northern estates brought them was compounded by the clannish nature

[60] Morgan, 'The King's Affinity in the Polity of Yorkist England', 19.
[61] Harl. 433, f. 284; CPR, 476; Morgan, op. cit., 19 (Lord Stanley, who was made constable of England with a fee of £100 p.a. in November 1483, CPR, 367). Sir William Stanley was appointed chief justice of North Wales on 12 November 1483, CPR, 368.

of northern society and the fierce traditional loyalties which this engendered, and by the lack of competition to their power, especially in the far north-east of the kingdom. The depth of this inherited strength is shown by the fact that successive kings could not do without them in the government of the north and the defence of the border. In spite of their comprehensive forfeitures for rebellion in 1405 and 1461, both Henry V and Edward IV had found it desirable and necessary to restore them to their former power: Edward even went so far as to allow them to recover former Percy lands which had been excluded from the act of restoration sanctioned by Henry V in 1418.[62] Yet their real influence in the north had been seriously eroded over five decades by the House of York and its allies, the Nevills, whose political successor in the north was Richard of Gloucester himself, first by the penetration of ambitious and greedy Nevills into Cumberland and Westmorland during the 1440s and 1450s, which greatly reduced the influence their wide estates should have commanded there, and secondly by the establishment of Richard of Gloucester to a commanding position in the north of England after 1471. Already by 1473 Gloucester and Henry, 4th earl of Northumberland, seem to have been at odds with each other, and it required the firm intervention of the king and his council to settle their differences. An 'appointment' between them reached in May 1473 was enshrined in a formal indenture in July 1474. In return for Gloucester's promise to stop poaching his retainers and followers, and thereby weakening his local influence, the earl agreed to become Richard's retainer and 'faithful servant'.[63]

This was scarcely a situation which could have commended itself to the head of an ancient and powerful family. Some indication of their relative strengths comes from a comparison between the retinues each took to France for Edward IV's invasion of 1475. Gloucester had 10 knights, 100 esquires or men-at-arms and 1,000 archers under his banner; Northumberland had 10 knights, 40 esquires and 200 archers. As time went on, the earl's position in relation to Gloucester became steadily worse. It was Richard, not Henry Percy, who became king's lieutenant in the north and principal commander when the Scottish wars began in the early 1480s; Richard's men began to predominate over Henry's in the commissions of array which raised troops for these campaigns; further grants of land and office to Richard in Yorkshire reduced Percy influence in this traditional region of their power; and the contrast between them is tellingly revealed

[62] J. M. W. Bean, *The Estates of the Percy Family, 1416–1537*, 69–80; Ross, *Edward IV*, 136, 144–5, 151.
[63] M. Weiss, 'A Power in the North? The Percies in the Fifteenth Century', *Historical Journal*, xix (1976), 501–9.

in their relations with the city of York, where, in their respective communications, Richard 'requires' and Northumberland 'prays'.[64]

Richard's accession to the throne brought no great relief to the pressure
on Northumberland. Although it left him as the most powerful man-on-
the-spot north of Trent, it did not bring a major recovery of Percy power.
The financial importance of the east march towards Scotland, traditionally an office which the Percies regarded as their own, had been declining.
In 1463, when occupied by John Nevill, Lord Montagu, the office of
Warden of the Marches had carried a fee of £3,000 yearly in peacetime,
but by 1477 this had fallen to £1,000, an insufficient sum for the earl,
whose landed revenues were far less than Duke Richard's, upon which to
support a large retinue. Some financial compensation was provided for
him, during the urgent days of the Protectorate, by his appointment on
20 May 1483 to the captaincy of the newly-recovered town of Berwick,
with the remarkable and inflated salary of £438 a month, or more than
£5,000 a year: it was therefore much more valuable than the wardenship
of the east march itself. But when the time came for the renewal of
Northumberland's incumbency of the office of warden (of the east and
middle marches), it was made for only one year, from 10 May 1483. The
subsequent renewal, in August 1484, was by Richard as king rather than
Protector.[65] This scarcely represents a vote of confidence by Richard in
Henry, since such appointments in the past had been regularly made for
five, six or ten years, sometimes to a father and son jointly in survivorship
for twenty years.[66]

The final blow to Northumberland's pride may have come from
Richard's decision to introduce a degree of devolution into the government of the north, especially in Yorkshire, and to nominate his nephew,
John de la Pole, earl of Lincoln, a 'foreigner' with no northern estates or
connections, as its president. All this may well explain why Northumberland seems to have been a somewhat tardy and reluctant supporter of
Richard during the usurpation, and only the pressures which Richard
put upon him forced him to come out into the open.[67]

He needed to be placated. It is true that he received rich rewards,

[64] Ross, *Edward IV*, 199–203; *YCR*, I, 34–5. Richard's predominance in relation
to York city is also sharply revealed in the thanks the city gave him for his good lordship, and its prayers that it should be 'of good continuance' (*ibid.*, 51–2), and in the
number and value of the presents given Duke Richard in comparison to those to the
earl.

[65] R. L. Storey, 'The Wardens of the Marches of England towards Scotland',
*EHR*, lxxii (1957), 615, for the wardenship of the east and middle marches (grant
wrongly dated to 9 April 1483); *Grants of Edward IV*, 19–23. (20 May, Richard as
Protector, for the captaincy of Berwick.)

[66] Storey, *op. cit.*, 615.

[67] See below, pp. 181 ff.

although not on the same scale as Buckingham or Norfolk. As Norfolk was made Admiral of England, and Stanley Constable, so Northumberland became Steward of England; he was given the valuable Buckingham lordship of Holderness in Yorkshire, worth well over £1,000 yearly, and upon terms which made it possible for him to provide for the future welfare and support of his younger son, Alan; and he was allowed to recover lands which he claimed by inheritance, the Brienne and Bures estates in south-west England.[68] But the grants were apparently not enough to offset Northumberland's sense of pique, and it is possible that he was already in treasonable correspondence with Henry of Richmond before the invasion of 1485.[69]

The political and military importance of these two great northern magnates can be illustrated simply and forcibly. If we accept the figures given by Polydore Vergil for the size of the contingents they brought to Bosworth (which may be exaggerated but can be related to the figures he gives for other forces at the battle), then the combined strength of Stanley's and Northumberland's followings exceeded that of the rest of Richard's army, and considerably surpassed the entire force at Richmond's disposal.[70] Here, if at all, lies any truth which may be contained in Sir Thomas More's remark that 'By great gifts [Richard] got himself unsteadfast friendship', and the behaviour of Stanley and (perhaps) Northumberland on the battlefield is a compelling illustration of the limitations of patronage when matched against the ambitions, fears or resentment of individual magnates. It is also a telling commentary on the inherent dangers of a political situation which had led, partly through the policies of kings, partly as a consequence of survivorship in an age of civil war, to the excessive concentration of power at the apex of English aristocratic society in the hands of so few men. Never again were the attitudes of just three or four over-mighty subjects able to exercise so decisive an influence on the survival or death of an English monarch.

[68] Harl. 433, f. 287v; CPR, 367, 409; and for the complicated question of the Brienne and Bures inheritance, Bean, op. cit., 116-23.

[69] A. Goodman and A. Mackay, 'A Castilian Report on English Affairs, 1486', EHR, lxxxviii (1973), 92-99, esp. 95-6.

[70] PV, 218, 223-4.

Chapter 9

# THE GOVERNMENT OF THE REALM

Richard III's reign was too short to allow him to make much significant change in the ways in which his realm was governed, even had he wished to do so. Political necessities forced upon him certain innovations, but for the most part his government was essentially conservative in character. He had no choice but to rely upon the tried and proven methods developed by his elder brother over the previous twenty years, which were to be maintained (after an initial hiccup due to his own inexperience) by that cautious statesman Henry VII for a further twenty-five years. Richard inherited from Edward IV a highly personal system of government, where a great deal depended upon the judgement, energy and application to business of the king himself, aided by a group of advisers whose importance derived less from any offices they might hold than from the degree of confidence which the king placed in them. Every kind of government business came to the king's attention and was decided by him and his councillors. Even the long-established departments of state, such as the chancery and exchequer, had little freedom of initiative, but were subject to regular and rigorous royal control.[1]

These features of Ricardian government may be illustrated, firstly, from the evidence provided by that unique and precious record known as British Library Harleian Manuscript 433, a collection of copies of documents which passed the signet during the reigns of Edward V and Richard III, bound up with a variety of memoranda and lists, mainly of financial interest, which were useful to the clerks of the signet office.[2] 'The signet was the king's own seal, kept by his secretary, and was used to authenticate documents originating with the king himself.' The document therefore directly illuminates the intense personal activity of the king in all matters of government, ranging from such affairs of state as preparations to resist invasion or high-level diplomatic negotiations down to instructions to

---

[1] Ross, *Edward IV*, 299–413, *passim*, and especially 299–307 on 'Personal Government'.

[2] The nature and importance of this MS is now fully explained by Rosemary Horrox, 'British Library Harleian Manuscript 433', *The Ricardian*, v (1979), 87–91, and her learned introduction to the printed edition, ed. Horrox and Hammond, I, ix–xlvix. Dr Horrox explains that, although the survival of the MS is fortuitous, it probably did not represent any administrative innovation (*op. cit.*, xvi).

19. The Admiralty Seal of Richard III.

20. James III of Scotland, a painting by Van der Goes, with his son,
the future James IV, kneeling behind him.

tenants on one of his wife's manors to practise their archery, stop playing tennis and bowls and desist from poaching the king's game or directions about the mowing of hay at Warwick.[3] It would not do to suggest that there was anything revolutionary about all this. Active kings had always shouldered a large share of the burden of decision- and policy-making.[4] But the level of the king's personal involvement certainly increased during the reign of the Yorkist kings, and there was innovation, too, in that so much of government action was now initiated by the king from within the context of his personal household, especially in matters of finance, rather than through established offices of state, such as the office of privy seal, the chancery and the exchequer.

Secondly, continuity of method is reflected in continuity of personnel. So personal a system of government depended on the initiative and expertise of trusted individuals rather than on the routine activities of bureaux, and Richard had necessarily to rely on the accumulated experience of men trained under his brother's regime. Changes were made only when politically necessary and desirable, and hence only in the higher echelons of government. The presumed loyalty of Edward IV's last chancellor, Thomas Rotherham, archbishop of York, to Edward's heir, and (if More is to be believed) his complacency in handing over the Great Seal to Elizabeth Woodville, led to his early dismissal.[5] Bishop Russell's preferment to the chancellorship made vacant his own office of keeper of the privy seal, which was filled by another former servant of Edward IV, John Gunthorpe, dean of Wells. The appointment of a new treasurer stemmed from natural causes: the long-serving Edwardian treasurer, Henry earl of Essex, died five days before his royal master, and was replaced by the under-treasurer from 1480 to 1483, Sir John Wood.[6] The loyalist sympathies of Edward IV's secretary, Oliver King, presumably explain his removal from office and imprisonment in the middle of June 1483, and his replacement by Richard's own private secretary, John Kendall.[7]

It was equally to be expected that, in a body of such political importance as the king's council, there would also be a number of changes. Men with loyalist or Woodville sympathies disappear. New men were introduced: some were northerners, but there was also a group of experienced estates officials and financial experts who had served in these capacities under King Edward but had not previously been councillors.

[3] Horrox, *Ricardian*, 88, 90.

[4] See, for example, for Henry IV's reign, A. L. Brown, 'The Authorization of Letters under the Great Seal', *BIHR*, xxxvii (1964), 125–56.

[5] Mancini, 85, and Armstrong's note 64; More, 22.

[6] Above, pp. 76–7.

[7] Horrox and Hammond, I, xvi; *Stonor Letters*, II, 161.

Even so, of fifty-four men named as councillors under Richard, no less than twenty-six had also been on Edward's council; nine were to continue in office under Henry Tudor.[8] It was unusual, even in this age of political upheaval, to disturb the judiciary, which was rightly regarded as apolitical. Richard found it necessary to make only one change: the Bishop of Ely's nephew, Robert Morton, was removed from his position as master of the rolls on 23 September 1483 and was replaced by one of Richard's own legal counsel, Thomas Barowe.[9] It was a similar story with the body of financial experts and estates administrators who managed the king's revenues. Sir Thomas Vaughan, who had been treasurer of the chamber to Edward IV, had also had very close associations with the leading Woodvilles and was executed together with Earl Rivers at Pontefract on 25 June 1483, his place being taken by Master Edmund Chadderton, a member of Richard's ducal council and his household chaplain, who was to become a member of the royal council.[10] Otherwise, Edward's professional servants accepted the new regime, and it has been suggested that their continuing loyalty to whoever held the crown was one of the reasons for the failure of Buckingham's rebellion. Even more than had been the case under Edward IV, these men – the receivers and auditors of the royal lands, including the Duchy of Lancaster, and those lands which came to the king by forfeiture – were freed from exchequer control and accounted to the officials of the king's chamber only: its treasurer had to account to the king in person.[11]

A medieval king was bound by the terms of his coronation oath to certain high moral duties – to keep the peace to clergy and people, to do justice in mercy and truth and to maintain the laws.[12] On a more pragmatic level, he had to defend his realm against outside attack, to repress disorder, which was only too often linked with sedition and the danger of rebellion, and to finance the administration of the realm.

[8] See the lists in Lander, *Crown and Nobility*, 318–20. The introduction into the council of financial officials such as Edmund Chadderton, Avery Cornburgh and Richard Salkeld may help to explain the attempts to tighten up financial administration (below, pp. 179 ff).

[9] Morton fled abroad to join Henry Tudor, returned with him in 1485 (*CC*, 502–3), and became bishop of Worcester in October 1486. It is interesting to notice that the date of Morton's dismissal (i.e. three weeks before Buckingham's rebellion broke out) coincides exactly with the seizure of the temporalities of Lionel Woodville's see of Salisbury (Harl. 433, f. 117v; Horrox, *Ricardian*, 89–90), which perhaps suggests that Richard already suspected that plots were being hatched against him.

[10] Wolffe, *Royal Demesne*, 181–2.

[11] *Ibid.*, 182–4.

[12] S. B. Chrimes, *English Constitutional Ideas in the Fifteenth Century*, 19 and 14–21 *passim*.

A good case has recently been argued that, for Richard, the maintenance of the law and the proper dispensing of justice was more than a mere well-intentioned aspiration.[13] Certainly, he was much concerned that justice should be seen to be done, even if this wish be interpreted as no more than a part of his campaign to present himself to his subjects in a favourable and beneficent light, and he made every effort to give full publicity to these good intentions. His first act on seating himself on the throne in Westminster Hall on 26 June 1483 was to call all the judges before him 'commanding them in right strait manner that they justly and duly minister his law without delay or favour'. A fortnight later, the coronation festivities completed, 'he sent home the lords into their countries' and commanded them that they should see 'the countries where they dwelled well guided and that no extortions were done to his subjects'.[14] Other well-publicized examples of the king's concern with law and justice are to be found in more than one of his royal proclamations. That issued, in the aftermath of Buckingham's rebellion, to the people of Kent makes a central issue of this concern:[15]

the king's highness is fully determined to see due administration of justice throughout this his realm to be had and to reform, punish and subdue all extortions and oppressions in the same.

It was the king's will that, during his visitation of the county,

every person ... that find himself grieved, oppressed or unlawfully wronged do make a bill of his complaint, and put it to his highness, and he shall be heard and without delay have such convenient remedy as shall accord with his laws. For his grace is utterly determined all his true subjects shall live in rest and quiet and peaceably enjoy their lands, livelihoods and goods according to the laws of this his land, which they be naturally born to inherit.

Another proclamation of December 1484 likewise stressed the king's love for the ministration of justice, and promised that any man who found himself wronged by a royal officer or other person should complain to the king, and 'according to Justice and his laws they shall have remedy'.[16]

Richard was regularly at pains to insist that legal remedy was readily at hand for all his subjects should they need it. Following a riot by the common people of York over disputed rights of pasture, the king sent

[13] Anne Sutton, 'The Administration of Justice Whereunto We Be Professed', *The Ricardian*, iv (1976), 4–15; Kendall, 306–8; but cf. the reservations noted below, p. 175.

[14] *GC*, 232–3; Vitellius A XVI, in Kingsford, *Chronicles of London*, 191.

[15] Harl. 433, f. 128v; ed. Horrox and Hammond, II, 48–9.

[16] Harl. 433, f. 273.

two letters to the city in October 1484, and it is interesting that his messenger was no less a person than Sir Robert Percy, the controller of the royal household.[17] That addressed to the mayor and the civic authorities merely expressed his displeasure at their failure to keep the peace. The much longer 'credence unto the commons' reproved them for taking the law into their own hands without submitting their demands to the mayor and his brethren. But if, the king continues, they had no lawful remedy in that quarter, then they should have brought their grievances before the earl of Lincoln or the earl of Northumberland (presumably as members of the Council in the North). If this too failed, then the king thinks they should have applied to himself, 'where you should have had convenient reformation and redress in every behalf according to right and conscience'. An extension of this was the added emphasis which Richard gave to what is nowadays called 'legal aid', that is, provision for the needs of poor persons who could not normally afford to go to law, a form of redress which later developed into the Tudor Court of Requests.[18]

Like many well-born young men of his time, Richard had enjoyed an education which probably included some instruction in the law.[19] Certainly, some legal knowledge was a desirable asset in any man called upon to control great estates in that land-hungry and litigious age. But Richard's interest in legal matters seems to have gone beyond the conventional. The best example of this facet of his character is his summoning a session of the Court of Exchequer Chamber, a grand legal assembly of all the judges and serjeants at law from the central courts which acted like a modern House of Lords, in its judicial capacity, as an ultimate tribunal on points of law. This meeting took place before Richard in person in the inner Star Chamber to answer three questions posed by the king, who cited the specific cases which had prompted his personal interference. They were not easily answered, and one provoked a complicated discussion: the king said that he was perturbed that offenders in this case should go unpunished, and was himself present in the court of king's bench at Westminster when four of the culprits were found guilty and fined.[20] It is not wholly unlikely that Richard's personal interest in legal matters had something to do with the pronounced emphasis on law reform which runs through the legislation of his only parliament.[21]

This evidence of Richard's proper concern with justice and the im-

[17] YCR, I, 104–5.

[18] CPR, 413, for John Harington's appointment as clerk of the council to deal with requests from poor persons.

[19] Ross, Edward IV, 8–9.

[20] Select Cases before the Exchequer Chamber, ed. M. Hemmant (Selden Society, 1948), II, xxxviii–xl, 86–94.

[21] Below, pp. 187–90.

partial administration of the law deserves its due consideration. It was at once morally laudable and politically shrewd. But it is important to remember the other side of the coin. We have already seen a number of instances which have a contrary weight. As duke of Gloucester, Richard was prepared to act without regard to either law or justice in his treatment of the countess of Oxford and his kinsman, George Nevill; as Protector, he did not hesitate to invade the lands of Earl Rivers and Thomas Grey, marquis of Dorset, although the council held that there was no case against them, and his seizure of the estates of the Holand Duchy of Exeter was in flagrant defiance of an act of parliament (later annulled).[22] As king, he had not scrupled to grant away the lands of the rebels of 1483 without authority of parliament, and to do so without the due taking of inquisitions which protected the rights of innocents: this process was in train when he was assuring his subjects in Kent of his concern for precisely these rights. In granting the estates of the Mowbray dukedom of Norfolk to John Howard and William Berkeley, he unlawfully disendowed the young Richard duke of York, since Richard's rights had nothing to do with inheritance or the fact that he was proclaimed a bastard, but depended upon an act of the parliament of 1483 – an act, moreover, which Richard could easily have caused to be repealed in his own parliament of 1484, but did not chose to do so.[23] Richard's apparently genuine concern with law and justice had its clearly defined limits. It was never allowed to override the demands of practical politics.

Richard proved himself an energetic and efficient king. He may have benefited from good advice from an experienced body of councillors and ministers, but the final responsibility was his own. His application to business certainly matched that of his elder brother, even if it could not quite parallel that of Henry VII. There is no hint in the administrative records of the reign of the nervous agonies or political palsy attributed to him by some of the chronicles and by his principal modern biographer.[24] He moved about his realm to an extraordinary degree and was rarely in one place for more than a few weeks at a time. To some extent, this

[22] For the Exeter inheritance, Ross, *Edward IV*, 336–7; Wolffe, *op. cit.*, 183–4. The act of 1483 is in *RP*, VI, 215–18, and Richard's annulment, *ibid.*, 242–4. The confiscation of the dower lands granted by Edward IV to Queen Elizabeth Woodville was authorized by a statute in the parliament of 1484, cap. 15 (*Statutes of the Realm*, II, 498).

[23] For the act of 1483, *RP*, VI, 205–7; Ross, *Edward IV*, 335–6.

[24] Fabyan's *Chronicle*, 673; PV, 191, 212; Kendall, 325, describes 1485 for Richard as 'a period of supension, the man turned inward upon himself ... these months represent a withdrawal, a lonely wrestling with the shapes of the past and the mocking, amorphous images of the future'.

peripatetic behaviour was imposed upon him by the necessities of the defence of the realm and resistance to internal threats to his regime, such as his westward journey to Exeter in the aftermath of Buckingham's rebellion.[25] But he well understood the political value of the official royal progress, most clearly demonstrated in his long tour of the midlands and the north in the summer and early autumn of 1483. To display to his subjects the majesty of the king's person and the splendour of his entourage was an exercise which still had a more than symbolic importance: the royal progress could also be used in a quasi-judicial fashion to assert the royal authority in the more distant parts of the realm.[26] By comparison with other kings, Richard spent little time in London or Westminster or the various royal residences in the Thames valley favoured by Edward IV. Nottingham Castle, with its modern residential apartments, seems to have been his preferred residence, but probably because of its strategic position as a centre to strike against invasion.[27] Richard's long absences from the capital are at least in part an explanation of the increased activity of the signet as a means of conducting the business of the realm.

Within the administrative framework he inherited from his brother, Richard and his advisers strove to tighten and improve existing procedures. In some degree, this also involved a further centralization, forced upon him by his acute shortage of reliable manpower. Many tasks could only be given to men close to the king and fully trusted by him. Thus much of the work of taking into the king's hands, organizing and administering lands went to his secretary, John Kendall, his chamber treasurer, Edmund Chadderton, and his solicitor, Thomas Lynom. Chadderton was also given personal charge, as receiver and surveyor, of most of Buckingham's forfeited lands. Royal manors in the south-east were placed in the control of Sir Robert Brackenbury, who had been treasurer of Richard's ducal household. The lands of Elizabeth Woodville, taken from her in 1483, were to be managed by John FitzHerbert, king's remembrancer of the exchequer. But the best illustration of this point lies in the orders sent

[25] Above, p. 117.

[26] Ross, *Edward IV*, 400–2.

[27] In 1484, for example, the king left Westminster early in March after a three-month stay (broken by an excursion into Kent in January). Moving north through Cambridge and Stamford, he then spent six weeks in Nottingham (where he heard of the death of his son). May saw him in York, Middleham, Durham, Scarborough (for naval preparations against the Scots) and York again; in June and July he was in Pontefract, Sandal, York and Scarborough, back again to Pontefract and York, reaching Nottingham on 30 July and not returning to Westminster until 9 August. Late August found him back in Nottingham where he remained (save for a brief visit to Tutbury) until early November, and did not return to the south until 13 November. The last few weeks of the year he divided between Westminster and Windsor. (Harl. 433, ed. Horrox and Hammond, II, 69–185 *passim*.)

to the men of Glamorgan to continue to be attendant upon Sir James Tyrell even after he had been sent to France in January 1485 as captain of Guisnes.[28]

Richard's efforts towards administrative improvement are especially noticeable in financial affairs, but not exclusively so. The good behaviour of his officials and a concern to assure the loyalty of his subjects are also obvious. A set of instructions issued to Sir Marmaduke Constable on his appointment as steward of the important Duchy of Lancaster honour of Tutbury was probably one of many such directives sent to the king's agents in similar positions.[29] It orders Constable to secure a special oath of allegiance from all the inhabitants of the honour: they were to be retained by the king and no one else. County bailiffs found guilty of extortions and oppressions were to be removed, and provision was made for the hearing of complaints against such persons; the king's own tenants were to be preferred to others in the granting of land-leases; local estate officials were to be fully attendant to their duties, and bailiffs were to be chosen from 'good and sufficient persons able to do the king service'.[30]

The distribution of patronage apart, the administrative records of Richard's reign are dominated by the problem of finance. The Croyland Chronicler believed that Richard was cushioned financially by his inheritance of a substantial treasure from Edward IV, although Mancini tells us that much of this was whisked away by the Woodvilles during the Protectorate; even Croyland admits that by 1485 Richard was running short of funds. The administrative records of his reign suggest that a financial crisis occurred much earlier, and this remained a constant preoccupation, especially given the expensive operations against the Scots during 1484.[31] Richard found himself in a position not dissimilar to but initially more advantageous than that of his brother, Edward IV, in

[28] Wolffe, *Royal Demesne*, 180–3, for the officials; for Tyrell and the men of Glamorgan, Harl. 433, fos. 201, 205; ed. Horrox and Hammond, II, 187–8, 197.

[29] Harl. 433, fos. 270–270v; printed in Gairdner, *Letters and Papers*, I, 79–81, and in Wolffe, *Crown Lands*, 131–3. The instructions were probably issued during the king's brief visit to Tutbury on 25 and 26 October 1484 (Harl. 433, f. 193).

[30] But cf. the comments of Horrox (Horrox and Hammond, I, xxix) on such clauses and similar ones in the general 'remembrance' on the king's revenues discussed below (p. 179) that they struck at the roots of the local patronage exercised by royal office-holders by depriving them of the right to appoint their own deputies. 'In practice,' she adds, 'the king could not insist on such recommendations' (which) 'had little impact on local patronage'.

[31] *CC*, 567, 571–2; Mancini, 78–9; Horrox, *op. cit.*, xxix; for the low levels of revenue handled by the exchequer (mainly customs duties, as from the 23 January 1484 and clerical subsidies), see A. B. Steel, *The Receipt of the Exchequer, 1377–1485*, 317–20, but the main part of Richard's revenues was being handled by the chamber.

1461. He had an unusually large amount of landed revenue at his disposal from the very beginning of his reign, whether it were royal, of his own family's or his wife's inheritance, or from the elimination of his political opponents in the process of his usurpation, and, by comparison with most other kings, the necessary financial burdens of supporting a royal family were slight indeed. Political necessities also compelled him to alienate the larger part of the great accession of revenue from land and offices which came to the crown as a consequence of the rebellion of 1483.[32] But this still left him with an income from land, according to a modern calculation, of some £22,000 to £25,000 annually, exclusive of a further £7,000, disbursed in fees and wages, derived from offices in the king's gift.[33]

But the very bouyancy of these landed revenues placed him at a disadvantage in seeking to supplement his income from direct taxation (as Edward IV had discovered in 1461).[34] In 1484 a reasonably docile house of commons was prepared to vote him indirect taxation for life (the customs duties), but he could not risk asking it for a lay subsidy, although he was successful in inducing the convocation of Canterbury to grant him two clerical subsidies, in 1484 and 1485.[35] But Edward IV's experience in 1482–3 had already shown the extraordinary difficulties of trying to conduct a war with Scotland without the help of direct lay taxation (to which Edward himself eventually had recourse), especially if offensives were to be mounted by sea as well as by land;[36] and Richard had, in addition, to prepare against foreign invasion and meet the expenses of suppressing domestic rebellion.

Financial stringency was apparent early in the reign. On 6 January 1484, Richard sent out letters to all the receivers of the various royal

[32] Above, pp. 118–24.

[33] Wolffe, op. cit., 188, 190.

[34] Ross, Edward IV, 348–9.

[35] J. H. Ramsay, Lancaster and York, II, 554–60, calculated the customs revenue at about £20,000 annually, and the yield of the Canterbury tenths at about £12,000 each. It is to be noted that, as well as being unable to ask parliament for direct taxation, Richard had thought it politic to remit the subsidy voted to Edward IV in the parliament of January 1483 (RP, VI, 401.)

[36] Ross, Edward IV, 386. It is quite impossible to calculate the costs of defence, but at times of threatened invasion quite large garrisons were maintained in strategically important castles: see, e.g., the orders of 6 March 1484 to pay Sir James Tyrell for the wages of 140 soldiers in his retinue at Carmarthen at the rate of 6d a day and of June 1484 for Sir John Huddleston's retinue of 40 soldiers at Beaumaris Castle (Harl. 433, fos. 163v, 179; Horrox and Hammond, II, 114, 143). Much money was also spent on repairs to a number of castles, e.g., York, Kenilworth and Tutbury (Harl. 433, fos. 183v, 192; Horrox and Hammond, II, 152, 168). In March 1485 bows, arrows, gunpowder and ordnance were being sent for the defence of Harwich (f. 217; II, 223).

estates and lands in the king's hands commanding them to pay in at once all monies due from them, 'not failing hereof as you will answer to us at your peril'. These followed upon the heels of others of similar content, which had not been complied with 'to our great marvel'.[37] No less significant is the well-known 'remembrance' for the 'hasty levy' of the king's revenues from lands, issued in October 1484. This directive, among other things, required the exchequer to be far more importunate in demanding early payment of sums due from royal officers, but it also discharged the exchequer of responsibility for a variety of receipts, on the grounds that these might be better administered elsewhere, by auditors answerable to the king's chamber. Such men were to exercise the greatest care in ensuring that all possible sources of income to the king were fully exploited, especially what were called casual revenues, such as might come from the felling of standing timber. The auditors themselves were to be men of quality and substance; lords, knights and esquires, 'many of them not lettered', were to be replaced as stewards of the king's lands by men learned in the law, who would not abuse their positions by 'taking great fines and rewards of the king's tenants to their proper use', and would not 'be wanting cunning and discretion' in exploiting the king's revenues to the full. Full annual accounts, a sort of budget, were to be presented by the treasurer of England and others.[38]

None of this staved off severe financial difficulties by the early months of 1485. The king had then to make recourse to allegedly 'forced' loans, although these were not the benevolences which Richard had condemned in parliament.[39] Ample data (carefully preserved) existed in government records about persons who could be called upon for administrative and (to use a modern term) 'party political' services. The right men were valued for a likely loan in letters entrusted to the usual agents. Thus the archbishop of York could lend £200, the bishop of Worcester £50, the abbot of Westminster 200 marks and the abbot of Cirencester £100. In the shires of Norfolk and Suffolk, John Wingfield, esquire, might be expected to supply £100, as also could Sir Edmund Bedingfield.[40] The surviving lists are not complete, and we have no means of knowing how much cash Richard raised by these means.[41] Yet, even if the loans were obtained by a mixture of placation and pressure, rather than outright

---

[37] Harl. 433, fos. 138v, 139; Horrox and Hammond, II, 70-1; Wolffe, *Crown Lands*, 124-6.

[38] Harl. 433, fos. 271-2; printed *Letters and Papers*, I, 81-4; summarized and discussed in Wolffe, *Crown Lands*, 62-3, 133-7; *Royal Demesne*, 186-8.

[39] For the benevolence, below, p. 189. Cf, *CC*, 498.

[40] Harl. 433, fos. 275v-277v.

[41] Ramsay, *Lancaster and York*, II, 532-4, 557, suggested £20,000 as a likely total; cf. Steel, *Receipt of the Exchequer*, 320-1, for a more sceptical view.

threat, they could scarcely have been popular even with those committed to the regime. If we may believe the *Great Chronicle of London*, Richard was having severe problems of cash-flow even a year earlier, and had been reduced to pledging a variety of crown jewels in order to obtain loans from prominent London citizens to meet the great charges he had incurred in the suppression of the rebellion of 1483. These loans were obtained by personal pressure from the king: 'he *instanced* them himself . . . to lend unto him certain sums,' says the Chronicle.[42] As with so much else concerning Richard's brief reign, revenue problems are a decapitated story, but it is permissible to suggest that the continuation of the war with Scotland in the summer of 1484 (especially since it involved costly naval operations) was an expensive error in view of Richard's financial position.[43]

Under Henry VII, as recent research has revealed, widespread use was made of a system of bonds and recognizances as a means of controlling and disciplining the king's subjects: Henry has been accused of holding them in awe by 'a terrifying system of suspended penalties'.[44] What has not been sufficiently appreciated is the extent to which such techniques were already employed by the Yorkist kings.[45] But, given the brevity of his reign, Richard used them far more intensively than Edward IV had done. As a weapon of political control, he directed them especially against those implicated in the 1483 rebellion.[46] Groups of men were made to stand surety, often in considerable sums of money, for the good behaviour of the principal offender, thus hanging financial penalties not only over him but also over his associates, friends or kinsmen. Thus the sureties for Thomas Leukenor had to find 1,000 marks that he would be of good and true bearing towards King Richard III and his heirs and serve him in peace and war when required; for Sir Richard Woodville the price was 2,000 marks, and the same for Sir William Berkeley. Often specific con-

---

[42] *GC*, 235–6. Although the chronology of the chronicle is here confused, the reference to the period following Buckingham's rebellion is clear, and the chronicler's first-hand knowledge of the proceedings is shown by his description of the king's pledges and his mention of the reward to the chamber of London for making these loans (a flat cup with a gold cover, garnished with diamonds and pearls, worth 100 marks).

[43] For these operations, see below, chap. 10. Richard's direct interest in the naval operations is shown by his repeated visits to Scarborough in the summer of 1484 and is stressed by the Croyland Chronicler (Harl. 433, fos. 174v, 181, 181v; Horrox and Hammond, II, 134, 146–7; *CC*, 571).

[44] J. R. Lander, 'Bonds, coercion and fear: Henry VII and the peerage', in *Crown and Nobility*, 267–300, especially 276.

[45] P. M. Barnes, 'The chancery corpus cum causa file, 10–11 Edward IV', in *Medieval Legal Records*, ed. R. F. Hunnisett and J. B. Post, 430–76, especially 438.

[46] Above, p. 113.

ditions were laid down: Leukenor was to abide with Sir John Wood, the treasurer of England, 'until the king's pleasure was known on his behalf'; Nicholas Gaynesford, esquire, was not to enter Kent without royal licence.[47] Bonds could also be used as a means of keeping the peace between powerful participants in private disputes. The abbot of Waltham had to find £1,000 to keep the peace towards Lord Ferrers, his servants and the inhabitants of Cheshunt, and Ferrers was bound over in the same sum in reverse fashion. A group of seven established Yorkists, including Edward Grey, Viscount Lisle, and Richard Redman, esquire, were bound over in August 1484 in sums ranging from 1,000 to 500 marks to keep the peace, meanwhile remaining within the city of London or no more than a mile outside. A feature of many of these penal bonds was the close interest taken by the king and council in the settlement of such private quarrels. For example, Thomas Grene, gentleman, of Green's Norton, Northamptonshire, was bound over in 1,000 marks – a very large sum for a man of his station – to appear before king and council and stand and obey the king's award in a long-standing dispute with the Delves family.[48] On one occasion at least Richard also anticipated a development much extended by Henry VII of taking bonds even from trusted servants for their loyalty and good conduct in the performance of their duties as royal office-holders: one of Richard's faithful Yorkshire-men, Sir John Saville, was bound over in 5,000 marks on his appoint-ment to be keeper of the vulnerable Isle of Wight 'to keep the island to the use and surety of our lord'.[49] As guarantees of political loyalty, the bonds taken from former rebels may have had a limited value in dis-suading them from giving active support to Henry Tudor in 1485, as Sir Walter Hungerford and Sir Thomas Bourchier (pardoned but not bonded) were to do. But his use of the system in general shows that Richard shared with Henry VII an awareness of the value of deploying the prerogative powers of the crown as a means of governing a lawless land.

Richard's one major institutional innovation was largely imposed upon him by the circumstances of his accession. In Wales and the Marches Edward IV had introduced a conciliar solution to the problem of regional disorder and disaffection by creating a council nominally under the prince of Wales, with the aid of members of the Woodville group and experienced professional administrators such as John Alcock, bishop first of Rochester and then of Worcester. In the north of England he chose instead to give semi-regal authority to Richard himself, especially in Yorkshire and the north-west.[50] Richard's departure to the throne left a power-vacuum in

---

[47] Barnes, *op. cit.*, 440; *CCR*, 365, 369.
[48] *CCR*, 388, 420, 426.
[49] *CCR*, 419.
[50] Ross, *Edward IV*, 193–203; and above, pp. 44 ff.

these notoriously troubled and rebellious areas. Clearly, there was no one with strength in the north whom he was prepared to trust, as he initially trusted Buckingham in Wales and the Marches, with the power north of Trent he had himself enjoyed. Instead, he chose to follow his brother's Welsh solution by creating a Council of the North. This may have been intended originally to have been nominally the council of his heir, Edward of Middleham, but with the prince's death in April 1484 he institutionalized it as a formal branch of the royal council proper under the presidency of his next male heir, John de la Pole, earl of Lincoln. His appointment was in itself an innovation, for Lincoln was a stranger to the north, having no experience of its affairs and possessing neither 'livelihood' nor 'conversement' in the region. Otherwise, the composition of the council is unknown, but it is likely that Lincoln had the support of a number of experienced northerners, who were among those appointed to the important commission of array for Yorkshire of 8 December 1484. These included the earl of Northumberland, Yorkshire barons like Lords Greystoke, Scrope of Bolton and Scrope of Masham, substantial local knights like Sir John Conyers and lawyers with northern connections such as Miles Metcalfe and Robert Danby.[51]

The area over which the council was to exercise jurisdiction is equally unclear. Its base was to be at Sandal Castle, near Wakefield in West Yorkshire. During his visit there in June 1484, Richard authorized the building of a new tower in the castle, presumably along the lines of the residential apartments at Nottingham Castle, and later (in October) the construction of a new bakehouse and brewhouse was authorized on the advice of Lincoln and others 'of the king's council lying there'.[52] The council was, however, already in residence by 20 July, when expenses were assigned for its maintenance, and in October a permanent assignment of 2,000 marks a year was made for 'the king's household' there, now under the control of John Dawnay, formerly treasurer of the prince's household: there is no evidence that it was ever based, as is sometimes claimed, at Sheriff Hutton.[53] The sessions of the council were, however, to be held at York, which makes it seem likely that its authority was

---

[51] For the council of the north in general, Rachel Reid, *The King's Council in the North*, especially 1–70 (which, however, contains a number of misconceptions); F. W. Brooks, *The Council of the North* (Historical Association Pamphlet, 1966), 3–12.

[52] Harl. 433, fos. 175v, 191v; Horrox and Hammond, II, 137, 168.

[53] Harl. 433, f. 183 (Horrox and Hammond, II, 150), f. 269v, summarized by Wolffe, *Crown Lands*, 131. Brooks, *op. cit.*, 11, is mistaken in saying that Richard's former ducal council was left at Sheriff Hutton (which he seems scarcely ever to have used a residence) and also in his statement that the new council *sat* at Sandal Castle.

intended to be exercised primarily in Yorkshire. Otherwise, we merely have the rather vague phrase 'in the Northe Parties' (which would tend to exclude the palatine counties of Durham and Lancashire), and it is possible that it had some authority in the north-west. Certainly, it would be wrong to assume that the border counties now came under the exclusive dominance of the earl of Northumberland. In spite of his title of warden-general of the marches, his authority was confined to the east and middle marches.[54]

The functions of the council were, however, well defined by a set of 'Regulations' issued in July 1484.[55] Councillors, whether lords or not, were to act impartially as 'the king's laws and good conscience' required, and were, moreover, to 'declare an interest', taking no part in discussions where their own private concerns were involved. The quorum was always to include 'our nephew' of Lincoln and two others who should be justices of the peace in the north parts. It was to meet at least quarterly at York, preferably with the whole council present. Its main duties were in the keeping of the peace and the punishment of lawbreakers, ordering and directing 'all riots, forcible entries, distress takings, variances, debates and other misbehaviours against our laws and peace'. Persons raising riots 'in the great lordships or otherwise' were to be jailed in one of the nearby royal castles, 'for we will that all our castles be our jail'. The council was to stand ready to resist and punish without delay any assemblies or gatherings made 'contrary to our laws and peace'. In addition, it was to have an equitable jurisdiction during its sessions at York, and could deal also with disputes over land if the parties involved agreed. Its status as an essentially autonomous branch of the king's council was emphasized: all its letters or writings were to be issued in the king's name and endorsed with the words *Per Consilium Regis* beneath the signature of the earl of Lincoln. Although we know little of its operations at the time, this council was perhaps Richard's most enduring monument, for its jurisdiction and procedure remained largely unchanged until its dissolution in 1641.[56] For no very obvious reason, no such conciliar solution was ever attempted in Wales and the Marches following the collapse of Buckingham's Cambrian empire in the autumn of 1483. A number of appointments to fill the vacuum were made in the weeks immediately following the rebellion. Richard's son-in-law, William Herbert, earl of Huntingdon, was made chief justice of South Wales on 15 November,

[54] M. A. Hicks, 'Dynastic Change and Northern Society: The Career of the Fourth Earl of Northumberland, 1470–89', *Northern History*, xiv (1978), 90–1, makes this point clear; cf. Reid, *op. cit.*, 59–61; Brooks, *op. cit.*, 11.

[55] Harl. 433, f. 264v; printed *Letters and Papers*, I, 56–9; Reid, *op. cit.*, 504–5, and (partially) G. R. Elton, *The Tudor Constitution*, 200–1.

[56] Reid, *op. cit.*, 66; but cf. Brooks, *op. cit.*, 12 ff. for a reconsideration.

but elsewhere Richard relied chiefly on outsiders, mainly northerners, for key positions, such as Sir William Stanley, chief justice of North Wales and with authority in the northern Marches and border counties, Sir Richard Huddleston as constable of Beaumaris and captain of Anglesey, Thomas Tunstall, esquire, as constable of Conway Castle and later sheriff of Cardigan, and Sir James Tyrell as guardian of the king's interests in Glamorgan.[57]

On 23 January 1484 Richard's first and only parliament met at Westminster. Originally summoned for the previous 6 November, the assembly had been postponed because of the rebellion. The king's purpose in calling it was threefold. Firstly, he sought to have his title to the throne ratified and publicly declared by a body which was unequivocally and undisputably parliamentary, unlike that which endorsed his assumption of the crown in June 1483. Secondly, he needed parliamentary authority, by now regarded as indispensable, for acts of attainder against the rebels of 1483 and the forfeiture of their property to the crown. In particular, he needed it to legalize the arbitrary procedures whereby he had already granted away rebel lands, sometimes in tail male, instead of merely giving temporary custody; and this had been done without the taking of proper inquisitions, which put at risk the rights of widows, dependants or others who had claims upon the lands in question. Thirdly, he wished to use parliament as a forum for reforming legislation which would give the fullest publicity to his beneficent intentions as king. An ancillary purpose was to permit the passing of a number of private acts which gave full rein to the land-hunger of some of his supporters and to provide sanction for measures like the dispossession of the dowager-queen, Elizabeth, of the dower settled upon her by Edward IV.

It is highly unfortunate that we know so little of the composition of this parliament. For the house of commons, no more than a handful of election returns have survived, and these only for the less politically important borough seats.[58] We cannot know, therefore, how far pressure was applied by the king and those lords connected with him to influence the elections and thereby procure a docile house, although attempts to do so had become a regular practice when important decisions were expected from parliament.[59] There are, however, clear indications that

---

[57] *CPR*, 367–9; Harl. 433, fos. 140v, 151 (Horrox and Hammond, II, 73–4, 91). Commissions of array against the rebels of 1483 were issued only to Herbert and Tyrell (*CPR*, 370; 5 November 1483).

[58] Wedgwood, *History of Parliament, Register*, 487–93. Only the names of 55 MPs, all borough members, are known for certain, out of a house of 296.

[59] Ross, *Edward IV*, 342–5.

parliament had either been efficiently packed in the royal interest or was in healthy fear of a king who 'had carved his way through slaughter to a throne' (as the poet Gray described it) and had just triumphed over a major rebellion. The Croyland Chronicler says roundly that 'such terror affected even the most stout-hearted among them' that the commons agreed to all the king's wishes. There may, however, be an element of clerical prejudice here, since the chronicler was shocked by parliament's willingness to endorse that part of Richard's royal title which derived from Edward IV's alleged pre-contract of marriage, an issue which he held (rightly) to be a matter for the church courts.[60] Another indication that Richard had managed to assemble a complacent house of commons lay in its choice of speaker. From the beginning of the Yorkist period at least it had become usual for the commons to select a man who was acceptable to the king, who was generally a royal councillor, who was paid a fee for his labours and who, therefore, tended to be rather more a government spokesman, rather like a modern leader of the house, than a defender of the commons' interests.[61] In choosing William Catesby, they provided a man who had all these qualifications, perhaps to an unusual degree, given the high favour in which he stood with the king. What was most unusual, for a speaker, was that he had never sat in parliament before, and therefore had no experience of its procedure. His selection was so politically convenient as to suggest that Richard had indeed been at pains to procure a biddable assembly. Certainly, it proceeded to execute his wishes without notable signs of dissent.

Some pressure was needed before parliament could be persuaded to take upon itself authority as a spiritual court (in the matter of Edward IV's pre-contract of marriage), but otherwise the ratification of the king's title passed through smoothly enough. A rather misleading significance has recently been attached to these proceedings, which have been seen as the high-water mark of 'constitutionalism' in the fifteenth century. The emphasis placed in the act on the authority of parliament in the making of a king, it is argued, 'put parliament well on the road towards supremacy or sovereignty'. The other emphasis given to Richard's having been 'elected' by the Three Estates of the realm makes him 'the most "parliamentary" monarch of the fifteenth century'.[62] But this is to ignore the

[60] CC, 570.

[61] J. S. Roskell, The Commons and their Speakers in English Parliaments, 1376–1523, especially 103, and for Catesby as speaker in 1484, 294–7, 351–2.

[62] W. H. Dunham, Jr, and Charles T. Wood, 'The Right to Rule in England: Depositions and the Kingdom's Authority, 1327–1485', American Historical Review, lxxxi (1976), 738–61, especially 755–9; B. Wilkinson, Constitutional History of England, 1399–1485, 162–3; but cf. J. W. McKenna, 'The myth of parliamentary sovereignty in late-medieval England', EHR, xciv (1979), 482–506.

true purpose of the operation, unless we are to disbelieve the specific
statements of the preamble to and conclusion of the parliamentary record
itself.[63] In 1483, it says, Richard had been asked to assume the throne by
a genuine assembly of the Three Estates of the realm, but one which was
meeting 'out' of parliament, not in the proper form of a parliament, for
which reason had

> divers doubts, questions and ambiguities been moved and engendered in
> the minds of divers persons, as it is said. . . .

Therefore parliament, whose authority 'maketh before all things most
faith and certainty' gives its blessing to the king's title,

> and quieting men's minds, removeth the occasion of all doubts and seditious
> language.

This was being done

> forasmuch as it is considered, that the most part of the people of this land
> is not sufficiently learned in the abovesaid laws and customs, whereby the
> truth and right in this behalf of likelihood may be hid, and not clearly
> known to all the people, and thereupon put in doubt and question.

In other words, the parliamentary declaration was made in the hope
of dispelling seditious rumours that Richard was not the lawful king of
England.[64] Richard's continuing anxiety on this point is emphasized by
the fact that in April 1484, more than a month after parliament had been
dissolved, the king summoned the leading members of the London livery
companies to Westminster to hear the 'king's title and right' declared to
them.[65] Similar declarations were to follow when no less dangerous

---

[63] *RP*, VI, 240–2.

[64] This is the argument put forward in Ross, 'Rumour, Propaganda and Public
Opinion during the Wars of the Roses', especially 20–2. McKenna, *op. cit.*, 499 n.
2, discounts the significance of references to 'doubts and ambiguities' on the grounds
that 'it is a commonplace phrase in the prologues of statutes and proclamations'.
This is in itself a questionable statement, but we are here dealing with no ordinary
statute but with the king's title to the throne. The significant comparison is with
Henry VII's parliamentary title (*RP*, VI, 270) which refers briefly, and only once,
to 'the avoiding of all ambiguities and questions': there is no harping on the theme,
and it is not mentioned in the colophon. No reference is made to such matters in the
rehearsal of Edward IV's title in 1461, except in regard to the validity of the judicial
acts of the three Lancastrian kings, then declared usurpers, where indeed legitimate
doubts might arise (1 Edward IV, cap. 1: *SR*, II, 380). Henry VII assures his subjects in general that 'for the quietness of his people' certain statutes and ordinances
have been established (*SR*, II, 477).

[65] Anne Sutton, 'Richard III's "Tytylle and Right": A New Discovery', *The
Ricardian*, iv (1977), 2–7.

21. A view of the battle of Bosworth from a modern diorama at the Battlefield of Bosworth Visitor Centre, near Market Bosworth.

22(a). Louis XI of France.

22(b). Charles VIII of France.

23(a). John Howard, duke of Norfolk, an original painting on glass from the church of East Tendring, Suffolk.

23(b). Brass rubbing of William Catesby from the church of Ashby St Ledgers, Northamptonshire.

24(a). Lady Margaret Beaufort, countess of Richmond, mother of Henry VII.

24(b). Tomb effigies of Henry VII and Elizabeth of York (daughter of Edward IV and niece of Richard III) by Pietro Torrigiano, *c.* 1512–19.

rumours circulated that Richard intended to marry his niece Elizabeth after the death of his wife in 1485.

Parliament made no bones at all about accepting an act of attainder against the rebels of 1483. A clause was inserted providing a legal process for those who might have suffered from the hasty taking of inquisitions, but, more important from the king's point of view, and at his insistence, the grants he had already made from the now forfeited lands were to be valid in law even though no inquisitions – the customary legal safeguard – had been taken.[66] The commons then gave their blessing to twenty-one 'private' acts, some of which were used to reverse, in arbitrary fashion, the scarcely less arbitrary act of Edward IV which had settled the descent of the Duchy of Exeter estates on the issue of the child marriage between the heirs of Thomas St Leger and Thomas Grey, an act wholly partial to the Woodville interest. Others admitted the inheritance claims of powerful men like Northumberland, Lovell and Sir James Tyrell, claims which were contentious by process of common law and gave rise to a series of law-suits.[67]

It is, however, the 'public' acts of Richard's parliament which have most attracted the attention of his modern admirers. One eminent modern jurist confessed himself baffled by the 'psychological notions' of latter-day historians in their efforts in trying to 'reconcile a ruler who was at once so solicitous for the common people and yet guilty of cruelty and parricides', and then, curiously, proceeds to admit that the ineffable Emperor Nero was capable of good law-making.[68] P. M. Kendall states his faith in the usual rhetorical terms:[69]

> In the grave and enduring pigment of parliamentary authority he had painted large for the whole realm to see his principle of rule by desert, his offer of peace and justice in exchange for a national allegiance to the Crown.

By implication if not by intent, Kendall was right in admitting some degree of political calculation in the legislation of Richard's parliament. It should

---

[66] *RP*, VI, 244–51. The king's insistence on the validity of his grants is shown by his reply to the general tenor of the act of attainder, as presented to him (officially) by the commons (*ibid.*, 249: 'Le Roy le voet toutz pointz, ovesque les deux Provisions cy assuantz' – of which this is the second).

[67] Wolffe, *Royal Demesne*, 193–4; *RP*, VI, 252–4 (Northumberland), 254–5 (Lovell), 255–6 (Tyrell).

[68] H. G. Hanbury, 'The Legislation of Richard III', *American Journal of Legal History*, vi (1962), 95–113, a paper rightly dismissed by S B. Chrimes, *Henry VII*, 182 n., as being 'of little historical value'. It is certainly loaded, for a legal author, with an astonishing pro-Ricardian bias.

[69] Kendall, 285.

be seen in the context of his overall search for support, not as a detached and immaculate indicator of his beneficent intentions as king.

By the later fifteenth century, English common law had become indecently complicated and technical, especially as regards land law and procedure, with its 'Bill of Middlesex', its 'Taltarum's Case' and the convolutions relating to use and entail.[70] Such complications have defied modern legal commentators almost as fully as they added to the bank-balances of practising fifteenth-century lawyers. Richard's legislation was brief, to the point, and designed to remove some of the most glaring irritations of the legal system. What Sir Francis Bacon called 'the politic and wholesome laws' of this parliament in fact concern only six of the sixteen statutes which emerged from its deliberations. Cap. 1, concerning enfeoffments to use, went some way towards establishing that the *cestui que use* (that is, the beneficiary in what is nowadays called, loosely, the establishment of a trust) should be regarded in law as the owner of the property involved, so that those involved in dealings with such property might have better assurance of an effective title. This, it has been claimed, although not in result as effective as planned, is 'nevertheless an important landmark in the history of the use of land', but this claim seems to miss the essential point of the act.[71] Cap. 3, by allowing bail to those suspected of felony, protected them from imprisonment before trial, and at the same time prevented their goods from being forfeited before conviction. Cap. 4 laid down standards of property qualification for men selected as jurors, so that they should be men of sufficient substance, but such qualifications applied only to the now almost moribund jurisdiction of the sheriff's tourn. Cap. 6 addressed itself to the problems of the courts of piepowder (those with summary jurisdiction over disputed transactions in markets and fairs): this reinforced an act of 1478, and introduced new penalties against the misbehaviour of officials in these courts, providing further protection for defendants. Cap. 7, concerning the conveyances known as fines, followed somewhat the same as cap. 1, on uses, in protecting the rights of purchasers to land by condemning the use of secret fines, which should be made fully public and therefore binding in law, once the formalities had been observed. Finally, in this group,

[70] No discussion of these complex problems can be attempted here. What follows is set forth in layman's language. For some idea of the difficulties involved, see (on the Bill of Middlesex), T. F. T. Plucknett, *Concise History of the Common Law* (3rd edn, 1940), 343–4; W. S. Holdsworth, *History of the English Law* IV (1924), 407–80; A. B. Simpson, *Introduction to the History of the Land Law*, 121 ff., on entails and collateral recoveries; H. W. Challis, *Real Property* (3rd edn, 1911), 309 ff., on Taltarum's Case; and J. M. W. Bean, *The Decline of English Feudalism*, *1215–1540*, an historical discussion which is vital for the history of the use.

[71] Hanbury, *op. cit.*, 98–100; Chrimes, *op. cit.*, 182 and *n.*; Bean, *op. cit.*, 235–40.

comes the best-known act of this parliament (cap. 2), which made illegal the arbitrary taxes known as benevolences, as levied by Edward IV in his later years. This prohibition was right and proper, but, given the manifest public annoyance caused by benevolences, it was also an overt – and quite reasonable – bid for popular approval.

The remainder of the public acts were essentially concerned with commercial matters, as was much of the legislation of the Yorkist and early-Tudor period. The most useful and important (cap. 8) was at once long and technical, designed, in a thorough review of existing regulations, to prevent commercial dishonesty in the cloth trade, obviously promoted by king and council in consultation with legal and commercial specialists. Others did no more than reaffirm and extend in time legislation already enacted by Edward IV.[72] Others again reflect a certain deliberate pliancy on Richard's part towards the economic chauvinism of English merchants, in being discriminatory against foreign merchants: there was nothing novel in this, since Edward IV had displayed a similar disposition when he thought it politically and financially desirable.[73]

H. G. Hanbury believed that he had succeeded in portraying Richard

> as a singularly thoughtful and enlightened legislator, who brought to his task a profound knowledge of the nature of contemporary problems, and an enthusiastic determination to solve them in the best possible way, in the interests of every class of his subjects.

This surely is to claim far too much, and is based upon a lack of understanding of Richard's immediate political situation.[74] For Hanbury, Richard's intentions are implausibly pure.

What, then, of Richard's government of England as a whole (immediate questions of defence and finance apart)? Here we have P. M. Kendall, surely the most respectable and scholarly of Richard's defenders:[75]

> In the course of a mere eighteen months, crowded with cares and problems, he laid down a coherent programme of legal enactments, maintained an orderly society, and actively promoted the well-being of his subjects.

Richard reacted, sensibly and intelligently, to the immediate demands of his own political circumstances, as a usurper who was given little breathing-space to affirm his good intentions as king, and for whom an immediate appeal to the goodwill of his subjects was of overall importance. Richard's protagonists will permit no separation between his supposedly

[72] The legislation is in *SR*, II, 477–98.
[73] Ross, *Edward IV*, 345–6, 356–61.
[74] Hanbury, *op. cit.*, 113.
[75] Kendall, 319, and see the comment by Pollard, 'Tyranny of Richard III', 153.

inherent beneficence and the legitimately pragmatic demands of his situation. His record as king cannot make him either far-sighted or idealistic. It is permissible to raise again Polydore Vergil's sly suggestion: 'he began to give the show and countenance of a good man, whereby he might be accounted more righteous, more mild, more better affected to the commonalty'. To say this is to do no injustice to a fifteenth-century usurper. It is doing no more than putting him in the context of his own place and time.

# Chapter 10

# FOREIGN POLICY AND THE DEFENCE OF THE REALM

For Richard III survival did not depend solely on the success of his domestic policies. Diplomatically, England was not an island, and could not afford to remain isolationist, at least as long as there was dynastic rivalry within the realm. Inevitably, she was enmeshed in the complicated diplomacy of her European neighbours, especially in the continuing rivalry between the kings of France and the dukes of Burgundy, in which English kings had played so important a part throughout the fifteenth century. For many years they had appeared to the French kings as potential conquerors of their realm, especially when aided by Burgundy and other dissident French feudatories, of whom the most important was the duke of Brittany. France had responded by aiding and supporting rival claimants to the English throne. This double legacy of hostility was hard to overcome. Anglo-French enmity always involved England's ancient enemy, Scotland. The Scots were usually ready to take advantage of weakness or division in England, and were no less concerned by recurrent English attempts to control Scotland, or at least to occupy parts of her territory. They could be further encouraged to take hostile action against England by French diplomatic pressure or the prospect of French military aid: the 'Auld Alliance' was already old by 1483. The diplomatic situation was further complicated by French interference in the tangled politics of Italy and by the policies of the rising dual monarchy of Ferdinand and Isabella in Aragon and Castile, but neither was of direct importance in 1483.

Richard inherited from his brother a difficult and delicate set of foreign relationships. Edward had somewhat wantonly provoked a war with Scotland (now temporarily halted by a truce) in the hope of establishing a complacent pretender, Alexander duke of Albany, brother of James III, on the Scottish throne and acquiring some Scots territory. Richard himself, with his reputation for military valour and his professed taste for war, may well have been a leading advocate of the idea that the war should be continued. Secondly, there was the eternal problem of whether England should pursue a policy of hostility or friendship towards an increasingly powerful and (under Louis XI) expansionist France. Between these alternatives Edward IV in his later years had wavered uncertainly and unsuccessfully. Bribed by a French pension and the prospect of a marriage between his eldest daughter Elizabeth and Louis XI's heir, later Charles VIII, he had tended to resist the increasingly desperate appeals of Maximilian duke of Burgundy for aid against French attack, only to find himself duped in the end when Louis and Maximilian came to terms with each other at the Treaty of Arras in December 1483. Edward's chagrin at being hopelessly cut out of the final settlement is said to have been so great that it brought him to a premature end, but this did not prevent a mighty anger with King Louis. In the last months of his reign, according to some contemporary writers, Edward was again contemplating open war with his ancient enemy. Relations with France, therefore, were as uncordial as those with Scotland when Richard came to the throne.[1]

To these uncertainties Richard's own violent seizure of power added a new and dangerous dimension. With the deaths of Henry VI and Edward prince of Wales in 1471, Edward IV had had no need to worry about possible claimants or pretenders to a now firmly established throne. A potential pretender survived in the person of Henry Tudor, earl of Richmond, now an obscure and penniless exile in Brittany. For Edward he was a nobody, and certainly not dangerous. Consequently, Edward made only the most half-hearted and sporadic attempts to secure Henry's person, and in the end was content with a promise from the duke of Brittany that he would keep Henry under ward and prevent him from doing anything which might endanger the Yorkist throne.[2] This situation changed radically in 1483, when Richard's seizure of the throne brought to power a king with a title which was dubious at best, who might be challenged by claimants who had remained insignificant while Edward was alive. When joined by a number of English exiles in the autumn of 1483, Henry Tudor's position improved yet again. The danger lay in the fact that any one of England's principal foreign neighbours might wish, for reasons of self-interest, to lend aid to a pretender. As the attitude of dissidents within England had clearly showed, Henry Tudor was the most obvious candidate.

It therefore became a major objective of Richard's diplomatic relations with the continental princes to secure their benevolence and persuade them not to lend support to the earl of Richmond. In this task he was to prove ultimately unsuccessful, yet the fault was only partially his own. To some degree, his failure sprang from the particular condition of politics in Europe at the time.

His most immediate problem concerned his relations with Scotland.

---

[1] For the general background, see Ross, *Edward IV*, 278–95; Ranald Nicholson, *Scotland: The Later Middle Ages*, 472–525; G. Donaldson, *Scottish Kings*, 96–129; Calmette and Perinelle, *Louis XI et l'Angleterre*, *passim*.

[2] Scofield, *Edward IV*, II, 166–73.

This was solved, eventually, in spite of rather than because of Richard's own policies.[8] Following the English invasion of 1482, the duke of Albany had been made lieutenant-general of Scotland, but had failed to consolidate his position, and King James III had gradually recovered control of his turbulent kingdom. Albany and his friends were charged with treason and were later formally condemned in the Scottish parliament on 8 July 1483. Albany fled to England and was welcomed and encouraged to do what he could by way of hostile action against Scotland, in company with another Scots exile, the earl of Douglas, to whom Richard gave an annuity of £200 on 12 February 1484. This action was taken in spite of the obvious desire of James III for peaceful relations with England. Peace missions came repeatedly from Scotland, in November 1483, and in March, April and August 1484, without receiving much response from the English government. Meanwhile, with official English backing, Albany and Douglas led a raid into Scotland, where they attacked Lochmaben in July 1484, when Douglas was captured. Albany escaped to France, only to die in a joust with the duke of Orleans in 1485. While lieutenant-general, Albany had installed an English garrison in the castle of Dunbar, which continued to hold out, against ineffective siege operations, until after the death of Richard himself at Bosworth.

The failure and flight of Albany, however, seems to have persuaded the English government at last to respond to Scottish overtures for peace. In September 1484 a meeting between English and Scottish delegations at Nottingham, where the king himself was in residence, surrounded by a powerful company of lords and bishops, reached agreement on a three-year truce between the two realms and on a marriage between James III's heir, the future James IV, and Anne de la Pole, Richard's niece and daughter of the duke of Suffolk. The obvious inference from all this must be that, given the opportunity, Richard would have preferred to continue the hostilities with Scotland in which he had himself played so large a part. He was deterred largely by a lack of money, for he would have needed a grant from parliament, for which he dared not ask, and, to a lesser extent, by his own domestic preoccupations and by his concern about his relations with the continental princes. Even as it was, Richard's latent hostility, or at least lack of warmth, towards James III of Scotland

---

[8] For what follows, see Nicholson, *op. cit.*, 508–17; Gairdner, 174–80; Kendall, 298–300. Inevitably, Kendall produces a flattering account of Richard's diplomacy, and places the credit for a settlement with Scotland – 'his greatest diplomatic success of the year' – on Richard. But cf. Nicholson, *op. cit.*, and Donaldson, *op. cit.*, for the persistent, if unpopular, Anglophile policy pursued by James III, from whom all essential peace initiatives came. Their view is supported by the relevant documents (*L & P*, I, 55–6, 59–67; Rymer, *Foedera*, XII, 207, 230–2, 235–42; *Cal. Documents Scotland*, IV, nos 1494, 1496, 1497; *Rotuli Scotiae*, II, 461–2, 464).

encouraged that king to improve his connections with the new king of France, Charles VIII, who succeeded Louis XI in August 1483. James's agreement to a truce with England did not prevent his sending a contingent of Scots to France. Under the command of Alexander Bruce of Earlshall, they were to fight at Bosworth on behalf of Henry Tudor alongside the larger French force under the Sire D'Aubigny. It can scarcely be said that Richard III conducted his relations with Scotland with much ability or discretion.

In terms of dynastic survival, Richard's relations with his continental neighbours were of far greater importance than those with Scotland. Early in his reign, while he was still at Warwick on his post-coronation progress, Richard received a friendly overture from Queen Isabella of Castile. A verbal communication from her ambassador disclosed the remarkable statement that she had been long estranged from England and the House of York because Edward IV had refused her hand in marriage in favour of 'a widow of England' (Queen Elizabeth Woodville). But with Edward dead, and now being offended by King Louis of France, she had returned to 'her natural kind and disposition' of friendship with England, and offered her active help against France. According to her ambassador, she could deploy the formidable force of 10,000 spears and 30,000 footmen in this venture. Since Richard at this stage did not wish to offend the French, and in any event was in no condition to undertake an attack on France, the matter was not pursued, and a promising dynastic ally was lost. To Queen Isabella, however, he wrote a friendly letter, and performed the polite gesture of knighting her ambassador, Geoffrey Sasiola, during his triumphal state visit to York in August 1483.[4]

Of more direct and immediate concern to Richard were his relations with France and Brittany. Here there were two pressing problems, especially as concerned Brittany. Relations between kingdom and duchy had always been bedevilled by the scourge of piracy, with faults on both sides. 1483 saw a marked resurgence in the activities of English pirates, mainly from Cornwall and Devon. The strong hand of Edward IV had gradually mastered the problem. Compared with the 120 recorded acts of piracy, some on a large scale and involving many vessels, which had marred the last decade of Henry VI's reign, there were only 58 during Edward's entire reign, and after 1471 the number of recorded acts of piracy had fallen to only four a year.[5] But with the temporary loosening of control after Edward's death, and apparently through the belief of 'diverse folks of simple disposition' that the various treaties for the protection of com-

---

[4] *L & P*, I, 31–3, 48 ff.; Rymer, *Foedera*, XII, 200.
[5] M. Meehan, 'English Piracy, 1450–1500' (Bristol M. Litt. unpublished thesis, 1972), 104–19.

merce which he had concluded were now no longer valid, English pirates took to the seas again, with devastating effects. Brittany responded by fitting out privateering flotillas. An unofficial war at sea developed. Soon the French also joined in. In 1484 an official French squadron, commissioned by the admiral of France and commanded by a veteran Breton captain, is said to have overwhelmed a privateering flotilla from Bristol, and indeed to have descended upon and pillaged Bristol itself.[6] Complaints about English piracy poured in also from Burgundy. Richard was at some pains to respond in friendly and cooperative fashion, and later he took vigorous action against the pirates on his own account.[7]

The second and most important problem in Richard's relations with Brittany arose from the presence of English exiles and refugees in the dominions of the duke of Brittany. Within weeks of his accession, the king despatched a confidential agent, Dr Thomas Hutton, to Brittany, to discuss with the duke not only the problem of the sea warfare, but also to sound out 'the mind and disposition of the duke against Sir Edward Woodville and his retinue, practising . . . to ensearch and know if there be any intended enterprise out of land upon any part of this realm'.[8] Although Henry Tudor was not mentioned by name in these instructions, it is clear from later correspondence that his position had been discussed by Hutton with the duke. This suggests that Richard was already at this early stage concerned by the potential danger from Henry Tudor, especially since Duke Francis had now relaxed the close restraints upon Henry and his uncle, Jasper, imposed at Edward IV's request.[9] The duke's response to Hutton's mission was superficially reassuring but essentially non-committal. He was clearly not about to surrender a bargaining counter which had increased so much in value with the change of dynasty in England. He also pointed out that he had several times refused to give

---

[6] *L & P,* I, 22.

[7] Meehan, thesis cited above; complaints about piracy on Breton ships are mentioned in Richard's instructions to his envoy Thomas Hutton, July 1483, *L & P,* I, 22-3, and, from the Breton side, in the duke's instructions to George de Mainbier, 26 August: 'a great number of vessels of the said kingdom of England have put themselves in warlike array upon the sea, and have threatened to take and plunder the subjects of the duke' (*ibid.,* 39). For the war at sea and the attack on Bristol, see Pocquet du Haut-Jussé, *François II, Duc de Bretagne, et l'Angleterre,* 253-5, 263-4. For Maximilian's complaints, *L & P,* II, 49, 51.

[8] The fleet which had put to sea under Sir Edward Woodville in May 1483 (above, p. 73) had soon disintegrated as a hostile force. The majority of captains, including the commanders of two powerful Genoese vessels under contract to the English, responded to Richard's overtures, and returned to port. Only two ships sailed on to exile in Brittany with Sir Edward, Mancini, 85-7; *L & P,* I, 22-3.

[9] *Ibid.,* 37-43.

Henry Tudor into the custody of Louis XI, who undoubtedly would have tried to make use of him against the interests of the House of York. At the same time, he could not alone risk offending the king of France. Lacking sufficient troops of his own, and with no naturally defensible borders, he was extremely vulnerable to French attack. He might consider defying France only with active assistance from England. He therefore asked Richard to supply him with 4,000 archers at English expense, and a further 2,000 or 3,000 at his own expense. There was something highly specious about this answer. Military aid to Brittany on this scale had been agreed during Edward IV's reign, in 1468, 1472 and 1475, but only within the context of a triple offensive alliance between England, Burgundy and Brittany, predicated upon an English invasion of France, and the duke must have been well aware that even six or seven thousand English archers could not hold back a French invasion, however formidable as fighters they may have been. Certainly, the duke's immediate professions of friendship had little to do with his later actions. Apart from supplying and equipping the small flotilla of five ships which took Henry Tudor on his abortive invasion of England in 1483, and supplying 325 fighting men to go with it, Duke Francis was also generous with cash. His treasurer-general was to pay expenses amounting to 13,000 *livres* (worth between £1,000 and £1,500) during October and November 1483, and he also advanced about £2,000 to Henry Tudor by way of loan on 30 October. He then welcomed Henry back into his domains after the failure of the expedition and also gave asylum to the other English exiles who fled there when the autumn rebellion had collapsed. Some of them, including the marquis of Dorset and that earlier refugee, Sir Edward Woodville, were in receipt of monthly pensions from the duke.[10]

For a nest of active and intriguing exiles to establish themselves on a friendly and convenient base for the invasion of England was precisely what Richard wished to avoid. Richmond's position was enhanced by this new accession of strength, and was further confirmed by the solemn ceremony which took place in the cathedral of Rennes on Christmas Day 1483, when the whole company of English exiles, former Lancastrians and Yorkist dissidents alike, witnessed his solemn pledge to marry Elizabeth of York once he gained the throne of England. They, in turn, pledged homage to Henry as though he were already king. This display of confidence apparently persuaded Duke Francis to promise them further assistance once an opportunity for a return to England arose. According to Polydore Vergil, Richard now became so worried about the danger from Henry Tudor and his confederates that 'he was vexed, wrested and

[10] Pocquet du Haut-Jussé, *op. cit.*, 249–53; Gairdner, 151–2.

tormented in mind with fear almost perpetually . . . wherefore he had a miserable life'.[11]

Richard, therefore, had to try to neutralize the danger from Brittany by whatever means he could. One method was to step up the level of English naval activity in the Channel in the continuing sea-war with Brittany, and hence to bring home to the Bretons the risks involved in their maintaining a hostile attitude. Duke Francis's unfriendly action in supporting Henry Tudor's invasion of 1483 was now repaid with great vigour. Soon after, the valiant Yorkshireman, Thomas Wentworth, was commissioned to take to sea a squadron 'to resist the king's enemies of Brittany and France', and, in March 1484, a similar commission was issued to John, Lord Scrope of Bolton. In January 1484 the king was engaged in the purchase of a Spanish ship, probably *La Garcia*, to make war upon his enemies of Brittany. Several officially sponsored and supported privateering ships and flotillas were at sea early in 1484. In January, Richard issued a letter to aid and assist one John Gost, merchant of the Staple of Calais, whom the king had commanded to do him service upon the sea 'against his enemies of France and Brittany'. In the same month, Spanish merchants were complaining about an attack upon their ships by John Benet, Charles Dinham, esquire, and 'others of the king's armament'. The master of that famous old ship, the *Grace Dieu*, in company with the *Mary* of Greenwich, was ordered to sea to resist the king's enemies in March 1484. The mayor and aldermen of London, and probably authorities within other ports, were commanded to seize all Breton ships and property within their jurisdiction, although later they had instructions to release them. English ships going to Iceland were firmly enjoined to sail only under convoy, known to contemporaries as a system of 'wafting'. Thus the English merchant marine was let loose against Breton, and, to a lesser extent, French shipping.[12] All this achieved some measure of success. Prizes poured into English ports, and the Breton marine suffered considerable damage. The duke of Brittany soon became alarmed for the safety of his duchy. Fearing an armed English seaborne descent upon his territory, he summoned all those of his subjects who owed him military service and ordered all coastal residents to maintain a constant watch for all hostile English vessels.[13] It is more than possible that Richard's vigorous action at sea may have strengthened the duke's growing wish for some sort of accommodation with the new regime in England.

[11] PV, 203–5.

[12] For these, and other similar activities, see Harl. 433, fos. 134–6v, 139v, 140, 143, 149v, 159v, 164, 180; CPR, 402, 426, 465; L & P, II, 287.

[13] Pocquet du Haut-Jussé, *op. cit.*, 254–5.

At home also Richard pursued diplomatic ends by seeking a rap-
prochement with the dowager-queen Elizabeth Woodville. It would be
of significant value to him if he could detach her from her support of
Henry Tudor, thereby depriving him of his intended bride, Elizabeth of
York, who formed the cement in the exiled Lancastrian-Yorkist alliance.
On 1 March 1484 he finally persuaded the dowager-queen to leave sanctuary in company with her daughters. By doing so, she was in a sense seen
to be publicly abandoning Henry Tudor's cause, and she was also
encouraged to persuade her son, the marquis of Dorset, to desert him
likewise. Dorset did indeed attempt to escape from France and return to
England, only to be checked by a French search party and induced to
change his mind.[14]

Finally, Richard tried to apply direct diplomatic inducement to get the
Breton government to withdraw its support for Henry Tudor. According
at least to Polydore Vergil, he sent an embassy to Duke Francis promising
to restore to him the title and estates of the earldom of Richmond, which
had been granted, a century earlier, to the Breton dukes when they were
allies of England in the reign of Edward III. He was also promised the
lands of the other English exiles if he would at least consent to put Henry
Tudor and his supporters under close ward, and hence prevent their active
intrigues against the interests of Richard himself.[15] In the event, it was
less the result of Richard's diplomatic pressure than of changes in the
political situation on the continent which induced the Breton government
to abandon its support for Henry Tudor. Here the internal politics of
Brittany and France and, to some degree, of Burgundy also enmesh with
their diplomacy, and a little explanation is necessary.

By 1483 Duke Francis of Brittany was an ageing and sickly man, subject
to fits of mental aberration. Even in his prime, he had not been a consistent or vigorous statesman. His duchy – the last great independent
feudal principality within France proper – faced a succession crisis upon
his death, since his issue was confined to a single daughter, Anne. While
Edward IV was still king of England, she had been promised in marriage
to Edward prince of Wales, but with his disappearance she became a likely
bride for the new king of France, the young but sickly Charles VIII. As
Henry VII was later to discover, no French government would readily
allow Brittany to pass into foreign hands. In France itself, however, there
was at this time a struggle for power between the houses of Bourbon, led
by the intelligent and skilful Regent, Anne of Beaujeu, and of Orleans, in

---

[14] Harl. 433, f. 308, printed in Ellis, *Original Letters*, 2nd ser., I, 149; Gairdner,
165–6; Kendall, 286–8. For Dorset's exploits, PV, 210, 214.
[15] PV, 205 (date perhaps June 1484).

the person of its duke, Louis (the future Louis XII). Orleans and his friends sought to establish themselves in control of the council of regency against the Beaujeus. There was a danger that they might revive the aristocratic League of the Public Weal which had menaced Louis XI in the early years of his reign. For this to be a success, Brittany's support was vital: hence the close interest of the Orleanists in that duchy's troubled affairs. Except during the occasional periods when Duke Francis asserted himself, real power in Brittany was wielded by his dominating but highly un-popular treasurer, Pierre Landais. Influenced by Orleans and by Maxi-milian of Austria, duke of Burgundy, and also by the attitudes of his many Breton opponents, who looked towards the Beaujeus in France, Landais gradually inclined towards the idea of a firm alliance with England which would bring him military support.[16] Accordingly, he despatched Jean de Salazar, a Burgundian agent and soldier who was later to play a part at Bosworth, to seek Richard's support. He followed this with a formal embassy in 1484.[17]

At first Richard seemed inclined to promise the large force of archers for which Duke Francis had earlier asked, but when a formal diplomatic agreement, establishing a ten-month truce, had been reached in June 1484, he proved willing to supply only 1,000 archers, instead of four or six times that number. John, Lord Grey of Powys was named as their commander, and a commission was issued to take a muster of the expedi-tionary force, by then assembled at Southampton, late in June. It is a most likely surmise that Richard's main condition for thus supporting Landais was that Henry Tudor should be placed under strict surveil-lance.[18] At least the English king's actions seem to have been sufficient to induce Landais to move against the rebel English refugees. Yet such was the elaborate network of spying and intrigue which pervaded Western Europe at this time that Henry Tudor was forewarned of the official Anglo-Breton plan, if only just in time. Bishop John Morton, who was then still in Flanders, learnt of it; his informant was probably Henry's mother, who had connections in Paris; she in turn may have had the information from her husband, Thomas, Lord Stanley, a member of Richard's council. In any event, the messenger from Morton reached Henry just in time to allow him, although not most of his followers, to escape from Brittany into France only hours ahead of the troopers sent to arrest him, but Duke Francis, now again recovering his wits, generously allowed the remaining Englishmen to follow Tudor into France. All this

[16] PV, 205; Chrimes, *Henry VII*, 31–3.

[17] For Salazar, see Wheeler and Nokes, *The Ricardian,* no. 36 (1972), 4–5.

[18] *CPR*, 446, 517, 547; Rymer, *Foedera*, XII, 226–7, 229; Pocquet du Haut-Jussé, 258–9; Kendall, 297.

seems to have taken place in September 1484.[19] By mid-October Henry
Tudor and his following were hopefully in attendance on Charles VIII
and the French court, then in the Loire valley. In November the French
council provided Henry with 3,000 *livres* to help him array his men.[20]

At this point, Richard's natural and sensible policy of trying to deprive
Henry Tudor of active Breton support brought a rather unexpected
Nemesis. Henry had now come under the protection of the greatest power
in Europe, far less vulnerable to English pressure than was Brittany, with
greater freedom of manoeuvre, and with far greater resources should its
government decide to support Richmond's invasion of England. Quite
why the French finally undertook to back Richmond's schemes remains
something of a mystery. They lived under the belief, ingrained in them
by long years of war and by Louis XI's teachings, that England was an
actively hostile power, eager to attack France with any allies she could
raise; and in 1484–5 rumours were circulating vigorously that hostile
action by the English was imminent. Until the autumn of 1484, French
policy had been correct if not friendly. Embassies, of the usual formal but
not purposeful kind, had been arranged to discuss a possible truce or an
improbable treaty of peace. Yet, as far back as the meeting of the Estates
General in January 1484, the minority government in France had raised
the spectre of an English invasion, and it may have been this fear which
caused it to support a Tudor venture. No doubt also the Beaujeu government was worried by Orleanist intrigues with Brittany and Burgundy, and
the danger that they might attract support from England.[21] However this
may be, Henry Tudor was certainly fortunate. French intervention in
Brittany procured the downfall of Pierre Landais, who was hanged from
the walls of Nantes on 19 July 1485. On 9 August, only two days after
Henry's invasion fleet had landed at Milford Haven, the French government signed a treaty of peace with Brittany. By then, having neutralized

---

[19] PV, 206–8; Gairdner, 167–9; Chrimes, 29–31. Margaret Beaufort's involvement
is reinforced by the fact that Morton's messenger, Christopher Urswick, was her
confidential agent. Gairdner dated Henry's escape to the spring of 1484, but cf.
Pelicier, *Essai sur le Gouvernement de la Dame de Beaujeu*, 86 n. 1, for record
evidence supporting the later date. The chronology of events on the continent involving Henry Tudor given in Chrimes, *Henry VII*, 31–5, is remarkably vague and
confused. I am indebted to Dr A. V. Antonovics, who is preparing a book on Charles
VIII, for drawing my attention to material in French sources bearing on the relations between Henry Tudor and Charles's minority government.

[20] Gairdner, 169–70.

[21] *Lettres de Charles VIII*, ed. Pelicier, 194–5. As late as June 1485, France is
said to have declared a general muster to resist an expected joint Anglo-Breton invasion (Pocquet du Haut-Jussé, *op. cit.*, 268–9). At the same time, Maximilian of
Austria was doing his utmost to persuade Richard to invade France, in collaboration
with Brittany (*L & P*, II, 3–51, especially 23–4).

Brittany, it had little need to bother about English intentions, still less to spend money and men on an invasion of England. One week later, and the Tudor dynasty might never have been born.[22]

It seems likely that a key figure in promoting the invasion of England and in persuading the French government to lend active aid was the Marshal of France, Philippe de Crèvecoeur, Seigneur d'Esquerdes, known to the English as Lord Cordes. In a funeral epitaph for Cordes, he is described as having been the veritable 'arbiter' of Richmond's fate.[23] An ardent advocate of French expansion to the north and east, and, in particular, of wresting Calais from the English grasp, he would gladly live seven years in hell, he said, to achieve this end. He had already clashed with England before Richard's assumption of power. Immediately after Edward IV's death, he launched a campaign at sea on the grounds that he had been unable to get restitution from the English for ships and goods which they had seized from him, and it was to resist Cordes's depredations that the English fleet under Sir Edward Woodville put to sea in April or early May 1483.[24] By 1485 he had become commander of the huge and expensive military base at Pont de l'Arche in the valley of the Seine. Some 1,500 discharged soldiers from this base formed the core of the 3,000, or perhaps 4,000, troops which the French government supplied to Henry Tudor. The men from Pont de l'Arche were professional soldiers, and scarcely deserve Commynes's contemptuous dismissal of them as a rabble, 'the worst that could be found'.[25] These men were provided at the wages of the king of France, and were placed by Henry Tudor under the command of an experienced soldier, Philibert de Chandée, who was an acquaintance and perhaps a personal friend of Henry, and who was soon to be rewarded with the earldom of Bath for his services on the Bosworth campaign. There was also a contingent of Scots, and a number of Breton adventurers, the 'beggarly Bretons' mentioned in the supposed address given by Richard to his men in the morning hour before Bosworth.[26]

[22] Chrimes, *Henry VII*, 37, and references there given.

[23] Lewis Thorpe, 'Philippe de Crèvecoeur, seigneur d'Esquerdes: two epitaphs by Jean Molinet and Nicaise Ladam', *Bulletin de la Commission Royale d'histoire*, cxix (Brussels 1954), 183–206, especially 201: one of the epitaphs reads: Par moy eust Richemont recouel en France terre/Se fus le moienneur qu'il fut roy d'Engleterre/ On m'ordonna le juge appoincteur e tournoy. See also Mancini, 118 (Armstrong's notes).

[24] Mancini, 81. There was subsequently extensive negotiation with Cordes about his alleged losses (*L & P*, I, 18–21).

[25] Commynes, II, 306; and for the base-camp at Pont de l'Arche, P. Contamine, *Guerre, Etat et Société à la fin du Moyen Age*, 300–1.

[26] PV, 562–3, also printed by Gairdner, 236–7. The 'beggarly Bretons' are here linked with 'faint-hearted Frenchmen'.

Finally, there was a body of some 300–500 English exiles,[27] who had recently been reinforced, at the level of high command, by that veteran Lancastrian, John de Vere, earl of Oxford, who made a spectacular escape from his prison at Hammes Castle, near Calais, accompanied by his gaoler, James Blount, probably late in 1484.[28] It was, therefore, very much an army of foreign troops which eventually set sail for England. In terms of the numbers of men deployed in the major battles of the English civil war, Henry's command was not large, but it was significantly larger than any invasion force which had assaulted English shores in the period since 1460. But its composition – Frenchmen, Bretons, Scots – provides something of a forceful comment on Richard's failure to win the neutrality of his immediate foreign neighbours. In addition to the troops, France supplied Henry Tudor with a loan of 40,000 *livres* and with the necessary shipping.[29] Thus, after twenty-two years of hopeless exile, and some eighteen months during which his potential as a rival claimant to the throne had risen steadily, Henry finally set sail from Harfleur on 31 July or 1 August 1485.

It remained a risky mission. Foreign support had made an invasion possible, but Henry's ultimate success depended on his ability to attract support within England and Wales. Without it he had little hope of defeating the king in battle. Certainly, he had not neglected this aspect of his venture, and had been in contact with various would-be or potential supporters. The major charge brought against the unfortunate William Collingbourne in 1484 was not his diffusion of the libellous lampoon on Richard and his advisers but the fact that he had been in treasonable correspondence with Henry Tudor, telling him that if Henry chose to

[27] This figure rests on the statements of Polydore Vergil that Henry had a retinue of some 300 Englishmen when he fled Brittany for France, and that these were later joined by others who had fled from England, and by English students living in France, probably from the University of Paris, among whom was Richard Fox, the future bishop of Winchester (PV, 207, 209).

[28] For Oxford's escape, and the subsequent upheavals at Hammes, see PV, 208–9, 212–13; Kendall, 301–2; Gairdner, 199–200; Chrimes, 34–5; Scofield, 'The Early Life of John de Vere, earl of Oxford', *EHR*, xxxix (1914), 244–5. Kendall (p. 486) is probably correct in questioning Polydore Vergil's story that the entire garrison of Hammes defied a force from Calais, and, on being relieved by Oxford, defected to Henry Tudor to a man: this is belied by the pardon granted to all of them in January 1485 (*CPR*, 526). The problems both at Hammes and at Guisnes, where a completely fresh garrison was installed, occasioned the despatch of a trusted supporter, Sir James Tyrell, to take charge of the defence of the Pale of Calais. (Harl. 433, fos. 200v, 201). Calais and the fortresses of the Pale remained loyal in August 1485, and presented no problems as they had done in 1460 and 1471.

[29] A. Spont, 'La marine française sous le règne de Charles VIII', *Revue des Questions Historiques*, lv (1894), 394; Pelicier, *Essai*, 103; Pocquet du Haut-Jussé, *op. cit.*, 270.

land at Poole in Dorset before Michaelmas next, his well-wishers in England would cause the people to rise in arms and levy war against Richard. Months later, on the eve of the invasion, messengers were slipping back and forth across the Channel exchanging messages and promises between Henry and several prominent Welshmen, notably Rhys ap Thomas and Sir Walter Herbert. Finally, according to an unsubstantiated Spanish source, he had been promised support by much more highly-placed persons.[30] Whether such promises would ever be honoured could only be discovered by the test of direct action.

Modern judgements on Richard's conduct of his diplomatic affairs have varied (inevitably) from the harsh to the flattering. James Gairdner, critical as ever, pronounced sentence against him: 'Of policy he knew nothing . . . continually unable to make war he was unwilling to make peace'. P. M. Kendall on the other hand saw the making of a 'genuine treaty of peace and amity' with Scotland as a major diplomatic achievement by Richard III (when all the evidence points to the impetus coming from the other direction), and excused Richard's failures with France and Burgundy on the ground that there was no dealing with them because of their internal divisions.[31] As so often, the truth lies between these extremes. It is unfair to say that he had no policy, but Gairdner was probably right to suggest that there was a certain inconsistency in Richard's relations with France and Brittany. By promising military aid to the anti-French faction in Brittany, he at once committed himself to an out-dated policy of continental aggression, and alarmed the French. Charles VIII's government had no motive to support Henry Tudor except in reaction to fears of English hostility, and had Richard been more actively friendly towards France it is likely that he would have been able to win from her at least the concession of placing Henry Tudor under strict ward where he could do no active damage. Neither the king of France nor the duke of Brittany or his ministers had the same active personal and dynastic interest in promoting the interests of a pretender to the English throne as the dowager-duchess of Burgundy was later to display in supporting first Lambert Simnel and then Perkin Warbeck against a Tudor monarch in England. Shifting, confused and uncertain the internal politics of both France and Brittany may have been between 1483 and 1485, but it can scarcely be said that Richard grappled with them either skilfully or judiciously.

If he could not obtain the goodwill of foreign powers, Richard could at least provide for the adequate defence of his realm, and the many references to defensive arrangements reveal the measure of his constant

[30] Gairdner, 186–7; PV, 215–16; and for the 'Spanish Letter', see below, p. 211, n. 3.

[31] Gairdner in L & P, II, introd. xiv–xv; Kendall, 295–8.

fear of a Tudor invasion. One major problem was to guess where on the coastlines of England and Wales the enemy might descend. Over the previous two decades of civil strife, invasion forces had landed in Northumberland, Humberside, Kent, south Devon and West and North Wales, and one abortive attempt had been made to effect a landing on the East Anglian coast. To poise himself, with what would obviously be his main army, to resist attack from any one of these many points of the compass, he chose Nottingham as his main base, where he was in residence when Henry Tudor finally made his landing. It was, perhaps, as sensible a choice as any, being fairly central to his kingdom, although he might have anticipated that Henry Tudor, with his Welsh connections through his uncle Jasper's long-standing relations with West Wales, might attempt a landing there. Richard's choice of Nottingham, however, was probably influenced by its proximity to the north, whence most of his reliable support would come: it provided a convenient point of mobilization for a northern army of which he could take personal command.

Richard further sought to secure early intelligence of an enemy landing by reviving, and perhaps expanding, the posting system, with riders stationed at regular intervals along the main routes, which Edward IV had instituted for the Scottish campaign of 1482. Unfortunately, such systems were extremely expensive to maintain, and the Croyland Chronicler clearly implies that it had to be dismantled or at least much reduced by 1485, when Richard began to run seriously short of funds. Even earlier intelligence of threatening enemy moves was to be obtained by a system of spies on the other side of the Channel, 'from whom he learned nearly all the movements of the enemy', at least in 1484, for spies too, the Chronicle tells us, were expensive. The English government could also make use of its last surviving bastion on the continent, Calais, for the rapid despatch of news of significant developments across the sea: thus, in 1483, its captain, Lord Dinham, sent off a pursuivant to Richard III within two hours of his receiving the news that Louis XI had died. Whatever the financial constraints may have been, Richard's intelligence system and arrangements for dispersing the news of an invasion seemed to work well enough when it actually came in 1485.[32]

How far Richard followed the example of his brother Edward in using naval patrols to detect or prevent an invasion is not known. Certainly, he seems to have learnt from Edward's example the importance of maintaining even a small *royal* navy, as distinct from the *ad hoc* procedures of

[32] *CC*, 571; C. A. J. Armstrong, 'Some Examples of the Distribution and Speed of News in England at the time of the Wars of the Roses', in *Studies in Medieval History Presented to F. M. Powicke*, ed. R. W. Hunt, W. A. Pantin and R. W. Southern, 429–54, especially 440; and below.

impressing merchantmen for particular tasks: there are several references to royal ships, and Richard was also engaged in buying ships to supplement those he had inherited from his brother. He had a fleet at sea in 1483 to resist the attacks of French and Bretons, and against the Scots in 1484. He is said to have won a considerable naval battle, 'through his own skill' (which suggests he may have been in personal command), with this northern fleet based on Scarborough, otherwise under the command of two tough and trusted Yorkshiremen, John Nesfield and Thomas Evering-ham. But fifteenth-century fleets could not be kept at sea for indefinite periods. Apart from problems of provisioning, they lacked the sailing capacity to manoeuvre against regularly hostile winds from the west, which was what made possible the prolonged English blockades of Brest and other French ports during the eighteenth-century and Napoleonic Wars. In any event, to equip and maintain a fleet at sea was enormously expensive and Richard may have been running short of funds by the summer of 1485.[33]

If other precautions failed, Richard's main hope lay in the speedy raising of a powerful army and in confronting the enemy in the field at the earliest possible moment. Experience during the years of civil war had shown that the longer invading armies were left unchallenged, the more dangerous they became, since it gave them the chance to acquire recruits, even if some were not wholly willing.[34] To this end Richard bent his full energies, and did all he could to see that the realm should be in a state of constant military preparedness. The use of field guns and, to a lesser degree, of hand guns, had become common during the civil war, and Richard, like his brother Edward, was well aware of the need for an adequate artillery. Already, in 1484, he was spending money both in purchasing guns and in the employment of specialists, some brought in from Flanders, to manufacture more in the Tower of London.[35] This

---

[33] Harl. 433, fos. 144v, 151v, 180v; *CC*, 571 (for the naval operations against the Scots: Harl. 433, fos. 174, 179v, shows that Richard himself was at Scarborough in May 1484 and again in July); C. F. Richmond, 'English Naval Power in the Fifteenth Century', *History*, lii (1967), 1–15, especially 14, for Richard's purchase of ships.

[34] E.g., in the campaigns of Barnet and Tewkesbury in 1471, of which Richard had had personal experience. Edward aimed to strike the rebels as far away from London as he could to prevent their gathering strength as they advanced, and the contemporary official account, *The Arrivall of Edward IV*, makes a special point of this: (the rebels) 'for that they would gather and array up the power of Devon-shire and Cornwall' (moved to Exeter) 'trusting that their *presence-showing in the country* should cause much more, and the sooner, the people come to their help and assistance' (my italics; *Arrivall*, 23; Ross, *Edward IV*, 162–70).

[35] Harl. 433, fos. 145, 157v, 163, 178v; Ross, *op. cit.*, 220, 272; *Wars of the Roses*, 112–16. Richard's purchases of hackbuts suggest that he relied more on the use of hand guns than had been usual in the past.

specialist arm apart, Richard relied upon two devices to put an effective army in the field – personal writs of summons to his principal supporters, and commissions of array, which empowered those named as commissioners to summon to the standards all able-bodied men within their county. The evidence rather suggests that these commissioners, instead of being appointed *ad hoc* for a particular occasion, were given more long-standing powers of supervision over their potential forces. Town levies were usually summoned by royal letters under the signet to the relevant mayors and corporations.[36]

Following the ignominious failure of Henry Tudor's projected seaborne landing in the wild autumn of 1483, there was something of a lull in defence preparations. No man would seriously attempt a cross-Channel invasion in the depths of winter. With the coming of the spring, however, Richard again seems to have become seriously alarmed about the danger of invasion. General commissions of array were issued on 1 May 1484.[37] The composition of these commissions reveals that Richard might hope for reliable support in the north, the midlands, in East Anglia and to some extent in the south-east. His main weakness lay in the south-west, where he was essentially dependent on outsiders like John, Lord Scrope of Bolton and John, Lord Zouche. Nothing came of these invasion fears, but Richard's renewed anxieties are fully revealed in a whole clutch of orders in December 1484, despite the season of the year. On 3 December Henry Tudor and his friends were denounced in a general proclamation, in phrases to be used all over again in the summer of 1485. General commissions of array were issued on 8 December. Then on 18 December there was a further general circular to the commissioners appointed in each shire 'for the defence of his most royal person and of this his realm'.[38] This is a document of considerable interest, since it reveals much of Richard's careful back-stage preparations of which otherwise we should know very little. First, it shows that many men of substance had been induced some time before to promise the king that they would supply a specified number of men whenever he required them. Among other tasks assigned to the commissioners was a demand that they should inquire 'of the number of persons sufficiently horsed, harnessed and arrayed as by every of them

[36] For the machinery of commissions of array, much revived during the Wars of the Roses, see M. R. Powicke, *Military Obligation in Medieval England*, 212–23. For signet letters, extensively employed during the Yorkist period, J. Otway-Ruthven, *The King's Secretary and the Signet Office*, 41 and 19–59 *passim*, and below, pp. 213–14; and the many examples of signet letters summoning troops among the York City records (*YCR*, I, e.g., 83–4 – Buckingham's rebellion). The York records are of interest in showing how the royal commands were implemented.

[37] *CPR*, 397–401.

[38] Harl. 433, f. 273v (cf. *PL*, VI, 81); *CPR*, 488–92; *L & P*, I, 85–7.

severally were granted to do the king's grace service before the old commissioners, whensoever his highness should command them, for certain
days in their said grants expressed, for the resisting and subduing of his
enemies, rebels and traitors'.[39] The reference to the 'old commissioners'
suggests that some such system of organized military standby had been in
existence for some time. Secondly, the instructions reveal that money had
already been levied from the king's subjects to provide for the payment
of these troops: the commissioners were to make sure that the money was
available when needed, that it was kept in proper official custody, such
as the constables' and bailiffs' hands, and that any who defaulted on payment should be tracked down and punished. Further, after thanking the
king's subjects 'for their true and loving disposition showed to his highness
the last year', the commissioners were, nevertheless, 'with straight com-
mandments' to instruct all their people that they should attend upon 'such
captains as the king's grace shall appoint . . . and none other'. Knights and
esquires were to be ready to do the king's service 'without any excuse', or
face his high displeasure. All private quarrels were to be laid aside, lest
they distract from the king's overriding concern with defence. In certain
parts of the country, such as palatine counties and marcher lordships,
where a normal royal administration did not exist, the king relied upon
the quasi-feudal authority of his great men to raise the shires. Thus, in
January 1485, he issued a warrant to all the knights, esquires, gentlemen
and others of the county of Chester to obey Lord Stanley, Lord Strange
and Sir William Stanley, 'who have the rule and leading of all persons
appointed to do the king service when they shall be warned against the
king's rebels'. Similar orders were issued in favour of Stanley and Strange
in Lancashire, and in Glamorgan in favour of Sir James Tyrell, the
people's 'governor and leader', despite his recent appointment to take
charge of the castle of Guisnes.[40] The instructions, therefore, clearly show
Richard's earnest endeavours to keep the country in a state of constant
military preparedness, although perhaps a certain unease is apparent in
the juxtaposition of his professed belief in his subjects' 'true and loving
disposition' and his injunction that they should serve only his appointed

[39] Independent confirmation of this point comes from two letters of August 1485.
John Howard wrote to John Paston asking Paston to join him with as many men as
he could at Howard's cost, 'beside that you have promised the king'. Richard himself wrote to Sir Henry Vernon commanding him to come 'with such number as you
have promised us' (*PL*, VI, 85; *HMC, Rutland*, I, 7).

[40] Harl. 433, fos. 201v, 205. Tyrell had been appointed to take charge of Guisnes
Castle during the absence of its captain, John, Lord Mountjoy (an ailing man who
died soon after), on 13 January 1485. Sir Ralph Hastings had already paid the king
1,000 marks for the reversion of the office of captain after the death of Mountjoy
(Harl. 433, f. 159).

captains 'and none other'. Taken in conjunction with the signs of Richard's unpopularity noted in the previous chapter, it suggests a certain mutual lack of trust between the king and his subjects.

Polydore Vergil would have us believe that (apparently early in 1485) Richard had learnt through his spies that Henry Tudor had had no success in gaining help from France and had become discouraged thereby. This lulled the king into a sense of false security, and he relaxed his vigilance: his ships were recalled from their stations, and the troops he had placed here and there to resist invasion were withdrawn, although he maintained a coastal defence force, especially in Wales, and a system of alarm beacons to carry news of any landing with all possible speed.[41] But the notion that Richard was thereby caught off balance when the invasion actually came is not borne out by the sober evidence of the records. The flurry of defence preparations in late 1484 and early 1485 was followed by yet another lull. But the next round of royal commands began on 22 June 1485, two months before Henry's landing. The commissioners of array were told that the king had learned of an impending invasion of the realm. The instructions of December 1484 were then repeated, except that all troops under their direct command were now to be ready at an hour's notice. Proclamations were to be issued for men in general to be prepared, also at an hour's notice, to obey the king's command. Again, all private quarrels were to be laid aside and disobedience would be severely punished. Letters were sent to all sheriffs ordering that they or their deputies should keep constant residence within the shire towns, so that they could act at once on any orders the king might send them.[42]

The following day Richard issued a general proclamation (again largely repeating that of December 1484), which deserves attention, both as an example of his propaganda and as a statement of the issues which he thought likely to command his subjects' loyalties. Henry Tudor's associates, Jasper Tudor, John de Vere, Sir Edward Woodville and Peter Courtenay, are first denounced as murderers, adulterers and extortioners.[43] They had taken refuge in France with Henry Tudor, a man of 'ambitiousness and insatiable covetousness', of bastard descent on both sides of his family, and therefore unfit to claim the throne, and had also submitted themselves to the obedience of the king of France, the king's ancient

[41] PV, 213–14.

[42] Harl. 433, fos. 220, 220v.

[43] Harl. 433, f. 220v, PL, VI, 81–4, where the various texts of the proclamation are collated. It is noticeable that Thomas Grey, marquis of Dorset, who had been denounced as a supporter of Henry Tudor in December 1484, was omitted from this proclamation of June 1485. Mistrusted by Henry Tudor, Dorset had been left behind in France as a hostage for the repayment of the money loaned to Tudor by Charles VIII.

enemy. Then follows an appeal to English chauvinism; to win French aid they had surrendered all the right of England to the throne of France, and had offered to give up Calais and its dependent fortresses to the French. Success for Henry Tudor, Richard firmly told his people, would mean disaster in other ways. Henry had promised to the king's enemies bishoprics, duchies, earldoms, baronies and the like. It was his purpose to change and subvert the established laws of the realm. If he achieved his false intent, every man's life, livelihood and goods would be in his hands, 'whereby should ensue the disinheriting and destruction of all the noble and worshipful blood of his realm for ever, and to the withstanding and resistance thereof every true and natural Englishman must lay to his hands for his own surety and weal'. If Henry and his friends came to power, it was their intent 'to do the most cruel murders, slaughters, and robberies, and disherisons that ever were seen in any Christian realm'. In marked contrast to the much more restrained, guileful and plausible propaganda employed both by Edward IV and his opponents, the sheer extravagance of Richard's dire prophecies of doom was surely self-defeating. Few of his subjects can have placed much credence in them.

This proclamation of 23 June 1485 was Richard's last public act in providing for the defence of his realm. He had surely done all he could, but he had to wait a further two months before his preparations were put to the test.

# Chapter 11

# AUGUST 1485

On 7 August 1485 Henry Tudor made a safe landfall at Mill Bay, on St Anne's Head, a few miles west of the modern deep-water port of Milford Haven. Thence, by means of a series of strenuous marches, he struck north through Cardigan to Machynlleth at the head of the Dovey estuary, and then turned due east across mid-Wales to reach the English-Welsh border at Shrewsbury by 15 August. From there he moved on, much more slowly and hesitantly, through Newport, Stafford, Lichfield and Tamworth, to arrive at Atherstone in Warwickshire by 21 August, a total marching distance of 170 miles.[1] Why did he take this much longer and more circuitous route through central Wales, rather than moving directly east from Milford Haven along the south coast of Wales to enter England at Tewkesbury, and then drive east again over the Cotswold Hills to London, the magnet, and the most important prize of all fifteenth-century invaders? It may have been that by going north he hoped to make contact with the main centres of Stanley power in north-east Wales, Cheshire and Lancashire, at least according to Polydore Vergil. Lord Stanley, he tells us, had been under suspicion during the rebellion of 1483, probably because of Richard's justified belief that his wife, Margaret Beaufort, had been a prime mover in the whole affair. Interrogated by the council, Stanley was acknowledged to be free of guilt, but told that he must remove all his wife's servants, and 'keep her so straight with himself that she should not be able from thenceforth to send any messenger neither to her son, nor friends, nor practise anything at all against the kings'. Independent confirmation that Richard remained wary of Stanley comes from the Croyland Chronicle, which says that when in 1485 Stanley asked permission to leave the court because he had been long separated from home and family, royal permission was given only on condition that he left behind him his eldest son, George, Lord Strange, virtually as a hostage.[2] According to one early but inaccurate source, Henry Tudor had

---

[1] S. B. Chrimes, *Henry VII*, 40–7; 'The landing place of Henry of Richmond, 1485', *Welsh History Review*, iv (1961), 173–80, and sources cited there.

[2] PV, 204, 217; *CC*, 573. Strange, who seems to have escaped death by a hair's breadth on 22 August, was later well rewarded by Henry VII, but predeceased his father, dying, perhaps by poison, in 1503: *CP*, IV, 207–8; XII (1), 356.

already been in secret correspondence with a number of highly-placed English nobles, who had pledged him their support, although only one 'Tamorlant' (probably the earl of Northumberland) is mentioned by name.[3] But Henry might well have hoped that his own stepfather, at least, would support his cause. On the other hand, given Lord Stanley's highly equivocal political record over the past twenty-five years, it would have been deeply naive to place any dependence upon a Stanley promise, and there were experienced men with Henry Tudor, like Jasper Tudor and John de Vere, earl of Oxford, who had ample reason to be aware of the risk of trusting this wily nobleman. Here, at least, they were at one with the king himself. Even when summoned by Richard to join him in arms, Lord Stanley declared himself ill with the 'sweating sickness', but this did not mean that he had committed himself to Henry Tudor, nor was he to do so.[4]

A more likely explanation is a testimony to the efficiency of Richard's defensive arrangements, and to the loyalty of the families of Herbert and Vaughan, who had no representatives at Bosworth, but who effectively straddled south-east Wales from Brecon to the coast. To attempt a direct advance east from Milford was to enter hostile territory, and, indeed, almost as soon as Henry left Milford Haven, there were rumours that Sir Walter Herbert was approaching from Carmarthen to attack him with a large force, although these later proved to be unfounded.[5] It was in all probability agents of the Herberts who made the long gallop of almost two hundred miles to Nottingham to advise the king of Henry's landing within five days.[6]

Secondly, although Henry encountered no opposition on his chosen route, equally he attracted little support. Circumstances of time, distance

[3] Elizabeth Nokes and Geoffrey Wheeler, 'A Spanish Account of the Battle of Bosworth', *The Ricardian*, no. 36 (1972), 1–5 (with translation and useful additional material); A. Goodman and Angus Mackay, 'A Castilian Report on English Affairs, 1486', *EHR*, lxxxviii (1973), 92–9, which more plausibly identifies 'Tamorlant' with Northumberland rather than Westmorland. The inaccuracy of the letter to Ferdinand and Isabella of Spain, dated 1 March 1486, is shown by its author's belief that the princes were murdered by poison before Edward IV died, at a time when Richard, not Edward, was on campaign in Scotland (Goodman and Mackay, *op. cit.*, 92 n.; Nokes and Wheeler, 2 n.), and by its reference to the totally unlikely manoeuvre attributed to 'Tamorlant'.

[4] *CC*, 573. For the epidemic of sweating sickness in 1485, L. Attreed, in *The Ricardian*, iv (1977), 2–16.

[5] PV, 216–17.

[6] Richard, at Beskwood Lodge, near Nottingham, knew of the landing by Thursday 11 August, as shown by his letter to Henry Vernon in Derbyshire (*Historical MSS Commission*: 12th Report, Rutland I, 1888, 7–8).

and the transmission of news may have prevented any one of the English magnates with whom he had been in contact from declaring himself so early in the day, although the Stanleys, who probably had early information, reserved their position to the bitter end, much to Henry's dismay. But Henry had to wait a clear week before the most important of the chieftains of West Wales, Rhys ap Thomas, declared his support: Rhys was probably being closely watched, and Richard had demanded the custody of his young son as a hostage. Probably because of his connections with the native Welsh, Rhys, once committed, was able to make his way north to join Henry by a far more direct route, skirting the county of Glamorgan, and then ahead through the lonely hills and vales of Radnorshire, to Shrewsbury. His adherence to Henry may have been induced by promises of substantial reward (later only partially made good), for he was very much a Welshman on the make, but what his support meant to Henry in terms of Welsh militia we simply do not know.[7]

At Shrewsbury, therefore, Henry's gamble was still as desperate as it had been at Milford Haven. The marked dice still lay unturned upon the board. Not until he reached Newport in Staffordshire did any Englishman declare for him, when Sir Gilbert Talbot, uncle of the young earl of Shrewsbury, rode in to join him with some 500 men. But it is unlikely that Sir Gilbert commanded the main allegiance of the Talbot connection, which was powerful hereabouts, because the young earl, George, seems to have been with the king and the royal army, and many Talbot followers and tenants may have held back for precisely this reason.[8] Lack of overt support may well explain the slowness of Henry's movements from Shrewsbury onwards. With only a slender force, he had still to reckon on confronting all the armed might which a king of England might assemble. Only if the Stanleys and perhaps Northumberland played traitor at the last had he any chance of success.

Meanwhile, Richard was making urgent preparations to resist the invader. Polydore Vergil – and here is evidence of his subtle literary bias – would have us believe that at first Richard took little notice of the news of the invasion, thinking that Henry was 'utterly unfurnished and feeble

[7] Chrimes, *Henry VII*, 42–3, and notes.

[8] The claim that Shrewsbury (then aged seventeen) was with the king ('Ballad of Bosworth Field', line 244) has been generally disbelieved, but is far from implausible. Custody of his person, and disposal of his marriage, had passed from Hastings to a small consortium headed by Elizabeth Woodville. With the disgrace of the Woodvilles, it is likely that he was brought under the king's personal supervision. Certainly, he was with Richard at Nottingham for the reception of the Scots ambassadors in September 1484. He was, however, already married to Hastings's daughter, by whom he later had eleven children (*CPR, 1467–77*, 539; *CPR*, 36; *CP*, XI, 706–7).

in all things', and that the king's men whom 'he had disposed for defence of that province [Wales] were ready in all respects'. Henry's small company would be annihilated by Walter Herbert or Rhys ap Thomas. He then (says Polydore) changed his mind, deciding it was 'a point of wisdom, not to contemn the forces of his enemy, though they were but small', but he only seriously became alarmed and 'began with grief to be in a fervent rage' when the news reached him that Henry had arrived at Shrewsbury.[9] Like so much of Polydore Vergil's account, this idea will not stand up to critical examination. It runs entirely counter to the careful if slightly feverish and anxious manner of Richard's defensive preparations.[10] On the very day, 11 August, when he first received the news of Henry's landing, he sent out a series of urgent letters to his supporters (to judge from those we know to survive), demanding their instant support. Sir Henry Vernon, of Derbyshire, a former retainer of the duke of Clarence, was told to 'come with such number as ye have promised . . . sufficiently *horsed* and harnessed', this to be done in all haste, with no excuses permitted, upon pain of forfeiture.[11]

To other supporters also, the news was sent 'in all haste'. The duke of Norfolk, who was probably then at Framlingham Castle in Suffolk, received the king's urgent requests at least by Sunday 14 August. Then, or on the next day, he wrote to John Paston, informing him that 'the king's enemies be on land'. But for 'Our Lady Day' (Monday 15 August, the Feast of the Assumption), the king would already have set forth. John Paston was told that the duke would lie at Bury St Edmunds 'as upon Tuesday night' (16 August), and that Paston should join him there 'with such company of tall men as ye may goodly make at my cost and charge, beside that ye had promised the king'.[12] Thus news of Henry's invasion had travelled some four hundred miles from West Wales to East Anglia within seven days of his landing. Given fifteenth-century conditions, this was no mean achievement. The duke of Norfolk's followers were already buckling their brigandines and honing their halberds before Henry Tudor's force had reached the English border on 15 August. The king's

---

[9] PV, 218–19. Polydore adds to the literary effect of his statement by adding that Richard ordered Brackenbury as lieutenant of the Tower to bring with him Thomas Bourchier and Walter Hungerford (leaders of the rebellion of 1483), together with 'many other gentlemen of the order of knighthood, whom he had in suspicion'; that these two and others escaped from Brackenbury's custody; that they joined Henry at Tamworth (probably true); and that, also at Tamworth, 'There flocked to him also many other noblemen of war, who hated . . . King Richard worse than all men living' (PV, 220). There is no evidence to support this latter statement.

[10] Chapter 10, above.

[11] See note 6 above (my italics).

[12] PL, VI, 85.

reaction to the invasion threat was thus sharp and swift. The apparent leisure of his movements was conditioned by the need to wait for some days at least for his forces to assemble from the far corners of his realm, especially from the north.

As to what was happening in the north, we are less well-informed. News of the invasion seems to have reached the city of York at least by Monday 15 August, but it was not until the following day that the city council met to consider its response to the king's message. The councillors agreed to send a messenger to Nottingham 'to the king's grace to understand his pleasure as in sending up any of his subjects within this city . . . for the subduing of his enemies', but their prime concern appeared to be (as so often with towns in this age) with the safety and defence of a self-interested York: 'Also' (says the minute) 'that every warden of this city search the inhabitants within his ward, that they have sufficient weapons and array for their defence and the weal of this City'. Not until Friday 19 August, only three days before the battle, did a messenger return from the king, who was then at Beskwood Lodge, near Nottingham. It was then decided that the city should send eighty men to the king's aid. They were to depart in all haste.[13]

One point, apparently hitherto unnoticed, which emerges from these various despatches, is that the royalist army which surrounded the king at Bosworth on 22 August must very largely have arrived there on horseback, even if it did not fight primarily as cavalry. Sir Henry Vernon was specifically instructed to have his men horsed as well as harnessed; the York contingent could not have marched 120 miles within three days; although it is possible that Norfolk marched his men about the same distance between the night of 16 August and the night of 21 August, it seems unlikely. The same applies even more strongly to other and perhaps more distant supporters of the king. We do not know when the news reached the earl of Northumberland, or even where he was at the time, although it is quite likely that he was at Wressle, in East Yorkshire. Even with the mightiest of gallops, he cannot have learned of the king's emergency before 13 August, and it took time for him to collect his men: one of his retainers, Sir Robert Tempest, had his seat some sixty miles away to the north-east at Skipton in Craven. By no means could such men have been mustered into a coordinated force, perhaps at Pontefract, before 19 August. A similar logic applies, with even greater force, to the powerful caucus of royal supporters in the far north-west, or to such of them as were not already in the king's company or coming from their appointed stations in the southern counties. It seems highly reasonable to assume that they were called upon by individual writs of summons like that sent to Sir Henry Vernon, but there was no way in which they could have

[13] Davies, *York Records*, 214–16; *YCR*, I, 17–18.

reached the battlefield in time unless they had been mounted. Certainly, the likely equine population of late-fifteenth-century England was capable of providing for the needs of some 8,000 to 10,000 men, even at harvest-time.[14] It was not, therefore, an especially weary army (as some commentators have assumed) which mustered under the royal banners at Sutton Cheney on the night before the battle.[15] Indeed, Henry's infantry, after their long march through Wales, may well have been more tired than the majority of Richard's men. Richard was also collecting men from close at hand. Richard Boughton, the sheriff of Warwick and Leicestershire, was raising the local levies of his shrievalty, and seems to have been slain on 20 August, the day on which Henry Tudor reached Tamworth, although whether his death occurred in some clash with Henry's forces is not known. His predecessor as sheriff, Sir Humphrey Beaufort, now constable of Warwick Castle, was also present at the battle, and, like so many of Richard's supporters, was to meet his death there.[16] Although primarily, it was not exclusively a northern army which stood and fought for the king on 22 August, but what does stand out is the lack of any reference to men from the southern and western counties of England, who had figured so largely in the rebellion of 1483, among the supporters of the House of York.

Like so much else connected with the battle of Bosworth, the size of the armies which eventually clashed there has been the subject of endless variance and dispute. Medieval chroniclers are notorious for their inaccuracy in estimating numbers, and in particular were prone to wild exaggeration.[17] Modern historians have not been much more successful in correcting their errors. In general, however, it can be suggested that the size of Henry's army has been underestimated and that of Richard's exaggerated. Allowing for the men he recruited en route from Milford Haven, Henry may have mustered some 5,000 men, perhaps more. Potentially, Richard could have gathered far more, but, given the hasty circumstances of his array, he may have had no more than 8,000 men in his command, although 10,000 is by no means unlikely, and we cannot wholly ignore the remark of the Croyland Chronicler that his number of warriors was 'greater than had ever been seen before in England collected

---

[14] A conservative estimate, based on nineteenth-century figures of the number of horses in England, when the human population was much larger but the dependence on horses for transport was much less, suggests that as many as 230,000 horses were available, even at harvest-time, since much harvesting was still done by oxen. I am indebted to Mr W. E. Hampton for expert advice upon this point.

[15] E.g., Kendall, 353. Kendall's account of the battle remains an astonishing mixture of imagination, speculation and purple prose, and his description of Richard's last moments seems to suggest that he was perched on the crupper of the king's horse.

[16] *Calendar of Inquisitions Post Mortem, Henry VII*, I, 11, 25–6, 52.

[17] Ross, *Wars of the Roses*, 135–9.

together on behalf of one person'.[18] The king, therefore, may be seen as possessing a substantial but not a decisive advantage in terms of numbers. More important, perhaps (treason apart), was that his own energy and military sense led him to assume a much superior tactical position in the initial stages of the battle. The confines of the terrain were later to turn against him in that he could not deploy all his admittedly superior forces at once.

There have been almost as many different accounts of the battle of Bosworth as there have been historians. The main problem arises from the fact that no reliable and first-hand account of the engagement was ever written, or, at any rate, has survived. The fullest description was given by Polydore Vergil, a foreigner writing twenty years after the event, although his account may have been based on what men actually present at the fight had told him. The Croyland Chronicler, writing early in 1486, devotes, unfortunately, but a few lines to the actual battle, although he attaches a note on the casualties.[19] The so-called 'Spanish Letter', written about the same time, is again the work of a foreigner working from second-hand information. It describes what appears to be an impossible man-oeuvre by the great English magnate 'Tamorlant' (that is, Northumberland), who moved out from the rear of Richard's position and then caused his array of 10,000 men to engage on Henry's behalf and attack Richard's vanguard. This can command no credence whatever, especially in view of the way Henry Tudor subsequently treated Northumberland.[20] 'The Ballad of Bosworth Field', so useful in many respects, offers little help as to the actual course of the battle. The author may have been present or nearby on 22 August, but he had an obvious propaganda intent, and his account is poetic rather than pragmatic. It does, however, help to confirm certain points of substance.[21]

[18] *CC*, 574, and see further below, p. 217. The idea that Richard's army was twice the size of Henry's rests entirely on PV, 223. For various modern estimates, see Chrimes, *Henry VII*, 40, 47–8; Makinson, 'The Road to Bosworth Field', 242; Ramsay, *Lancaster and York*, II, 544; D. T. Williams, *The Battle of Bosworth* (1973), 1–24, especially 8–9). See also A. H. Burne, *The Battlefields of England*, 135–55, especially 139, which I have tended to follow. For the size of Henry's invasion army, see above, pp. 201–2 and *n*. 25. Curiously, James Gairdner, 'The Battle of Bosworth', *Archaeologia*, lv, I (1896), 159–78, makes no reference at all to the size of the armies involved.

[19] PV, 221–4; *CC*, 574–5.

[20] Above, *n*. 3; below, pp. 222–3.

[21] 'Ballad', lines 545–604. It says (1) that the military intervention in the battle was undertaken by William Stanley, and not by him and Lord Stanley jointly, although here the purpose of Richard's ultimately fatal charge is represented as being to seize all three Stanleys, Thomas, William, and Humphrey, the younger son, and not Henry Tudor; (2) that Northumberland was not engaged; (3) that Richard might have escaped from the battle had he accepted the offer of a horse: instead, he demanded his battle-axe and his crown, below, pp. 224–5.

Amid all this uncertainty, some facts seem clear. Richard III awoke in his camp at Sutton Cheney early in the morning of 22 August, after a night troubled by uneasy dreams. We need not suppose they were of quite the violent, ghostly and portentous sort envisaged by Shakespeare, although some contemporary support exists for the notion that he appeared 'pale and death-like . . . as though surrounded by a host of demons'.[22] For Richard, as for Shakespeare, dawn brought relief. He recovered his nerve, and was up and about early enough to move his men forward to what, in a mildly rolling landscape, was to prove a commanding height, the modest and rather narrow plateau of Ambien Hill, some 400 feet in elevation. Thence he would have a good view of the disposition of the enemy forces advancing from the west, and certainly would have been able to pick out the location of particular commanders by their great battle-standards. Such standards, in the mellays of English fifteenth-century battles, were the only means by which the rank-and-file of an army contingent could keep in touch with their individual commanders.[23] Whether he could also have discerned the intentions and movements of Sir William Stanley, who seems to have taken up a position on another modest eminence called 'Hanging Hill', a mile or so north of the scene of the battle, near the village of Nether Coton, is less clear, but he would certainly have been well placed to identify any direct intervention by Sir William in the fighting going on in advance and below. Equally, Sir William himself had a useful vantage point from which to survey the entire field.[24]

The king had entrusted command of a powerful vanguard to his most reliable major supporter, John duke of Norfolk. His force consisted mainly of archers, perhaps some 1,200 strong, flanked and protected by spearmen and buttressed by the artillery, whose guns are said to have been linked together by chains in order to prevent enemy penetration of their position.[25] Behind the duke lay the main 'battle', commanded by Richard himself, possibly some 2,000 or 3,000 strong, and including a significant mounted element. In the rear, stood the forces of the earl of Northumberland, with a force of at least the same size. One of the earl's sixteenth-century successors, according to his own bailiff, could raise at least 9,000 men from his Yorkshire and Cumberland estates alone, including 3,000 horse, but his levy in August 1485 had been organized in a matter of days and over considerable distances. However, if Polydore Vergil is

---

[22] Shakespeare, *Richard III*, V, iii; *CC*, 574.

[23] Ross, *Wars of the Roses*, 119.

[24] Hutton, *op. cit.*, 245–6; Gairdner, *op. cit.*, 174–5. Williams, *Bosworth Field*, 13, places both Stanleys there, but it scarcely amounts 'to a vantage point between the two armies'. This is one of many inaccuracies in this account.

[25] 'Ballad', lines 489–92.

correct in crediting the Stanley contingent with 3,000 men, it is reasonable to assume that Northumberland, even at short notice, could raise at least as many.[26]

It was usual for fifteenth-century armies going into battle to fan out so that they ended in opposing lines abreast, as at Barnet or Tewkesbury in 1471. But the physical confines of Ambien Hill precluded any such familiar arrangement, especially if cavalry were involved. Armed horsemen need at least six feet between them to undertake a charge, and even if Richard had as few as 3,000 men horsed, they could not have been deployed in line without spilling over the edges of Ambien Hill.[27] Hence Richard's army was in column, one 'battle' behind the next, and this provides at least part of the explanation for the eventual outcome of the fighting. Only Norfolk's vanguard was directly involved in heavy fighting, unless we assume that Richard took the whole of his main 'battle' into his charge upon Henry Tudor. Northumberland's rearguard was never seriously engaged, nor could be, whatever the proclivities of its commander. Fainthearts and deserters from Richard's cause there may have been, but once Richard himself had been seen to die in the fighting against Henry Tudor's entourage, a fact which could have been observed from the top of Ambien Hill as the royal standard fell, the issue was settled anyway, especially since Norfolk had probably been killed already. No fifteenth-century battle in the civil war continued after the leaders of either party had fallen in the fighting.[28]

Rather similar logistical problems affected Henry Tudor's army. Despite all his hopes, he had failed to obtain any definite commitment from the Stanleys, and now had little choice but to engage his inferior force against a well-positioned enemy.[29] Much confusion about his movements has been

[26] M. E. James, 'A Tudor Magnate and the Tudor State', *Borthwick Institute of Historical Research Papers*, no. 30, p. 27 and *n.*

[27] The peak of the hill is at 393 feet. Taking the contour of 375 feet as being generally the top of the hill, on which an army might be assembled, we are left with an area 1½ miles long and only 352 yards wide. In no way could any substantial force of cavalry have been deployed except in column in this limited space.

[28] Ross, *Wars of the Roses*, 119–21.

[29] PV, 220–2. Henry's apparently joyous meeting with the two Stanleys at Atherstone on the previous day, as described by Polydore, had no sequel in terms of any immediate commitment from them, and his early-morning message to their camp had met with a rebuff. The equivocal nature of the Stanleys' replies to Richard himself bears all the marks of Lord Thomas's inherent caution. It is most unlikely that Lord Stanley (even if he were not genuinely ill with the sweating sickness) took part in the battle at all: he had already managed to avoid Towton, Barnet and Tewkesbury. If Henry Tudor, with Sir William's help, won the battle, then Thomas, as Henry's father-in-law, could claim credit; if not, his own non-intervention might save the family fortunes from Richard's wrath. Sir William had already been declared a traitor.

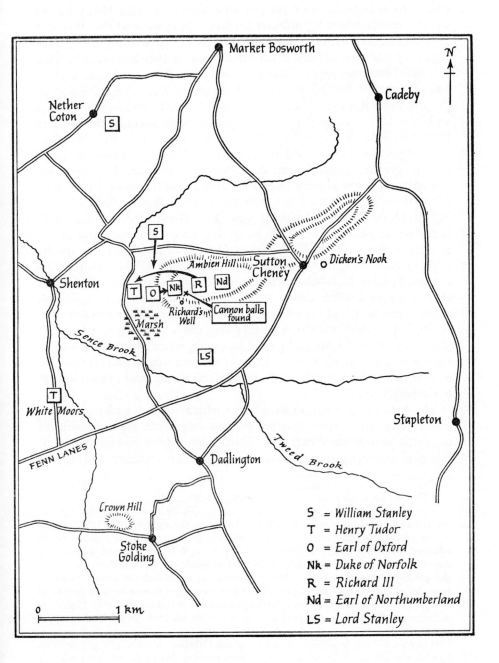

Market Bosworth

N

Cadeby

Nether
Coton

S

Shenton

S

Ambien Hill    Sutton
Cheney

Dicken's Nook

T  O  Nk  R  Nd

Richard's
Well

Cannon balls
found

Marsh

Sence Brook

LS

T

White Moors

FENN LANES

Dadlington

Tweed Brook

Stapleton

Crown Hill

Stoke
Golding

0        1 km

S  = William Stanley
T  = Henry Tudor
O  = Earl of Oxford
Nk = Duke of Norfolk
R  = Richard III
Nd = Earl of Northumberland
LS = Lord Stanley

caused by two statements from Polydore Vergil, one that Henry had to avoid a marsh, which lay athwart his line of advance, and the other that his men marched with the sun upon their backs. Tireless but inconclusive ingenuity has been lavished upon the location of Polydore's marsh. That delightful antiquary, John Nichols, visited the scene of the battle in 1838, full of romantic sensibility: 'the blossom of the hawthorn, assuming its deepest vermeil tincture . . . the red and the white rose full-blown (apt emblems of the scenery we contemplated) were literally entwined in beauteous embrace . . . the flaunting woodbine, thrusting forth in luxuriant stem, began to exhibit delicious fragrance'.[30] Alas for history, he could offer no evidence about the marsh, because by then it had been dried up. On balance, it would seem that the marsh lay to the south and west of Richard's position on the hill, forming an effective flank protection. Skirting this obstacle probably made it difficult for Henry's forces to fan out in battle order, and compelled his vanguard, under the command of the veteran soldier John de Vere, earl of Oxford, to attack directly up the slope of Ambien Hill into the fire of Norfolk's men.[31] No less tortuous arguments have been advanced in an endeavour to explain Polydore's claim that an English army, advancing from the west on an English summer morning, had the sun upon its back. A circuitous route around a variously-positioned marsh? A battle which did not begin until two in the afternoon, when the sun had passed its zenith, when all available sources suggest that the fighting began early in the morning? It seems safest to assume that Polydore had simply got his facts wrong, and to turn instead to the battle itself.[32]

The engagement seems to have begun with a vigorous exchange of fire, both of guns and arrows, between the two vanguards. Some accounts of the battle have assumed that only Henry Tudor's force possessed artillery, collected, according to conjecture, from the nearby ancient and disused

[30] Hutton, *Bosworth Field*, 142–3; *Excerpta Historica*, 105.

[31] Polydore Vergil's confusing account (p. 223) of Henry Tudor's disposition places the van under Oxford, *flanked* by Gilbert Talbot on the right and Sir John Savage, a very recent deserter from Richard, on the left, thus suggesting a line abreast in advance, while Richmond himself, with only a small force, followed in the rear. Any such arrangement would have been most unusual: it was invariable practice for the principal commander, here Henry himself, to command the centre battle, at least during the Wars of the Roses, although not among some continental armies. It is also curious that he makes no reference to any command for the other highly experienced soldier apart from Oxford on Henry's side, his uncle Jasper Tudor, earl of Pembroke.

[32] For conflicting discussions of this issue, see Gairdner, *op. cit.*, 162–3, supported by Chrimes, *op. cit.*, 46–7, whose version relies too slavishly on the suspect testimony of Polydore Vergil; Kendall and Makinson, *op. cit.*, both of whom reject outright the statement about the sunshine; Burne, *op. cit.*, 144, 149–50.

castle of Tamworth, although why it should have contained up-to-date artillery has not been explained.[33] Even more unlikely is the idea that Richard had no such support. Apart from the vigorous lines of the 'Ballad of Bosworth Field', describing the size of Richard's artillery train, which included not only serpentines and bombards ('like blasts of thunder did they blow'), but also the comparatively new-fangled use of hand-gunners ('harquebusiers'),[34] the supposition that they could not have been brought along on his rapid march is not convincing. Horse-drawn guns could certainly keep pace with an army containing infantry. Twenty miles a day amounts to a very minor achievement compared with some later feats. All the later battles of the Wars of the Roses had involved the use of field-guns, and Richard, who had fought at Barnet (where hand-guns also had been used) and Tewkesbury, had direct experience of this comparatively modern arm of warfare. It is highly unlikely that he would not have seen fit to equip himself accordingly, and, as king, he had the resources to avail himself of what was still a very expensive form of weaponry, which few private persons could afford.[35]

In the event, this exchange of missiles proved inconclusive. Even if we ignore the use of rival artilleries, which were still not only expensive but rather inefficient, English armies using bows and arrows tended to cancel each other out. Neither side had the decisive tactical advantage which the English had possessed against the mounted French armies during the Hundred Years' War, displayed with such devastating effect at Crecy, Poitiers, Agincourt and Verneuil. Hence the armies had tended to become involved in a straightforward hand-to-hand fight, or mellay, so characteristic of the battles of the civil war, with almost every man fighting on foot, whether originally mounted or not. Because of his formation, and the limited space on the top of Ambien Hill, Richard could not deploy all his superior forces at once. His own rearguard, for example, was completely out of touch. The Croyland Chronicler specifically states that, although fierce fighting was going on before the king's position, from 'where the earl of Northumberland stood, with a large and well-equipped contingent, no adversary could be seen; no blows were given and none received'.[36] Communications in medieval armies were bad, once battle had been joined, and Northumberland's men could only have been committed to the fighting by way of a sophisticated right-hook flanking

---

[33] Gairdner, *op. cit.*, 167–9; cf. the comments of Burne, 154–5. It is much more likely that, if Henry picked up artillery en route, he did so at Lichfield, where, as the 'Ballad' says (ll. 397 ff.), the guns 'cracken on hye' to greet Henry's arrival. The Act of Attainder of 1485 (*RP*, VI, 276) specifically says that Richard's army had guns.

[34] 'Ballad', ll. 489–94, 571–4.

[35] Ross, *Wars of the Roses*, 112; *Edward IV*, 160, 167, 171.

[36] *CC*, 574.

manoeuvre, which even disciplined modern armies find hard to achieve. In the fields below the forward end of Ambien Hill, Henry's commanders may have found it easier to deploy the right and left wings of the rebel vanguard, and thereby engage the larger part of his forces. This may well have brought Norfolk's troops under heavy pressure.

It seems to have been at this stage of the battle that Richard decided to make a direct attack upon the person of Henry Tudor himself. Experience had shown clearly that no enemy force would go on fighting once its principal commanders had been killed or captured. A contemporary chronicle says of the first battle of St Albans in 1455 that once the chief leaders on the royalist side had been slain, the fighting ceased abruptly, and much the same seems to have happened in the hard-fought battle of Barnet, where Richard had commanded a division. As soon as it became clear to the rank-and-file that Warwick and his brother Montagu were dead, the opposition to the royal army of Edward IV disintegrated.[37] If Richard could slay Henry Tudor, then the day would be his.

His intention in making the charge, therefore, is clear enough, his reasons for deciding to make it far less so. In this most historiographically inchoate of battles, many reasons may be suggested, but none can be proved. It may have been that he saw Norfolk's troops already in trouble against the main bulk of the Tudor forces, and that he could not readily engage the remainder of his own forces. It may have been that, already angered by the equivocal replies he had received from the Stanleys, and, seeing from his vantage point that Earl Henry was 'afar off' with only a small force of soldiers about him, 'all inflamed with ire, he struck his horse with his spurs, and runneth out of the one side without [i.e., around] the vanguard against him'. It was, therefore, so Polydore Vergil would have us believe, an impulsive and ill-considered act.[38] Equally, he may have discerned that Sir William Stanley was preparing to engage, or had already engaged, on Henry's behalf, and that it was essential to attack Henry personally before the full weight of the substantial Stanley contingent came in from the north and was committed against him (although this is *not* what Polydore would have us believe).[39]

Another possible reason is that Richard had already learned that the earl of Northumberland was not prepared to commit his men on the royalist side, and, again, that early action was needed. Northumberland's alleged prevarications have often led him to be regarded as one of the great traitors of English history. It is a view which commands little

---

[37] *English Chronicle*, ed. Davies, 72, for 1st St Albans; Ross, *Wars of the Roses*, 119, for Barnet and Tewkesbury.

[38] PV, 224.

[39] *Ibid.* Polydore stresses that Sir William joined in only when he saw Henry in imminent danger of being overwhelmed by Richard's charge.

credence. We have already seen that the physical confines of the terrain did not allow him to engage and this is supported by the evidence of the Croyland Chronicler.[40] Two days after the battle, the corporation of York believed that the earl was already back in his East Yorkshire castle of Wressle, hardly the action of a man who had conferred a signal favour on the new king by withholding his troops at a vital stage of the battle, but this report proved to be unfounded.[41] In fact, he was taken into custody, along with Thomas Howard, earl of Surrey, and probably placed in the Tower.[42] There he seems to have remained until admitted into favour in the spring of 1486.[43]

Finally, Richard may have faced the prospect of low morale, or even mass desertion, among his own forces. Desertions there had been, but before the battle, and from men whom Richard already had under suspicion and had placed under guard.[44] Yet two contemporary sources allege that Richard was in the event betrayed by his own people. A report reaching York two days after the battle, by the hands of its own agent, John Spooner, states that Richard 'late mercifully reigning upon us, was, through the great treason of the duke of Norfolk, and many other that turned against him, piteously slain and murdered, to the great heaviness of this City'.[45] The Croyland Chronicler points up this claim by adding that many of those who deserted Richard were the northerners in whom he had placed such trust; but the chronicler's intense dislike of northerners is clear and repeated, and there is here an obvious element of bias in an otherwise reliable authority.[46]

Among these alternatives we may only guess, but cannot know. On balance, it seems probable that Richard's action was a combination of

[40] Above, p. 218.

[41] *YCR*, I, 119.

[42] *CC*, 575; PV, 225.

[43] He is wholly missing from all the usual commissions (e.g., commissions of the peace in Yorkshire and Northumberland) on which his presence was normally mandatory during the remainder of 1485, and did not reappear in public life until reappointed warden of the east march towards Scotland on 3 January 1486 (Storey, 'Wardens', 615).

[44] Above, p. 181, 213 *n*.

[45] *YCR*, I, 119 (where 'lawfully reigning' is wrongly given instead of 'mercifully'); Davies, *York Records*, 218. I am much obliged to Miss Lorraine Attreed for her careful scrutiny of the York House Books, II–IV, fos. 167 ff., including the supposedly missing folios, on this and other points. The report reaching York was incorrect as regards Norfolk: see following note.

[46] *CC*, 574. For the anti-northern bias, Pollard, 'Tyranny of Richard III', 150, 162. Like the York records, *CC* describes Norfolk as a traitor, but this has recently been shown to be no more than a printer's error (Hanham, 'Early Historians', 100). This in turn invalidates the reliability of the York report, especially since Norfolk was killed in the battle.

impulse and calculation. To dispose rapidly of his rival, especially if he had become separated from the main body of his troops, was to be certain of victory. Whether he would have done better to wait until he was able to bring his superior force fully into action is again a matter of speculation. Whether desperate, ill-advised or merely premature, Richard's charge came remarkably close to success. It seems likely that he took with him only his own household men and the immediate personal friends who were beside him at the time, rather than the main 'battle' of '1,000 or more knights', as some have supposed.[47] Most of these committed supporters were to share his own fate in the subsequent hand-to-hand fighting. Nevertheless, this small but determined squadron swept through the enemy ranks to close with Henry's immediate bodyguard. Richard himself cut down Sir William Brandon, Henry's standard-bearer – the only casualty of note on Richmond's side – who could not have been more than a few feet from Henry himself.[48] He then engaged and finally overbore Sir John Cheyne, described as a man of outstanding strength and fortitude. At this stage his horse seems to have been killed under him. Two contemporary sources state that he had the chance of a fresh horse and of escape, but refused. In a series of loaded sentences, Polydore Vergil says:

> when the matter began manifestly to quail, they brought him swift horses; but he, who was not ignorant that the people hated him . . . is said to have answered, that that very day he would make end of either war or life, such great fierceness and such huge force of mind he had . . . wherefore, knowing certainly that that day would either yield him a peaceable and quiet realm or else perpetually bereave him the same, he came to the field with the crown upon his head, that thereby he might either make a beginning or end of his reign.

The 'Ballad of Bosworth Field' is more direct. A knight appeared at his elbow ('I hold it time for to flee/ For yonder Stanleys dints they be so wight'):

> 'Here is thy horse at thy hand ready;
> another day thou may thy worship win. . . .'
> He said, 'Give me my battle-axe in my hand,
> Set the crown of England on my head so high!
> For by him that shaped both sea and land,
> King of England this day will I die!'

[47] Williams, 'Bosworth Field', 18; cf. the comments of P. W. Hammond, *The Ricardian* (1973), 19–20; (1975), 5–6.

[48] The significance of the standard-bearer is underlined by Oxford's order to the men of his vanguard that 'no soldiers should go above ten foot from the standards' since he feared that 'his men in fighting might be environed of the multitude' (PV, 223).

So great was the threat to Henry at this crucial point of the battle that his own soldiers 'were now almost out of hope of victory', until Sir William Stanley's intervention turned the tide. Richard continued to fight on bravely, 'making way with weapon on every side', until he was finally overthrown. Even his hostile critics did not stoop to deny his martial prowess on that day. 'Alone,' says Polydore, 'he was killed fighting manfully in the press of his enemies.'[49]

Casualties seem to have been heavy, especially among the circle of Richard's immediate supporters. Howard of Norfolk, Ferrers of Chartley, Robert Brackenbury, Richard Ratcliffe, Robert Percy all fell in the battle; Catesby was captured, to be executed in Leicester two days later; Lincoln, Lovell, Humphrey and Thomas Stafford all escaped to make more trouble another day; Northumberland and Surrey were placed in honourable imprisonment. But in the immediate aftermath of battle all sorts of rumours flew about as to who was alive and who was dead: neither the informants of the city of York nor even Henry Tudor himself were quite certain.[50] Polydore's speculative estimate of 1,000 dead among the rank-and-file may not be too wide of the mark.[51]

For Richard himself, prolonged posthumous humiliation was in store. The crown which he had worn into battle was found on the field (according to a later legend, upon a thornbush)[52] and placed upon Henry's head. The king's dead body was stripped, carried naked across a horse to the house of the Franciscans in Leicester, exposed to public view for two days to prove that he was indeed dead, and then buried without stone or epitaph.[53] Some years later, Henry VII provided the miserly sum of £10 is to provide a coffin of sorts for the dead king's remains. When,

[49] PV, 224–6; 'Ballad', ll. 585 ff. Shakespeare's famous line (Act V scene iv) – 'A horse! A horse! My kingdom for a horse!' – seems to have the facts in reverse.

[50] On 27 August York received a royal demand for the arrest of Robert Stillington, bishop of Bath and Wells, who was certainly alive, and of Sir Richard Ratcliffe, who almost certainly was not (YCR, I, 122). Confirmation of Vergil's list of casualties is provided by CC, 574, which adds the names of Robert Percy and of John Kendall, the king's secretary.

[51] PV, 224.

[52] Chrimes, Henry VII, 49 n., follows S. Anglo, 'The Foundations of the Tudor Dynasty', Guildhall Miscellany, II (1960), 3, in dismissing the whole story of the crown in the thornbush as apocryphal. Whilst it is true, as Dr Anglo points out, that it is not mentioned in any contemporary or early-Tudor source, nor even in Shakespeare, who might have made good dramatic use of it, it is hard to see why it became such a common element of Tudor iconography: it appears, for example, on Henry VII's tomb, in the east windows of Henry VII's chapel at Westminster, and on contemporary representations of Tudor badges (e.g., Ross, Wars of the Roses, plate 12). It is a somewhat unlikely badge to have been the subject of pure heraldic invention.

[53] Kendall, 368–9.

during Henry VIII's reign, the Franciscan convent was dissolved, the bones were thrown out and the coffin became a horse-trough outside the White Horse inn. By 1758, even that had disappeared; the broken pieces had come to form part of the inn's cellar-steps.[54] It is an indication of the continuing hostility of the Tudors towards Richard, as well as of their bad manners, that no move was ever made to give him fitting burial. Whether for reasons of policy or piety, previous 'second-generation' usurpers had done public penance. Henry V had had Richard II's remains transferred from King's Langley to a stately tomb in Westminster Abbey beside his first wife, Anne of Bohemia. Richard III himself had caused the corpse of Henry VI to be moved from Chertsey Abbey to lie across the choir of the Garter Chapel in Windsor from the sepulchre of his old rival, Edward IV. No such generous move came from an uncaring Henry VIII. With the problematic exception of Edward V, Richard III is the only English king since 1066 whose remains are not now enshrined in a suitably splendid and accredited royal tomb.

[54] Hutton, *Bosworth Field*, 142–3.

# CONCLUSION

Richard III has been the most persistently vilified of all English kings. In the century after his death, no one of note had any great interest in defending his name, or could risk doing so. Henry VII and Henry VIII meted out a brutal fate to each potential claimant to the Yorkist throne, even the aged and innocent Margaret countess of Salisbury. This was sufficient deterrent to any prudent person (not least Norfolk's heir, Thomas Howard) to keep silent about the king the Tudors most loved to hate, which meant that the Tudor tradition was built, perforce but not wholly, on the opinions and reminiscences of Richard's enemies. This does not mean that it is wholly untrustworthy, since it contains very strong echoes of what Richard's contemporaries thought about him. Scarcely less important was the fact that the Yorkist dynasty died with Richard himself on 22 August 1485. He left no direct heir. The dynasty itself had not lasted long enough to establish any great tradition of loyalty. Attempts to unseat Henry VII in the name of the House of York were largely organized and inspired by self-interested foreigners. They attracted no significant support in England. The Lincoln-Lambert Simnel invasion of 1487 provided Henry VII with the most serious threat he ever had to face. The battle of Stoke proved to be a very close-run affair, but the army which Henry confronted was overwhelmingly a mixture of tough German mercenaries and wild Irish levies. In 1487 few Englishmen of rank were prepared to support a now moribund Yorkist cause. Yet it is worth remembering that many more had backed Richard III at Bosworth when he too confronted an army of assorted foreigners and some Welshmen. Had 'the judgement of God' (to use Henry Tudor's own official phrase) gone the other way at Bosworth, Henry Tudor would have been no more than an inconsiderable footnote in the record of English history. Richard suffered also, in historical retrospect, from Henry Tudor's politic marriage to Elizabeth of York. This diverted much lingering Yorkist sentiment to Henry Tudor, although, for good and politic reasons, he did not wish to emphasize the point to the English public. Many people regarded the Princess Elizabeth as the true heiress of York: the projection of her marriage with Henry had been an essential element in winning support for the rebellion of 1483. The very frequency with which the double white-and-red-rose badge, symbolizing this union, appears in Tudor iconography, is testimony to the political importance of the marriage. Yet it helped to make the cause of Richard III, and his good name, more forgettable to his former adherents, who now had to live with a new king.

Richard's reputation has suffered scarcely less from the attentions of his own defenders. His career is full of drama. Here is the wicked uncle, waiting in the wings to take advantage of his innocent nephews when the chance came. Here was the man who cut his way to the throne and lived only to pay the penalty for his crimes. The theme was irresistible to Tudor dramatists and historians alike, all of them, in one degree or another, concerned 'to point a moral and adorn a tale'. Nowadays, we know better than to believe that the hostile Tudor version of Richard was the product of official propaganda. Yet the result was the same. Richard emerged as a wicked king. It has been a persistent and serious weakness of much that has been written about Richard III to concentrate on the sequence of violent events which attended his acquisition of the throne, and, in particular, his responsibility (or lack of it) for his nephews' death. This is to confront the enemy on his own chosen battleground. Because the more hostile of the Tudor writers, and Shakespeare, chose to select Richard as an object-lesson in villainy and tyranny is no good reason to view him in isolation from the conditions in which he lived. No one familiar with the careers of King Louis XI of France, in Richard's own time, or Henry VIII of England, in his own country, would wish to cast any special slur on Richard, still less to select him as the exemplar of a tyrant.

This attention to ultimately insoluble problems of historical detection ignores an entire dimension of critical evaluation of his life and reign. Richard was born into a violent age. At the age of eight, he was to learn that his father, Duke Richard of York, had been killed in battle, and that his elder brother, Edmund of Rutland, then aged seventeen, had been brutally murdered afterwards. Twice he was himself to suffer exile as a consequence of the civil war. Most of the men he had known in youth were either killed in battle or judicially murdered for their alleged treason, among them his mentor, Richard Nevill, earl of Warwick, himself no mean practitioner in the arts of political ruthlessness, and another brother, George duke of Clarence, killed in the Tower in 1478. Warwick had taught Richard Plantagenet lessons in the killing without trial of his political opponents, especially in his illegal despatch of William Herbert, earl of Pembroke, in 1469. Edward IV himself had little hesitation in disposing of Henry VI once it became convenient to do so, and as he became more high-handed in his later years, had taught Richard further lessons in arbitrary procedures, even in regard to inheritance, which he did not forget. Both the execution of Rivers, Grey and Vaughan at Pontefract without trial in 1483 and Richard's various illegal actions in regard to property committed both during the Protectorate and after the failure of the 1483 rebellion, may appear as a direct legacy of this instruction. To put Richard thus into the context of his own violent age is not to make him morally a better man, but at least it makes him more understandable. In the climate of high politics of his own day, his mistakes may then be seen as errors of judgement rather than moral failures.

The admirable William Hutton (with whom this book began) believed that Richard III 'of all English monarchs . . . bears the greatest contrariety of character'. By this fine eighteenth-century term 'contrariety', we might nowadays understand 'complexity' or even 'discordancy' of character. But we do not know Richard well enough to indulge in such psychological complexities. Any discordancy arises from his behaviour patterns (notably his pronounced loyalty to Edward IV and his disloyalty to Edward's sons). He does not appear to have been a complex man. He may not have been a particularly intelligent man, yet it is hard to fault his conduct of government once he became king. Sir George Buck's idea that he should have killed off or otherwise disposed of his political opponents lacks practical reality in Richard's position. So, too, does the notion that he should have pre-empted Henry Tudor's claim to the throne by marrying his niece, Elizabeth of York, since this (it would appear) would have risked the precious allegiance of his northerners: perhaps his one fault as king was an undue reliance on his former servants from north of Trent. In the end, any 'contrariety of character' of Richard III stems not from what we know about him, but from what we do not know about him.

APPENDICES
GENEALOGIES
SELECT BIBLIOGRAPHY
INDEX

Appendix I

# ON THE BONES OF 1674

The bones now in Westminster Abbey, assumed to be those of the princes, were examined by the anatomist Professor Wright when the tomb was opened in 1933, and the conclusion was reached that, on the medical evidence, they were likely to have been those of the sons of Edward IV. Later, in his book published in 1955, P. M. Kendall cited the opinions of no less than four medical experts, three American, one English (Kendall, 497–8), based upon the findings of the 1933 examination. One, a professor of Physical Anthropology, gave his view as 'All things considered, the total age range of all the material is such that both children could have met their deaths as historically stated (i.e. in August of 1483).' The dental evidence, in the opinion of another expert, supports the view that the elder child's teeth would suggest an age of 11½, but that he could be anywhere from 11 to 13 years. Professor Kendall himself concluded that 'the skeletons interred in Westminster Abbey cannot be flatly and incontrovertibly identified with the sons of Edward IV'. 'It must be acknowledged,' he continues, 'that their identification with the princes can only be expressed in terms of probability' (Kendall, 498). About the same time, Professor A. R. Myers ('Character of Richard III', p. 125) cited the opinion of R. G. Harrison, Professor of Anatomy in the University of Liverpool, on the findings of Professor Wright: 'In spite of some difficulties in the evidence which he does not discuss, he [Wright] appears to be correct in his conclusion that the bones were consistent with the sizes and ages of the two princes in 1483.'

I am indebted to three experts in the University of Bristol for allowing me to quote their judgements. Dr Juliet Rogers, who has made a special study of ancient bones, expresses reservations on the identification with the princes: she points out (a) that the sex of the bones cannot be determined from the existing remains, and (b) that 'the only certain evidence here available is that they are pre-1674. . . . They might equally well have been less than a hundred years old or date from a much more remote period of the past, for the area has been the scene of vigorous human occupation since a very early period of time, and the finding of skeletal remains at a depth of 10 feet could just as well be consistent with a very much greater age. After all, we are digging up Romano-British skeletons at lesser depths at this moment.'

Dr J. H. Musgrave, of the Anatomy Department of Bristol University, was more confident. He reports that Professor Wright's 'assessment of the age of Edward V from the state of development of his axis or second cervical vertebra alone is very convincing indeed'. He adds two points: (a) that Professor Wright's comments on the stain on Edward's facial bones are not conclusive: 'It may well have been a blood stain but one couldn't tell for certain without the aid of modern biochemical analysis'; (b) 'The skeletal – as opposed to dental – remains of Richard duke of York are perhaps less informative. But the dental evidence is strong.'

Support for this latter point came from Professor E. W. Bradford, Professor of Dental Surgery in Bristol University, who, on the evidence of the molars and canines in the older skull (Edward V) concluded 'that with one-third of the crown [of the third molar] formed' this 'would put the child at more than 11 years . . . if one assumes the child is about average then the best guess at age would be 12 years old'. Of the younger skull, he further observes, on the basis of the eruption of the permanent incisors, that the child was '8 years old plus or minus 2 years, i.e., somewhere between 6 and 10'. However, other evidence, set forth in Professor Bradford's letter, would add '1–1½ years to the above figures, i.e., the child would be between 7 and 11½'. He adds that not 'very much credence can be attached to evidence of consanguinity' and that 'tooth development seems to be on a time-scale of its own somewhat independent of the overall development of the individual'.

The medical evidence, therefore, is not conclusive, but, on balance, it suggests that the bones of 1674 might well have been those of the princes, and it certainly does not rule out the possibility or even the probability that they were. The onus of 'proof' therefore comes back firmly into the historians' court, but with some support from modern medical expertise.

# THE BALLAD OF BOSWORTH FIELD

Much reliance has been placed in the later chapters of this book on the narrative poem known as 'The Ballad of Bosworth Field', especially for the extent of Richard's support on 22 August 1485. The Ballad was printed in *Bishop Percy's Folio Manuscript*, III (1868), edited by J. W. Hales and F. J. Furnivall, pages 233–59, from a British Library manuscript, now Harleian 542. In its present form this is a seventeenth-century copy of an early original. Many fifteenth-century personal names became mangled in the copying, and it ends with some joker's dedication to '*James* of England that is our King'. Considering the dearth of reliable information about the battle and those who took part in it, this source has been curiously ignored by historians. For example, James Gairdner, in his detailed discussion of the battle in *Archeologia*, lv (1893), 319–64, makes several references to 'The Song of the Lady Bessiye' (printed by Bishop Percy, 319–63), a romanticised and probably later version of the more sober Ballad. P. M. Kendall (491–2) made some use of it, from Nichols's edition of Hutton's *Bosworth*, but was essentially dismissive ('probably not altogether reliable'), even though the information it provides would well have suited his defence of Richard III. A. H. Burne (*Battlefields of England*, 138) refers to what he calls 'this curious document'. But, entirely without warrant, he makes Lord Stanley the author, and his misquotation of the source is only one of a whole series of errors and anachronisms which largely deprive his account of the battle of serious credibility, although he does at least recognize the possibility (p. 151) that Richard had field-guns. In general, however, Burne lacked any proper understanding of the logistics of medieval warfare, and was cavalier in his handling of evidence. Sources were all very well when they fitted in to his personal doctrine of 'Inherent Military Probability'; otherwise not. These references apart, the Ballad has barely been mentioned.

Yet, on both historical and literary grounds, the Ballad deserves most serious consideration as a major historical source. Despite its poetic form, it is above all an early and well-informed source, as compared, say, with Polydore Vergil's description of the battle written some twenty years afterwards and based on necessarily second-hand information. It seems unlikely that the author of the Ballad was present in person at the battle (in line 471, with reference to Sir William Stanley, he remarks 'men said that day that dyd him see'), but it can be shown that he was, nevertheless, a knowledgeable and very contemporary author.

The historical reasons for this opinion may be summarized as follows:
1.   In all, he cites the names of ninety supporters of Richard at the battle. Of these, twenty-three were noblemen and the rest were gentry, mainly from the north of England. Several names listed in the text are now so distorted as to be unidentifiable, but the great majority represent men whose support for Richard can be regarded as almost automatic. Some had been knighted by Richard in the Scottish campaign of 1482, many others had received favours from him. Their close connections with the king can be confirmed from contemporary record sources. Only a well-informed northerner writing soon after the event could have produced this battle-roll of nobles and gentry from the north.
2.   The Ballad mentions a significantly large number of gentry from Nottinghamshire, whence Richard started his campaign. These include Sir Gervase Clifton and Sir Henry Pierpoint, with whom we know he had close associations. More important is the number of local men cited by name. Whatever their possible loyalties, they could not risk ignoring the commands of a king then sitting upon their own doorsteps.
3.   Among the many northerners listed as supporters of Richard in 1485, the Ballad mentions only one southerner. This was Sir Richard 'Chorlton' (*rectius* Charlton), of Edmonton, Middlesex. It is not without significance that he was the only southerner known to have been slain at Bosworth, and was afterwards attainted by Henry VII (*RP*, VII, 276).
4.   Of Sir Richard Ratcliffe, the author of the Ballad observes, 'of King Richard's council was he'. This might well have been common and not specialized knowledge. But of another northerner, Sir Marmaduke Constable, he remarks 'of King Richard's council was he nigh'. The incomplete official records do not reveal Constable as a member of the royal council, but he was clearly high in Richard's favour, and was very well rewarded for his support. Only a well-informed contemporary would have been likely to possess such knowledge.
5.   The Ballad's brief list of casualties on 22 August 1485 seems to be accurate, with the exception of a reference to Sir William Conyers. His name does not appear among the many writs of *Diem Clausit Extremum* issued by Henry VII later in 1485 and early in 1486 (*CFR, 1485–1509*, 1–7), which include nearly all the known victims of the fight at Bosworth. Conyers seems to have been alive in March 1490, when he was succeeded by his grandson, William, later Lord Conyers (*CP*, III, 404).
6.   According to the poem, four men 'did assay them with their chivalrye' and 'went to the vaward with our kinge' (i.e., Henry Tudor). John Savage, Hugh Persall and Humphrey Stanley (a member of the family) all had close Stanley connections. The fourth, Sir Richard Tunstall, K.G., was a

former long-term Lancastrian, who turned coat to the Yorkists after he had been compelled to surrender his command of Harlech Castle in 1468, but he too was essentially a Lancashire man. Tunstall, Savage and Stanley all survived to prosper considerably under Henry VII.

7.   The poem was clearly written in the Stanley interest, but provides clues as to its own date. A revealing phrase (line 340: '2 Shires [Lancashire and Cheshire] against all England to Fight' suggests its north-western provenance. The poem includes lavish praise of both Lord Stanley ('stern and stout') and of his brother, Sir William Stanley (lines 68–72: 'a better knight never umstrode strede . . . a more nobler Knight att neede'; line 469, 'wise and worthye', repeated in line 565). Sir William Stanley was executed for treason by Henry VII in 1495. It would have been impolitic in the extreme to have written of him in such terms after 1495.

All this points to a knowledgeable northerner writing within ten years of the battle.

The literary evidence, so far as it goes, supports the historical evidence. On this issue, I am much indebted to Professor V. J. Scattergood, of Trinity College, Dublin, for his expert advice. He points out that 'umstrode', meaning bestrode (line 68), is only known to have been mentioned twice, in texts of c. 1352 and c. 1400, both of northern origin. 'Min' (line 398), meaning 'less' ('Guns in Lichfield they cracken on hye/ To cheer the countye both more and min'), always occurs in this combination, is now obsolete, and the majority of quotations of its use occur in northern or Scottish authors. 'Throwlye' (lines 494, 574), meaning violently, furiously or eagerly, was mostly used by northern and Scottish authors, but not after 1535. 'Swee', for 'sway', is used before 1500, and not after, and its use is largely northern. Other examples of northern usages abound (e.g., 'busked' = set out, line 113; 'bowned' = prepared, line 121; 'wight' = brave, bold, valiant, lines 236 ff.). Moreover, it is clear also that in various parts of the text the original rhymes could have been perfect only in northern forms. Professor Scattergood concludes: 'One might reasonably expect that the poem predates 1495 (the death of Sir William Stanley) and that it is of northern provenance . . . it seems to me almost certain that the author of this poem was a northerner: northern vocabulary comes easily to him, and he rhymes like a northerner.'

# Table 1   YORK AND LANCASTER

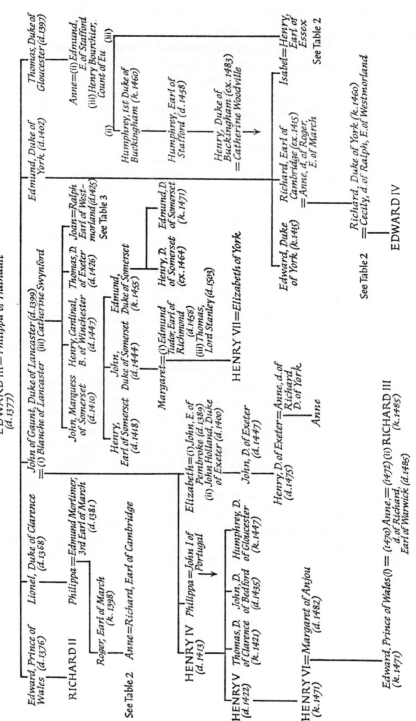

Table 2   THE NORTHERN CONNECTION

Richard Nevill, Earl of Salisbury (d.1460) = Alice Montagu

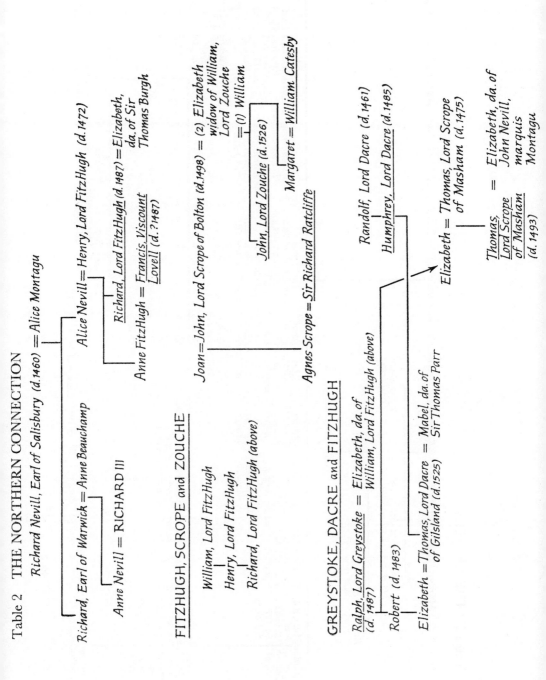

Richard, Earl of Warwick = Anne Beauchamp

Anne Nevill = RICHARD III

Alice Nevill = Henry, Lord FitzHugh (d.1472)

Richard, Lord FitzHugh (d.1487) = Elizabeth,
da. of Sir
Thomas Burgh

Anne FitzHugh = Francis, Viscount
Lovell (d.?1487)

Joan = John, Lord Scrope of Bolton (d.1498) = (2) Elizabeth
widow of William,
Lord Zouche
= (1) William

John, Lord Zouche (d.1526)

Margaret = William Catesby

Agnes Scrope = Sir Richard Ratcliffe

Randolf, Lord Dacre (d.1461)

Humphrey, Lord Dacre (d.1485)

Elizabeth = Thomas, Lord Scrope
of Masham (d.1475)

Thomas,
Lord Scrope
of Masham
(d.1493)
=   Elizabeth, da. of
John Nevill,
marquis
Montagu

### FITZHUGH, SCROPE and ZOUCHE

William, Lord FitzHugh
Henry, Lord FitzHugh
Richard, Lord FitzHugh (above)

### GREYSTOKE, DACRE and FITZHUGH

Ralph, Lord Greystoke = Elizabeth, da. of
(d. 1487)                   William, Lord FitzHugh (above)

Robert (d. 1483)

Elizabeth = Thomas, Lord Dacre = Mabel, da. of
of Gilsland (d.1525)   Sir Thomas Parr

# Table 3  THE NEVILLS

Margaret d. of Earl of Stafford (i) = Ralph Nevill, 1st Earl of Westmorland = (ii) Joan Beaufort, d. of John of Gaunt and Catherine Swynford
(d.1425)

John = Elizabeth, d. of Earl of Kent
(d.1423)

Many other children

Ralph = Elizabeth d. of Henry Percy (Hotspur)

John (d. 1461)

Ralph, 3rd Earl (d. 1499)

Richard, Earl of Salisbury (ex.1460) = Alice, d. & h. of Thomas Earl of Salisbury

William, Lord Fauconberg, Earl of Kent (d.1463)

George, Lord Latimer (d.1469) = Elizabeth, d. & coheir of Richard, Earl of Warwick

Robert, Bishop of Salisbury (d.1427) Durham (1438) (d.1457)

Edward, Lord Abergavenny (d.1476) = (i) Elizabeth, d. & coheir of Richard, Earl of Worcester = (ii) Catherine, sister of John, Lord Howard

Catherine = (i) John, 2nd Duke of Norfolk (d.1432) = (ii) Thos. Strangeways = (iii) Viscount Beaumont = (iv) John Woodville (ex.1469)

Anne = (i) Humphrey, D. of Buckingham (k.1460) = (ii) Henry, Earl of Northumberland (d.1455)

Eleanor = (i) Richard, Lord Despenser (d.1444) = (ii) Henry, Earl of Northumberland (d.1455)

Richard = Cecily Duke of York (k.1460)

EDWARD IV

Richard, Earl of Salisbury & Warwick (k.1471) "The King-maker" = Anne, s. & h. of Henry, Duke of Warwick

Thomas = Maud, widow of Lord Willoughby (k.1460)

John, Earl of Northumberland, Marquess Montagu (k.1471)

George, Archbishop of York (d.1476)

George, Duke of Bedford (d.1483)

Joan = William, Earl of Arundel (d.1487)

Cecily = (i) Henry, D. of Warwick (d.1446) = (ii) John, E. of Worcester (ex.1470)

Alice = Henry, Lord Fitzhugh (d.1472)

Eleanor = Thomas, Lord Stanley (d.1503)

Catherine = William, Lord Hastings (ex.1483)

Margaret = John, Earl of Oxford (d.1513)

Isabel = George, Duke of Clarence (ex.1478)

Anne = (i) Edward, Prince of Wales, son of Henry VI (k.1471) = (ii) RICHARD III (k.1485)

See Table 2

Table 4 THE WOODVILLES

Richard Woodville, Lord Rivers, 1st Earl Rivers = Jacquetta of Luxemburg, sister of Louis, Count of St. Pol,
(ex. 1469)                       widow of John of Lancaster, Duke of Bedford
(1466)

Anthony, =(i) Elizabeth,  John = Catherine  Lionel,  Richard,  Edward  Sir John Grey (i) = Elizabeth = (ii) EDWARD IV
Lord Scales,  d. & h. of  (ex. 1469)  Nevill  Bishop  Earl Rivers  (d. 1488)  son of Lord      See Table 2
Earl Rivers  Lord Scales  Duchess of  of  (d. 1491)  Ferrers of
(ex. 1483)  =(ii) Mary, d. of  Norfolk  Salisbury      Groby
Sir Henry      (1482)      (k. 1461)
Fitzlewis      (d. 1484)

Richard
(ex. 1483)

Thomas, =(i) Anne, d. of
Marquess of  Duke of
Dorset  Exeter
(1475)  =(ii) Cecily, d. & h.
of Lord
Borville
(d. 1501)

Thomas

Margaret = Thomas,  Anne =(i) William,  Jacquetta = John,  Catherine =(i) Henry,  Mary = William,  Eleanor = Anthony,
Earl of  Viscount  Lord  Duke of  2nd Earl  Lord Grey
Arundel  Bourchier  Strange  Buckingham  of Pembroke  of Ruthin
(d. 1524)  (d. 1482)  of  (ex. 1483)  (d. 1491)  (d. 1480)
      =(ii) George,  Knockin  =(ii) Jasper Tudor,
      Earl of  (d. 1479)  Duke of
      Kent      Bedford
      (d. 1503)      (d. 1495)
                  =(iii) Sir Richard
                  Wingfield

# SELECT BIBLIOGRAPHY

This bibliography is intended to provide details of printed works and unpublished theses cited in the footnotes to the book, and is in no sense designed to provide an exhaustive book-list. To facilitate ease of reference from books, articles and manuscripts cited in the book, both primary and secondary sources have been combined in a single alphabetical list.

*Acts of Court of the Mercers' Company*, ed. L. Lyell and F. D. Watney (1936).

ANDRÉ, BERNARD, *Historia Regis Henrici Septimi*, ed. J. Gairdner (Rolls Series, 1858).

ANGLO, S., 'The Foundations of the Tudor Dynasty', *Guildhall Miscellany*, ii (1960).

ARMSTRONG, C. A. J., 'The Piety of Cecily, Duchess of York', in *For Hilaire Belloc*, ed. D. Woodruff (1942).

——, 'Some Examples of the Distribution and Speed of News in England at the time of the Wars of the Roses', in *Studies in Medieval History Presented to F. M. Powicke*, ed. R. W. Hunt, W. A. Pantin and R. W. Southern (Oxford 1948).

——, 'L'échange culturel entre les cours d'Angleterre et de Bourgogne à l'époque de Charles le Téméraire', in *Cinq-Centième Anniversaire de la Bataille de Nancy* (Nancy 1979).

——, and see below, under MANCINI.

ATTHILL, W., ed., *Documents Relating to the Collegiate Church of Middleham* (Camden Society, xxxviii, 1867).

ATTREED, LORRAINE, 'The Relations between the Royal Government and the City of York, 1377–1485' (unpublished thesis, University of York, 1979).

——, 'The Epidemic of Sweating Sickness in 1485', *The Ricardian*, iv (1977).

'Ballad of Bosworth Field', *Bishop Percy's Folio Manuscript*, III (1868), ed. J. W. Hales and F. J. Furnivall, pp. 233–59.

BALCHIN, NIGEL, 'Richard III', *British History Illustrated*, i, no. 4 (October 1976).

BALDWIN, J. F., *The King's Council in England during the Middle Ages* (Oxford 1913).

BARKER, N. and BIRLEY, R., 'Jane Shore', *Etoniana*, no. 125 (June 1972).

BARNES, P. M., 'The Chancery Corpus cum Causa File, 10–11 Edward IV', in *Medieval Legal Records*, ed. R. F. Hunnisett and J. B. Post (1978).

BEAN, J. M. W., *The Estates of the Percy Family, 1416–1537* (1958).

——, *The Decline of English Feudalism, 1215–1540* (Manchester 1968).

BELTZ, G. F., *Memorials of the Most Noble Order of the Garter* (1841).

BEVERLEY SMITH, J. and PUGH, T. B., 'The Lordship of Gower and Kilvey', in *Glamorgan County History*, ed. T. B. Pugh, III (Cardiff 1971).

'Brief Latin Chronicle', in *Three Fifteenth-Century Chronicles*, ed. J. Gairdner (Camden Society, 1880).

BROOKS, F. W., *The Council of the North* (Historical Association Pamphlet, 1966).

BROWN, A. L., 'The Authorization of Letters under the Great Seal', *BIHR*, xxxvii (1964).

——, 'The Reign of Henry IV', in *Fifteenth-Century England, 1399–1509*, ed. S. B. Chrimes, C. D. Ross and R. A. Griffiths (Manchester 1972).

BROWN, R. ALLEN, COLVIN, H. M. and TAYLOR, A. J., *The History of the Kings' Works*; II, *The Middle Ages* (1963).

BUCK, SIR GEORGE, *The History of King Richard III*, ed. A. N. Kincaid (1979).

BULLOUGH, G., *Narrative and Dramatic Sources of Shakespeare*, III (1966).

BURNE, A. H., *Battlefields of England* (1950).

——, *More Battlefields of England* (1952).

*Calendar of Chancery Proceedings, Richard II to Elizabeth* (Record Commission, XC, XCI).

*Calendar of Charter Rolls*, VI, *1427–1516* (1927).

*Calendar of Close Rolls: Edward IV*, I–II, *1461–1468* (1949, 1953); *Edward IV–Edward V–Richard III, 1476–1485* (1954).

*Calendar of Documents Relating to Scotland*, ed. J. Bain, IV, *1357–1509* (1888).

*Calendar of Fine Rolls: XX (Edward IV, 1461–1471,* 1949); XXI (*Edward IV–Richard III, 1471–1485,* 1961).

*Calendarium Inquisitionum Post Mortem sive Exceatarum*, ed. J. Cayley and J. Bayley (Record Commission), IV (1828).

*Calendar of Patent Rolls: Edward IV*, I–II, *1461–7, 1467–77; Edward IV–Edward V–Richard III, 1476–85* (1897, 1899, 1901).

*Calendar of State Papers and Manuscripts existing in the Archives and Collections of Milan, I (1385–1618)*, ed. A. B. Hinds (1913).

CALMETTE, J. and PÉRINELLE, G., *Louis XI et l'Angleterre* (Paris 1930).

CAMPBELL, LILY B., '*Shakespeare's "Histories"*', (San Marino, California, 1947).

*The Cely Papers*, ed. H. E. Malden (Camden Society, 3rd series, i. 1900) (see also under HANHAM).

CHALLIS, H. W., *Real Property* (3rd edn, 1911).

CHRIMES, S. B., *English Constitutional Ideas in the Fifteenth Century* (Cambridge 1936).

——, 'The Landing Place of Henry of Richmond, 1485', *Welsh History Review*, iv (1961).

——, 'The Fifteenth Century', *History*, xlviii (1963).

——, 'The Landing Place of Henry of Richmond, 1485', *Welsh History Review*, iv (1964).

——, *Lancastrians, Yorkists and Henry VII* (1964).

——, *Henry VII* (1972).

*Chronicle of the Rebellion in Lincolnshire, 1470*, ed. J. G. Nichols (Camden Society, 1847).

*Chronicle of John Stone*, ed. W. G. Searle (Cambridge Antiquarian Society Publications, xxxiv, 1902).

CHURCHILL, G. B., *Richard III up to Shakespeare* (Berlin 1900; reprint Gloucester 1976).

CHURCHILL, WINSTON S., *A History of the English-Speaking Peoples*, I (1956).

CLARK, G. T., *Cartae et alia munimenta quae ad dominium de Glamorgancia pertinent* (6 vols, Cardiff 1910).

COBBAN, A. B., *The King's Hall Within the University of Cambridge in the Later Middle Ages* (Cambridge 1969).

COLEMAN, C. H. D., 'The Execution of Hastings: A Neglected Source', *BIHR*, liii (1980).

COLES, G. M., 'The Lordship of Middleham, especially in Yorkist and Early Tudor Times' (unpublished M.A. thesis, Liverpool University, 1961).

COMMYNES, PHILIPPE DE, *Mémoires*, ed. J. Calmette and G. Durville, 3 vols (Classiques de l'Histoire de France au Moyen Age, Paris, 1924–5).

*Complete Peerage of England, Scotland, Ireland and the United Kingdom*, ed. G. E. Cokayne: new edn by Vicary Gibbs, H. A. Doubleday and others, 13 vols (1910–59).

CONTAMINE, P., *Guerre, État et Société à la fin du Moyen Age: études sur les armées des rois de France, 1337–1494* (Paris 1972).

CONWAY, A. E., 'The Maidstone Sector of Buckingham's Rebellion, October 18th, 1483', *Archeologia Cantiana*, xxxvii (1925).

COOPER, J. P., 'The Social Distribution of Land and Men in England, 1436–1700', *Economic History Review*, 2nd ser., xx (1967).

CRAWFORD, ANNE, 'The Career of John Howard, Duke of Norfolk, 1420–1485' (unpublished M. Phil. thesis, University of London, 1975).

——, 'John Howard, Duke of Norfolk: A Possible Murderer of the Princes?', *The Ricardian*, v (1980).

CROTCH, W. J. B., *The Prologues and Epilogues of William Caxton* (Early English Text Society, 1928).

DAVIES, R., *Municipal Records of the City of York during the Reigns of Edward IV, Edward V and Richard III* (1843).

DOCKRAY, K. R., 'The Troubles of the Yorkshire Plumptons', *History Today*, xxvii (1977).

DONALDSON, G., *Scottish Kings* (1967).

DRAKE, FRANCIS, *Eboracum* (1736).

DUNHAM, W. H., Jr., 'Lord Hastings' Indentured Retainers, 1481–1483', *Transactions of the Connecticut Academy of Arts and Sciences*, xxxix (New Haven, Connecticut, 1955).

——, and WOOD, CHARLES T., 'The Right to Rule in England: Depositions and the Kingdom's Authority, 1327–1485', *American Historical Review*, lxxxi (1976).

ELLIS, H., *Original Letters illustrative of English History* (1824–46, 11 vols in 3 series).

ELTON, G. R., *The Tudor Constitution* (1960).

——, *England, 1200–1640* (*The Sources of History*) (1969).

EMDEN, A. B., *A Biographical Register of the University of Oxford to A.D. 1500* (3 vols, Oxford 1957–9).

——, *A Biographical Register of the University of Cambridge to 1500* (Cambridge 1963).

*English Chronicle of the Reigns of Richard II, Henry IV, Henry V, and Henry VI, written before the year 1470*, ed. J. S. Davies (Camden Society, 1856).

EVERITT, ALAN, 'The County Community', in E. W. IVES (ed.), *The English Revolution, 1600–1660* (1968).

*Excerpta Historica*, ed. S. Bentley (1831).


FABYAN, R., *New Chronicles of England and of France*, ed. H. Ellis (1811).

*Fifteenth-Century England, 1399–1509*, ed. S. B. Chrimes, C. D. Ross and R. A. Griffiths (Manchester 1972).

FLENLEY, R., ed., *Six Town Chronicles of England* (Oxford 1911).

FLETCHER, BRIAN, 'Tree Ring Dates for Some Paintings in England', *Burlington Magazine*, cxvi (1974).


GAIRDNER, JAMES, *Letters and Papers Illustrative of the Reigns of Richard III and Henry VII* (2 vols, Rolls Series, 1861, 1863).

——, 'The Battle of Bosworth', *Archaeologia*, lv (i), 1896.

——, *History of the Life and Reign of Richard III* (Cambridge 1898).

GOODMAN, A. and MACKAY, A., 'A Castilian Report on English Affairs, 1486', *English Historical Review*, lxxxviii (1973).

*Grants from the Crown during the Reign of Edward V*, ed. J. G. Nichols (Camden Society, 1854).

*The Great Chronicle of London*, ed. A. H. Thomas and I. D. Thornley (1938).

GREEN, V. H. H., *The Later Plantagenets* (1955).

GRIFFITHS, R. A., *The Principality of Wales in the Later Middle Ages*: I, *South Wales, 1277–1536* (Cardiff 1972).

——, 'The Sense of Dynasty in the Reign of Henry VI', in *Patronage, Pedigree and Power in Late Medieval England*, ed. Charles Ross (Gloucester 1979).

——, ed., *Patronage, The Crown and the Provinces* (Gloucester 1981).


HALL, EDWARD, *Union of the Two Illustre Families of Lancaster and York*, ed. H. Ellis (1809).

HALSTED, C. A., *Richard III as Duke of Gloucester and King of England* (2 vols, 1844).

HAMMOND, P. W., *Edward of Middleham, Prince of Wales* (1973) and below, see HORROX.

*Handbook of British Chronology*, ed. F. M. Powicke and E. B. Fryde (2nd edn, 1961).

HANBURY, H. G., 'The Legislation of Richard III', *American Journal of Legal History*, vi (1962).

HANHAM, ALISON, 'Richard III, Lord Hastings and the Historians,' *English Historical Review*, lxxxviii (1972).

——, 'Hastings Redivivus', *English Historical Review* (1975).

——, *Richard III and his Early Historians* (1975).

——, *The Cely Letters, 1472–1488* (Early English Text Society, no. 273, 1975).

HARRISON, F. L., *Music in Medieval Britain* (1958).

HAY, DENYS, *The Anglica Historica of Polydore Vergil, A.D. 1485–1537* (1950).

——, *Polydore Vergil: Renaissance Historian and Man of Letters* (1952).

——, 'History and Historians in France and England during the Fifteenth Century', *Bulletin of the Institute of Historical Research*, xxxv (1962).

HICKS, M. A., 'The Career of George Plantagenet, Duke of Clarence, 1449–1478', (unpublished D.Phil. thesis, University of Oxford, 1974).

——, 'Dynastic Change and Northern Society: The Career of the Fourth Earl of Northumberland, 1470–89', *Northern History*, xiv (1978), and 'The Career of Henry Percy, 4th Earl of Northumberland, with special reference to his retinue' (unpublished M.A. dissertation, University of Southampton, 1971).

——, 'The Changing Role of the Wydevilles in Yorkist Politics to 1483', in *Patronage, Pedigree and Power in Late Medieval England*, ed. Charles Ross (1979).

'Historiae Croylandensis Continuatio', in *Rerum Anglicarum Scriptores Veterum*, ed. W. Fulman (1684); English translation by H. T. Riley, *Ingulph's Chronicles* (1893).

*Historical Manuscripts Commission*, 11th Report, Appendix III (1887); 12th Report, Rutland Manuscripts, I (1888).

*Historie of the Arrivall of Edward IV in England*, ed. J. Bruce (Camden Society, 1838).

HOLDSWORTH, W. S., *A History of English Law*, IV (1924).

HOLMES, G. A., *The Later Middle Ages, 1272–1485* (1962).

HORROX, R. E., 'The Patronage of Richard III' (unpublished Ph.D. thesis, University of Cambridge, 1975).

——, and HAMMOND, P. W., eds, *British Library Harleian Manuscript 433*, 2 vols (Gloucester, 1979–80, in progress).

HOUGHTON, K., 'Theory and Practice in Borough Elections to Parliament during the later fifteenth century', *BIHR*, xxxix (1966).

*Household Books of John, Duke of Norfolk and Thomas, Earl of Surrey, 1481–1490*, ed. J. P. Collier (Roxburghe Club, 1844).

HUTTON, W., *The Battle of Bosworth Field* (1788).

*Inquisitions Post Mortem, Henry IV and Henry V*, ed. W. P. Baildon and J. W. Clay, Yorkshire Archaeological Society, Record Series, lix (1918).

IVES, E. W., 'Andrew Dymmock and the Papers of Anthony, Earl Rivers, 1482–3', *BIHR*, xli (1968).

JACOB, E. F., *The Fifteenth Century* (Oxford 1961).

JALLAND, P., 'The Influence of the Aristocracy on Shire Elections in the North of England, 1450–1470', *Speculum*, xlvii (1972).

JAMES, M. E., 'A Tudor Magnate and the Tudor State: Henry fifth earl of Northumberland', Borthwick Papers, no. 30 (York 1966).

——, 'Obedience and Dissent in Henrician England: The Lincolnshire Rebellion, 1536', *Past and Present*, no. 48 (1970).

JENKINS, ELIZABETH, *The Princes in the Tower* (1978).

KEEN, M. M., *England in the Later Middle Ages* (1973).

KENDALL, P. M., *Richard III* (1955).

KINGSFORD, C. L., *Chronicles of London* (1905).

——, *English Historical Literature in the Fifteenth Century* (1913).

KIRBY, J. L., *Henry IV of England* (1970).

KNECHT, J., 'The Episcopate and the Wars of the Roses', *University of Birmingham Historical Journal*, vi (1957).

LANDER, J. R., *Crown and Nobility 1450–1509* (1976)–includes reprints of 'Attainder and Forfeiture, 1453–1509' (1961), 'Marriage and Politics in the Fifteenth Century: The Nevilles and the Wydevilles' (1963), 'Bonds, Coercion and Fear: Henry VII and the Peerage' (1972).

——, *The Wars of the Roses* (1965).

——, *Government and Community: England 1450–1509* (1980).

LESLAU, JACK, 'Did the Sons of Edward IV outlive Henry VII?', *The Ricardian*, iv (1978).

LEVINE, MORTIMER, 'Richard III: Usurper or Lawful King?', *Speculum*, xxxiv (1959).

——, *Tudor Dynastic Problems, 1460–1571* (1973).

LOWE, D. E., 'The Council of the Prince of Wales and the Decline of the Herbert Family during the Second Reign of Edward IV (1471–1483)', *Bulletin of the Board of Celtic Studies*, xxvii (1977).

LULOFFS, MAAIKE, 'King Edward in Exile', *The Ricardian*, iv (1974).

MCFARLANE, K. B., 'Parliament and Bastard Feudalism', *TRHS*, 4th series, xxvi (1944).

——, *The Nobility of Later Medieval England* (1973).

MCKENNA, J. W., 'The Myth of Parliamentary Sovereignty in late-medieval England', *EHR*, xciv (1979).

MCKISACK, M., *The Fourteenth Century, 1307–1399* (Oxford 1959).

MACRAY, W. D., *The Register of Magdalen College* (Oxford 1894).

MAKINSON, A., 'The Road to Bosworth Field, August 1485', *History Today*, xiii (1963).

MANCINI, DOMINIC, *The Usurpation of Richard III*, ed. and translated by C. A. J. Armstrong (2nd edn, Oxford 1969).

MARKHAM, C. R., *Richard III: His Life and Character* (1906).

MEEHAN, M., 'English Piracy, 1450–1500' (unpublished M.Litt. thesis, University of Bristol, 1972).

METCALFE, W. C., *A Book of Knights Banneret, Knights of the Bath and Knights Bachelor* (1885).

MILLES, JEREMIAH, 'Observations on the Wardrobe Accounts for the year 1483', *Archaeologia*, i (1779).

MORE, SIR THOMAS, *The History of King Richard III*, ed. R. S. Sylvester (*Complete Works*, Yale Edn, II, 1963).

MORGAN, D. A. L., 'The King's Affinity in the Polity of Yorkist England', *TRHS*, 5th series, xxiii (1973).

MYERS, A. R., *The Household of Edward IV* (Manchester 1959).

——, 'Richard III', in *Encyclopaedia Britannica* (1964 edn).

——, 'The Character of Richard III', originally published in *History Today*, iv (1954), reprinted in *English Society and Government in the Fifteenth Century*, ed. C. M. D. Crowder (Edinburgh and London 1967).

——, 'Richard III and Historical Tradition', *History*, liii (1968).

——, *English Historical Documents*, IV, 1327–1485 (1969).


NELSON, W., *John Skelton Laureate* (New York 1964).

NICHOLSON, R., *Scotland: the Later Middle Ages* (Edinburgh 1974).

NOKES, E. M. and WHEELER, G., 'A Spanish Account of the Battle of Bosworth', *The Ricardian*, no. 36 (1972).


O'REGAN, MARY, 'Richard III and the Monks of Durham', *The Ricardian*, iv (1978).

OTWAY-RUTHVEN, J., *The King's Secretary and the Signet Office in the XV Century* (Cambridge 1939).


*Paston Letters, 1422–1509*, ed. J. Gairdner, 6 vols (1904).

*Patronage, Pedigree and Power in Late Medieval England*, ed. Charles Ross (Gloucester 1979).

PELICIER, P., *Essai sur le Gouvernement de la Dame de Beaujeu* (Geneva 1970).

——, ed., *Lettres de Charles VIII*, 5 vols (Société de l'Histoire de France, 1898–1905).

PLUCKNETT, T. F. T., *Concise History of the Common Law* (3rd edn, 1940).

*Plumpton Correspondence*, ed. T. Stapleton (Camden Society, 1839).

POCQUET DU HAUT-JUSSÉ, B. A., *François II, Duc de Bretagne, et L'Angleterre* (Paris 1929).

POLLARD, A. J., 'The Northern Retainers of Richard Nevill, Earl of Salisbury', *Northern History*, xi (1976).

——, 'The Tyranny of Richard III', *Journal of Medieval History*, iii (1977).

——, 'Richard Clervaux of Croft: A North Riding Squire in the Fifteenth Century', *Yorkshire Archaeological Journal*, li (1978).

——, 'The Richmondshire Community of Gentry during the Wars of the Roses', in *Patronage, Pedigree and Power in Late Medieval England*, ed. C. Ross (1979).

POWELL, J. ENOCH and WALLIS, KEITH, *The House of Lords in the Middle Ages* (1968).

POWICKE, M. R., *Military Obligation in Medieval England* (Oxford 1962).

PUGH, T. B. and ROSS, C. D., 'The English Baronage and the Income Tax of 1436', *BIHR*, xxvi (1953).

PUGH, T. B., ed., *Glamorgan County History*, III (The Middle Ages) (Cardiff 1971).

——, 'The Magnates, Knights and Gentry' in *Fifteenth-Century England* (above).

——, *The Marcher Lordships of South Wales, 1415–1536* (Cardiff 1963).


RAMSAY, J. H., *Lancaster and York* (2 vols, Oxford 1892).

RAWCLIFFE, CAROLE, *The Staffords, Earls of Stafford and Dukes of Buckingham, 1394–1521* (Cambridge 1978).

*The Register of Thomas Rotherham, Archbishop of York*, ed. G. G. Barker, (Canterbury and York Society, lxix, 1976).

*Registrum Thome Bourgchier, 1454–1486*, ed. F. R. H. Du Boulay, 2 vols (Canterbury and York Society, liv, 1955–6).

REID, R. R. *The King's Council in the North*, (1921).

RHODES, PHILIP, 'The Physical Deformity of Richard III', *British Medical Journal* (1977).

RIBNER, IRVING, *The English History Play in the Age of Shakespeare* (Princeton 1957).

RICHMOND, C. F., 'English Naval Power in the Fifteenth Century', *History* lii (1967).

——, 'Fauconberg's Kentish Rising of May 1471', *EHR*, lxxxv (1970).

ROSENTHAL, J. T., *The Purchase of Paradise: gift-giving and the aristocracy, 1307–1485* (1972).

ROSKELL, J. S., 'The Office and Dignity of Protector of England, with special reference to its origins', *EHR*, lxviii (1953).

——, *The Commons in the Parliament of 1422* (Manchester 1954).

——, *The Commons and their Speakers in Parliament, 1376–1523* (Manchester 1954).

ROSS, C. D., *Edward IV* (1974).

——, 'Forfeiture for Treason in the Reign of Richard II', *EHR*, lxxi (1956).

——, 'Rumour, Propaganda and Popular Opinion during the Wars of the Roses', in *The Crown, Patronage and the Provinces*, ed. R. A. Griffiths (1981).

——, 'Some "Servants and Lovers" of Richard III in his youth', *The Ricardian*, iv (1976).

——, *The Wars of the Roses* (1976).

*Rotuli Parliamentorum*, ed. J. Strachey and others, 6 vols (1767–77).

ROUS, JOHN, *Joannis Rossi Antiquarii Warwicensis Historia Regum Angliae*, ed. T. Hearne (Oxford 1745).

——, *The Rous Roll* (1859, reprinted Gloucester 1980).

ROWSE, A. L., *Bosworth Field and the Wars of the Roses* (1966).

RYMER, T., *Foedera, Conventiones, Literae . . . et Acta Publica* (etc), 20 vols (1704–1735).


SACCIO, P., *Shakespeare's English Kings* (1977).

SCOFIELD, C. L., 'The Early Life of John de Vere, Earl of Oxford', *EHR*, xxxix (1914).

——, *The Life and Reign of Edward the Fourth*, 2 vols. (1923).

SEARLE, W. G., *The History of the Queens' College of St Margaret and St Bernard* (Cambridge Antiquarian Society, 1867).

*Select Cases before the Exchequer Chamber*, ed. M. Hemmant (Selden Society, XXXVIII–XL, 1948).

SIMPSON, A. W. B., *Introduction to the History of the Land Law* (Oxford 1961).

SMYTH, J., *Lives of the Berkeleys*, ed. J. Maclean, 3 vols (Gloucester 1883–95).

SOMERVILLE, R., *History of the Duchy of Lancaster, 1265–1603* (1953).

SPONT, A., 'La marine française sous le règne de Charles VIII', *Revue des Questions Historiques*, lv (1894).

*Statutes of the Realm*, ed. A. Luders and others, 11 vols (Record Commission, 1810–28).

STEEL, A. B., *Richard II* (1941).

——, *The Receipt of the Exchequer* (Cambridge 1954).

*The Stonor Letters and Papers, 1290–1483*, ed. C. L. Kingsford, 2 vols (Camden Society, 3rd series, xxix–xx, 1919).

——, 'English Officers of State, 1399–1485', *BIHR*, xxxi (1958).

——, *The End of the House of Lancaster* (1966).

——, 'The North of England', in *Fifteenth-Century England, 1399–1509*.

SUTTON, ANNE, 'The Administration of Justice Whereunto We be Professed', *The Ricardian*, iv (1976).

——, 'Richard III's "Tytylle and Right": A New Discovery', *The Ricardian*, iv (1977).


TANNER, L. E. AND WRIGHT, W., 'Recent Investigations Regarding the Fate of the Princes in the Tower', *Archaeologia*, lxxxiv (1934).

TAYLOR, J., 'The Plumpton Letters, 1416–1553', *Northern History*, x (1975).

THOMPSON, A. H., *The English Clergy and their Organization in the Later Middle Ages* (Oxford 1947).

THOMSON, J. A. F., 'The Courtenay Family in the Yorkist Period', *BIHR*, xiv (1972).

——, 'Richard III and Lord Hastings', *BIHR*, xiviii (1975).

THORNLEY, I. D., 'The Destruction of Sanctuary', in *Tudor Studies Presented to A. F. Pollard*, ed. R. W. Seton-Watson (1924).

THORPE, LEWIS, 'Philippe de Crèvecoeur, Seigneur d'Esquerdes: two epitaphs by Jean Molinet and Nicaise Ladam', *Bulletin de la Commission Royale d'Histoire*, cxix (Brussels 1954).

TILLYARD, E. M. W., *Shakespeare's History Plays* (1944).

TOUT, T. F., 'The Captivity and Death of Edward of Carnarvon', *Collected Papers*, III (1920).

TUCKER, MELVIN J., *The Life of Thomas Howard, earl of Surrey and second duke of Norfolk, 1443–1524* (The Hague 1964).

TUDOR-CRAIG, PAMELA, *Richard III* (1973).

TURNER, S., *The History of England during the Middle Ages*, 3 vols (3rd edn, 1830).

VERGIL, POLYDORE, *The Anglica Historia of Polydore Vergil, A.D. 1485–1537*, ed. and translated by D. Hay (Royal Historical Society, Camden Series, lxxiv, 1950).

——, *Three Books of Polydore Vergil's English History*, ed. H. Ellis (Camden Society, 1844).

*Victoria History of the Counties of England: Durham*, II (1907); *Cambridgeshire*, III (1959); *Yorkshire*, III (1913); *Yorkshire, City of York* (1976).


WALPOLE, H., *Historic Doubts on the Life and Reign of Richard III* (1965 edn).

WARREN, W. L., *Henry II* (1973).

WAURIN, JEAN DE, *Anchiennes Cronicques d'Engleterre*, ed. E. Dupont, 3 vols (Société de l'histoire de France, Paris, 1858–63).

WEDGWOOD, J. C., *History of Parliament, 1439–1509: Biographies* (1936); *Register* (1938).

WEINBAUM, N., *British Borough Charters, 1307–1660* (Cambridge 1943).

WEISS, M., 'A Power in the North? The Percies in the Fifteenth Century', *Historical Journal*, xix (1976).

WEISS, R., *Humanism in England during the Fifteenth Century* (3rd edn, Oxford 1967).

WIGRAM, ISOLDE, 'The Death of Hastings', *The Ricardian*, no. 50 (1975).

WILKINSON, B., *Constitutional History of England in the Fifteenth Century, 1399–1485* (1964).

WILLIAMS, D. T., *The Battle of Bosworth* (Leicester 1973).

WILLIAMS, M. E., 'Richard III: Chantry Founder', *Notes and Queries*, clxviii (1934).

WILLIAMSON, AUDREY, *The Mystery of the Princes (an Investigation into a Supposed Murder)* (Dursley, Gloucestershire, 1978).

WILKINS, D., *Concilia Magnae Britanniae et Hiberniae, A.D. 466–1718*, 4 vols (1737).

WOLFFE, B. P., *The Crown Lands, 1461–1536* (1970).

——, *The Royal Demesne in English History* (1971).

——, 'When and Why did Hastings lose his head?', *EHR*, lxxxix (1974).

——, 'Hastings Reinterred', *EHR*, xci (1976).

WOOD, CHARLES T., 'The Deposition of Edward V', *Traditio*, xxxi (1975).

——, 'Who Killed the Little Princes in the Tower?', *Harvard Magazine* (January–February 1978).


*York Civic Records*, ed. A. Raine, I, II (Yorkshire Archaeological Society, Record Series, XCVIII, 1939, CIII, 1941).

*York Records: Extracts from the Municipal Records of the City of York*, ed. R. Davies (1843).

# INDEX

# INDEX